Born in Sussex, **Douglas Streatfeild-James** grew up in Malta, Britain and Canada. In 1986, before going up to Oxford University, he spent six months in India and Nepal where he caught the travel bug. Since then, during periods of extended travel, he has trekked in South America, canoed across France and motorcycled across Europe.

Douglas is currently researching and writing a new Trailblazer guide, *Trekking in the Pyrenees*. He has contributed to *Silk Route by Rail*, also from Trailblazer, and is the author of Lonely Planet's *Goa* guide.

China by Rail
First edition: October 1997

Publisher
Trailblazer Publications
The Old Manse, Tower Rd, Hindhead, Surrey, GU26 6SU, UK
Fax (+44) 01428-607571
E-mail: trailblazer@compuserve.com

British Library Cataloguing in Publication Data
A catalogue record for this book is available from the British Library

ISBN 1-873756-15-1

Quotations from *The Travels of Marco Polo* (translated by RE Latham) are
reproduced by permission of Penguin Books, quotations from *Wild Swans* by
Jung Chang are reproduced by permission of HarperCollins and Simon &
Schuster (© 1991 by Global Flair Ltd), quotations from *Peking Story* by David
Kidd are reproduced by permission of Eland, quotations from *My Bodhi Tree* by
Zhang Xianliang (translated by Martha Avery, Secker & Warburg) and *Behind
the Wall* by Colin Thubron (Heinemann) are reproduced by permission of Reed
Consumer Books, quotations from *A Traveller in China* by Christina Dodwell are
reproduced by permission of Hodder & Stoughton.

Editor: Patricia Major
Typesetting: Robert Stotherd
Cartography and index: Jane Thomas

Every effort has been made by the author and publisher to ensure that the
information contained herein is as accurate and up to date as possible. However,
they are unable to accept responsibility for any inconvenience, loss or injury sus-
tained by anyone as a result of the advice and information given in this guide.

Printed on chlorine-free paper from farmed forests by
Technographic Design & Print (☎ 01206-303323) Colchester, Essex, UK

CHINA
BY RAIL

DOUGLAS
STREATFEILD-JAMES

WITH ADDITIONAL MATERIAL BY
DOMINIC STREATFEILD-JAMES

TRAILBLAZER PUBLICATIONS

Acknowledgements

There are, inevitably, many people to thank, including those who helped out along the way: Bruno (Italy), Karen (Canada), David (Australia), Karsten (Germany) and Vic (England). Thank you, too, to Jane McGregor and Scott McEwan for your help and advice. The biggest thank you's go to Richard and George for putting up with me in Hong Kong, and to Simon, (yet again) for letting me stay for so long in Beijing. Thanks too, to the Beijing crew: Coquita, Hamish, Lena, Theresa and Sarah, for being great company.

Nearer to home, thanks to Anna and Chris for enduring three months of chaos while the dining room table was commandeered, to my parents for putting up with the mess for the rest of the time, and to Qiang Huang who did sterling work with the translation.

Finally, of course, thank you to Patricia Major for editing the final version, to Jane Thomas for all the work on the maps, to Dominic for advice (and about 100 pages of text), and to Bryn for giving me the job.

A request

The author and publisher have tried to ensure that this guide is as accurate and up to date as possible but things change quickly in China. If you notice any changes or omissions please write to Douglas Streatfeild-James at Trailblazer Publications (address on p2). A free copy of the next edition will be sent to persons making a significant contribution.

Front cover: The Qian Jin or QJ class are the largest steam engines still in use in China. This one, carefully maintained by its crew, is pictured in the railway yards at Harbin.

CONTENTS

PART 1: PLANNING YOUR TRIP

PART 2: CHINA

PART 3: THE CHINESE RAIL SYSTEM

PART 4: GATEWAYS – BEIJING AND HONG KONG

Beijing

Hong Kong

PART 5: THE EASTERN PROVINCES – BEIJING TO HONG KONG

PART 6: THE WESTERN PROVINCES – HONG KONG TO BEIJING

PART 7: HARBIN TO BEIJING – THE NORTH EAST

PART 8: BEIJING TO ÜRÜMQI – THE NORTH WEST

APPENDICES

INDEX

INTRODUCTION

China, with all its paradoxes and contradictions, is a country that often defies comprehension. It is the last great bastion of Communism yet it also has the world's fastest growing economy. It holds a quarter of the world's population but huge areas are practically uninhabited. Terraced paddy fields are still ploughed using water buffalo, while whole cities are crammed with high-rise buildings and satellite dishes. Literally tens of millions of peasants are still estimated to live below the poverty line, yet China is a nuclear superpower whose industries include commercial satellite launching. The juxtaposition of ancient and modern is fascinating and sometimes baffling.

For the last two centuries the Chinese have tried to keep the West at arm's length but now, after an era of wars and internal fighting, the world's third largest country is opening up, and both tourists and business people are being welcomed. Though this doesn't mean you can go absolutely everywhere without restriction, probably more of China is accessible today than it has been at any other time. Increasingly, too, there's more to see when you get there; the Chinese have at last realised that their historical sites are of tremendous value. Artefacts are now being properly restored and displayed. Indeed, with its density of exciting new finds, China may well harbour the last and greatest archaeological sources in the world today.

The rapid development of tourist facilities means that the reputation of the People's Republic as a difficult place to travel is also being overcome. No one would describe a trip to China as relaxing but neither is it the case of unremitting hardship people imagine. There are luxurious hotels and fully-guided tours for those who want them, while the adventurous can explore independently.

There's something for everyone, from fabulous Buddhist cave sculptures to treks in remote national parks. You can savour the peace, colour and variety of the minority areas. For the energetic, there's mountain climbing, caving and walking. More sedentary attractions include a night at the opera or a meal in a top class restaurant. There's even a thriving nightlife in some of the larger cities. Most importantly there are plenty of chances to meet and talk to the Chinese themselves. There have been enough Western tourists through most places now for the staring to have stopped and for local people to have become more confident about being open and friendly. Increasing numbers of Chinese are learning English and are only too keen to practise on any foreigner who comes to hand.

For those who are travelling between countries on a long trip, China is a natural stopover. Sharing borders with, among others, Vietnam, Laos, Nepal, Pakistan, Kazakhstan and Russia, there are numerous opportunities to travel through the Central Kingdom en route to, or from, other places.

Not only more accessible than it has ever been before, China is rapidly becoming one of the most important nations in the modern world....and yet side by side with the trappings of a new superpower rest the remains of one of the world's oldest and greatest civilisations. A visit here is truly unforgettable.

PART 1: PLANNING YOUR TRIP

Routes, costs and making a booking

ROUTE OPTIONS

The choice of possible routes around China is infinite; there's so much to see, and such wide variety on offer. To simplify travel planning this book is organised around four routes, each covering a different part of the country and taking in the most interesting sights. Each of the routes is very different in character from the others, and all of them tie in with likely travel connections at either end. The routes can be combined in any number of ways.

Keep your travel plans flexible; it's more fun that way. Do some preliminary planning and, once in China, talk to other travellers and then modify your route accordingly.

COSTS

China is not, as many people believe, a particularly cheap place to travel. In the last few years the authorities have been making great efforts to foster an increasingly lucrative tourist trade. While prices in budget hotels are cheaper than in Western cities, the cost of entrance fees, transport, and accommodation can mount up quickly. While researching this book, I was staying generally in budget accommodation, going to visit three or four tourist sights a day, and travelling by train every two or three days. Without spending much on luxuries, I found that I was getting through US$150 per week. You can, of course, travel more cheaply than this if you try, and likewise you can pay top Western prices and enjoy luxury.

❑ **Sample budgets**

A possible daily breakdown of costs (excluding travel costs, souvenirs, taxi rides etc) is as follows:

	Low	Mid-range
Hotel	US$4-5/£3-3.5 (dorm/cheap dble)	US$20/£13 (dble room)
Breakfast	US$0.50-1/50p (street snack)	US$2.5/£1.70 (hotel)
Lunch	US$1.20/85p (street snack)	US$1.20/85p (street snack)
Supper	US$2.40/£1.70	US$6/£4.20
Sightseeing	US$3.70/£2.50 (entrance fees only)	US$12/£8.30 (guided tour)
T o t a l	US$13/£9	US$41.5/£28

Hotel accommodation

In most places there is a range of accommodation available, from top class hotels, right down to cheap hostels with basic three- or four-bed dormitories. If you are on an organised tour or have booked your accommodation through a travel agent in advance, you will find yourself in the former of these. Budget travellers, on the other hand, will have to hunt around for a good bargain at the latter end of the scale. In some cities there is only one budget hotel, and the prices can be higher than you might expect. In Shanghai, Guangzhou, Kunming and Chengdu, for example, you will pay a minimum of US$6/£4 for a dormitory bed.

One of the problems is that hotels must have a licence to accept foreigners, and in some cities the police restrict the number of licences. Though you may not mind living in a fleapit and the reception might be happy to have another room filled, they may not be allowed to take you; 'We're full' can often be taken as a euphemism for 'No foreigners allowed here'. Unfortunately it also gets used if the receptionist simply can't be bothered to help you, so it pays to be persistent (while remaining polite!). A little friendly bargaining can be worth a try too. Staying with a Chinese family is a non-starter, and even in cheap hotels Chinese and foreigners are not permitted to stay in the same room. Although a small hotel may have a dormitory, if there are already Chinese in it, you will have to take a private room.

Transport costs

In many places foreigners are charged more for their train, plane or bus tickets than the local Chinese, and although this custom seems to be dying out, where you do come across it there is little you can do except pay. Despite this, transport is reasonably priced considering the vast distances involved. Tickets are cheaper if you buy them yourself but doing so takes time. Many travellers, therefore, use a ticket agency at some time during their visit. They pay more for the ticket but the commission (typically US$6-10/£4-6) can be a reasonable trade for not having to stand in line for several hours. Train tickets have the price printed on them, so it's easy to check whether the travel service has been fair with you.

Ticket prices depend not only on what type of ticket you buy (Soft

❑ Sample rail fares				
Beijing to:	Distance	Soft sleeper	Hard sleeper	Hard seat
Shanghai	1463 km	US$63/£43	US$42/£29	US$22/£15
Hangzhou	1664 km	US$67/£46	US$44/£30	US$24/£17
Xi'an	1165 km	US$52/£36	US$34/£23	US$19/£13
Harbin	1288 km	US$54/£37	US$35/£24	US$19/£13
Guangzhou	2295 km	US$86/£59	US$56/£38	US$31/£21

Sleeper, Hard Sleeper, Soft Seat or Hard Seat – see opposite) but also on the type of train. A ticket on an express or international train will cost you more than a ticket on a fast or local train. Slower trains stop everywhere and tend to be fairly grotty, while express and international trains make far fewer stops and are more comfortable.

Air tickets are much easier to get hold of than train tickets but, of course, cost more. Large hotels are usually willing to book them for you, or you can arrange them yourself at the local CAAC office and avoid the commission. Examples of air fares can be found in the Moving On section at the end of each city guide. Long distance bus prices are also reasonable.

Accommodation on the train

A night spent on the train saves you both time and money, and assuming that you manage to get a sleeper ticket, travel on Chinese trains is pretty relaxing. If, on the other hand, you decide to rough it in the Hard Seat carriages you are likely to have an interesting but rather more tiring journey. There are four types (or classes) of rail ticket:

● **Hard Seat** is the cheapest form of travel and has gained a bad reputation with many foreigners as it can be horrendously overcrowded. It consists of rows of very slightly padded seats in an open-plan carriage. Actually it isn't too bad as long as you manage to secure a reservation for a seat, and don't try it for much longer than seven or eight hours. Hard Seat carriages are the only ones where the number of passengers allowed is unlimited. On busy trains, therefore, they simply keep filling up until no more people can physically squeeze inside. Capacity crowding is pretty unpleasant when it occurs.

● **Soft Seat** carriages are only found occasionally, on short distance intercity trains. The seats are cushioned and the number of passengers is limited to the number of seats – luxury.

● **Hard Sleeper** tickets are generally the most difficult to obtain because they offer a good compromise between comfort and price. The carriages are laid out in sections accommodating six people in two banks of triple bunks. Again the number of passengers is limited. The bunks do not fold up or down, so unless you've got the bottom bunk, which serves as the communal seat in the daytime, you can sleep all day if you like.

● **Soft Sleeper** is the most expensive and luxurious way to travel. Each compartment has four berths with soft mattresses, and there's usually air conditioning. This is the class that most travel services including CITS will try to persuade you to use – mainly because it's too expensive for many Chinese and hence tickets are more easily available. In some ways Hard Sleeper is preferable: if you don't hit it off with the others in your Soft Sleeper compartment the atmosphere can get quite claustrophobic.

Other costs

The other major cost for most tourists is entrance fees. It is a universal policy across China that foreigners pay more to visit tourist sights. In some cases this will be double what the Chinese pay but it's not uncommon to pay three, four, or even five times as much. The entrance fees are actually not particularly high by Western standards, it's just that every place you go to has its own admission charge. Some even have two – one ticket gets you into a courtyard area where you find that you have to buy another to see what you came for. Unless you speak Chinese it's not always clear what you're paying for. The Temple of Heaven in Beijing, for example, has a ticket for foreigners which includes entrance to all the buildings. If you just want to walk in the park the ticket is a fraction of the price but the more expensive ticket is the one that's pressed on you.

There is nothing you can do about paying the entrance fees. An International Student Card rarely works, and you just have to accept the system. If you're studying or teaching in China, however, an official ID card will secure you massive savings – see under Documents in the Practical Information for the Visitor section. Having said all this, there are signs that the foreigners' pricing policy may be about to change. In August 1997 it was announced that the entrance fees to the Great Wall at Badaling would be standardised for foreigners and Chinese. It remains to be seem whether other tourist sites will follow suit.

WHEN TO GO

In all but the south of the country winters are extremely cold, and summers are very hot in all but the mountainous areas. True, there is a difference between the extreme dry heat of the far north-west in midsummer and the humid heat of central China, but basically from May to September it's hot everywhere except in the mountains. (For temperatures in different regional centres, see p29). Although the rainy season varies slightly across the country, the rains occur mainly in June, July and the first half of August and do not affect the far north west.

In theory, then, the best time to visit China is either in the spring (April/May) or autumn (September/October). Most Chinese agree that autumn is the best time of all – the temperature is warm, the skies are clear, and the crowds have gone. Note that the spring can be particularly dry and windy in the north.

WITH A TOUR OR ON YOUR OWN?

Group tours

For those short on time and not particularly strapped for cash a tour may be the best option. Your itinerary will be organised for you, travel tickets provided and all hotel reservations prebooked. Without having to worry

❑ **Useful Web sites**

Sites which can be helpful for planning a trip include the following:

• China Railways Home Page, at **http://severn.dmu.ac.uk/~mlp/crsg.html**, is the best site for information on steam trains in China and has links to other sites of interest. In the railfanning section there are reports by recent rail travellers; there are also lists of related books and videos, and information on the China Railways Study Group.

• There are several forums of interest to rail travellers, such as CompuServe's **TrainNet Forum**.

• Get the latest rates of exchange on **http://www.xe.net/currency**

• At Lonely Planet's site (**http://www.lonelyplanet.com**), you can leave messages for other travellers on their 'Thorn Tree'.

• For health information check out the pages of the World Health Organisation (**http://www.who.ch**) and the Centre for Disease Control (**http://www.cdc.gov/travel/travel.html**).

about where you're going to stay, or whether you'll be able to get your next train ticket organised, you can enjoy what you came for: the sights. Tours to China are becoming big business, and operators vie with each other to offer the definitive itinerary. Perhaps the most compelling argument for taking a tour, however, is simply that you will be accompanied throughout by guides who know what they're talking about. Without a decent understanding of what you're looking at, travelling around China can be incredibly frustrating.

The disadvantage of taking a tour, of course, is that you sacrifice your independence. You are required to conform to the timings of the rest of the group, and there is rarely enough time allowed simply to wander around and discover things for yourself. China is a huge place, and in order to fit everything in to some of the more ambitious tours, the timetables can be punishing – by the end of your fortnight you will have seen an awful lot, but you may feel like taking another holiday to recover.

Semi independent travel

Many travel agents now offer to organise tailor-made tours, allowing you to specify how long you want to spend in each place. Accommodation and transport bookings are then made, so that you have some security and structure to your visit. Although this arrangement generally works well, it is not always foolproof. The problem is that most bookings go indirectly through the China International Travel Service (CITS), who are more interested in group tours than in individual arrangements. Occasionally the system breaks down, and staff can be less than helpful in sorting out problems. If you do make bookings in advance, ensure that you are carrying all your vouchers with you to prove that you have not only booked in advance but that you've paid, too.

Fully independent travel

This is definitely the way to go if you have the time. For all the frustrations of backpacking around China, having the freedom to adjust your plans at short notice is rewarding. If you meet other travellers who have just visited somewhere excellent, you can change course; likewise if you feel that a place is overrated you can get back on the train and go elsewhere. Travelling independently will allow you the time to explore the cities or just go walking in the countryside. It can, however, be as frustrating as it can be fun and if you hate the idea of queuing for a couple of hours to buy each train ticket, you may be better off taking a tour.

Visas

Obtaining a Chinese visa is not a problem in most countries where there is a Chinese embassy (see Making a Booking for listings). Tourist visas generally last one month from the day of entry and are valid for up to three months. They are usually extendable by one month at any large Public Security Bureau (PSB) office in China. Beijing, paradoxically, is a bad place to extend your visa (see p85).

MAKING A BOOKING IN BRITAIN

Prices and options change, so the information provided below is for guidance only. Note that almost all the travel agents listed here will handle visa applications for you if you have booked through them. If you are just looking for flights, try the bucket seat shops on Earl's Court Rd, in London. The **China National Tourist Office** (☎ 0171-935 9787) is at 4 Glentworth St, London NW1 5PG. They will probably advise you to take a tour but they also hand out loads of brochures and free city maps of various Chinese cities. A visit here is worthwhile if only to pick up the one really essential bit of travel equipment – an English language rail timetable (phone to see if they've got any left, first).
● **Regent Holidays** (☎ 0117-921 1711; fax 0117-925 4866, e-mail: 106041.1470@compuserve.com; http//www.regent-holidays.co.uk), 15 John St, Bristol BS1 2HR This friendly company organises independent and small group travel throughout China and can book all accommodation and rail/air travel.
● **The Imaginative Traveller** (☎ 0181-742 8612, fax 0181-742 3045, e-mail: imagtrav@aol.com) 14 Barley Mow Passage, Chiswick, London W4 4PH, is the UK agent for Sundowners (see p19). This efficient company specialises in small group tours but is also prepared to make individual travel arrangements.
● **China Travel Service** (☎ 0171-836 9911, fax 0171-836 3121, e-mail: CTS@ukcts.demon.co.uk, web site http://www.wtgonline.com/cts), 7 Upper St Martin's Lane, London, WC2H 9DL. As well as offering some good standard tours, CTS can tailor individual tours in China for the

semi-independent traveller. The helpful staff offer useful advice on all aspects of Chinese travel.

● **China Travel Service and Information Centre** (☎ 0171-388 8838, fax 0171-388 8828), 124 Euston Road, London NW1 2AL. Despite the name, this organisation is a travel agent rather than an information centre; it specialises in tours and tailoring independent travel arrangements.

● **Jasmine Tours** (☎ 01628-531121, fax 01628-529444), High St, Cookham, Maidenhead, Berks SL6 9SQ. Although this company specialises in tours, they can also make independent travel arrangements if required. They have several standard tours to China.

● **Intourist** (☎ 0171-538 8600, e-mail: info@intourus.demon.co.uk), 219 Marsh Wall, Isle of Dogs, London E14 9PD. Although their main interest is in Russia, they can organise tours and independent travel in China.

Companies specialising in organised tours

● **Voyages Jules Verne** (☎ 0171-616 1000, fax 0171 723 8629, e-mail: sales@VJV.co.uk), 21 Dorset Square, London NW1 6QG. If you want to travel in style, this is the way to go. VJV offer a number of standard tours and often come up with some interesting one-off trips, too.

● **Bales Tours** (☎ 01306-885991 for tours, ☎ 01306-884397 for individual bookings, fax 01306 740048), Bales House, Junction Rd, Dorking, Surrey, RH4 3HL. Bales offer various two or three week tours to China.

● **Explore Worldwide** (☎ 01252-319448, fax 01252-343170), 1 Frederick St, Aldershot, Hants, GU11 1LQ. Explore specialise in small group tours with a difference. If you fancy being carted through some of the more remote parts of the country, in the company of other adventurous sorts, this could well be for you.

● **Exodus Expeditions** (☎ 0181-675 5550, fax 0181 673 0779), 9 Weir Road, London, SW12 OLT. Exodus run adventurous holidays but with a reasonable degree of comfort throughout. They have several tours to south-west and central China.

Rail enthusiasts' and specialist interest tours

● **Great Rail Journeys** (☎ 01904-679969, fax 01904-679961) 71 The Mount, York YO2 2AX, have a three-week fully-guided rail trip from London to Beijing with a possible add-on to Vietnam. Accommodation is in three- and four-star hotels.

● **Occidor Adventure Tours** (☎ 01243-582178, fax 01243-587239) 10 Broomcroft Rd, Bognor Regis, West Sussex PO22 7NJ

● **Enthusiast Holidays** (☎ 0181-699 3654, fax 0181-291 6496, e-mail: vicallen@polxpres.itsnet.co.uk), 146 Forest Hill Rd, London SE23 3QR.

● **Dorridge Travel Service** (☎ 01564-776252, fax 01564-770117), 7 Station Approach, Dorridge, Solihull, B93 8JA.

● **Industrial Railway Society** (☎ 01734 475 949, fax 01734 475 656), 16 Berrylands Rd, Caversham, Berks RG4 8NU

● **TEFS** (☎ 01509 262745, fax 01509 263636), 77 Frederick St, Loughborough, Leics LE11 3TL
● **Warwickshire Railway Society** (☎ 01564 826143), 145 Fulford Hall Rd, Tidbury Green, Solihull, West Midlands
● **LCGB**, Flat 5, 91 Albemarle Rd, Beckenham, Kent BR3 5JZ
● **Steam & Safaris** (☎ 01433 620805, fax 01433 620837), Eccles House, Eccles Lane, Hope, nr Sheffield S30 2RW
● **Leva** (☎ 01582 421203), 5 Hartley Rd, Luton, Beds LU2 0HX

Chinese embassies in Britain

The embassy of the People's Republic of China (☎ 0891-880808 visa information line), is at 31 Portland Place, London, W1N 3AG. There is also a consulate in Manchester, at Denison House, Denison Rd, Victoria Park, Manchester M14 5RX. Getting a Chinese visa is straightforward, and takes three to five days if you apply in person. Tourists are normally given a one-month single entry visa, valid for three months from the date of issue. It is quite possible, however, to apply for a double entry visa, and up to two months duration. The single entry visa costs £25 (or £35 if applying by post), and on application the following must be presented: a completed aplication form, two passport photos, and a passport which is valid for at least six months from the date of application.

For help obtaining your visa, try Travcour (☎ 0171-223 7662) and Overseas Business Travel (☎ 0171-702 2468, fax 0171-488 1199).

Getting to China from Britain

● **By air** Flights to Beijing are around £250 one way, £460 return. Air China are usually a good bet for cheap seats and can be booked from CTS (☎ 0171-388 8838).
● **By rail** To get from London all the way to Beijing by rail will cost around £450 (less if you're under 26) and will require a change of train in Brussels and Moscow. Alternatively you could go to Moscow and then head south into Central Asia to enter China via the Silk Route. For more information on these journeys see *Trans-Siberian Handbook* and *Silk Route by Rail,* both from Trailblazer.

MAKING A BOOKING IN CONTINENTAL EUROPE

From Austria

● **Rail Tours** (☎/fax 43 1450 1488), Rosensteing 92/20, A-1170 Wien.

From Belgium

● **Intourist Benelux** (☎ 02-502 4440, fax 02-502 7913), Galerie Ravenstein 2, 1000 Brussels.
● **Boundless Adventures** (☎ 02-426 40 30, fax 02-426 03 60), Ave Verdilaan 23/15/1080 Brussels - Ganshoren.

From Denmark
● **Kilroy Travels** (☎ 33 11 00 44, fax 33 32 32 69), Skindergade 28, DK-1159 Copenhagen K. Offices in Aarhus (☎ 86 20 11 44), Aalborg (☎ 99 35 11 00), Odense (☎ 66 17 77 80) and Lyngby (☎ 45 88 78 88).
● **Albatros** (☎ 33-32 24 88), Frederiksberggade15, DK-1459, Copenhagen K.
● **Chinese embassy** (☎ 625806, fax 625484) Oregards Alle 25, 2900 Hellerup, Copenhagen

From Finland
● **Kilroy Travels** (☎ 90-680 7811), Kaivokatu 10 D, Helsinki; also in Oulu (☎ 981-372 720) Pakkahuoneenkatu 8; Tampere (☎ 931-223 0995) Tuomiokirkokatu 36; and Turku (☎ 921-273 7500) Eerikinkatu 2.

From France
● **Office de Tourisme de Chine** (☎ 01-42 96 95 48), 116 ave des Champs Elysées, 75008 Paris.
● **CTS**, 32 rue Vignon, 75009 Paris.
● **Chinese embassy** (☎ 47233677, fax 47202422) Ambassade de la Republique Populaire de Chine, 11 ave George V 75008, Paris.

From Germany
● **Travel Service Asia Gmbh** (TSA-Reisen) (☎ 07371-8522; fax 07371-12593, e-mail 100140.3174@compuserve.com) Schulgasse 1, D-88499 Riedlingen. Also specialise in Trans-Siberian travel to China.
● **Fremdenverkehrsamt der Volksrepublik China** (☎ 069-528465, fax 069-528490) Ilkenhans Strasse 6, 6000 Frankfurt/M.
● **Lernidee Reisen** (☎ 030-786 50 56; fax 030-786 55 96) Dudenstrasse 78, 10965 Berlin.
● **STA Travel** STA has many branches some of which include: Hamburg (☎ 040-450 38400), Berlin (☎ 030-311 0950), Frankfurt/Main (☎ 069-703035), Cologne (☎ 0221-442011) and Heidelberg (☎ 06221-23538).
● **SRS** (☎ 030-281 6741), Studenten Reiseservice GmbH, Marienstrasse 25, 1040 Berlin.
● **China Tourist Office** (☎ 069-520135), Ilkenhanstrasse 6, D-60433 Frankfurt/Main.
● **CTS** (☎ 069-250515), Dusseldorferstrasse 14, D-6000 Frankfurt.

From the Netherlands
● **Eurocult** (☎ 030-243 96 34, fax 030-244 24 75, e-mail: euro.cult @inter.nl.net, http//www.xs4all.nl/~eurocult/13GRORUS.html) Balderikistraat 83 Utrecht. Check their Web site for the latest prices.
● **Global Travel** (☎ 020-696 75 85, fax 020-697 35 87) Anne Kooistrahof 15, 1106 WG Amsterdam; can make train reservations in 51 countries – worth contacting even if you don't live in the Netherlands.

● **Kontakt International** (☎ 020-623 47 71, fax 20-625 80 57, e-mail: kontakt@tip.nl) Prins Hendrikkade 104, 1011 AJ Amsterdam, specialise in tailor-made individual tours, and small groups.

● **NBBS** (☎ 071-25 33 33), Schipolweg 101, PO Box 360, 2300 AJ Leiden; branches in Groningen (☎ 050-12 63 33), Amsterdam (☎ 020-20 50 71), Utrecht (☎ 030-31 45 20) and Rotterdam (☎ 010-414 9822)

● **Chinese embassy** (☎ 3551515, fax 3551651) Adriaan Goekooplaan 7, 2517 Jx Den Haag.

From Norway

● **STA** (☎ 22 42 10 20, fax 22 33 21 02, e-mail: Kilroy@Kilroy.no), Nedre Slottsgate 23, 0157 Oslo 1.

● **Kinareiser** (☎ 47 22-110 057), Hegdehaugsveien 10, 0167 Oslo.

From Spain

● **China National Tourist Office** (☎ 0034-1-5480011, fax 0034-1-5480597) Gran Via 88, Grupo 2, Planta 16, 28013 Madrid.

● **Chinese consulates**: Madrid (☎ 519-4242), Arturo Sonal 113, 28043; Barcelona (☎ 455-6060), Travesera de Gracia 342.

From Sweden

● **Frank Stenvall** (☎ 40-127 703, fax 40-127 700), Foreningsgatan 67, S-211 52 Malmo.

● **Fram Resor AB** (☎ 08-215934. fax 08-214060), Box 64, Kingsgaten 56, 11132 Stockholm.

● **STA** (☎ 08-234515), Box 7144. Kingsgatan 4, 10387 Stockholm.

MAKING A BOOKING IN NORTH AMERICA

From the USA

● **China National Tourist Office** (☎ 212-867-0271, fax 212-599-2892), Lincoln Building, 60 E 42nd St, Suite 3126, New York, NY 10165 and in Los Angeles, 333 West Broadway, Suite 201, Glendale, Los Angeles, CA 91204, ☎ 818-545-7505).

● **Safaricentre** (☎ 310-546-4411; fax 546-3188; e-mail: info@safaricentre.com) 3201N Sepulveda Blvd, Manhattan Beach CA 90266. Agents for the popular Sundowners Adventure Travel trips (see p19).

● **China Voyages** (☎ 415-398-2244, 800-914-9133, fax 399-0827, e-mail: info@chinavoyages.com, http://www.chinavoyages.com/siber.html 582 Market St, San Francisco, CA 94104. They market a range of independent and group tours in Russia, Mongolia and China.

● **World Rail Travel Specialists Inc.** (☎/fax 516 878 2260), PO Box 732, E Moriches, NY 11940-0732.

● **Rail Study Tours** (☎ 703 998 2362, fax 703 528 0356), PO Box 3468, Alexandria, VA 22302.

● **General Tours** (☎ 800-221-2216), 53 Summer St, Keene NH 0343.

- **Rahim Tours** (☎ 561-585-5305; fax 561-582-1353, toll free ☎ 800-556-5305), 12 South Dixie Highway, Lake Worth, Florida 33460. Offers tours and will also arrange individual itineraries.
- **STA** (☎ 415-391-8407) 51 Grant Avenue, San Francisco CA 94108. STA has many branches in North America, some of which include: Boston (☎ 617-266-6014; 297 Newbury St), Santa Monica (☎ 310-394-5126; 120 Broadway, Apt 108), New York (☎ 212-627-3111; 10 Downing St – 6th Avenue and Bleecker), Washington DC (☎ 202-887-0912; 2401 Pennsylvania Ave G), Chicago (☎ 312-786-9050; 429 South Dearborn St), Seattle (☎ 206-633-5000; 4341 University Way NE) and Miami (☎ 305-461-3444; 3115 Commodore Plaza).

Chinese consulates in USA New York (☎ 212-330-7400, 520 12th Ave), Washington DC (☎ 202-328-5205), Houston (☎ 713-524-0780), San Francisco (☎ 415-533-4885), Los Angeles (☎ 213-380-2506) and Chicago (☎ 312-346-0288).

From Canada

- **Travel by Rail** (☎ 416-701-0756, fax 701-0751) 72 Prescott Ave, Toronto, Ontario M6N 3GS. Agents for Sundowners (see p19).
- **Exotik Tours** (☎ 514-284-3324, fax 514-843-5493), Suite 806, 1117 Ste Catherine St West, Montreal, Quebec, H3B 1H9
- **CTS** (☎ 604-872-8787), 556 West Broadway, Vancouver, BC
- **Travel Cuts** (☎ 416-979-2406, web site http://www.travelcuts.com), 187 College Street, Toronto, Ontario, M5T 1P7
- **Adventure Centre/Westcan Treks** has several branches in Canada and can arrange group tours as well as individual itineraries. There are offices in Toronto (☎ 416-922 7584, e-mail info@tor.trek.ca), 25 Bellair St; Vancouver (☎ 604-734 1066, e-mail: info@van.trek.ca), 1965 West 4th Ave, Edmonton (☎ 403-439 9118), 8412 109th St, and Calgary (☎ 403-283 6115), 336 14th St NW.

Chinese consulates in Canada Ottawa (☎ 613-789-3434), 515 St Patrick's St, Ottawa, Ontario K1N 5H3. There are representatives in Vancouver (☎ 604-734 0704), 3380 Granville St; and Toronto (☎ 416-324 6466), 240 St George St.

MAKING A BOOKING IN SOUTH AFRICA

- **Student Travel** (☎ 11-447 5551), The Arcade, 62 Mutual Gardens, Corner of Oxford Rd and Tyrwhitt Avenue, Rosebank, Johannesburg 2196 and at 62 Strand St, Cape Town 8001 (☎ 21-418 6570).
- **Concorde Travel** (☎ 11-486 1850), 3rd fl, Killarney Mall, Riviera Rd, Killarney, Johannesburg 2193. Agents for Iris Hotels (see p19).
- **Travelvision** (☎ 11-482 5222), PO Box 4779, 9th fl, Metal Box Centre, Johannesburg 2000. Agents for Sundowners Adventure Travel (see p19).

MAKING A BOOKING IN ASIA

From Israel
● **China National Tourist Office** (☎ 522 6272) 19 Frishman St, Tel Aviv, 61030

From Hong Kong
● **China International Travel Service** (☎ 2732 5888), Room 1213-1215, 13/F, Tower A, New Mandarin Plaza, 14 Science Museum Road, Kowloon

● **Monkey Business/Moonsky Star** (☎ 2723 1376; fax 2723 6653, e-mail: MonkeyHK@compuserve.com, http://www.monkeyshrine.com) E-Block, 4th floor, Flat 6, Chungking Mansion, 36-44 Nathan Rd, Kowloon. Monkey Business do not deal with transport or bookings inside China but specialise in bookings for the Trans-Siberian – which may be of use if you're planning to arrive in or leave China this way. They provide the vital visa support you'll need for stopovers in Russia and Mongolia. They also have an infocentre (see Tours: p86) in Beijing.

● **Phoenix Services Agency** (☎ 2722 7378; fax 2369 8884), Room A, 7th floor, Milton Mansion, 96 Nathan Rd, Kowloon.

● **Time Travel Services** (☎ 2366 6222, e-mail: timetrvl@hkstar.com), Block A, 16th floor, Chungking Mansions, 40 Nathan Rd, Kowloon.

● **Wallem Travel** (☎ 2876 8231, e-mail: wtlhk@wallem.com), Hopewell Centre, 46th floor, 183 Queen's Rd East, Wanchai.

From Japan
● **CTS** (☎ 03-3273 5512), Nihombashi-Settsu Building, 2-2-4, Nihombashi, Chuo-ku, Tokyo

● **Japan China Tourist Office** (☎ 03-3433 1461), 6F Hachidai Hamamatsu-cho Bldg, 1-27-13 Hamamatsu-cho, Minato-ku, Tokyo

● **STA** Tokyo: 2nd Floor, Toko Bldg, 1-5 Yotsuya, Shinjuku-ku, Tokyo 160, (☎ 03-5269 0751). Branches also in Osaka (☎ 06-262 7066).

● **Japan-China International Ferry Co** (☎ 03-5489 4800, fax 03-5489 4788), Daikanyama Pacific Bldg, 10-14 Sarugakucho, Shibuya-ku, Tokyo 150 and Room No 201, San-ai Bldg, 1-8-6, Shinmachi, Nishi-ku, Osaka 550. Services from Kobe or Osaka to Shanghai operate all year, from ¥18,400 one way.

● **Chinese embassy** (☎ 03-3403 3381, fax 03-3405 3345), 3-4-33 Moto Azabu, Minatu-ku, Tokyo 106.

From Singapore
● **China National Tourist Office** (☎ 221-8681), 1 Shenton Way, 17-05 Robina House, Singapore 0106.

● **Chinese embassy** (☎ 7343361), 70 Dalvey Rd.

MAKING A BOOKING IN AUSTRALASIA

From Australia

● **China National Tourist Office** (☎ 02-299 4057) 19th floor, 44 Market St, Sydney, NSW 2000

● **China Travel Service** (☎ 02 9211 2633) 757-759 George St, Sydney NSW 2000.

● **Sundowners Adventure Travel** (☎ 03-9600 1934, fax 9642 5838, e-mail: sundownr@ozemail.com.au), Suite 15, 600 Lonsdale St, Melbourne, Vic 3000, has been recommended by several readers. They offer escorted and semi-independent trips. On their independent trips all bookings on the train and in hotels are made for you to a tailor-made itinerary but you travel independently. The itinerary can also include Vietnam using the Beijing-Hanoi rail-link.

● **Iris Hotels Pty Ltd** (☎ 02-9580 6466; fax 02-9580 7256, e-mail iristour@mpx.com.au), PO Box 60, Hurstville, NSW 2220.

● **Passport Travel** (☎ 03-9867 3888, fax 03-9867 1055, e-mail bmccunn@werple.mira.net.au, http://www.travelcentre.com.au/) Suite 11, 401 St Kilda Rd, Melbourne, Victoria, 3004.

● **Russia-Rail Internet Travel Service** (http://www.russia-rail.com/, e-mail russia-rail@russia-rail.com). Useful if you're continuing through Russia as they can book tickets, organise visas and provide timetables.

● **Adventure World** North Sydney (☎ 02-9956 7766), 73 Walker St; Melbourne (☎ 03-9670 0125) 3rd Floor, 343 Little Collins St.

● **Gateway Travel** (☎ 02-9745 3333, fax 02-9745 3237, e-mail: gatrav@magna.com.au, http://www.magna.comau/~gatrav), 48 The Boulevard, Strathfield NSW 2135.

● **STA** (☎ 02-9212 1255), 1st Floor, 732 Harris St, Ultimo, Sydney NSW 2007. There are dozens of branches including Adelaide (☎ 08-9223 2426) 235 Rundle St; and Canberra (☎ 06-247 863) 13-15 Garema Place.

● **Safeway Travel** (☎ 03-9534 4866, fax 03-9534 4206) 288 Carlisle St, Balaclava. Offers tours and hotel arrangements.

● **Access Travel** (☎ 02-9241 1128) 5th floor, 58 Pitt St, Sydney.

● **Classic Oriental Tours** (☎ 02-9261 3988) Level 4, 491 Kent St, Sydney, offers escorted and semi-independent trips.

Chinese consulates in Australia
At 539 Elizabeth St, Surry Hills, NSW 2010 (☎ 02-9698 7929), 75-77 Irving Rd, Toorak Vic 3142 (☎ 03-9822 0607), and 15-17 William St, Perth WA 6000 (☎ 08-9481 3278).

From New Zealand

● **Eurolynx** (☎ 09-379 9717), 3rd floor, 20 Fort St, Auckland, is the agent for Sundowners Adventure Travel (see Australia).

● **Suntravel** (☎ 09-525 3074) PO Box 12-424, 407 Great South Rd, Penrose, Auckland. Specialises in China, Russia and Mongolia.

● **Adventure World** (☎ 09-524 5118), 101 Great South Road, Remuera, PO Box 74008, Auckland.
● **STA** (☎ 09-309 9995), 10, High St, Auckland. STA also has branches in Christchurch (☎ 799 098) and Wellington (☎ 850 561).

Chinese consulate in New Zealand The Chinese Consulate (☎ 04-472 1382) is at 2-6 Glenmore St, Wellington.

Before you leave

WHAT TO TAKE

As a general rule it pays to travel as light as possible, although if you're part of a tour this is less important than if you're backpacking.

Clothes

In mid winter, even as far south as Shanghai you need warm clothes – and lots of them. In Beijing the temperature can easily fall to minus 10° centigrade or below and in the far North-East they hold a festival on the metre-thick ice of the Songhua River. The best garb in these conditions is several layers of warm clothing – and thermal underwear. Don't forget gloves and a hat, anything, in fact, to keep in the heat. If you're travelling for any length of time, you don't necessarily have to carry all this stuff with you: excellent padded jackets and other warm clothing are widely available.

In the summer you need loose, lightweight clothes that allow your skin to breathe. Take clothes that are easy to wash and that will dry quickly, as this can be a problem when it's very humid. If you're visiting during the rains, you may as well accept that you're going to get soaked at some stage. It pays to wear clothing that will dry on you relatively easily. A lightweight waterproof is useful but nothing will keep you dry in a real downpour. Sunglasses and a hat are both essentials if you're visiting in the mid summer: the sun can be intense particularly in the deserts of the north west.

China is not a particularly clean place and a single train journey can leave you covered in grime; don't bring white clothing or you will spend every evening doing the laundry. Light-coloured clothing does, however, reflect the sun while faded colours or patterned clothing often disguise the dirt best.

Although there is something of a fashion movement in cities like Beijing and Shanghai, most Chinese are far from fashion-conscious, and the Western backpacking community hardly has high dress standards, so you don't need to bring smart clothes. Most travellers wear shorts or slacks in summer, and sandals. If you're going up into the mountains, to Dali or Emeishan, or perhaps into Tibet you will need at least one warm piece of clothing (even in summer) – a fleece jacket, or a jumper is ideal.

Luggage

For those taking a tour, a suitcase is the obvious choice – there's loads of space, clothing can be kept flat, and you won't be carrying it very far. For independent travellers, the choice is generally between a grip and a rucksack. Whatever you choose, ensure that it's rugged and will survive a few knocks. It's not essential to be able to lock it – the Chinese are fairly honest, and besides, if anyone really wanted to get into your luggage they'd manage anyway. If you're considering doing some walking, a rucksack is likely to be much easier to carry over any distance. It's a good idea to have a small shoulder bag, too, just large enough to carry the essentials when you're out sightseeing.

Passport, travellers' cheques, air tickets and other vital documents should be carried in a money belt worn under your clothing. Putting them all in a plastic bag first will protect them against moisture.

Medical supplies

China is pretty well up on medical supplies, but it's far easier to bring your own, rather than try to explain to a Chinese pharmacist what you're after. Essentials include: aspirin; suntan lotion; insect repellant; something for an upset stomach (eg Imodium, see p25); antiseptic cream and plasters/bandaids, and an anti-AIDS kit containing sterile syringes and swabs for emergency medical treatment. Other items you might want to bring include: lipsalve; multivitamins; toilet paper (although it's available it's often not up to Western standards); moisturising cream and water purification tablets. Those planning to stay any length of time in China may want to bring Lemsip and throat pastilles, as there seems to be a permanent cold going around which can be hard to shake off. Don't forget to stock up on tampons and contraceptives, too. Finally, anyone who has seen the barber's-shop-style dental clinics in China, will balk at the thought of getting repair work done here. It's a good idea to have your teeth checked before you come away.

General items

Some items which come in handy are: a plastic or metal mug (train travel in China revolves round constant cups of tea); a small jar of instant coffee; a penknife (essential to peel fruit, and to open bottled drinks); a small sewing kit; a few metres of string to use as a clothes line; a universal bath/sink plug; a water bottle; an alarm clock; a compass (nothing fancy, but accurate enough to make sure you've got the map the right way round); a small torch; a foldaway umbrella (you can buy these in China); writing paper and envelopes; an address book (not your main one, in case you lose it); something to read; photos of family/friends/girlfriend/boyfriend/house/car etc (these will get instant attention on the train); a small bike lock (to secure your luggage if you're going to sleep); earplugs; washing powder; a walkman. Last of all, don't forget the Chinese phrasebook – it's essential.

Gifts

It's important not to appear patronising. China has all the badges, biros and gimmicks that you're likely to be able to find at home, and probably more. Unless you intend to give something special, it's probably best just to give something that's a curiosity. A lot of people collect foreign coins and banknotes – and if nothing else they make an interesting conversation piece on the train. There's a particular fascination for US$ bills – not just for the cash value, but because they denote 'worldliness'. Stamps are also a good bet – there are large philately sections at many post offices and stamp collecting is popular. If you want to buy a special gift for someone in advance, you can't go far wrong with Western alcohol or perfume.

Money

It's easy to cash travellers' cheques in China these days, and in most large cities you can get a cash advance on your credit card too (though it's unwise to rely on this, as the service sometimes breaks down). Travellers' cheques actually command a higher exchange rate than hard currency in most places in China, and the banks give almost the same rate as the black market, so there really is no point in carrying huge amounts of cash around with you or in getting involved with the illegal money changers. Take a well-known brand of cheques: American Express are probably the most widely recognised in China, although other large names are also acceptable .Keep a record of your travellers' cheque numbers separately from the cheques themselves.

It is still a good idea to carry part of your money in hard currency in case of emergencies. This comes into its own particularly if you're nowhere near a Bank of China; most large hotels are quite happy to change hard currency for non-residents but will change travellers' cheques only for residents. US$ bills are the best choice and you should ensure that they are in pristine condition. They must also be 1990 issue or later. Try to carry a few lower denomination notes – they might be handy to pay for a taxi ride in an emergency. Keep your money in your money belt at all times, except for the small amount you need in your wallet, and a reserve (perhaps at the bottom of your rucksack) for emergencies.

❑ **Rates of exchange**

US$1	Y8.29
UK£1	Y13.17
Can$1	Y5.94
Aus$1	Y6.20
NZ$1	Y5.37
DM1	Y4.57

For up-to-the-minute rates of exchange check the Web on **http://www.xe.net/currency**

Photography

Print film is widely available in China, although it is often stored in direct sunlight and kept well beyond its sell-by date. Better to bring what you need with you. Specialist films, including slide film are hard to come by. A useful accessory is a lead lined bag to protect films from X-ray machines at airports and at railway stations.

Be sensible about taking pictures; shooting photos of the police or military is likely to get you into trouble, and at the very least you will probably have the film removed from your camera. Likewise in temples and religious sites, the monks and pilgrims will be extremely offended if you take pictures of the statues.

Ask permission before you start pointing your camera at people, too. Take a lead from the Chinese themselves; you may well find that you are the curiosity in many places, and when Chinese tourists want to take photos of you they'll ask first.

VACCINATIONS AND HEALTH SAFEGUARDS

Vaccinations

No vaccinations are listed as official requirements for Western visitors in China but you should give serious thought to some of the following. Since some injections may have to be given separately you should start planning well in advance.

Up to date health information and on the spot vaccination services are available in London at **Trailfinders** (☎ 0171-938 3999) at 194 Kensington High St, and at **British Airways Travel Clinic** (☎ 0171-439 9584), at 156 Regent St. **Nomad Travellers' Store & Medical Centre** (☎ 0181-889 7014) at 3-4 Turnpike Lane (Wellington Terrace), London N8 0PX offers travel medical advice, inoculations and supplies.

In the USA, the **Center for Disease Control and Prevention** (☎ 404-332 4559) in Atlanta is the best place to call for information. If you have a fax an automated service is provided on the above number to fax you back the latest health information for the countries you are visiting.

● **Diptheria** Check with your doctor that you were given the initial vaccine as a child and a booster within the last ten years. The WHO recommends a combined booster dose of tetanus-diptheria toxoid. If you've never had the diptheria vaccine in any form, you'll need two jabs one month apart, followed by a booster after six months.

● **Tetanus** Tetanus vaccine needs renewal every 10 years. If you cut yourself and you haven't had one, you may have serious trouble trying to get the right treatment abroad, so check.

● **Hepatitis A** The most commonly contracted serious travellers' ailment, this is spread via food, water and infected eating utensils; though it probably won't kill you, it can lay you out for anything up to a couple of

> ### ❑ Drinking water
>
> You would be extremely unwise to drink, or even brush your teeth with, tap water in China. Simple precautions you should take include avoiding ice cubes, salads, and unpeeled fruit (all of which may have come into contact with contaminated water). Drink bottled drinks, or drinks made with boiled water; if you are given a dirty glass for tea or beer, wash it before use with boiling water, or hot tea.
>
> Luckily there is absolutely no problem with obtaining safe drinking water. Bottled water is sold on every street in the country, and the Chinese national pastime of drinking tea means that there are hot water boilers on every train and in every hotel. Add to this the fact that thermoses are supplied to every hotel room, and you should never find yourself without easy access to safe drinking water.
>
> It can still be useful to have the means to purify water should you need to do so either by boiling or by adding a purifying chemical. Tincture of Iodine is available at most chemists: add four drops of 2% Tincture of Iodine to each litre of water, and allow to stand for 20 minutes before drinking. If you don't like the strong chemical taste, add fruit juice powder or a Vitamin C tablet to disguise it. Iodine-based purification tablets such as Potable Aqua or Coghlan's are an alternative. Note that chlorine-based purification tablets are ineffective against the bugs that cause amoebic dysentery and giardia.

months. Gamma globulin, given just before departure, affords protection for up to six months. Havrix Monodose lasts twice that time, and a second shot, given a year after the first, extends protection for up to 10 years.

● **Polio** The vaccine lasts 10 years and is administered orally, usually in a sugar cube; check whether you are up-to-date.

● **Typhoid** A new vaccine, Typhim Vi, gives protection for three years.

● **Rabies** It's debatable whether to have this one or not – speak to your doctor, or the staff at the vaccination centre. The vaccine consists of two (or in some cases three) shots a month apart and means that if you get bitten you won't have to go through the ordeal that others will be enduring. Medical treatment will be necessary but this vaccine buys you time.

● **Japanese Encephalitis** The disease is now rare but if you're heading down to the south west of China, near the Vietnamese border, it might be a good idea. It's given in three shots over the course of a month.

● **Hepatitis B** This is usually only given to those who are going to live or work in China. A single jab, given 10 days before departure, gives three years' protection.

● **Malaria** If you are travelling to central or south China, anti malarial treatment will be necessary. The type of tablets you take depends on which area you're going to – your doctor will have details.

Potential health problems

Two potentially serious problems with which you may come into contact are sunburn and diarrhoea. Prevention is the key to **sunburn**. In the north west, the desert sun is incredibly hot; always wear sunglasses and a hat and get into the shade long before you think you may be burning. If you are badly burned and feel nauseous or dizzy, consult a doctor immediately as you may have sunstroke. Drink plenty of fluids.

With **diarrhoea**, the best thing to do is simply to wait, as it is far better to let your body sort itself out than to mess around trying to 'cure' it. Most people will get an upset stomach at some point, if only as a reaction to the spicy food. Don't panic, drink plenty of water, and if it doesn't start to clear up in a couple of days, then Imodium is usually effective. Don't take too much as it has a very binding effect.

The only other ailment which commonly afflicts those travelling in China is a local **'flu bug**, which can leave you with a very sore throat, and feeling pretty lousy for several days. Lemsip, throat pastilles and aspirin will alleviate the symptoms, but the only real way to get over it is to rest. Some people carry a course of antibiotics with them for just such occasions but it's wiser to let nature take its course and keep drugs for an emergency.

Unless you speak Chinese, the best way to find a doctor fast is via the tourist agencies (CITS) or the large hotels used by foreigners. It is a wise precaution to have travel insurance so that, should you need urgent treatment, or even need to be flown home, your costs are covered.

Travel insurance
You would be foolish not to take out a combined medical and travel insurance policy (available at any travel agent) before you leave.

BACKGROUND READING

Travel narratives
● *Riding the Iron Rooster* – Paul Theroux. Theroux visited China just after it had opened its doors to foreigners, and spent several months travelling the railways to almost all parts of China. This really is essential (and very enjoyable) reading.
● *Behind the Wall* – Colin Thubron. Along the same lines as Paul Theroux's book. Colin Thubron visited China in the mid 1980's. Although he travelled less extensively than Theroux, in many places his accounts of conversations with the Chinese are more poignant and revealing. The result is an unforgettable book which, ten years later, still sheds light on the way modern China really operates.
● *A Traveller in China* – Christina Dodwell. Although Dodwell doesn't write with the style of Thubron or Theroux, this account makes good reading. Arriving in northwest China, she embarks on a remarkable trip, by every means of transport available, including her inflatable canoe.
● *In Xanadu* – William Dalrymple. During a summer break from university, William Dalrymple set out to retrace the steps of Marco Polo's jour-

ney from Jerusalem to the fabled palace of Kubilai Khan. A combination of historical comment, and anecdote make this account fascinating, amusing and exciting, by turns.

● *News from Tartary* – Peter Fleming. A classic travel book. Just before the outbreak of the Second World War, Fleming set out to travel from Peking to Kashmir, across an area of northwest China and the Himalaya which was hardly explored at the time.

● *A Forgotten Journey* – Peter Fleming. This is out of print, now, but is a great book to dip into, if you can find a second hand copy. It is basically a reprint of his diary of 1934-1935 when he travelled from Europe, across the north of Russia and then down through China, as a correspondent for The Times. He writes brilliantly.

● *The Great Game* – Peter Hopkirk. A fascinating account of the covert operations carried out by Russian and British spies in Central Asia during the last century. There's not really much about China, although Kashgar and Tibet feature slightly, but it's great reading about the political machinations of the time.

● *The Gobi Desert* – Mildred Cable and Francesca French. These venerable female missionaries travelled through Xinjiang province in the early 20th century. Another book by them on the same subject is Through the Jade Gate (but The Gobi Desert is better). Both books are overtly religious at times but give an excellent insight into the area. They are out of print, but can be found quite easily if you look around.

● *Buried Treasures of Chinese Turkestan* – Albert von Le Coq. German archaeologist and explorer von Le Coq, travelling across Xinjiang in the early 20th century, took along a case of Veuve Cliquot for special occasions. This account of his expeditions is wonderfully understated and makes excellent reading.

● *China-Burma Vagabond* – Harold B Rattenbury. Although this is hardly likely to make the best seller lists (partly because it's out of print) it's an interesting book, and worth a read if you find a copy anywhere. In 1939 Rattenbury, a missionary with over 30 years' experience of China, returned to visit the mission stations to see how they were doing. He travelled extensively for nine months, through a country racked by war.

● *The Travels – Marco Polo* (translated by RE Latham in the Penguin Classics series). Some may find it rather heavy going for travel reading but this is, after all, the classic travel book, and it's all about China.

● *Did Marco Polo go to China?* – Frances Wood. If you're after a bit of intellectual controversy you should pack this one. Frances Wood, despite her own scepticism about 'Il Milione's' honesty, puts the cases for and against fairly, and in doing so covers some extremely interesting ground about other early visitors to China.

Twentieth century China

● *Wild Swans* – If you were only to read one book about China, it should be this one. The history of 20th century China is told through the (real) experiences of three generations of women. After reading this firsthand account of the violence and madness that China has experienced in the last 100 years you will look at the place, and people, in a different way.

● *My Bodhi Tree* – Zhang Xianlang. This is actually the second book of the series – the first being *Grass Soup*. Zhang Xianlang spent 22 years of his life in labour camps, and these books are the published and expanded versions of his diaries. They offer a bleak personal account of the suffering of millions of internees in the late 1950's and 1960's. Above all they offer a clue to how the Chinese came to terms with this period, both at the time and in retrospect.

● *Peking Story* – David Kidd. Seldom can someone have been in such an ideal position to give a unique account of China. In the late 1940's David Kidd, an American studying in Peking, married the daughter of a high ranking Chinese judge. He lived with the family in their Peking mansion, and watched as the old order disintegrated with the arrival of the Communists. Fascinating.

● *Red Star Over China* – Edgar Snow. In the summer of 1936 Edgar Snow travelled to the Communist stronghold at Yan'an, armed with a letter of introduction. He was the first Western correspondent to interview Mao in these years, and his book was for some time the only firsthand account of 'Reds' in China.

● *The Soong Dynasty* – Sterling Seagrave. A fascinating and very readable history of twentieth century China. Seagrave describes just how unbelievably corrupt a period this was – and how the West was duped time and again. This is another book which is likely to alter the way you think about China.

● *Mandate of Heaven* – Orville Schell. Most visitors to China speculate about what the future holds in store for the country. Starting with an excellent account of the 1989 Tiananmen Square massacre, Schell reveals the facts about China today. There are several recent books which take on the same subject matter, but Schell is probably one of the best qualified 'China-watchers' to give us an accurate assessment.

Guidebooks

Lonely Planet's *China – a travel survival kit* is recommended if you're exploring more widely. The *Blue Guide to China* by Frances Wood contains less practical advice but the history sections are excellent. Odyssey illustrated guides also produce a number of guidebooks which may be of interest, including guides to Shanghai, Beijing and the Yangtse River.

For books about the **railways in China** see p71.

PART 2: CHINA

Facts about the country

GEOGRAPHICAL BACKGROUND

With a total area of 9.6 million square km, the People's Republic of China is the third largest country in the world after Russia and Canada. From north to south Chinese territory stretches 5500km, while from east to west it covers 5200km. China's land borders stretch 22,800km (along frontiers with Korea, Russia, Mongolia, Kazakhstan, Kyrgyzstan, Tajikistan, Afghanistan, Pakistan, India, Nepal, Bhutan, Myanmar, Laos and Vietnam), and it has 18,000km of coastline.

Although it has a huge geographical area, China is, in parts, one of the most crowded countries in the world. It is home to over 1.2 billion people – about a quarter of the entire world's population. The crowding problem is exacerbated by the fact that much of China's terrain is inhospitable and only 10% of it is suitable for farming. A census in 1990 showed that the population density averaged 360 people per square kilometre in the eastern coastal areas, while in the western plateau areas there were fewer than 10 people per square kilometre. Put another way, 95% of the population live on 45% of the land.

Topography

Basically, China's surface slopes from west to east. In the west is the high Qinghai-Tibetan plateau with an average elevation of over 4000 metres. Below this lie the Yunnan-Guizhou plateau and the Inner Mongolian plateau, as well as the Tarim, Yunggar and Sichuan basins, all of which are around 1000 to 2000 metres above sea level. The North China plain, the North-East and the Lower Yangtse Plains, are all between 500 and 1000 metres, while at the bottom of the scale, the coastal plains form part of the continental shelf and are very close to sea level. The low level of the coastal plains has traditionally been the cause of problems. In the case of the Yellow River, the minimal gradient has led to a constant risk of flooding. The river is kept in check by dykes which rise at times over 10 metres above the level of the plain.

The predominantly west to east slope of the land means that most of the rivers also flow towards the east. At 6300km long, the Yangtse is the longest river in China, with a catchment area of nearly two million square km. It is the subject of considerable controversy at the moment as the government pushes ahead with plans to build a hydroelectric plant in the middle of the naturally stunning Three Gorges area. This is due for completion in 2009. The Yellow River, stretching over 5400km across north and east China is the country's second longest river.

Climate

The majority of the Chinese land mass experiences a continental climate. In winter, north and east China are cold and dry with little snowfall; the southern provinces never get very cold. In spring, as the land begins to warm up, strong winds can be generated in the north, causing dust storms. Maritime tropical air starts to return to the south from about March onwards. Where the front forms between the southern tropical air and the northern continental air, cloud and rain are formed. The rains gradually move northwards through China during May, June and July. Extremely heavy rain is experienced, along with consistently humid weather, and there can be considerable flooding. Between July and September typhoons can strike the south and south-east coast. From September onwards as the continental land mass begins to cool, a high pressure centre begins to establish itself over Mongolia, and autumns are generally calm and sunny with low humidity.

There are, of course, extremes. The North-East and North-West experience the coldest weather in winter. In the summer, the North-West usually gets little or no rain and has China's hottest town, Turfan, where the highest recorded temperature was 49.3°C. Xinjiang Autonomous Region which contains both the Tarim Basin and the Dzungarian Basin is dominated by the Taklamakan Desert. In the South-West, by contrast, Kunming, on the Yunnan plateau, is known as the Spring City because of its mild temperatures all year round.

❑ Average rainfall (mm) and temperatures (°C)

City	December mm/°C		March mm/°C		July mm/°C		October mm/°C	
Harbin (north-east)	5	-15.8	20	-5.8	180	22.7	40	5.9
Beijing (north)	5	-2.8	10	4.4	240	26.0	20	12.5
Ürümqi (north-west)	5	-8.7	20	-3.8	20	14.7	50	1.9
Shanghai (central)	50	6.2	85	8.3	150	27.9	75	17.9
Guangzhou (south)	30	15.2	80	14.6	280	28.7	120	23.0
Kunming (south-west)	5	8.3	25	13.2	210	19.9	100	15.0

Transport and communications

China's railways are well developed. Figures for 1993 show that there were 53,800km of track, which, during the year had carried 1.627 billion tons of freight, and 1.054 billion passengers. In addition, 1409km of new track were laid, and 1113km of line were double tracked. There are two major trunk lines, one from north to south the other from east to west. The north-south line with Beijing as its key link consists of the Beijing-Guangzhou railway and the Beijing-Harbin railway. The east-west line, with Zhengzhou as its key link, consists of the Lianyungang-Lanzhou railway and the Lanzhou-Ürümqi railway.

The network of roads is being expanded rapidly, and roads are, for the most part, of good quality. Freight movement by road is necessary in areas not served by the railways and in 1993, there were 1.084 million km of highways open and 8.28 billion tons of freight were carried. The Chinese have perfected the art of loading trucks to the absolute limit of their capacity, and in areas such as Xinjiang and Gansu it is not unusual to see convoys of enormous lorries along the roads. Although private car ownership is becoming slightly more common, most Chinese are restricted to either motorbikes or bicycles.

Transport of both freight and, to a lesser extent passengers, is still very much an option on China's waterways. Over 110,000km of China's inland waterways are navigable and the Yangtse has 6000km navigable throughout the year.

Air travel is increasingly becoming a possibility for wealthier Chinese, and most large cities are well served by a nearby airport.

The economy

In the three decades following Liberation, China's economic development was stopped almost dead by a series of disastrous political movements. The Great Leap Forward and the Cultural Revolution in the 50's and 60's destroyed much of China's infrastructure and removed the intellectuals, while most of the 70's was spent not being able to admit that there had been dreadful mistakes. Bearing in mind the turmoil in which China was embroiled such a relatively short time ago, its recovery, the result of reforms introduced by Deng Xiaoping since 1982, has been remarkable. Throughout the 1990's China has had the fastest growing economy in the world. The official target for economic growth, set by the government, is 8%, but for most of the last six years real GDP growth has hovered between 10-13%.

China's economic growth is, however, posing a number of social and political problems. Socially the gap is widening rapidly between the wealthy cities of the east coast and the poorer western provinces. Two consequences of this are social unrest in minority areas, and migration from the countryside to the cities, which are unable to support the huge growth in numbers. Politically, Deng Xiaoping trod a fine line when he introduced his reforms in the early 1980's. Without contradicting Party policy, he propounded a theory that economic development was a necessary evil which should not be blocked by ideology. Although agriculture and industry have both benefited from being allowed a degree of profit-making, China's leadership is having a hard time reconciling its socialist creed with capitalist business interests. The question now is whether to free the rules still further or reassert Party doctrine. There are obvious implications for reform. China has been applying for the last decade to join the World Trade Organisation but one likely requirement will be that it loosens its own trade regulations, which insist that Western businesses must trade only with government firms. It is already proving difficult to keep Western influences out of the country, and there is a fear that freer contact with the West will lead to greater calls for individual freedom.

Despite the fact that China's economy is booming, the overriding concern of feeding the vast population is still a central issue. Recently released World Bank figures suggest that one third of China's population is below the poverty line. Unemployment and social welfare are also problems which the Chinese government must address in the next few years. Officially the unemployment rate has edged up to 2.9%, but these figures ignore large numbers of city dwellers who are only theoretically employed. If these are added to the equation, some estimates put unemployment as high as 8%. The average monthly wage in China is about Y440 (US$53) per month.

HISTORICAL OUTLINE

Prehistory

According to Chinese mythology, (there are actually several different myths), the creator of the world, Pan Gu, was formed from Chaos before heaven and earth came into being. On his death his body formed the earth, while the fleas on his body became the human race. After Pan Gu came four generations of divine rulers, who invented elements of culture and gave them to their subjects as gifts. The third and most famous of these rulers was Huang-ti, the Yellow Emperor, who is reputed to have invented boats, carts, pottery, armour and medicine.

For those of a more scientific bent, however, early hominids are known to have been living in China about half a million years ago. In the 1920's, fossilised remains of Homo Erectus were discovered in limestone caves at Zoukoudian, to the south-west of Beijing. The remains became known as Peking Man and although the originals went missing during the Japanese occupation, more have subsequently been found and dated to 500,000-210,000 BC. Subsequent finds elsewhere in China suggest that there were several similar cultures at the time. Peking Man was a hunter, who ate cooked meat and berries, and possibly also practised cannibalism. Although he used basic stone tools, there is no similarity between the tools found here and those used by contemporary cultures in parts of Africa, Europe and West Asia. Hence, archaeologists conclude, Chinese Homo Erectus developed separately from his counterparts elsewhere in the world.

Several Chinese sites have yielded examples of remains that fall between Homo Erectus and Homo Sapiens, somewhere in the period 100,000 to 30,000 years ago. Fully modern Homo Sapiens' remains of about 30,000 years old have been found in Shanxi, and of about 20,000 years old in the upper cave of Zoukoudian. Thus it is known that by about 20,000 years ago several parts of China were populated with Homo Sapiens. Neolithic culture was well established in many areas of China by 5000 BC, and from sites such as Banpo near Xi'an, archaeologists have gained a good idea of these Neolithic people's lifestyle. Living in small communities and occupying wooden huts, they kept domestic animals and practised farming, as well as hunting and catching fish. Both weaving and pottery were used, and jade carving was carried out with intricate designs.

The First Dynasties

According to tradition, the first royal house in China was the **Xia Dynasty**, which is reputed to have lasted for approximately 400 years from the 21st century BC to the 16th century BC. Until recently archaeologists have been sceptical about the existence of the Xia, but new finds are now beginning to lend credibility to this earliest of reigns.

Much safer ground is reached in the case of the **Shang Dynasty**. Zhou and Han texts have it that the dynasty lasted from the 16th century BC to the 11th century BC, and that its 31 rulers exercised power over an area covering much of present day northern China. The Shang were a superstitious people who practised religious divination by reading oracle bones which had been deliberately cracked with heat. Much of what we know about the Shang is due to these bones, for the practice was to inscribe the subject of the enquiry, the interpretation and sometimes even the outcome on the bones themselves, over 100,000 of which have been found.

❑ Chinese dynasties

Xia	21st century – 16th century BC
Shang	16th century – 11th century BC
Western Zhou	11th century BC – 770 BC
Eastern Zhou	770 BC - 221 BC
Qin	221 BC - 207 BC
Western Han	206 BC - 24 AD
Eastern Han	25 - 220 AD
–	220 - 581 AD
Sui	581 - 618 AD
Tang	618 - 907 AD
Northern Song	960 - 1127 AD
Southern Song	1127 - 1279 AD
Yuan	1279 - 1368 AD
Ming	1368 - 1644 AD
Qing	1644 - 1911 AD

The Western and Eastern Zhou

The Western Zhou succeeded the Shang in the 11th century BC and established a capital in Hao, not far from present day Xi'an. In 771BC, following repeated attacks by northern tribes, the capital was moved to Lo-yi (near modern day Luoyang), where internal rivalry over succession threw the kingdom into turmoil for 20 years. Although peace was eventually restored, the Eastern Zhou dynasty was so weak that a new style of government resulted. Individual states formed a loose alliance which was led by the most powerful noblemen, acting as protectors to the royal household.

The period was one of considerable turbulence. During the Spring and Autumn Period (722-421BC), scholars were preoccupied with philosophies which attempted to dictate how society and government should operate. Confucianism and Taoism are both products of this time. The latter half of the Dynasty is commonly labelled the Warring States Period (453-221 BC). The name is self-explanatory; by the middle of the fifth century BC, the alliance of states was splitting apart, and neighbours vied for power.

The unification of China

Although a number of small kingdoms existed, it was the state of Qin which became predominant. Its rise started in the 4th century BC, although it wasn't until King Zheng took power in 246BC that the real expansion began. Conquering each of the small states in turn, Zheng finally overcame the Chu in 223BC and the Qi two years later. Thus in 221BC, for the first time, China was unified, and Zheng pronounced himself the First Emperor (Qin Shi Huangdi).

Having gained control, Zheng appointed regional governors and enacted a series of reforms. A universal system of weights and measures was introduced, and a standard script for official documents was adopted. Work was also carried out to enhance the hitherto piecemeal northern defences of the country. Existing stretches of fortifications were joined to form a much larger system which was the forerunner of the Great Wall.

Emperor Qin's rule was also characterised by severity, however, as he attempted to discourage potential challengers by a harsh system of punishments. He suppressed dissent about his style of government by ordering all philosophical books to be burned, and a large number of Confucian scholars to be killed. When he died, his chief minister, Li Si, placed one of the emperor's younger sons on the throne. Although this allowed Li Si to retain his influence, it also meant that there was no one sufficiently strong to hold the empire together. After a period of rivalry between several factions, Liu Bang took power in 206 BC and founded the Han Dynasty.

The Former/Western Han Dynasty

The Han Dynasty is widely regarded as one of the golden periods of Chinese history. In the early stages of the dynasty, Liu Bang, who took the title Emperor Kao-ti, strengthened his existing position. Rivals were disposed of and members of his close family were placed in key positions. Liu Bang's successors, Emperors Wen-ti and Ching-ti, continued strengthening the empire, and by 135 BC the state was strong enough to take a more aggressive stance in foreign affairs. Campaigns were mounted against the Xiongnu to the north, although success was limited because the nomadic tribes were difficult to pin down. The northern defences were strengthened and were extended much further west than they had previously gone; at the same time Han forces pushed west, forging new diplomatic and trade links. Expansion also took place to the south and south-west, and information about territories even further afield was gained from the travels of, among others, Zhang Qian, whose journeys took him as far as north India. By this stage, however, the dynasty was weakening and in 90 BC the capital Ch'ang-an was the scene of violent rivalry.

Attempts to get the situation back under control were partially successful but the Han line was eventually broken in 9 AD. When an infant ascended the throne, a court official named Wang Mang secured for himself the position of regent to the child; later he took the throne for himself and proclaimed his own dynasty.

The Later/Eastern Han Dynasty

Wang Mang didn't last long, however, finally being put to death by rebels in 23 AD. Disorder reigned for a couple of years before Liu Hsiu re-established the Han line in 25AD. The house that he founded is commonly known as the Later Han dynasty, or the Eastern Han, because the capital was moved east to the city of Luoyang.

The dynasty, initially strong, was riven by power struggles. In 184 a rebellion by the Yellow Turbans had to be suppressed and eventually the empire divided into three powerful states: Shu-han in the west, Wei in the north and Wu in the south. The last Han emperor, Hsien-ti, with nothing left to rule, abdicated in 220. Despite the turbulence of the times, however, the Han dynasty had witnessed some major developments. The first Buddhist establishments were founded in China in the second century, and paper was first presented to the court by Ts'ai Lun in 105.

Between the fall of the Han in 220 and the arrival of the Sui dynasty in 581, China was racked by rivalry and instability. Warfare was bitter, and hundreds of thousands died. The names given to the various states which held power during this period are extremely complicated. In outline the three-way split between the Shu, Wu and Wei remained, although small states rose and fell within each. Particularly notable were the

Northern Wei who left remarkable cave art around their capitals – today the Buddhist carvings at Yungang (Datong) and Longmen (Luoyang) are two of the most famous groups of carvings in China.

The Sui Dynasty

In 581, finally, a general named Yang Chien gained supremacy in the north, proclaimed himself the first Sui emperor, and went on to pacify the south. As Emperor Wenti, he effected sweeping reforms including reshaping the bureaucracy, balancing civil and military power, and using a mixture of Confucianism, Taoism and Buddhism to help bring the shattered populace together. A new tax system was instigated and China's northern defences were strengthened.

Although Wenti presided over a remarkable rebuilding of the fortunes of the empire, his methods could be none too savoury. To ensure his claim to the throne he eliminated 59 other members of the royal household, and was reputed to have suffered terrible fits of rage, even beating some of his ministers to death.

The new Sui capital was established slightly to the south of the old Han capital at Ch'ang-an. With walls measuring some 37km in circumference, this was by far the largest city in the world at the time.

Yang Kuang, Wenti's son, succeeded him in 605. Despite an initially successful rule, he embarked on a series of overambitious projects including rebuilding large sections of the Great Wall and work to complete the Grand Canal. It is said that when the canal was completed, the Emperor sailed its length on a tour of inspection in a flotilla which stretched 100km. Yang Kuang's final mistake, however, was to engage in a series of three costly and unsuccessful campaigns against Koguryo (present day North Korea). After a period of large scale revolts, the Emperor was assassinated in 618.

The Tang Dynasty

During the chaos that surrounded the collapse of the Sui, the Tang dynasty emerged. Li Yuan, a high ranking official of the Sui court, was in command of the Luoyang garrison when the rebellions started. Seeing his chance, he used his troops to secure Ch'ang-an, and installed a Sui child as a puppet emperor. He subsequently took the throne for himself, only to be deposed by his son, Li Shimin, in 626, after the latter had arranged for his brothers to be murdered so that he could take power. Despite his apparent brutality, Li Shimin was a good ruler, and the empire flourished. Tang dynasty China was an unbelievably cosmopolitan place; merchants from around the Middle East settled and traded in the large cities, and monks such as Xuan-Zhang travelled as far afield as India to bring back original Buddhist scriptures. Xuan-Zhang's journey was later immortalised in the Chinese classic novel *Journey to the West*.

Li Shimin was succeeded by his son, who proved to be scarcely up to the task of ruling, and the reign ended in crisis caused by overspending, external threats, and natural disasters. After the emperor's death his widow, Empress Wu Chao, took the throne, becoming the only female ruler in Chinese history. The dynasty gradually recovered, and the subsequent reign (712-756) of Ming-huang (Brilliant Emperor) is often seen as the high point of the Tang dynasty, and one of the peaks of Chinese culture. Military operations met with success, taxes were collected fairly, and the arts thrived. Court intrigue and power politics were beginning to take their toll, however. In 755 An Lushan, a powerful and trusted general who had become bitter at the machinations of the ministers at court, started a rebellion. A disastrous defeat inflicted on the imperial forces led the emperor to flee to Sichuan. Although the rebellion was put down in 763, the troops used had been withdrawn from garrisons elsewhere and a series of other rebellions followed. Over the next hundred years the dynasty never regained its control.

Five Dynasties, Ten Kingdoms and the Song Dynasty

The Tang dynasty officially came to an end in 907, although the process of disintegration had been going on for some 20 years. The ensuing years are often known as the Five Dynasties and Ten Kingdoms period, because the north of China experienced five major states while south and central China divided into ten tribes. The last of the major northern states was the Chou. In 960, when a seven year old emperor came to power, the palace guard rebelled and placed their commander on the throne, thus founding the Northern Song Dynasty. By a mixture of diplomacy and force, the new emperor T'ai-tsu brought back under central control all the states bar two. His brother, who succeeded him, finished the job and implemented a series of reforms. Unfortunately the third Northern Song emperor was less successful largely, it is often claimed, because of his own extravagance. Rebellions in 1120 and 1121 signalled an end to his popular support, and at the same time the Chin, a powerful tribe from the north, launched an attack. The capital, Kaifeng, was taken, the court fled south, and Emperor Hui-tsung was made prisoner, eventually ending his days in captivity.

Hui-tsung's ninth son, Kao-tsung, was away on a mission at the time of the defeat. On his return he began the process of rebuilding the dynasty's power in a new southern capital of Hangzhou. This phase of the Song dynasty is often known by historians as the Southern Song Dynasty, for despite gaining control of much of south and central China, the Song never managed to win back the north. After a dozen years of fighting, the Emperor and his chief minister, Qin Hui, opted for a peaceful settlement and signed a treaty with the Chin in 1141. A victim of this new policy was the patriotic general Yue Fei, whose military successes had so nearly fulfilled Song aims; he was put to death and has since become a national hero. Qin Hui, held to blame for his death, is still reviled as a traitor. Although the Song and their new capital thrived, the peace was short lived, for the Mongol invasion at the start of the 13th century made previous alliances and treaties worthless.

The Mongols

In 1206, Genghis Khan, having finally managed to unite the northern tribes, started pushing south into China. In 1209 the Mongols took on the Chin and, having defeated them by 1234, they then turned their attentions to the Southern Song. Fighting continued until the late 1270's, when Kubilai Khan finally brought all of China under his control, and the Yuan dynasty was formed. The Mongols, despite their tendency to leave a trail of destruction behind them, were surprisingly good rulers. Most of the real power was retained in the hands of Mongol officials at all levels, but the new arrivals quickly adapted themselves to the Chinese way of life.

After China had been re-unified, public works were carried out and private enterprise became accepted. International trade, in particular via the Silk Route flourished, and it was at this time that Marco Polo visited China. His account of being able to travel widely in Central Europe through Mongol affiliated states indicates how the Pax Mongolica which existed at this time, allowed unprecedented freedom of movement and cultural exchange.

The Ming Dynasty

Despite the awesome power of the Mongol empire at its height, the Yuan dynasty survived for only a century or so. In 1355 an orphan and former novice monk named Zhu Yuanzhang became the de facto leader of a powerful faction of southern rebels. Consolidating his power throughout the 1360's he finally proclaimed himself emperor on 23 January 1368, in Nanjing. He named his new dynasty Ming (Radiance) and took for himself the title of Hong Wu (meaning Great Military Achievement). He was a conscientious but ruthless leader, eliminating tens of thousands of officials and their families whom he believed to be a threat.

Hong Wu was succeeded by his grandson, but after only four years the boy's uncle seized power, installing himself as the Yung-lo emperor. He established a northern capital in Beijing and thenceforth the dynasty operated the two capitals in tandem, leading to the names they still have today, which mean literally north and south capitals. The Ming dynasty saw a revival of the threat from the north and much work was done on the Great Wall at this time. In the later Ming dynasty Matteo Ricci, a Jesuit missionary, reached Peking. Having found favour with the court, where he was much admired for his knowledge and phenomenal memory, he remained there, teaching.

Decline of the Ming and start of the Qing

The Ming dynasty's decline began in the 16th century, at a time when the Manchus to the north-east were consolidating their power and becoming a serious threat. However, although the Ming demise came at a time when the Manchu tribes were gathered ready for war near China's eastern defences (the gate at Shanhaiguan), the end of the dynasty was actually caused by an internal rebellion. As the rebel army approached Peking in April 1644, the last Ming emperor hanged himself. Opinions as to what happened in Shanhaiguan vary. Some accounts have it that the general in charge, in a last desperate bid to quell the rebellion, agreed to let the Manchus through the defences. Others say that the Manchus had already succeeded in breaching the Wall, and the Ming commander, faced with a fait accompli, surrendered. At all events, the Manchu leader Dorgon entered Peking without opposition and the Qing dynasty was born. By the 1660's the new rulers had finally suppressed the last rebels, and a period of peace, overseen by three excellent emperors, ensued. A century later, in 1750, China was possibly the strongest and wealthiest nation on earth.

Paradoxically, the seeds of China's downfall were sown at this time. In the four centuries since the departure of the Mongols, the empire's population had grown hugely, and food production was falling behind actual requirement; no adequate measures were taken to remedy this. The Imperial government also failed to perceive the threat posed by the arrival of the Western nations.

Direct trade with Europe had started with the arrival of the Portuguese, who in 1557 had been granted the concession of Macau. By the late 1700's other nations were cashing in, and initially trade was very much in China's favour. Western merchants, however, were keen to find a product that they could exchange, rather than having to pay for everything in silver, and they introduced the opium trade. By the late 1820's opium consumption had rocketed, while money was flowing out of China. Poverty, unemployment and a series of bad harvests all exacerbated by widespread corruption, led to a number of rebellions. At the same time, the Chinese found that they could no longer make the rules with the Western powers.

The First Opium War

After a number of minor incidents, the Emperor decided to take the situation in hand. In 1838, he appointed a high ranking official, Li Zexu, to deal with the opium problem in Canton. Li was convinced that if he threatened the foreign merchants with stopping trade altogether, they would back down. On arrival in Canton, in March 1839, he demanded that all opium held by foreign merchants should be handed over. Further to this he declared that traders would in future have to sign a promise never to deal in opium again. A fortnight later he stopped trade altogether, blockaded the warehouses, and held hostage 350 foreigners including the British Superintendent of Trade, Captain Charles Elliot. Eventually 20,283 chests of opium were handed over, and Elliot and the entire British community left Canton for Macau shortly afterwards.

While the Emperor congratulated Li, the British were assembling an expeditionary force, which was ready off Macau by June 1840. The justification for reprisals was claimed to be the unlawful confiscation of goods and the taking of British hostages. In January 1841 the Chuenpee Convention was drawn up and promptly rejected by both sides – by the Chinese for being too harsh, and by the British for being too lenient. Following a number of attacks by the British, four coastal cities were captured and finally, in early summer 1842, the fleet sailed up the Yangtse to within striking distance of Nanjing. On 29 August 1842 the Treaty of Nanjing was signed. Under the treaty's terms, the Chinese were forced to pay 21 million Mexican dollars, and to open Canton and four other ports to foreign trade. In addition there were to be equal relations between Britain and China, and Hong Kong was to be surrendered to Britain.

The Taiping Rebellion – Heavenly Kingdom of Great Peace

The Chinese were also facing a serious internal threat at the time. The Taiping Rebellion originated in the southern province of Guangdong where members of the Hakka minority had formed a pseudo Christian sect. The group was led by Hong Xiuquan, a failed scholar who came to believe that he was the second son of God, and therefore the brother of Jesus. Appealing to the anti-dynastic sentiments of the peasants, Hong envisaged forming a Heavenly Kingdom of Great Peace, in which land and wealth would be divided equally.

Gradually the rebellion spread across the south of China, until in 1853 Nanjing was captured and became the Heavenly Capital. Opium, wine and tobacco were prohibited and land was redistributed. The rebellion lasted until 1864 when the Imperial army, backed up by irregular forces, and with foreign assistance, finally stormed Nanjing. The fighting left a trail of devastation and millions were killed. To make matters worse a famine in the north in 1877-79 is estimated to have led to the deaths of 10 million people.

The Second Opium War

Meanwhile foreign relations had gone from bad to worse. In October 1856, a Hong Kong registered vessel, the *Arrow*, which was supposedly immune from searching by the Chinese, had been boarded and searched by Chinese police. Several crewmen were arrested and a British flag was torn. When the Chinese failed to apologise for this indiscretion, the British bombarded Canton, and with the assistance of the French occupied the city. A joint force then sailed on Tianjin. Faced with the threat of further violence, the Chinese signed the Treaty of Tianjin in June 1858.

The terms of the settlement were once again crippling: ten more treaty ports were to be opened, diplomatic residence in Peking was to be permitted, and large financial settlements were to be made to both France and Britain. The matter didn't rest here. The next year, a British emissary attempted to get to Peking to ratify the Treaty, despite Chinese insistence that it should be signed in Shanghai. Ignoring Chinese protests, he tried to force his way to the capital, and ran up against an armed blockade. In response, Anglo-French forces occupied Peking and burned the Summer Palace. The Conventions of Peking were signed in 1860.

Continued decline

By this stage the combination of China's weakness in the face of foreign military power, and the widespread unrest within the country had led most Chinese intellectuals to conclude that urgent reform was required. In 1861, however, a five year old boy came to the throne, and his mother, the Dowager Empress Ci Xi became his regent. By manipulating the Imperial succession, the Dowager Empress effectively held power for the next forty years. Her main preoccupation was retaining her position, and she actively blocked reform wherever possible. Thus, at a point when China's fate might have been improved by timely action, the situation simply got worse.

In late 1884 China half-heartedly agreed to assist its southern neighbour against the French annexation of Indo-China. Thus ensued the Sino-French war, which further drained resources. Ten years later in 1894 China got dragged into the Sino-Japanese War, which was fought over control of Korea. The Chinese were beaten and forced to pay a large indemnity. In 1900 there was another large internal rebellion – the **Boxer Uprising**. The movement was not only anti-government but anti-foreigners, too. The Dowager Empress, thinking that it could be turned to her advantage, diverted the rebels' anger towards the foreign legations in Peking and then pretended to ignore what was going on. In August 1900, as the situation was getting really serious, European forces arrived and put an end to the Boxer threat. In order to signal their displeasure at the way in which the Chinese government had failed to act, the forces then went on to demolish the Summer Palace. In the Peace Protocol of September 1901, such a huge payment was demanded of the Chinese, that the foreign powers rather ashamedly agreed to spend much of it on educating Chinese students abroad.

Manchuria

Throughout the nineteenth century the Russians, worried that they might be falling behind in the global power struggle, had had designs on northeast China. In 1860 the Chinese government, already harried by the British and French, and trying to deal with the Taiping rebellion, had tried to settle the issue with a treaty. The agreement ceded a large portion of north-east China which still belongs to Russia today. What the Russians really wanted, however, was an ice-free port and access to the mineral resources of Manchuria. The chaos surrounding the Boxer Uprising gave them the excuse they needed and they seized the area. The Russian actions prompted yet more complications, for the Japanese had long harboured plans for their own occupation of Manchuria. Faced now with accepting the status quo or using force, the Japanese struck on the night of 7-8 February 1904, with a submarine attack on the Russian fleet in Port Arthur. Russian resistance crumbled, and by 1905 the USA had to step in to broker a treaty. Characteristically, it was a negotiating process over which China itself had little influence.

Foundation of the Republic

In 1908 the Dowager Empress died and the last emperor, **Henry Puyi** ascended the throne, aged two. By this stage, even if he had been old enough to take control there was little that could have been done to save the dynastic system. Attempts at reform, which Ci Xi had been persuaded to enact after the shock of seeing Peking occupied in 1901, had all faltered because of overcautiousness and corruption.

For the previous decade, revolutionaries such as **Dr Sun Yatsen** had been studying and fund-raising abroad. Sun Yatsen himself was elected head of the Tungmenhui (Revolutionary Alliance, the precursor of the Kuomintang) in Tokyo in 1905. After a series of badly organised and unsuccessful attempts at starting a revolution, an opportunity finally presented itself in 1911. When riots broke out in Sichuan, troops were removed from the garrison at Wuchang, and the factions made their move. On 10 October 1911, Wuchang was seized and separate uprisings around the country followed. On 12 February 1912 the Emperor was forced to abdicate.

Despite having the new presidency within his reach, Dr Sun Yatsen voluntarily stepped down, realising that in order to stand any chance of succeeding, the new Republic must have the full support of the military. In his place, the most powerful military figure in China, General Yuan Shi-kai, was elected to be the first president. The move was a mistake, for Yuan subsequently tried to make himself emperor and to suppress the Kuomintang (KMT). Dr Sun Yatsen started building up his own power base again, but by this stage the country was fragmented and under the control of a number of regional warlords. Unable to master the situation with his own resources, he accepted Russian assistance. In 1923 a Russian adviser, Michael Borodin arrived to help organise the party and its army, which would be used to regain control of the country.

Alliance of the Kuomintang and the Communists

Under Russian insistence, Dr Sun Yatsen was persuaded to let Chinese Communist Party (CCP) members, whose organisation was still largely embryonic, into the KMT. There were grave doubts about the alliance on both sides, but Moscow advised that it was for the best, and Sun Yatsen was powerful enough to quell disagreements. Thus in late 1923 the KMT and CCP were allied. In 1925, however, Sun Yatsen died and Chiang Kaishek, who was much less well disposed towards the Communists, came to be the most powerful figure in the KMT. Both parties held conferences in late 1925 and proposed withdrawing from the alliance; from the KMT point of view Communist influence was growing alarmingly, and from the Communist viewpoint, Nationalist ideology was flawed. Again Moscow exerted its influence. The differences were papered over, in favour of planning the joint military campaign to regain control of the whole country.

The Northern Expedition started in June 1926, and lasted for two years. With Chiang Kaishek as Commander-in-Chief, the armies swept north defeating the forces of local warlords or buying them off where possible. By the end of 1926 fighting stopped to allow time to reorganise; a Communist-led force was based in Wuhan, while a Nationalist army, led by Chiang, was in Nanchang. In early 1927, Chiang's force struck out to the north and north-east; Shanghai fell on 22 March and Nanjing on 24 March. It was at this stage that Chiang, who had been threatened over the previous months by Communist attempts to curtail his power, decided to get rid of the opposition.

Suppression of the Communists

Over the preceding months the Communists had built up a power base in Shanghai, and a carefully co-ordinated uprising allowed the KMT army to enter the city with little or no opposition. Having disarmed the Chinese police, however, the workers were reluctant to hand over control to the KMT commanders. Stalin himself got involved, ordering them via a telegraph message to bury their weapons for use at a more convenient time but the workers refused to comply. Chiang Kaishek was not the only one worried by the prospect of Shanghai falling into the hands of the Communists; business leaders and foreign administrators urged him to take action. Chiang used his underworld connections to hire several hundred gunmen, who were disguised as workers. Before dawn on 12 April 1927 they passed through the barricades and ambushed the unsuspecting Communists. Hundreds died, and leaders of the movement were immediately executed.

In May 1927 the co-ordinated drive northwards continued, but by midsummer the KMT forces were joined by General Feng Yuxiang's army. The general threw his support behind Chiang Kaishek, thus swinging the balance of power against the Communists, who withdrew from the alliance. A number of small-scale Communist revolts were easily quashed by the KMT forces, and in June the following year, Peking finally fell to the Nationalists. On 10 October 1928, the National Government of China was declared in Nanjing, with Chiang as president. Despite the continuation of the Nanjing Government for some nine and a half years, however, China was still not under central control. The government slowly extended its power but even by 1937 large areas were in the hands of warlords or Communists. Chiang's determination to finish off the latter led him largely to ignore a far greater threat that grew throughout the 1930's – the Japanese.

Manchukuo and the Last Emperor

Following the end of the Russo-Japanese war, the Japanese had retained a foothold in Manchuria. Having expanded their holdings in both Manchuria and Shandong during the 1920's, in September 1931 they staged a full-scale invasion of Manchuria. Although China appealed to the League of Nations, Chiang was unwilling to fight, being fully occupied with the Communists whose guerilla tactics defeated his KMT army in a succession of campaigns throughout 1930-2. In February 1932 the Japanese proclaimed the state of Manchukuo and installed Henry Puyi, the last Qing emperor, as the head of state. It was a puppet regime in which the senior Japanese military commander called the shots.

The Long March

Meanwhile, in south China, Chiang's fifth campaign against the Communists, in which he fielded a massive force of three quarters of a million soldiers, finally met with success. The Communists, unable to fight their guerilla war in the face of such numbers, decided to retreat to a safe area in the north. Different groups followed separate routes towards Shaanxi province, Mao's group covering 9600km, averaging some 27 km a day, and arriving in late 1935 after a year on the move. Other groups, however, were still arriving in late 1936. Constantly harassed by Nationalist troops, the dangers and hardships took a devastating toll: only a tenth of those who set out from Jiangxi province reached Shaanxi. On the way, however, the forces had laid important groundwork with peasant groups throughout the country.

The Anti Japanese War

By late 1935, the CCP were appealing to the government to join forces with them against the Japanese. Chiang showed little sign of coming round until, in December 1936, his generals took it into their own hands to act. In the **Xi'an Incident**, Chiang was seized and held captive (by his own commanders) until he agreed to the alliance against the Japanese. In July 1937 all-out war commenced, with the Japanese occupation of Peking and Tianjin. Shanghai fell in November, Nanjing in December and Canton the following year. By 1939 the situation had stabilised with the Japanese controlling east China, and the Chinese government based in

Chongqing. Although a united front operated between the Communists and Nationalists from mid-1937, it was never free of suspicion. The agreement broke down almost completely after January 1941; Chiang's government withdrew all financial aid and even used troops to blockade the Communists' stronghold in Yan'an.

The war years in Yan'an saw the Communists grow rapidly in strength. Not only did the numbers in Yan'an increase to over one million by 1945, but important groundwork was laid elsewhere in China. The Communist soldiers were adept at guerilla war and hence were suited to operating against the Japanese in large areas of occupied China. While they moved around areas which were largely off limits to the Nationalists they converted the peasants to their cause. During this period, too, the leaders emerged and were confirmed; Mao was undisputed leader, Liu Shaoqi became recognised as his right-hand man, and Zhou Enlai as the efficient and personally charming administrator who was able to mediate when required.

Civil War

Following the end of the war, there was a brief period of peace. From August to October 1945 Mao and Chiang met in Chongqing to discuss the future. General George C Marshall, the US Presidential ambassador, arrived in December 1945 to try to mediate between the leaders. He succeeded in making some headway in early 1946, but by June fighting had broken out. The war went in favour of the Nationalists for the first year but by late 1947 the tide began to turn. By early 1949 the Communists had taken Peking, and the Nationalists were on the run. Eventually Chiang Kaishek fled to Taiwan. From the balcony of Tiananmen Gate on 1st October 1949, Mao proclaimed the birth of the People's Republic of China.

The People's Republic of China

For the new government, and Mao, there were two main priorities in the months following October 1949. Firstly the country's infrastructure had to be repaired, and agricultural production returned to normal. Secondly, in order to maintain the support of the masses, there had to be seen to be reform and redistribution of the land. The restoration of manufacturing and agricultural output was achieved remarkably quickly, and it is estimated that by 1952 China was back to pre-war levels. In Mao's first Five Year Plan, released in 1955, the emphasis was placed on investment and building up industry. Russian aid was sought and Soviet machinery was provided in return for agricultural goods and raw materials. The concentration on industry, however, put a heavy strain on agricultural production, and returns were slow.

The Great Leap Forward

In 1958, in order to regain the momentum of the revolution, Mao initiated the Great Leap Forward. His plan, which was opposed by most of the rest of the leadership, was to boost production massively by collectivising farming and motivating the people in the pursuance of a great national aim. It was a disaster. Not only were the people less motivated by being grouped in large communes, but the effort coincided with a number of years of poor harvests.

The withdrawal of Russian aid in 1960 following a long-standing disagreement proved too much. Literally millions of Chinese starved to death during the years surrounding 1960 – some estimates put the number as high as 30 million.

The Cultural Revolution

By late 1961 China was back on a more sensible heading, with a policy which advocated a slower rate of growth, concentrating on agriculture as a priority. Mao by this stage was becoming sidelined within the government. Watching events unfold in Russia, where Kruschev was advocating a closer relationship with the United States, he felt that Communism was losing its way. He needed both to reassert his personal position, and ensure that the original ideals of the revolution remained paramount. By his reasoning 'You learn to swim by swimming, you learn to make revolution by making revolution'. Thus, in 1962 he instituted the Socialist Education Programme, designed to seek out those who were subverting the true course of the revolution. In November 1965 the Great Proletarian Cultural Revolution started.

Famously directed by the **Gang of Four**, a group which included Mao's wife, Jiang Qing, the revolution encouraged citizens to seek out and denounce capitalist roaders. At the same time the young were encouraged to join the Red Guards, who were in turn exhorted to violence; 'To rebel is justified,' Mao declared, 'bombard the headquarters'. Students were encouraged to denounce teachers and workers turned in their bosses; horrifying physical and mental persecution was carried out, often on the basis of no more than a personal grudge. Members of the Red Guards

> ❏ In January 1961 Zhang Xianlang, who was serving a sentence in a labour camp, escaped only to find that conditions were far worse outside the camp than inside. In *My Bodhi Tree*, he recalls the brief time he spent on the run before voluntarily returning to the camp:
>
> 'I experienced personally the trauma of there being absolutely nothing at all to eat, anywhere. No wonder Su Ruixin had run away once and then not tried again; no wonder that during the 'three years of natural disaster' in some regions entire villages shut themselves into their homes and starved to death. Only within an organized social structure such as a labour camp could you, with great difficulty, find enough to eat to keep you alive.'

were practically invulnerable, and they were able to burn and destroy as they pleased. In a country where Confucianism had advocated respect for the old for nearly two and a half millennia, this was a devastating new order.

> ❑ 'Lin Biao...made a speech calling on the Red Guards to charge out of their schools and "smash up the four olds" – defined as "old ideas, old culture, old customs and old habits".
>
> Following this obscure call, Red Guards all over China took to the streets, giving full vent to their vandalism, ignorance and fanaticism. They raided people's houses, smashed their antiques, tore up paintings and works of calligraphy. Bonfires were lit to consume books. Very soon nearly all treasures in private collections were destroyed. Many writers and artists committed suicide after being cruelly beaten and humiliated, and being forced to witness their work being burned to ashes.' *Wild Swans* Jung Chang

From 1969 onwards order began to be restored, but it wasn't until after Mao's death that the Cultural Revolution was officially declared ended.

Recovery

In the 1970's, steered by Zhou Enlai, work began on rebuilding the economy. Ever since his days as a mediator with the KMT, Zhou had been held in high esteem as a man of principle. His reputation had been enhanced during the Cultural Revolution by his personal intervention to curb the worst excesses of the Red Guards. When he died in 1976 the people used the excuse to lodge a very public protest against the government by filling Tiananmen Square with wreaths. The flowers were removed overnight but the next day saw yet more portraits and tributes. The protest was ended after fighting between protesters and the security forces.

Mao died shortly afterwards at the end of 1976, and one of the first actions of the new premier, Hua Guofeng, was to have the Gang of Four arrested. After a brief interlude, the most popular of the Chinese leaders, **Deng Xiaoping** came to power in 1982 and started a process of reforms and opening up to the West which had immediate effect. As foreign trade began to expand, increasingly there were calls for political reform.

Tiananmen Square

In April 1989 a student protest occupied Tiananmen Square, and over the course of the following weeks, the gathering rapidly grew to become a huge pro-democracy rally. Under the glare of the world's media, the ageing Chinese leaders were divided as to how to handle the situation. Deeply distrustful of mass youth movements, after the experiences of Cultural Revolution, they were unwilling to be embarrassed in front of the world's press. Equally, however, many were reluctant to use force, particularly since the event was rapidly becoming worldwide news. The affair was allowed to escalate to the point where only brute force or political submission could have provided a solution. Eventually, the leaders chose the former and on the night of 3rd/4th June Tiananmen Square was stormed with tanks and troops. Estimates of the dead and wounded vary wildly. In the confusion that followed some of the students' and workers' leaders managed to escape to Hong Kong or Taiwan. Others were not so lucky, and even today their persecution continues: in November 1996, Wang Dan was sentenced to a further 11 years in prison.

After Tiananmen

Despite the international outcry following Tiananmen, trade and political links quickly returned to normal, boosted to a large extent by worldwide recognition of the strength of the Chinese economy and the potential market that China seemed to offer.

There are still a number of trouble spots in China, particularly Tibet, which China formally annexed in 1950, and Xinjiang, where there are continual disturbances in support of independence. Social tensions are also caused by the widening trade gap between the wealthy coastal cities of the south-east and the rest of the country. Similarly, the Politburo are facing a tough period ahead in which calls for democracy are likely to get ever stronger. Now perhaps more than ever, China is facing the dilemma of reconciling its own orthodoxy with the ways of the rest of the world.

THE PEOPLE

China is the most populous nation on earth, with somewhere over 1.2 billion people. Despite a massive drive towards birth control the figure is still rising and some estimates put the likely population at 1.5 billion by the year 2030. Traditionally the Han Chinese see themselves as the original Chinese race, tracing their lineage back to the Han Dynasty; they constitute about 95% of the population, while the other 5% belongs to any of 55 ethnic groups. This means that some 60 million inhabitants are looked down upon as non-Chinese.

China is divided into 22 provinces, three special municipalities which have the status of provinces (Beijing, Shanghai and Tianjin), and five autonomous regions. The autonomous regions are designed to allow a certain amount of freedom to important minorities. Below the provinces, there are two further administrative levels: prefectures and counties. There is some provision here, too, for local minorities. In 1994 there were 30 autonomous prefectures and 124 autonomous counties.

Government

China has a rather murky political system, in that there is a marked difference between the way power is exercised theoretically, and the way in which the country is actually ruled. In theory, the highest body in the land is the National People's Congress (NPC), which contains 2970 delegates, who have been elected to represent their provinces, municipalities, autonomous regions, or sections of the armed forces. The NPC elects a Standing Committee, which meets when the Congress is not in session, and also elects the executive (a 15-member state council) and the president. Elections of the State Council members and of the president are held every five years.

In reality, the NPC is pretty much redundant and serves only to rubber-stamp policies. Real power rests in the hands of the Party. The Politburo of 20 members controls all administrative, legal and executive appointments, and its seven member Standing Committee makes all the important decisions. Theoretically the president must be re-elected every five years by the NPC but the incumbent generally enforces his own authority to the point where his position as head of state is unassailable. Jiang Zemin, the current president, occupies the three most influential offices in China: he is President, General Secretary of the Communist Party, and Chairman of the Military Commission (in other words, head of the military). In addition it is widely rumoured that he is keen to reinstate the office of Communist Party Chairman, a position that is associated with Mao, and which was abolished in 1982.

There are hints that the system may be changing slightly. Over the last decade local elections at village level have been encouraged, and results have been free of interference from the Party. Since the results seem to have been successful with genuinely competent representatives elected and a consequent rise in productiveness, there is speculation as to whether such free elections will be allowed to take place at county or even prefectural level. On the other hand, Jiang Zemin has recently been keen publicly to reassert Party doctrine, and stamp on the idea of freer speech. Only time will tell.

Education and social welfare

Since 1976 education has been high on the national agenda and now there is near 100% school attendance rate. Schooling is free and compulsory for six years at the primary stage and two years at the secondary stage. Following the Cultural Revolution, all students went to work in industry for two years before they were eligible for further education. Their academic ability was then coupled with employers' assessments of motivation, both political and practical, to vie for university places. This all changed in 1977 and now university entry is based entirely on the results of entrance exams. Although there are over 1000 colleges, universities and institutes, competition is fierce; since 1985, moreover, further education is no longer free apart from teacher training.

China's main health problem this century has probably been opium addiction, for which the Western nations are largely to blame. After 1949 a major operation was mobilised to purge the country of its drug dependence. This was fuelled by zeal and sheer manpower and was so effective that by 1955 it was claimed that literally no addicts remained. This was only one of a series of campaigns against specific problems, however; another example of this type of action was the crusade against bilharzia, a debilitating disease often termed snail fever, since the parasite responsible develops in snails before passing into the water supplies. Vast numbers of Chinese were mobilised to destroy the snails manually, twice a year. It was a typical labour intensive strategy but it worked, as did other campaigns against lice, mosquitoes, cockroaches and rats.

Traditional Chinese therapies have long been considered archaic by the West but it seems that the more researchers investigate them the more they are impressed; this is the case in particular with acupuncture, which is still used in the East for its anaesthetic qualities during surgical operations. Western know-how has flooded in, however, and Chinese medicine now flourishes on a mixture of the two cultures' knowledge. Workers' medical care is usually financed by their employers, while those working in communes often pay a fixed premium into their group's funds annually, and from this fund comes the money for treatment.

Religion

Confucianism and Taoism are the sources of traditional beliefs in China and with Buddhism form the foundations of Chinese culture. **Taoism**, founded by Lao Tze in the 6th century BC, posits a sense of all pervading unity behind objects and their ideal state. This is the Tao or Way. Life should be lived in accordance with the Tao in order to promote oneness and harmony. Various ways of doing this are prescribed, including such diverse disciplines as yoga, meditation, philosophical dispute and magic. **Confucianism** was also founded in the 6th century BC by Confucius himself, who wrote numerous discourses on the art of successful government. Although he was largely unrecognised in his own lifetime his writings were adopted by virtually all Chinese dynasties later as models for civil service training recruitment and practice. See p347 for information on **Buddhism**.

Since 'Liberation' in 1949, China has had an ambivalent attitude towards religion. Despite Mao's 1954 guarantee of the individual's rights to freedom of belief there is considerable evidence of suppression over the last 40 years, The Cultural Revolution stopped all overt religious activity and was responsible for the wholesale destruction of religious centres and symbols. Thus it appears that institutional religion may have suffered severely, although whether this is reflected in individuals' beliefs is a matter for debate. Following the trial of the Gang of Four in 1976 religious practices became more open. Amongst the ethnic minorities, Islam is strong with about 12 million adherents. There are about 60 million Christians and evangelical sects are reported to be making new recruits.

Practical information for the visitor

DOCUMENTS

You will obviously need to bring all booking vouchers for any advance bookings that you may have made, and your passport. Some travellers also bring other forms of ID card (library card/student card etc) as places such as bike hire stalls usually ask for proof of ID to be left with them as security. On arrival in China you will be asked to show your health documents. In practice, all that most foreigners can show are their vaccination certificates, but as long as you can show something they seem to be happy. Very occasionally hotel regulations state that a man and woman who want to share a room should produce a copy of their marriage certificate but I've never heard of this being enforced.

The *really* useful document to have when travelling around China is a Chinese student/teacher's card, as this entitles you to get into all tourist sites at a fraction of the normal foreigners' price. Obviously you are only entitled to one if you are studying or teaching in China, but there are several places in larger cities which offer to procure fake cards at a price. Many people seem to think that this is worth a try and will insist that you are foolish not to get hold of one. It is obviously illegal, however, and reportedly some travellers were caught recently in Xi'an because the local university, unbeknownst to the forgers, had changed the style of its ID cards. A US$100 fine was, apparently, levied on the offenders.

Customs declaration form

On entering China you will be asked to complete a customs declaration form stating what valuables you are carrying and how much currency you are bringing into the country. This form must be presented when you leave China to prove that you still have all the valuables in your possession, and that you have valid exchange certificates to account for the money. It seems unlikely that the exchange certificates will ever be a problem, partly because it is so easy now to get money on credit cards, that it's impossible to keep track. In practice, however, it's best to play safe: keep hold of the declaration form and the currency exchange slips.

HOTELS AND GUEST-HOUSES

Most cities boast a range of accommodation varying from four- or five-star luxury hotels (starting prices are US$80-100/£50-65), to cheap guest-houses in which you can get a dormitory bed for US$3-5/£2-3. Expensive hotels offer Western facilities, including a choice of restaurants, bars and leisure facilities. Note that all mid- and top-range hotels in China, will have a surcharge which will automatically be added to the quoted price of the room. Sometimes this is justified as a service charge, and at other times as government or city development tax, and sometimes as all three. In most cases you can expect the surcharge to be about 15%, although it can occasionally be even higher.

At the budget end of the market there are no surcharges, and the price you pay largely depends on whether you want a private room, and if you require a private bathroom and/or air conditioning.

Checking in

You'll be asked to show your passport, so that your identity and your visa can be checked. Usually the registration form is in English, but occasionally you may be presented with a form entirely in Chinese. If no help is forthcoming you can probably bluff, simply filling in your details in any order, as the receptionist won't understand much of what you've written anyway. Your passport is returned to you before you leave reception, and you will be asked to pay for at least one night, plus possibly a deposit. The amount of the deposit is at the discretion of the hotel, but it is receipted and is invariably returned without argument on departure.

You are unlikely to be given a key to the room. Instead you will receive a piece of paper or a room card which you present to the attendant on your floor who will unlock your door for you. If you're going backwards and forwards to the room this can get quite annoying, particularly for the floor attendant, but that's the system.

Hotel rooms

Rooms in all hotels come with sandals (flip-flops) for you to shower in, and a thermos of boiling water, as well as mugs for hot drinks. The supply of boiling water is unlimited – you can either refill the thermos yourself from the boiler (usually somewhere near the bathrooms) or get the attendant to fill it for you. Rooms nearly always have a TV (even in the cheap places) and a ceiling fan. Basic bed linen is provided, although in cheap hotels this may only be a huge towelling sheet, and a pillow. In the winter excellent duvets are usually provided. If they're not immediately visible they're likely to be found tucked away in the cupboards.

Medium-priced and expensive hotels have private bathrooms (with Western-style toilets) but cheaper places tend to have communal bathrooms and toilets. In some places the showers are in a separate building, and in many the hot water comes on for only a couple of hours in the evening. The lavatories vary from smelly to absolutely foul, and are usually a row of squat-style toilets with small partitions between them. Many Chinese seem to suffer temporary amnesia when it comes to flushing the toilet after use, so the smell can really build up. As in practically all Asian countries, no toilet paper is provided, so bring your own. The plumbing will not handle the paper, so it goes in the basket provided.

CITS, CTS, CYTS, FITS

CITS (China International Travel Service) is the organisation which foreign tourists deal with when they are in China. In fact, however, CTS (China Travel Service), CYTS (China Youth Travel Service) and FITS (Foreign Individual Travel Service) also perform much the same functions although they were originally set up to cater for overseas Chinese visitors. Tours booked from abroad generally run through CITS or CTS when you get to China. It is worth noting that just because CITS is the official tourist organisation this does not mean that their tours will go like clockwork. What you are guaranteed if you book with them is that the difficult organisation will be done for you and that the trip will go as smoothly as is possible at the time. Whatever happens, if something goes wrong don't create a scene midway through your tour – you are unlikely to accomplish anything and it will only spoil your holiday; wait until you get back and then try for a refund.

The tourist organisations can be useful for the independent traveller. In virtually every Chinese town which is open to foreigners there will be a tourist office run by CITS, CTS, CYTS or FITS. These offices should be staffed by foreign language speakers qualified to assist tourists, and services offered include tours, interpreters and ticket booking.

Recent additions to the scene are privately run travel services, which are springing up in major tourist centres. They are often much more attuned to what tourists actually want, and their services are worth investigating, though you should be careful about parting with your cash if you have any doubts about the honesty of the operators.

PUBLIC SECURITY BUREAU (PSB)

If you get into trouble in China, CITS may well help but will probably refer you direct to the Public Security Bureau. When something has been stolen try to get a signed official declaration to that effect, partly because customs may want proof that you haven't simply sold all your fancy Western gadgets, and partly because you will need a letter if you want to claim on your insurance when you get back. Visa extension is handled by the PSB and is usually a straightforward procedure which takes as little as ten minutes (except in Beijing see p85).

LOCAL TRANSPORT

For information on **trains** within China see the next chapter.

Buses

Long distance buses depart both from the bus station and from outside the railway station. Services are bumpy and crowded but are also frequent and reasonably priced. Generally tickets bought at the bus station ticket counter are fixed price, whereas with private buses and minibus services you need to agree a price. The co-driver will cajole, humour and even force people into the bus until it is so overloaded that passengers are hanging out of the door. Get a definite price before you squeeze in; the less scrupulous bus crews will demand four or five times the real price as soon as they see a tourist, so you must bargain. Although private buses may depart more frequently than public buses and are capable of higher speeds, this doesn't always mean that they'll get you to your destination quicker. Profit is the overriding consideration: the driver will stop for anyone who looks as though they've got a yuan to their name.

In the cities, public buses, trolley buses and minibuses are all convenient ways of getting around. As soon as you arrive in a new place buy a local map since most include bus routes; in most cities vendors will meet you as you leave the station. The only problem with all of the above is that they are often extremely crowded. Many of the buses use a system which is meant to lessen the pushing and shoving by nominating an 'in' and 'out' door (often labelled in English 'up' and 'down'). In theory this is great but on a crowded vehicle it means that as soon as you get on the bus you have to start pushing your way through the crowd to be ready near the exit. Although travel on public transport is generally very safe, it's only common sense to keep a close eye on your belongings.

Typically city buses divide into two types – either you pay money to a conductor once you're on the bus, or else you put the money in a box by the door as you board. Generally Y0.5 is about right if you're only going a few stops, and Y1 is ample if you're going a fair way across town, but if in doubt slot a Y1 note into the box by the door as you get in and no one's likely to argue. If it's a bus with a conductor, keep your town map to hand so that you can show him or her where you're going.

Taxis

Taxis are remarkably standardised around the country. The most common three are Miandis, Tianjins and VW Santanas.

Miandis are little minivans which usually charge about Y10 to pick you up and take you the first 5km, after which it's Y1.4 per km. **Tianjins** (so called because the little Daihatsu-style cars are manufactured in Tianjin) are slightly more expensive. At the top of the range are the **VW Santanas**, many of which are air-conditioned, and which have a flag-fall of about Y20, with a per km charge of Y1.8-2 thereafter. Of course, all this is assuming that they have a meter. In large tourist centres like Xi'an and Beijing, taxi drivers are generally quite fair, but in smaller towns you may have to insist on the meter being used, or start bargaining. Sometimes the prices quoted are ridiculously high, and a good warning sign that you're about to get ripped off is if they have got a meter and don't want to use it. An interesting variation on the normal taxis are the large number of **motorbike** and **motorbike/sidecar taxis**. Generally reports of these are pretty negative: apart from the possibility of crashing because of someone else's irresponsible driving, the riders seldom seem to have a clue where they are going. A ride in a sidecar or on the back of a bike can be a quick and exhilarating way to get around town but they're probably best used when you're going somewhere well known.

At the bottom end of the scale are the **rickshaws**, both motorised and bicycle type. These should be the cheapest of all but the price quoted is usually several times the actual price, so hard bargaining is required.

Bicycle

In many places you can hire a bicycle, and brave the traffic for yourself. It's a cheap and convenient way of getting around: typically bike hire for a day costs Y10-15, and you will be required to leave a deposit of Y100-200, or some form of ID. Some places will ask you to leave your passport, which is not a good idea, but you can often persuade them to take another form of ID (a student card for example), or persuade them to take a cash deposit. Before accepting the bike, check it for serviceability: brakes that work, a saddle that doesn't tip up when you sit on it, and pedals that remain in place when you move off are all an advantage. All hire bikes should also have a lock on them. Lock the bike before leaving it, and in towns ensure that it is parked in a designated bike parking area. You pay a few jiao to leave your bike in a supervised bike park.

ELECTRICITY

The mains electricity supply throughout China is 220V/50 cycles, and there are two main plug types in use: the North American style two and three pin plugs. Many cities in China are prone to power cuts, and when you see the amazing amount of neon on display you can understand why.

TIME

Beijing time is eight hours ahead of GMT. Despite stretching over 5000km from east to west and covering an area which should include three time zones, China operates entirely on Beijing time. This is the cause of understandable frustration to inhabitants of the furthest provinces to the east and west but it makes life a lot easier for travellers. In the extreme areas (Xinjiang in particular) it's worth checking bus times etc, as local time sometimes operates unofficially.

MONEY

Foreign Exchange Currency has now been abolished and tourists and Chinese alike use People's Money or 'Renminbi' (RMB). The basic unit of currency is the yuan (nicknamed the kwai). This is subdivided into 10 jiao (also known as mao), and one jiao is in turn divided into 10 fen. In practice fen are worth so little that they are rarely used, although there are still some fen coins and notes in circulation, just to confuse tourists. The largest banknote is the Y100 note after which there are banknotes for Y50, Y10, Y5, Y2, and Y1 as well as a Y1 coin. For jiao there are both banknotes and coins for 5 jiao, 2 jiao, and 1 jiao. At the bottom end of the scale there are 1 fen notes and 2 fen coins. For exchange rates see p22.

POST AND TELECOMMUNICATIONS

Post

The postal system is both cheap and reliable. It costs Y3.50 to send a letter to Europe and Y2.30 for a postcard to anywhere in the world. It's worth buying the stamps and fixing them on to your postcards before you start writing, as you are frequently given two or three large stamps which end up covering a sizeable part of whatever you've just written. The stamps and envelopes are ungummed, and small pots of glue are available at the post office. An enterprising move in the last couple of years has been to produce packs of ten postcards complete with stamps: check before you buy these as on some the postage is only sufficient to carry the card to an address inside China.

Sending packages home is also straightforward. Business documents can be sent quickly via the Express Mail System (EMS), although it's much cheaper simply to send a parcel in the standard mail. There's usually a wrapping service in large post offices. Note that anything going out of the country has to be inspected by customs, and large post offices will also contain a customs desk. The procedure is a formality but has to be adhered to, so don't seal your package up until they've had a look inside.

A poste restante service is generally operated in large cities, with varying degrees of reliability. Some poste restantes are excellent (Beijing, Guangzhou, Shanghai and Kunming for example) whereas some others are rather slapdash (Chengdu). Addressing mail to 'Name, Poste Restante, General Post Office, City, Province, People's Republic of China' seems to work OK. Get your potential correspondents to ensure that your name is unmistakable – using capital letters and underlining the surname should do the trick.

Telephone

The telephone service is generally very good, and both Domestic Direct Dial and International Direct Dial facilities are widely available. For domestic calls the simplest thing to do is to get a magnetic phone card and use one of the Western-style phone boxes that are springing up everywhere in large cities. The phone cards cost Y20, Y50 or Y100 and are widely available. Note that while China Telecom cards will work throughout China, if you buy a Shanghai or Beijing telecom card it will work only on phones in that city. Alternatively, many Chinese shops have a phone which you can use. You'll see the telephone symbol displayed outside countless places; the owner will meter the call.

International calls, which are relatively expensive, are best made from the post/telecom office, or, if you don't mind the extra expense, from a large hotel. A convenient alternative is to register with an organisation like BT chargecard, AT & T or Sprint, both of which will allow you to reach a local operator and thence be put through to an international service, the bill being sent to your home address.

NATIONAL HOLIDAYS

- 1-2 January: New Year's Day
- January/February: 2-3 days for Spring Festival (Chinese New Year)
- 8 March: International Women's Day
- 1 May: International Labour Day
- 4 May: Youth Day
- 1 June: International Children's Day
- 1 October: National Day

BUSINESS HOURS

Officially, banks are open 09.00-12.00 and 14.00-17.00 daily (except Sunday), government offices open 08.00-11.30 and 13.00-15.00 Monday to Saturday, and shops do business from 09.00-19.00 daily. However, hours may alter according to local customs, the weather, or just the whim of those concerned. Restaurants tend to close relatively early except in large cities or popular tourist haunts.

❑ COPING WITH CHINA

It would be foolish to travel this far across the world and believe that the people and customs you encounter are going to be exactly the same as they are at home. Actually there are far more similarities than you might imagine but as it's the differences which stand out, it doesn't always seem this way. There are a number of Chinese behavioural quirks which tend to annoy travellers so it would be as well to be ready for these.

Money – the two tier system

First, there is the matter of money: the Chinese have absolutely no qualms about charging foreign visitors two, three or even ten times the price that they would expect a local person to pay. Occasionally you will come across a bus conductor who will make a point of asking you for the correct fare, or a passer-by who will argue on your behalf. Generally, however, the system is accepted: foreigners can afford it, so they should pay more. There is little you can do about official overpricing, and you will occasionally find yourself the victim of gross overcharging in the markets. Bargain where possible, but otherwise grin and bear it; losing your temper will only spoil your day.

The problem of saving face

When you come across a cheap hotel which refuses to take you 'because all the rooms are full', ask them if you can book a room for tomorrow, next week, or even next month. The answer is always that this is impossible because they are booked up months in advance. Actually the real reason is that they don't take foreigners but it seems too embarrassing to say this. Examples of the same syndrome are found elsewhere; waitresses will smile and tell you that your food is definitely coming, CITS staff will confirm that they are certain to be able to get you a ticket, and that if you travel down to the museum it will certainly be open. Double and even triple check the answers you receive.

Sometimes, unfortunately, travellers meet with the exact opposite of this behaviour. Either because the person approached doesn't believe that he or she can help you, or because they don't want to lose face if they are unable to do so, the answer is a blanket refusal. 'Mei yo' are the magic words, and can mean anything from 'I don't understand' to 'I don't speak English' to 'Before you ask the answer is no'. The only thing you can do is remain polite, and finally, if you're really being blanked out, go elsewhere.

Being the centre of attention

Somewhat unnerving can be the national habit of staring. The Chinese will stare at anything, and after a few weeks in the country, you'll probably find yourself doing it too. Huge crowds gather in the street to gawp silently at a road accident, an argument, or any other unusual event. How convenient then, if on a long and boring train journey there's a foreigner in your carriage – particularly if he or she has some particularly non-Chinese characteristic – a big nose, hairy arms or a large breasts; this is ready-made entertainment. No harm is meant by all this, and although you may find complete strangers poring over your letter as you write it, it's only out of curiosity. Smile and try some Chinese words – you'll make a lot of friends.

Spitting

For many foreigners one of the most off-putting habits in China is the constant spitting. Waking in the morning in any low budget hotel, you are likely to be met by the sounds of a chorus of fellow residents, all hawking up their guts, as part of their morning ablutions. It's an age old tradition. Marco Polo recorded that, in the palace of Kubilai Khan: '...every baron or nobleman continually carries with him a little vessel of pleasing design into which he spits so long as he is in the hall, so that no-one may make so bold as to spit on the floor.' It isn't considered rude to spit in public – in fact it's necessary; everybody has the 'flu bug, and consequently everybody needs to clear their tubes. This, of course, means that germs get passed around and many travellers who spend more than a short time in China catch some sort of flu bug, – hence the advice to bring throat pastilles and Lemsip.

Lighten up – you're on holiday!

Finally, remember that, as in any country, a smile, a little patience and any attempt to communicate in the local language will go a long way. The Chinese are, for the most part friendly, courteous and hospitable.

FOOD

There is a wide regional variation in food across the country. Very broadly speaking, in the north and north-west the staple food is **noodles**, while the south traditionally has more **rice** dishes, but since food is now easily transported around the country these traditions have become less important. In addition each province has its own style of cooking: **Sichuan** food is renowned for being particularly spicy, **Guandong** for having great seafood and **Shanghai** for being something of a melting pot for everyone else's styles. In effect there are literally hundreds of dishes and styles of cooking – the Chinese love their food and eating out is a national past time. The easiest way to get over the language problem and also to find out what's best in a new town is simply to find a restaurant that's well patronised by local Chinese and try whatever they're eating that looks good. One problem with this is that you're unlikely to find out what you're eating (but then this might also be seen as an advantage).

The Chinese don't bother too much with **breakfast**, so fruit or cooked snacks make a good alternative to keep you going through the morning. The big meal for the Chinese is **supper**, eaten anytime between 6.30 and 8pm, although many places will serve later than this.

Escalope of scorpion?

Often the more bizarre Chinese dishes are the best known, simply because of their rarity. Snake, camel's hump, shark's fin, dog, scorpion, – if you really want to try something different head for an expensive restaurant or the Chinese restaurant in any large hotel. Many of these dishes are probably overrated and will set you back a suitably large amount of money.

One of the pleasures of travelling in China is that there are also great **snacks** available – anywhere near a market you'll find a huge choice of steamed dumplings (*baotse*), fried ravioli (*jiaotse*), hard boiled eggs (often boiled in tea), sweet breads, sweet potatoes, spicy omelettes, rice wrapped in leaves, pancakes, and more. Dig in – things rarely cost more than a few jiao, so if you don't like them it's no problem. Moreover since they are usually cooked in front of you, there's little danger of stomach bugs. There is also an excellent variety of fresh **fruit** available. In the summer, literally everything you can imagine is on offer.

DRINKS

Non alcoholic

The staple drink is tea (*cha*), though for the uninitiated it may come as a surprise to find that there are so many varieties of tea. Generally the Chinese drink **green tea**, without milk or sugar. Variations on the standard green tea are widely available and include a flower tea, which seems to include bits of everything and has a wonderful sweet fruity taste. Tea houses are an institution and are places where people congregate to sit and chat, and play cards or chess and, of course, drink tea. You pay Y2-3 for a cup with some tea leaves in it, and then get unlimited free top-ups of boiling water.

Coffee hasn't really caught on in China, although caffeine addicts will be relieved to hear that it's widely available in department stores. **Soft drinks** are also available everywhere, and an excellent Chinese soft drink worth trying is Jian Libao – the Chinese equivalent of Lucozade. Look out, too, for the small milk churn shaped bottles that are available in some street stalls and contain delicious **fresh yoghurt**. Finally, small bottles of **mineral water** are on sale everywhere for Y2-3.

Alcoholic

The Chinese are great beer drinkers, and excellent local **beers** are brewed in each city, with a large bottle costing less than a can of Coke. The most famous beer in China is Tsing Tao which is made in the city of the same name (although in Pinyin it's spelt Qingdao) in Shandong Province. The brewery was originally built when the Germans set up shop in Shandong at the turn of the century. While Tsing Tao will set you back a few extra yuan (in the market it costs Y5-6), the local beers are often just as good. Despite some fairly appalling **wines** that have previously been available, things have improved since the establishing of joint venture companies. Two wines worth a try are Dynasty and Dragon Seal. There's a wide selection of **spirits** – typically different provinces each seem to have their own variation on a theme. What most of them have in

> ❏ Marco Polo commented on the Chinese liquor in *The Travels*, thus: 'You must know that most of the inhabitants of Cathay drink a wine much as I will describe to you. They make a drink of rice and an assortment of excellent spices, prepared in such a way that it is better to drink than any other wine. It is beautifully clear, and it intoxicates more speedily than any other wine, because it is very heating'.

common is that they are extremely strong, and in some cases probably also fairly bad for your health. The most famous liquor of all is Mao-Tai. Apart from the better known brews, however, you're unlikely to be drinking any of these for pleasure.

WHAT TO DO IN THE EVENING

A traditional **Chinese opera** is a must and likewise, in the big cities, the **acrobatic troupes** are really worth a visit for an hour and a half of pure fun.

The Chinese are completely hooked on **karaoke** as you soon realise from the number of bars with 'OK' written over the door, and the dreadful noises that emerge once the evening gets under way. It could be entertaining if you know the songs but you may find a browse in the **night market** more interesting. There's no lack of things to do in the evening but, except in Beijing and Shanghai, there's a dearth of English-language newspapers telling you what's available. For information, try the reception at more upmarket hotels.

SHOPPING

In all towns of any size there is at least one department store, where things like soap, coffee and writing paper can be bought. Apart from such basics, there is little else that will be of interest in the big stores. Increasingly, smaller shops now have price labels on goods which eliminate the need to haggle, but once in the markets, bargaining is the norm. Whatever happens when you start bargaining, it's important to have a sense of humour and keep smiling, firstly because if you start getting angry the stall keeper is unlikely to back down for fear of losing face. The second and equally important reason is that shopkeepers, with some justification, know that you've got more money than they have, so while good-humoured bargaining is welcomed, losing your temper over something you can obviously afford is rude. Ideas for good things to buy are listed at the end of each city guide.

SPECULATION

The idea of making money by bringing anything desirable to China for resale is a non-starter. As you realise soon after you arrive, Chinese shops are extremely well stocked both with imitation Western goods, and very frequently with the real items.

CRIME

Generally speaking, China is a remarkably safe place to travel but there are occasional instances of foreigners getting robbed. One businessman I met had been the victim of a particularly unpleasant credit card rip off in Shanghai, and there are occasional reports of bags being slashed on crowded buses. Generally, however, the Chinese are friendly and honest, often to the extent of openly sticking up for you if they think you're being ripped off, and returning money that has fallen out of your pocket. Having said this, it's worth ensuring that you take some basic precautions and don't present too much temptation. Always keep a close eye (and hand if possible) on your bag. Carry your money, passport and tickets in a money belt worn under your clothing, and only keep a small amount of cash in your pockets. Illegal money changers have gained a reputation for being violent in some places, so it's best not to try playing around with black market exchanges.

PART 3: THE CHINESE RAIL SYSTEM

Using the railways

China Railways logo

China's railway network is one of the most heavily used in the world, and its importance to the Republic's infrastructure cannot be overestimated. Not only are the railways the prime means of mass transportation but more importantly they are crucial to China's industry and to food distribution. Minerals such as coal and iron are transported from mines in the north and north-east, while grain and farm products can be distributed from the fertile southern and western provinces. The railways are central to China's defences, too, and much of the effort to expand the system as fast as possible has been driven by military expediency. This is particularly important in such a large country, where memories of internal rebellion and foreign invasion are still relatively fresh.

Although Chinese trains can at times be noisy, dirty and uncomfortable, rail travel in China has an element of excitement that is unlikely to be found on the networks of the West. The enormous distances covered, the complexity of the system and the importance attached to its smooth running all give China's railways a glamour which is reminiscent of turn-of-the-century rail travel in Europe or the United States. There is undeniably something romantic about the notion of a train which has travelled for two days from the mountains of South-West China to the ancient capital of Xi'an in the north; and there is the train which leaves Shanghai on the east coast bound for Ürümqi on the edge of Central Asia, or the international service which leaves Beijing, bound for Moscow, via Mongolia.

The image is intensified by the fact that China is one of the last countries in the world where steam trains are still in regular use. The huge engines that you are likely to see in any large station around China are seldom employed nowadays for passenger services but are depended upon for shunting freight. For those willing to go looking, there are some rare locomotives still in use. In the North-East particularly, the number and variety of steam engines used for forestry, mining operations, and for industrial work should keep even the most ardent enthusiast busy.

Most importantly, however, rail travel in China offers the visitor a number of unique opportunities. First and foremost there's the opportunity to meet a wide variety of Chinese people. You may be approached by someone who speaks English, or just be the centre of attention for everybody in the carriage who doesn't; either way you are likely to meet a bunch of friendly and hospitable people. Smile a lot and offer to share some of your food and you will make a host of new friends.

Secondly, travel by train offers a grandstand view of the Chinese countryside. Air travel may get you there quicker but did you come all this way to see the landscape from 30,000 feet? Finally, even the most unmechanically-minded traveller is likely to wonder at the engineering that went into building these railways – some of which run through incredibly difficult terrain. The history and politics that surrounded their construction are a study in themselves. China's railways provide an unusual and fascinating insight into the formation of the modern nation.

Buying a ticket

In most places buying a ticket is a simple process, as long as you've got plenty of time and a heap of patience. Tickets are generally not released for sale until three days before the day of departure, so don't try to book a place more than three days in advance (unless it's through CITS, who can take your order and arrange the reservation through their own channels). With the exception of large cities (Beijing, Shanghai etc) there is no centralised computer system, and most reservations are therefore managed by issuing slips of paper which detail the date, train number and seat/sleeper reservation. One of these slips is glued onto the standard price ticket when it is sold. Because there are often several outlets for tickets in one city (eg CITS may get a quota, and various ticket offices around the city each get a quota), it is possible that although there may not be tickets available at the railway station, another ticket office in the city may still have some reservations. It is very difficult, if not impossible, for small stations along the way to issue reservations. For this reason try to plan your itinerary so that you set off on any particularly long journeys from a large city, as it will be much easier to get sleeper tickets. Small stations are likely to sell only hard seat tickets which will get you onto the train, after which you can ask to upgrade.

Common sense dictates that, in busy destinations, it pays to get to the ticket office early on the first day that tickets are offered for sale. Find out in advance the details of the train you want to catch before you start queuing, and use the ticket booking form (see p380). Finally check with other people in the ticket hall that you're standing in the right queue – not all windows sell tickets for all trains.

Upgrading a ticket

Should it prove impossible to get the ticket you want at the station, it is possible to buy a hard seat ticket and then upgrade it once you are aboard. Upgrading is done on the basis of vacancies – if people got off the train at the last station, or if not all sleeper tickets were sold originally, your chances are reasonable. The extra fee which you are charged to upgrade is worked out, quite fairly, on the distance you intend to travel on the upgraded ticket. Should your berth be reclaimed by someone who has a proper reservation for it, you should be reimbursed according to how much further you have to travel. The guard's compartment (which is probably little more than a desk and a secure area) is usually in the Hard Seat carriage nearest to the centre of the train. Get there as early as possible, as in a crowded train lots of other people will have had the same idea.

Catching the train

Once you've got the ticket, the rest is simple. Try to arrive at the station between half an hour and an hour in advance of departure time. At the main entrance to most stations there is an X-ray machine to check passengers' luggage for inflammable materials – if you're worried about your films you can get past it by just putting your rucksack through and keeping hold of your hand baggage. The procedure for waiting for and boarding the train is extremely regimented and it would be nearly impossible to go wrong. A waiting room, or part of it, is clearly marked as the area for your train (the train number and departure time are displayed). When it's time to board, inspectors check tickets. Once on the platform you must show your ticket again to carriage attendants.

On board the train

Once the train is moving, if you're in any class other than hard seat, the carriage attendant will collect your ticket from you and give you a token in return. This collection of tickets helps the staff to see at a glance how many vacancies are available to allow other passengers to upgrade. The ticket is returned to you just before you get off the train – keep it to hand as you need to show it again to get out of the station.

In most carriages there is a water boiler, as well as a toilet and a wash basin (which invari-

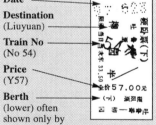

❏ **Deciphering your ticket**
The small cardboard rail tickets come in a number of versions. The front of the ticket usually shows:

Date

Destination (Liuyuan)

Train No (No 54)

Price (Y57)

Berth (lower) often shown only by a berth number on the back of the ticket. There are up to three berths:

下 Lower
中 Middle
上 Upper

A reservation slip may be glued to the **back** of the ticket (or, alternatively, the information may be written directly on the ticket). This will show: train time, month and day of travel, followed on the next line by the carriage number, berth number (and sometimes also the position of the berth – lower, middle or upper).

ably becomes clogged with remnants of pot noodle within a couple of hours). In Hard Sleeper and Soft Sleeper carriages there are thermoses between the bunks and bedding is supplied. The restaurant car (which is typically open 07.00-09.00, 12.00-13.00, and 18.00-20.00), is normally situated near the centre of the train, and the food, though slightly overpriced, is quite reasonable. It is also usually brought around the train in trolleys. This is cheaper than eating in the restaurant (usually Y5-10), and the food is good, but can be pretty cold by the time it gets to you. At each station there are also vendors on the platform selling everything from pot noodles to beer and roast chicken.

Stops
Trains generally stop at stations for anything between one and thirty minutes but it is worth noting that however long your train may be supposed to stop at a particular station, it will wait only as long as the driver feels like waiting. Consequently I have not indicated how long stops last, as this is impossible to predict. Take your cue from the carriage attendant if you want to get off for a wander but never go far from the train itself. At smaller stations you may have to climb over the track in order to get to the platform; do not allow a different train to get between you and your carriage, or you won't be able to get back in.

Kilometre marker posts
The route guide sections of each chapter in this guide refer to the marker posts along the railway line. These can be on either side of the track, although usually they're all on one side along a particular stretch of line. Near a junction, however, the numbering sometimes changes abruptly. Another source of confusion is the approach to, or departure from cities, where numbering can reverse itself several times before finally settling into logical sequence. Finally, there are often long stretches where the numbering either disappears or is so close to the side of the track that it's almost impossible to see.

Using the route guide
In the route guide sections, where something of interest appears on one side of the train only it is designated by the letter (R) or (L) for right or left. Obviously, if you are heading in the opposite direction to this guide, all sights will be on the other side. Note that some of the distances quoted in the text are approximations, so it is wise to be ready for a particular sight a couple of kilometres before it is due. Watch out for two or three markers in succession every now and then so you know which way the numbers are counting, and roughly where you are.

(**Opposite**) An engineer dwarfed by the huge wheels of a QJ locomotive at Harbin.

Railway history

Initial overtures

Although the Chinese had heard about trains long before they actually made their appearance in the Central Kingdom, they were initially less than keen to have the new invention in China. Much of this reluctance stemmed from a general distrust of the foreigners who proposed to import the technology. In 1864, only four years after the occupation of Beijing, the first formal bid was made to obtain a railway concession. Sir Rowland Macdonald Stephenson, fresh from building India's first railway, tried to persuade the Imperial court to let him design a national network. Perhaps unsurprisingly, his proposal was politely but firmly turned down.

There were several practical reasons behind this refusal. The government, beset with the costs of foreign indemnities and suppressing the Taiping Rebellion, had little money available for large scale projects. The road and waterway network which had served so well for centuries would, it was argued, do well enough for a few more years. Equally there were fears of large scale unemployment which could lead to further civil unrest; literally millions of Chinese were employed in the transport business, from muleteers to coolies, and it was feared that the railways would make them redundant. Most important, however, was the concern that allowing foreigners to build railways would only help them to bring larger military forces against the Chinese. The debate was to rage for several years, with one side arguing that railways favoured defence of the country, and the other side claiming that they would help attackers. Overall the official policy was to ignore the issue.

The first lines

Two years after Stephenson's visit, in 1866, a group of British merchants in Shanghai applied to build a short railway from the city to the docks at Woosung to assist with unloading cargo. The request was refused but the project was resurrected nine years later by a syndicate of Chinese and Western businessmen who saw a way to circumvent the ruling. Having obtained permission to build a road to Woosung, they began its construction with narrow gauge track laid alongside. The line, which stretched 10 miles, opened in July 1876 but was short-lived. After a man was run down and killed, the local magistrate objected and closed the operation. In late 1877, the track and equipment were bought from the merchants, torn up and shipped to Taiwan where they were left to rot. The following

---

(**Opposite**) The Great Wall at Jinshanling near Beijing (see p83).

year saw a more successful attempt to bend the rules. The owner of a coal mine in Tangshan, near Tianjin, applied to build a railway to shift coal from the mine to the nearest canal. Initially the trucks were hauled by mules to stave off any objections but finally permission was granted to use a small engine. The home-built locomotive, christened *The Chinese Rocket*, was constructed by the engineer who had built the line itself, Mr CW Kinder. Kinder later went on to build further railways in the North-East, and his six mile stretch of track became part of the Beijing-Shenyang railway. It is perhaps indicative of his intentions from the beginning that the line to and from the coal mine was built with a gauge of 4 ft 8½ ins – standard railway gauge.

Acceptance of railways

In 1880 there was a change in policy when an official paper was presented at court. The report emphasised the benefits of a rapid transport system to the Empire's defences and also stressed that railways would help famine relief and the transport of minerals. It recommended that a number of lines should be built; although agreement was obtained in principle there was little money to fund the projects. Not much was done for the next five years but, following China's defeat in the Sino-French War (1884-85), national security suddenly took on a new importance. The Chinese admiralty applied to extend the Tangshan line east to Shanhaiguan and west to Tianjin to aid the movement of supplies. Under Kinder's supervision, the line reached Tianjin in July 1888, and Shanhaiguan in the early 1890's. In 1889 the proposal, made by a Chinese courtier, Chang Chih-tung, to build a line south from near Peking to Hankow (Wuhan) on the Yangtse river was accepted. The project made little progress because of lack of funds but was the precursor of the line from Peking to Canton. By the start of the Sino-Japanese war in 1894, China still had only some 300 miles of railway. Defeat at the hands of the Japanese made it clearer than ever that modernisation was a priority.

The scramble for concessions

The fact that China did not have the experience or the cash to do the job alone was clear, and the government quietly became amenable to the idea of foreign-built railways. Thus began the scramble for concessions between the various Western nations.

The motivation to build railways in China was not necessarily the profitability of the railways themselves but the spin-offs offered. Railway surveyors were the first to carry out geological surveys along prospective routes and consequently there was the lure of gaining mineral rights. Also, railways promised to carry Western goods to a larger market throughout China: whoever controlled them controlled the trade. Above all, the main motivation may simply have been distrust of the opposition. What Rudyard Kipling termed the Great Game was being played out in

China using railways. Railway colonialism was a way of quietly carving larger empires in the last available large piece of real estate in the world.

Spheres of influence – Manchuria

In order to maintain a pretence of decorum, the foreign powers devised an agreed system of spheres of influence, where each country would press its own interests. The French, continuing their drive north through present day Vietnam, claimed south-west China; the Germans claimed Shandong, the British the Yangtse valley. In particular, the Russians coveted Manchuria. In 1891 work had begun on the Trans-Siberian line which was to connect Moscow with Vladivostok. The Russian engineers soon realised that they could save money and effort if the eastern part of the line could be laid across the flat territory of Manchuria. The Russian Minister of Finance, Sergei Witte, already understood the political implications of the Trans-Siberian which, he believed, would allow Russia 'important advantages over all the other states of Europe'. The chance to get a foothold in Manchuria made the prospects even better. Not only would the railway to Vladivostok be easier to build, but the Russians would have a legitimate excuse to be in north-east China, which offered the prospect of an ice-free port, Port Arthur. Russian aspirations nearly came to nothing when Japan claimed a chunk of Manchuria as its settlement after the Sino-Japanese war. Adept diplomacy followed, as Russia teamed up with Germany and France to persuade the Japanese to give up the territory in favour of a larger cash settlement. Having thus restored Manchuria to the Chinese and ingratiated themselves in the process, all three countries applied for and received railway concessions.

The Trans-Siberian was duly routed across Manchuria, and, since it was guarded by Russian soldiers along the way, became effectively a military corridor through the North-East. At the same time, Russia started work on a line leading directly to Port Arthur, despite earlier assurances to the Chinese that it would not attempt to do so.

Other concessions

Almost simultaneously, France began work on the line which today still runs across the border from Hanoi to Kunming. It was a venture which the Governor-General of Indo-China claimed would be 'an instrument of development and power'. Meanwhile, Belgium put together a consortium of bankers and signed a contract to fund the stalled Peking to Hankow railway. King Leopold foresaw the day when the railway would eventually run all the way from Peking to Canton, and he hankered to be the one who controlled *la colonne vertebrale*. Belgian plotting to achieve this aim continued for several years, and included attempts, eventually successful, to buy out the American firm which was building the southern part of the line. In their turn, the British insisted on being allowed to build six new lines, five of them around the Shanghai/Nanjing/Hangzhou area and one between Kowloon and Canton. The diplomatic and strategic importance which all the main players attached to the railways was demonstrated during the Boxer Rebellion in 1900. The Russians used the excuse to annex the whole of Manchuria in order to protect their interests. Having reached Tianjin, they attempted to carry their advantage still further by insisting that of all the Western forces waiting to advance on Peking they were the best suited to run the rail link from Tianjin to Peking. Things came to a head when they approached the important Fengtai Junction just to the south of the capital. The British feared that control of the junction would effectively mean control of the railway leading south through China. The confrontation lasted for nearly a week while British troops, dug in around the railway junction, held the Russians at bay. Finally the situation was defused when the Germans were appointed to run the railway instead.

The early twentieth century

After the Boxer Rebellion, railway construction continued apace. Following the Russo-Japanese War of 1904-5 the Japanese took control of 700km of the north-south branch of the Chinese Eastern Railway, renaming it the South Manchurian Railway and converting it to standard gauge. They also rapidly built new lines from Mukden (present day Shenyang) south-east to Korea and north to Xinmin. According to Japanese diplomats it was at this time that promises were received from the Chinese that no other lines would be built in competition with the existing ones. Although this agreement was never committed to paper, it was later to be used as an excuse to annex the whole of Manchuria.

In 1905 a line was started north-west from Peking towards Zhangjiakou. Built entirely by Chinese engineers through extremely difficult terrain, the 200km line was completed two years ahead of schedule, and was proof that the Chinese possessed the skills to build their own railways. The engineer in charge of the project, Zhan Tianyou, went on to invent the automatic coupling that is still used today. Unfortunately this home-grown project was one of very few at the time, and despite calls for all railways to be built by the Chinese themselves, other attempts by landowners and businessmen to build local lines often foundered because of poor research and funding. As contracts were consistently awarded to foreigners, anger began to mount at the way in which the rights to China's own transport links were owned by other nationals. The Viceroy of Wuchang, Chang Chih-tung, who had conceived the idea of the Peking to Hankow railway, notably compared the foreign railways to a number of scissor cuts, by which China was being divided up into pieces. Anti-dynastic sentiment was mixed with the indignation of the local dignitaries and businessmen and the Railway Protection Movement was born. This became a focus for malcontents and there were a number of riots in the western provinces. Troops were rushed to Sichuan to control the worst of the violence, leaving other areas thinly garrisoned. The withdrawal from

Wuchang gave would-be rebels the chance they needed. An uprising took place which led to the seizure of power and the formation of the Republic.

The Republic

After the Revolution, the railways came under the control of the central government, and a new Ministry of Communications began the herculean task of standardisation. Sun Yatsen, having stood down from the presidency in favour of Yuan Shikai, became Director General of National Railways. He drew up ambitious plans for a national railway system that he hoped would stretch over 100,000 miles – a tall order when one considers that at this stage China had approximately 5500 miles of line. In order to speed up the work, international consortiums were formed to complete the Hankow to Canton line, and to extend the Long Hai line to Xi'an in the west and to the sea in the east. Although considerable lengths of track were laid in this period, events conspired against swift progress, work being hampered initially by WWI and then by the Northern Expedition. By the start of the 1930's the task of repairing China's railways after years of neglect was a formidable one. Engineers found that sleepers had rotted, bridges were seriously weakened and steam engines which hadn't been serviced for years could not be run at full power for fear of explosions. To complicate matters further no one was sure what holdings the individual railway companies had had, and local warlords were loth to give up rolling stock which they regarded as rightfully theirs.

The Anti-Japanese War

In 1930, relations deteriorated between the Japanese and the warlord in Manchuria, Chang Xueliang. He began to obstruct Japanese plans to build new railway lines, while himself planning new links in competition to the existing Japanese ones. On 18 September 1931, the Japanese created an incident, in which a bomb exploded in front of a South Manchurian train near Mukden. Using this as an excuse, the Japanese army occupied all South Manchuria, proclaiming the new state of Manchukuo in March 1932. Immediately they initiated a spate of railway building to further their plans for developing Manchuria as a commercial and mining centre. Elsewhere in China, although the early 1930's saw considerable expansion of the railways, plans were curtailed by events in the latter half of the decade. In 1937 the Anti-Japanese War started and the Chinese retreated westwards taking with them as much of the rolling stock, workshop machinery, and even track itself, as was possible.

Post Liberation

After 1949, under the Communists, restoration and expansion of the railways became a priority. In 1949 there were 21,000km of line, whereas by 1990 the total railway length was over 88,000km. Among the major projects undertaken, the Trans-Mongolian line through Ulan Bator was built in association with the Russians, and the main east-west trunk line, the

Long Hai Line, was extended west to Lanzhou. Following the breakdown of relations with the USSR, this line was rapidly extended towards the frontier with Russia in the North-West, taking it through Ürümqi. In 1992 the line was finally linked with Central Asian railways across the border.

Just as important was the extension of rail links to South-West China. The first of the new lines ran from Hengyang to Liuchow and Nanning but other lines soon followed linking Liuchow to Guiyang, and Guiyang to Kunming and Chongqing. Later the line from Baoji to Chengdu was completed. The feats of engineering involved in building these lines, which pass through some of China's most mountainous countryside, are staggering. So, too, is the size of the work force; considering that many of the lines were built during the Cultural Revolution it seems highly likely that much of the labour used was forced. In 1968 the famous road and rail bridge was completed in Nanjing. Even today it remains a source of Chinese pride and the most visible sign of their achievements in building their own railways. Work continues at a steady pace on expanding the railway system throughout China, and the latest ambitious project is the high speed link connecting Beijing and Hong Kong.

Steam in China today

For many people the golden age of railways was ruled by steam. Even for the uninitiated, coming face to face with some of the 4000 simply huge machines that still operate in China is a experience not to be forgotten. The country's major locomotive factory in Datong stopped building steam engines in 1988 and steam traction is gradually being phased out. There are persistent rumours, however, that a few steam locomotives are still being made in Tangshan. Despite the fact that the country is now slowly moving towards entirely diesel and electric traction, the steam engines that are still in use are being carefully maintained.

Quite apart from the chance to see steam in everyday use, another fascination of China's railways is the variety of the engines to be found. The international origin of the rail system has led to a distinctive mix of influences. Whereas most of the engines still operating belong to two or three classes, the railway museums in Shenyang and Datong testify to a much richer heritage with trains from Britain, Russia, Japan, Poland, Hungary and the United States. A visit to any of the major remaining steam yards may well reveal a number of unusual models still in operation.

Two classes of steam locomotive are still in common use on the railways today. The most frequent sight around stations is the huge (133 tons) **Qian Jin** (literal meaning Advance Forward) or QJ. The QJ was based on a Soviet design and construction started, with Soviet aid, in the late 1950's. The sheer power of these engines has ensured their continued value: they are still widely used for freight movement. By way of comparison, the QJ has a tractive power of over 33,000kg, while the nearest challenger, the JS, has a tractive power of just over 25,000kg. In layman's terms, the QJ compares favourably for sheer power with any other steam locomotive built anywhere in the world. QJ's were in regular production until 1988. **Jian She** (literal meaning Construction) or JS class locomotives are still a relatively common sight and are descended from the American JF design. The original JF dates from the First World War, and Japan continued its production between the wars. In 1957, with only a few alterations, the design became the JS class, and production continued until 1987. **Small gauge** (762mm) steam locomotives are still in constant use on the forestry railways in the North-East.

Specialist steam enthusiast tours (see p13 and p16) have been operating for several years, and the range of contacts which the best operators have now established ensures not only fair prices but also access to industrial sites where individual travellers would not be allowed to go.

Further reading
- *China's Railways* Colin Garratt (Patrick Stephens, 1988)
- *Industrial Locomotives of the PRC* (Industrial Railway Society, 1996)
- *To China for Steam* Robert Adley (Blandford Press, 1983)
- *The Railways of China* Lt Col Kenneth Cantlie (China Society, 1981)
- *The Dragon and the Iron Horse, The Economics of Railroads in China 1876-1937* Ralph William Hueneman (Harvard University Press, 1984)
- *Railway Enterprise in China* PH Kent (Arnold, 1907)

❑ Railway museums
Special mention must be made of China's two railway museums in Datong and Shenyang. The Chinese have not really perfected the art of presenting the museums well and many of the engines to be seen are rusting away quietly but the selection is probably unique.

Datong contains China's oldest locomotive and the Dowager Empress's carriage which it reputedly pulled. (This may be rather fanciful, since the Type 0 locomotive was brought to China from Britain in the early 1880's and the Dowager Empress's first train journey is believed to have been in 1901, by which time there were undoubtedly more powerful engines available for the task). Also on show are examples of the Sheng Li (SL) 601, and the Renmin (RM) 1001, both of which were built in China in the 50's and 60's. There are also a JF and a QJ on display. **Shenyang** has a much larger and more varied selection than Datong, including a Pacific class SL7, built in Japan in 1934. Other exhibits include a DL 220 and DB 28, both from the United States and built in 1907. There are also other locomotives from Czechoslovakia, Romania, Poland, Japan and Russia. Further details about each of the museums is given in the relevant section of this book.

PART 4: BEIJING AND HONG KONG

Beijing
北 京

No trip to China would be complete without a visit to the capital city, Beijing. It epitomizes modern China. It is the last major Communist capital in the world, and yet it boasts a wide range of five-star hotels. Within a short distance of the city are some of China's finest historical sights, while at the same time Beijing itself is being comprehensively rebuilt as a metropolis of gleaming skyscrapers. In the same market you can bargain for 'genuine' Ming antiques or pirated CDs. Tiananmen Square is dominated by Mao's mausoleum but flanked by American fast food restaurants.

The sights in Beijing are so numerous that no matter how long you stay you are unlikely to see them all. Most visitors allow three or four days here during which time they see the main attractions: Tiananmen Square, the Great Wall, the Forbidden City and the Temple of Heaven. Although Beijing is a hectic, modern city and it can be far from relaxing, travellers tend to agree that it is also one of the highlights of their trip.

HISTORY

In 1921 the earliest evidence of human settlement around Beijing was found at the Zhoukoudian site, 48km to the south west of the city. Here archaeologists unearthed the remains of a hominid cave dweller, believed to have lived up to 500,000 years ago. This earliest ancestor of the Chinese people became known as Peking Man. Historical records, of course, didn't start for another few hundred thousand years. The first written accounts state that during the Zhou Dynasty (11th century BC to 221BC) the feudal state of Yen covered this area, and that the capital Chi was near to the site of present day Beijing.

During the struggles to unify China in the third century BC, the city was destroyed by the First Emperor Qin Shi Huangdi. It was quickly rebuilt and by the time of the Han Dynasty (206BC-220AD), it was recognised as being of strategic significance. The threat of attack by the barbarian tribes from the north was a very real one, and the city was taken and retaken a number of times. The major invasion, of course, was perpetrated by the Mongols under Genghis Khan in 1215. Having torched the place they proceeded to build their own capital here, calling it

Khanbalik (City of the Khan). The Chinese knew it as Ta-Tu (Great Capital) and it was during the Mongol rule that the first Westerners entered the city, including Marco Polo, who described the Khan's palace:

'The palace itself has a very high roof. Inside, the walls of the halls and chambers are all covered with gold and silver and decorated with pictures of dragons and birds and horsemen and various breeds of beasts and scenes of battle. The ceiling is similarly adorned, so that there is nothing to be seen anywhere but gold and pictures. The hall is so vast and so wide that a meal might well be served there for more than six thousand men. The number of chambers is quite bewildering. The whole building is at once so immense and so well constructed that no man in the world, granted that he had the power to effect it, could imagine any improvement in design or execution...'.

The Ming dynasty and the Forbidden City

When the Mongols fell in 1368, Zhu Yuanzhang, founder of the Ming dynasty, established his capital in Nanjing. A generation later, however, Zhu's brother, having usurped the throne from his nephew, moved the capital back. He renamed the city Beijing (Northern Capital), while the southern city became Nanjing (Southern Capital). It was during the Ming dynasty that most of the present Imperial City was designed, and that the Temple of Heaven was built.

Although establishing a Northern Capital was convenient politically, the risk involved in being so close to the north-east border had not diminished. In the end a combination of internal rebellions and external threat from the Manchus in the North-East led to the establishment of the Qing Dynasty. Despite a strong start to the dynasty, the period overall was one of decline. For much of the next three hundred years the last Chinese dynasty, ensconced in the security of the Forbidden City, presided over the slow disintegration of the Empire.

Although a handful of missionaries such as Matteo Ricci were permitted to live in Beijing in the 17th century, foreigners in general were not welcome. When Lord Macartney and his retinue arrived in the capital in 1793 to discuss possible trade links, he was accorded little respect and no trade concessions.

Shortly afterwards, however, the capital began to feel the effects of the foreigners' new influence. Having been humiliated by the outcome of both the First and Second Opium Wars, in 1860 Beijing itself was the target of Western violence. The city was occupied by a joint Anglo-French force and the Summer Palace was ransacked. The government had no option but to concede to demands that foreigners should be allowed to live in Beijing. European embassies began to spring up, and parts of the city were declared foreign areas. During the Boxer rebellion of 1900, the foreign legations were besieged for two months. When reinforcements finally arrived, punitive measures were taken, including the burning down of the recently rebuilt Summer Palace.

BEIJING – KEY

Where to stay

1	Palace Hotel	1	王府饭店
2	Peace Hotel	2	和平饭店
3	Taiwan Hotel	3	台湾饭店
4	Beijing International Hotel	4	国际饭店
5	Beijing Hotel	5	北京饭店
6	Munzhu Hotel	6	明珠饭店
7	Qian Men Hotel	7	前门饭店
8	Bei Wei Hotel	8	北纬饭店
9	Long Tian Hotel	9	泷天饭店
10	Qiaoyuan Hotel	10	侨苑饭店
11	Jingtai Hotel	11	京泰饭店
12	Jing Hua Hotel	12	京华饭店

What to see

13	Tiananmen Square	13	天安门广场
14	Forbidden City	14	圆明园遗址
15	Temple of Heaven	15	天坛
16	Beihai Park	16	北海公园
17	Taorantang Park	17	陶然亭公园

Where to eat

18	Bin Yi Fang Roast Duck Restaurant	18	便宜坊烤鸭店
19	Qianmen Roast Duck Restaurant	19	前门烤鸭店
20	Sichuan Restaurant	20	四川饭馆
21	Kentucky Fried Chicken	21	肯塔基烤鸡店
22	McDonald's	22	麦当劳
23	Pizza Hut/Vie de France	23	比萨饼屋
24	The Sunflower Club	24	太阳花俱乐部

Shopping

25	Friendship Store	25	友谊商店
26	Silk Market	26	丝绸市场
27	Pearl Market	27	珠宝市场
28	Wanfujing Dajie	28	王府井大街

Other

29	Central Railway Station	29	中心火车站
30	Main Post Office	30	中心邮局
31	CAAC	31	民航
32	CITS (Beijing Office)	32	北京国际旅行社
33	PSB	33	公安局
34	Visa Service	34	签证办事处

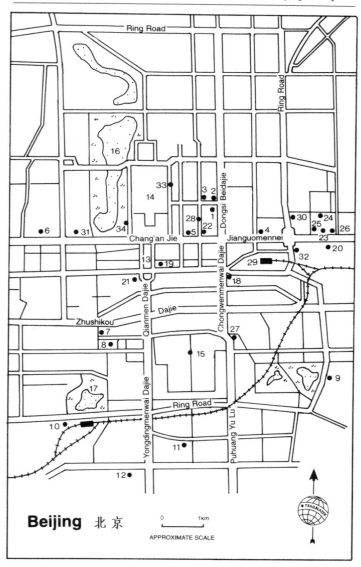

Ring Road

Ring Road

16

33

3 2

Dongsi Beidajie

14

28 1

22

5

34

Chang'an Jie

6

31

30

25 24

26

4

23

Jianguomennei

20

13

19

29

32

21

18

Qianmen Dajie

Dajie

Chongwenmenwai Dajie

Zhushikou

7

8

27

15

17

9

Yongdingmenwai Dajie

Ring Road

10

Puhuang Yu Lu

11

12

Beijing 北京

0   1km

APPROXIMATE SCALE

★ TRAILBLAZER

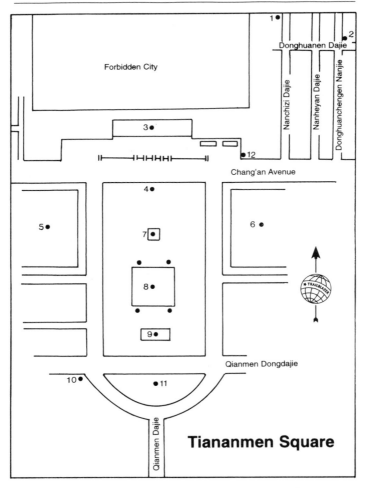

Tiananmen Square

1 PSB
2 Bank of China
3 Tianan Gate
4 Flagstaff
5 Great Hall of the People

6 Museums of Chinese History and the Revolution
7 Monument to the People's Heroes
8 Mao's Mausoleum

9 Qianmen Gate
10 Kentucky Fried Chicken
11 Arrow Castle
12 Bicycle Park and lavatories

Revolution and beyond

After the abdication of Puyi, the city remained at the heart of the country until the Kuomintang moved the capital to Nanjing in 1928. It was renamed Pei Ping (Northern Peace), as it had been during the first years of the Ming rule. The city was occupied by the Japanese in 1937, and after the World War, was held at first by the KMT and then by the Communists. On 1st October 1949 Mao proclaimed the formation of the People's Republic of China, from the balcony of Tianan Gate. Beijing was the capital again, although the order was changed. David Kidd, who was living in Beijing at the time, describes the preparations for the ceremony in *Peking Story*:

'In the middle of the plaza [Tiananmen Square], workmen had drilled a hole as big as a well. It had turned out to be the foundation for a huge flagpole, on which now waved the flag of the People's Republic – one large and four small gold stars on a red field. The cosmic heart of Peking had been pierced with a flagpole. (Years later, the mausoleum of Mao Tse-tung was also to be built on this same sacrosanct axis). The meaning of the flagpole was clear to all who lived in Peking. The old city had been struck its deathblow'.

Although the old order might have been changed, Tiananmen Square has remained the symbolic heart of China since 1949. Whenever a great political statement has been made, it has been made here. In the late 1960's it was the scene of mass rallies of the Red Guards. In 1976 the flowers and wreaths for Zhou Enlai that covered the Monument to the People's Heroes reflected the political opinion of the masses. Most recently in 1989 the pro-democracy movement which ended in the Tiananmen Massacre, occupied the square for nearly two months before its abrupt and bloody dispersal.

WHAT TO SEE

Tiananmen Square

The ideal starting place for a tour of Beijing, the square itself is vast (40 hectares) and has been the site of a number of important movements in 20th century Chinese history, from the declaration of the Chinese Republic in 1949, through the massive fanatical reviews of the Cultural Revolution to the massacre of the pro-democracy protesters in 1989. If you include the Forbidden City to the north, the numerous sights in and around the square will take at least a day.

Chairman Mao's Mausoleum In the centre of the square, this is the best place to visit first, as it is open only from 8.30am to 11.30am. It was completed in May 1977 and is still pulling the crowds in, with well over a million Chinese visitors coming each year. The mausoleum is hemmed in north and south by four statues, each representing historical struggles of the Chinese people. Queues can be long but the line moves surprisingly fast, so you shouldn't have to wait for more than 10-20 minutes. Inside, guards bark at you if you slow down or look as if you are about to stop for a better view. Bags and cameras must be left in the booths on the east side of the mausoleum.

National Museum of Chinese History On the eastern side of the square, this huge building also houses the Museum of the Chinese Revolution. Entry to each museum is Y10. They are open 08.30-15.30, closed Monday.

The **National Museum of Chinese History** contains extensive relics from every period of China's history, with occasional English labelling, making a visit here something of a guessing game. Easily recognisable are the prehistoric tools, early jewellery and terracotta warriors.

The **Museum of the Chinese Revolution** contains many hundreds of relics from pre- and post-WWII struggles: everything from photographs, flags and cannon to a cloth cap once worn by Mao. Also in this building is a display of gifts given to the Chinese government by foreign dignitaries, which is less culturally exciting but still pretty interesting: check out the Brazilian teatray surfaced entirely with butterfly wings, and the fearsomely tacky Shakespeare plate from the UK.

Great Hall of the People Covering an area of 170,000 square metres, this hall is used for meetings of the National People's Congress but is open to the public from 08.30 to 15.30 when meetings are not being held. Unless you enjoy looking at vast, empty rooms give this a miss, saving yourself Y30. Photographers may decide to avoid the place because of the X-ray machine at the door, through which all bags must pass.

Qianmen Gate This was the main entrance to the northern half of the city. It was built in 1419 and at 42m is the tallest of the old buildings here. It's possible to get inside for Y5 to see the photograph museum (no English labels). Continue climbing for a good view of the square and its surroundings, and to visit the huge souvenir shops; although items in here have price tags on them, it's sometimes possible to haggle.

Other sights in Tiananmen Square The monument to the People's Heroes stands directly north of Mao's mausoleum; this was the centre of the wreath-laying protests in 1976 (see p46). It is decorated with Mao's and Zhou Enlai's calligraphy and the base contains carvings which illustrate suitably revolutionary events in Chinese history. Directly to the north of this flies the PRC flag from sunrise to sunset, and if you get here early or late enough you can catch the Colours ceremony. Finally, note that there are toilets and a bicycle park just to the east of the Tianan Gate.

Tiananmen (Gate of Heavenly Peace)
On the northern side of Tiananmen Square sits the entrance to the Imperial (Forbidden) City. This famous gate was also used as a podium

from which imperial decrees were read and from here, on 1 October 1949 Mao proclaimed the foundation of the People's Republic of China. The front is embellished with a huge picture of the man himself, and the inscriptions read 'Long live the People's Republic of China', and 'Long live the unity of the peoples of the world'.

Inside is an exquisite ceiling, a couple of paintings of Mao and his acolytes and a few bits of furniture. Entry, at Y30, is somewhat over-priced. Open 09.00-17.00.

The Imperial Palace (Forbidden City)

The Imperial Palace, comprising more than 178 acres, 1000 buildings and 9000 rooms, is so vast that it's difficult to know where to start. It would be impossible to do justice to it in a short guide such as this, so what follows is merely a brief overview. To explore the whole thing you'd need to spend days inside; half a day is about all most people can take in.

The palace itself, also known as the Purple Forbidden City, was built in the reign of the Ming emperor, Yong Le, between 1406-20, and since then has been the home of 24 emperors, right up until 1911. It has been destroyed by fire and rebuilt a number of times but reconstruction has always followed the original designs, so the integrity of the place is retained.

Maps of the Imperial City are common, and many city maps have them on the back. For those not taking private tours, it is worth hiring the cassette tour outside Meridian Gate: for Y30 a rather droll Roger Moore guides you round the sights. After the tour, of course, there's nothing to stop you exploring other areas on your own.

The Imperial Palace is open 08.30-16.30 but ticket offices close at 15.30. Entrance is Y55.

● **Entering the city** There are five bridges over the Golden Waters River leading to Tianan Gate. The middle one and the central path throughout the city were reserved exclusively for the emperor's personal use. Emperors were not expected to soil their feet with the ground, how-ever, and so the central path through the palace was constructed entirely of marble; this was known as the Imperial Way. Moreover, just to be sure that no dirt ever touched the imperial feet the emperor was carried every-where in a sedan chair. Tianan Gate leads you to Duanmen (Upright) Gate and then to the Meridian Gate, which is the entrance to the Forbidden City proper. Ticket offices are on the right.

Although you cannot see the water from the Meridian Gate, you should be aware that you are crossing over the moat, which is fifty metres wide, and through the walls, which are seven metres thick. Emperors used to stand inside Meridian Gate to supervise the flogging of errant courtiers in the eastern half of the square inside; records tell of one such session in 1534 when 134 men were beaten here. Seventeen died.

● **Central halls** Heading north, you will pass through the Gate of Supreme Harmony, to face the largest structure inside the city, the **Palace of Supreme Harmony**. From the throne in this palace, the emperor surveyed the most important court pageants. Nearly 100,000 state officials could fit into this square. Passing on, you will come to the **Hall of Complete Harmony**, which was used as a preparation room for the emperor and for occasional state functions; there are two original sedan chairs in here today.

Behind this is the **Hall of Preserving Harmony** which was used for less significant banquets and for the final stage of the highest civil service examinations. Of the ten shortlisted candidates (drawn from all over China) three would be chosen by the emperor. These three were allowed to follow the Imperial Path through the city only once. Behind the Hall of Preserving Harmony, note the vast carved marble slab decorating the stairway; this is the largest single piece of marble in the city, weighing over 200 tons. It is 16.5m long, 3m wide and 1.5m thick, and it was dragged to the palace in winter when water was thrown over the roads to make them icy.

● **Inner court** To the north of this ramp lie the living quarters of the emperor – the élite part of the city – and there are three successive palaces here. The first, the **Palace of Heavenly Purity**, was the emperor's bedroom until the mid 18th century, when it was converted into a meeting room for foreign dignitaries. The second, the **Hall of Union**, was the empress's quarters, while the third, the **Palace of Earthly Peace**, was used, among other things, for the consummation of imperial marriages. The blocked-up hole against the wall of this building was part of a charcoal underfloor heating system. Behind the palace you will find the Imperial Garden, which was laid out in the Ming dynasty. From here the path leads straight to the Hall of Imperial Peace, and then to the Shenwumen Gate, the northern exit from the Forbidden City.

❏ Marco Polo was particularly impressed with the emperor's harem, noting that selection was generally governed by physical appearance, but that suitable candidates were handed out to baron's wives to be examined. They were under the strictest orders to 'observe them carefully at night in their chambers, to make sure that they are virgins and not blemished or defective in any member, that they sleep sweetly without snoring, and that their breath is sweet, and they give out no unpleasant odour'.

● **Other sights** It would be a mistake to wander through the palace only from south to north. Other sights of interest in the eastern part of the city include the **Museum of Clocks**, the **Dragon Screen**, the **Jewellery Museum** and **Qianlong's Garden** (this contains a tiny artificial river along which cups of wine were floated; whenever the cup stopped moving with the flow the person nearest it had to compose a poem or drink the contents). Look out for the **Imperial Opera House** and the **well** in which Guangxi's favourite concubine, Zhen Fei, was drowned on the orders of his aunt, Ci Xi.

Immediately to the north of the Forbidden City is **Jingshan Park**, built on an artificial hill made out of earth removed to create the palace moat. Most palace visitors go straight into the park after leaving the north gate, for the top of the hill affords a great view of the city. If you are not totally overloaded with Forbidden City architecture, there are a couple of interesting buildings on the northern side of the park, too. As Beijing's parks go, however, this is not one of the most peaceful. Entry is Y0.3.

Tian Tan – The Temple of Heaven

Tian Tan was the site at which the most auspicious imperial ceremonies were held. Although there were altars here for many years before, the temple as we know it was built in 1420 at the order of Yong Le (who was also responsible for the Forbidden City) and since then emperors have visited regularly to pray for good harvests and to celebrate the winter solstice. Invariably the emperor would enter the complex through the western gates, spending at least one night fasting in the **Hall of Abstinence**. South-east of this hall stands the marble **circular altar** constructed in 1530 and later rebuilt in 1740. It is worth noting of this altar, as of every building in the ensemble, that construction dwelt upon the sacred numbers three and nine, each being representative of heaven. Thus virtually any statistic you can think up about the buildings here (apart from their construction dates, of course), will be a multiple of three. Try counting the number of tiers, steps, or the posts around the edge.

Just north of the altar is the **Imperial Vault of Heaven** which contained the sacred ancestral tablets, to be produced for each ceremony. The **circular wall** around this vault is said to have been designed for its acoustic properties, which should ensure that a whisper towards the surface of one side of the circle is clearly audible on the opposite side. What it actually ensures is that there is always a deafening rumpus here as everyone claps and bellows frantically at the wall.

To the north is the **Hall of Prayer for Good Harvests**; this is the most important building of the complex, and it is particularly impressive. It was built entirely without glue or nails.

The temple is well worth seeing, and the park which provides its setting is lovely, too. Get here as early as possible in the morning or late in the evening when the place will be more or less quiet, otherwise it will be swarming. It's a 10-minute cycle ride south of Tiananmen Square, and bus Nos 35 and 36, among others, run past the northern entrance. Entry to the park itself is only Y1.5, but tourists are pressed to take the sightseeing ticket, which gains you entry to all the buildings and costs Y30 (keep your ticket, as it is needed for access to different areas). The park is open from 06.00-22.00, the temple from 08.30-17.00.

The Summer Palace

The palace and its grounds together clock in at a hefty 290 hectares – four times the size of the Forbidden City. Three quarters of the area, however, is taken up by Kunming Lake (the Lake of Superior Brightness). Originally this was a small pond but it was converted into a reservoir in 1292 to provide drinking water for the area. In 1750, Qianlong built a garden here to celebrate his mother's birthday and the lake was further expanded. Since that time the site has been used by the imperial households as a summer retreat. Following the Opium Wars the palace was sacked by Anglo-French troops in 1860. It was rebuilt on its present site by Ci Xi just in time for it to be burned to the ground again in 1900 after the Boxer Rebellion. As with the Forbidden City, there is far too much on display to cover adequately here but you should try to see the following.

From the East Palace Gate the visitor steps into the royal residence areas. Here, in the late 19th century, the Empress Dowager Ci Xi lived and received guests. Her unfortunate nephew, Guang Xu, was imprisoned here, despite the fact that he was the legitimate heir to the throne, and the wall she built to stop him from escaping can still be seen. In this area you will find Ci Xi's private theatre and a number of living quarters which have been converted into museums (Ci Xi's car, clothing, carriages and make-up are all on display). On the left as you reach the lake you will see the small Perceiving of Spring Jetty/Island, so called because the ice melts here first at the end of winter. Passing to the south along the shore you come to the beautiful 17-arch marble bridge leading to South Lake Island, which is the setting for the Dragon King Temple.

Heading north and west, you will be approaching Longevity Hill. Turning left around the lake you find the Long Corridor, which, measuring 730m from end to end, is the longest covered walkway in the world. It is very impressive, with unique artwork on every eave. This brings you to the main architectural structures of the complex, the Cloud Dispelling Hall and the Tower of Buddhist Fragrance, which at 41m high is the park's dominant non-fluid feature. In the former building Ci Xi used to celebrate her birthdays, and there are a number of museums here, each of which charges an entry fee; in one of them is the famous portrait of her in 1905 by Dutch artist Voss Hubert. Entry to the hall and tower is Y10.

Most visitors see about this much and then visit the famous marble boat further to the west but there is a good deal more exploring to do if you have the time. It would be easy to spend a whole day here. You could walk around the lake, or row across it, and find a quiet spot on the south-eastern side for a picnic.

To get to the Summer Palace take the metro to Xizhimen station. Walk west along Xizhimenwai Dajie towards the zoo. Then either take bus No 332 west to the end of the line or catch a minibus, whichever comes first; the terminal is right next to the entrance. There is a good, clear, aerial map of the complex on the right as you go in. Entry to the palace is Y45.

❏ Excursions to the Great Wall

China's most famous tourist attraction has a long and venerable history. As far back as the Warring States period individual principalities were building walls to protect themselves. With the unification of China by Emperor Qin Shi Huangdi in 221BC, however, it was decided to link the extant stretches of wall together in order to protect the Chinese against their one common enemy: the barbarians from the north.

The Wall has been periodically revamped, usually at times when the northern threat was particularly serious. Despite the huge work undertaken by the Ming, the wall did little to stop the Manchurian invasion in the 17th century, which led to the foundation of the Qing dynasty. While the Wall may be considered a failure for defensive purposes, it acted as a very effective means of communication, allowing envoys to travel through dangerous country safely, and messages to be quickly relayed across the country.

Which section to see? The Wall makes an easy day trip from Beijing, and the majority of visitors head for the stretches at either Badaling or Mutianyu. This in itself is an excellent reason for going somewhere else, a good choice being Simatai, which is harder to get to by yourself but is the destination for the reasonably priced tour run by the travel service at the Jing Hua Hotel. Most exclusive of all, at the moment, is the area around Jinshanling, and it's likely to remain this way. Jinshanling is not easily reached unless you have your own transport, so either hire a minivan between several people, or don't bother. Wherever you go, allow a full day, to give time for a good 2-3 hour wander when you get there (it's a two-hour drive to both Mutianyu and Badaling). Be prepared for some serious stair climbing, although there are cable cars at Mutianyu and Badaling. Being lazy will cost you at least Y50.

Mutianyu, Simatai and even Jinshanling get very busy in the summer and there are numerous stalls selling souvenirs. Badaling outdoes them all, however; here you can buy a 'Not a plucky hero until one reaches the Great Wall' certificate for a thoroughly reasonable Y15.

Getting there Bus tours to Mutianyu and Badaling run from virtually every hotel. CITS currently organise a day tour to Badaling and the Ming Tombs for Y320, and an afternoon tour to Mutianyu for Y230. To get to Badaling on your own, take a train from Xizhimen (north) railway station. It's about a three-hour ride each way, so you can catch an early morning train out and a late afternoon train back. For Simatai, take the 07.00 bus from Dongzhimen station (don't miss it: it's the only one all day) or try the travel service in the Jing Hua Hotel, who will arrange to take you there and back for Y80.

While most visitors spend long enough at the Wall to have a wander and take some pictures, there is the scope here for longer excursions. If the weather is nice, radical student-types bring guitars and sleeping bags, and yomp off to the further reaches to camp; this has been highly recommended by some. The more energetic and those who have their own transport recommend a day walk along the Wall between Jinshanling and Simatai – it's about five hours of hard walking and not for the faint hearted. Bring lots of water, and make sure you're wearing strong shoes, as the Wall descends almost to rubble in places. Finally, there are occasional special events which can be quite fun – 'Jazz on The Wall' and 'Hamlet on the Wall' were two recent examples. The best place to find out about these is in the listings of *Beijing Scene*.

Beihai Park

Located just to the north-west of the Forbidden City, Beihai Park is pleasant place in which to while away an afternoon, although it can get rather crowded, especially at weekends. Entry is Y10 and the boat to the island costs Y2. Its history considerably predates the Imperial Palace, for it was on the southern side of the lake here that Kubilai Khan lived. Construction of the lake, which accounts for over half of the park's area, originally started in the 10th century, the rocks being piled up in the middle to form Qionghua (Jade Flower) Island. The Yuan dynasty remodelled the place, while the ever-busy Qianlong conducted major reconstructions here, too. The buildings were sacked and burned by foreigners in 1900 following the Boxer Uprising.

Entering the park from the south you will find all that remains of Kubilai Khan's Stately Pleasure Dome: a huge carved **jade bowl** from which, apparently, he used to drink wine (he must have been some drinker, because it's about a metre across). Behind the bowl, in the Chengguandian (Hall for Receiving Light) is an impressive Buddha figure encrusted with jewels, hewn from a single piece of white jade. The figure originally came from Burma and was presented to Ci Xi in the late 19th century.

Crossing the Yong'an Bridge you come to the park's most famous construction, the 35m high **White Pagoda**, which was built in 1651 to commemorate the first official visit of a Dalai Lama to Beijing. In fact the top half of it only dates to 1977 and it had been rebuilt a number of times before this as the result of earthquake damage.

Other notable sights, both on the island and off it, include the **dew collecting plate**, which was used to gather pure dewdrops for the emperor's various potions, and a **nine-dragon screen** on the northern shore. The **Five Dragon Pavilions** which line the shore are so-called because their roofs look like the spine of a huge swimming serpent. There are also **botanical gardens** on the northern side, and it is possible to rent rowing boats in summer. In winter the lake becomes a huge **ice-rink**.

Museums

Apart from the museums in Tiananmen Square there are numerous other museums including the **Museum of Peking Man** (the skull here is a replica), Zhoukoudian, Fangshan District; the **Museum of Buddhist Sutras and Relics** (Fayuansi Temple), Xuahwu District; **Cultural Palace for Nationalities** on Fuxingmennai Dajie; **Beijing Art Museum**, Wanshousi St, West District; **Beijing Stone Carving Museum**, Wutansi (Five Pagoda Temple), Xizhimenwai; **Memorial Hall of the Chinese People's Anti-Japanese War**, near Lugou Bridge, Fenghai District; **Observatory** (astronomical instruments dating back to 1442), Jianguomen; **National Art Gallery**, Wusi St, East District; **Natural History Museum**, Tianqiao Lu.

PRACTICAL INFORMATION
Orientation and services

Despite the size of the city, orientation is made considerably simpler by the fact that streets head either east-west or north-south. There are excellent maps available, and the streets are all clearly named in Pinyin, so it doesn't take too long to get the hang of it. Street names, however, can be confusing at first because there are often several of them. The main east-west thoroughfare, for example, starts off in the west as Fuxing Lu, then becomes Fuxingmenwai Dajie, Fuxingmennei Dajie, Xi Chang'an Jie, Dong Chang'an Jie, Jianguomennei Dajie and then Jianguomenwai Dajie.

CITS staff can be found in many of the up-market hotels, notably the Beijing Hotel. The two main offices, however, are at opposite ends of the Chang'an Rd: CITS head office (for all China) is at 103 Fuxingmennei Dajie (☎ 6601 1122), while CITS Beijing is at 28 Jianguomenwai, in the building next to the Gloria Plaza Hotel. CITS Beijing are fairly helpful and are the ones that you are most likely to want to speak to. They can book **air tickets** here (☎ 6515

8564) and **train tickets** (☎ 6515 8565), and can also advise on city tours and all aspects of booking a trip onwards through China. Both offices are open 08.30-17.00. There is also a CITS **ticketing office** (☎ 6512 6688 ext 1751), which deals with air tickets only, in the Beijing International Hotel. The service here is surprisingly good and you may find that they can provide you with the cheapest air tickets in town. They are open: (weekdays) 08.30-11.30, and 13.30-17.00; (Saturdays) 08.30-12.00, (closed Sundays).

The **Public Security Bureau (PSB)** is immediately to the east of the Forbidden City on Beichizi Dajie and the visa office here is open 08.30-11.30 and 13.00-17.00 (closed Saturday afternoon and Sunday). Beijing, however, is not the place to extend your visa, if you can help it. Although the prices are cheap, the system here demands that you leave your passport for a week which is clearly extremely inconvenient for any tourist. The alternative is to go to the **Beijing Consultation Centre for**

❑ Embassies

Australia (☎ 6532 2331) 21 Dongzhimenwai Dajie, San Li Tun
Austria (☎ 6532 2062) 5 Xiusui Nan Jie, Jianguomenwai
Belgium (☎ 6532 1736) 6 Sanlitun Lu
Canada (☎ 6532 3536) 19 Dongzhimenwai Dajie, Chaoyang District
Denmark (☎ 6532 2431) 1 Dongwu Jie
France (☎ 6532 1331) 3 Dongsan Jie, Sanlitun
Germany (☎ 6532 2161) 5 Dongzhimenwai Dajie
Kazakhstan (☎ 6532 6182) Sanlitun
Mongolia (☎ 6532 1203) 2 Xiushui Beijie, Jianguomenwai
Netherlands (☎ 6532 1131) 4 Liang Ma He Nanlu
New Zealand (☎ 6532 2732) 1 Dong Er Jie, Ritanlu
Norway (☎ 6532 1329) 1 Dong Yi Jie, Sanlitun
Pakistan (☎ 6532 6660) 1 Dongzhimenwai Dajie
Russian Federation (☎ 6532 2051) 4 Dongzhimen Bei Zhong Jie
Sweden (☎ 6532 3331) 3 Dongzhimenwai Dajie
UK (☎ 6532 1961) 11 Guang Hua Lu
USA (☎ 6532 3831) 3 Xiushui Bei Jie, Jianguomenwai
Uzbekistan (☎ 6532 6854) 2-1-92, Ta Yuan Diplomatic Compound

Private Overseas Trip (sic), on Taiyanle Hutong, on the west side of the Forbidden City, where they will get you a visa extension in two working days – but at a very hefty charge. It is bound to be cheaper and quicker to extend your visa anywhere other than Beijing.

The **CAAC office** (☎ 6601 7755), 15 Fuxingmen Dajie, is open 08.00-20.00. It's to the west of the Forbidden City. There is a bus service to the airport from here; the trip takes about an hour, depending on traffic, and you will have to buy a ticket before getting onto the bus (there's an English sign by the kiosk). First buses go at 05.30 but it would be safer to get a taxi at this time.

The main **post office** is on Jianguomenbei Dajie, immediately to the east of the Beijing International Hotel. There is an efficient poste restante counter here. There's also a new post office almost directly opposite the Beijing International.

The CITIC Industrial Bank will change travellers' cheques into US$ and also allow you US$ withdrawals on major credit cards. They have a branch next to the Friendship Store on Jianguomenwai Dajie, which is open from 09.00-12.00 and 13.00-16.00. This is also a good place to try if you need to have money transferred from abroad.

If, after months on the road, you're desperate to read an English paper, pay a visit to the British Council who have a reading area with papers and news magazines. They are at: 4th Floor, Landmark Building, 8 Dong San Huan Beilu, Chaoyang District. A limited selection of Western newspapers and magazines is also available in the Friendship Store.

Local transport

Many travellers rent **bicycles** from their hotels and since the city is flat this is a convenient way to get around, although some sights are a long way apart.

Buses are generally very good but can be frighteningly overcrowded, so be very careful with your valuables. Don't even try to get on at rush-hour unless you enjoy being elbowed in the ribs. One bus to look out for is bus No1, which runs east-west along Chang'an Ave and is particularly useful for getting from the West railway station (where trains from Xi'an and Luoyang arrive) to the city centre. You should have no problem spotting this one: it's a double decker. The **metro** is simpler, but won't take you back to your hotel unless you are staying right in the centre of town. Station names are also in English, making life relatively easy, and the set fee for any trip is Y2.

Taxis are easily available and drivers are usually good about using the meter – though you may need to remind them. The price per km should be advertised on a sticker in the side window. Motor- and cycle-rickshaws are another matter, and you'll have to bargain to get a reasonable price.

Tours

Tours to virtually anywhere are available from the leading hotels and CITS. A lot of the main sights are not actually too far away though, so it's probably worth ignoring tours to, say, the Forbidden City, the Summer Palace or the Temple of Heaven. It is worth taking a tour to see the Wall, however, and the Ming tombs. The best place to organise the Wall trip is at the travel service in the **Jing Hua Hotel**, where a day trip to Simatai costs Y80. Likewise, **Monkey Business** (☎ 6329 2244), who specialise in Trans-Siberian train travel, have also run good tours in the past and are worth contacting. They're at Beijing Commercial Business Complex, No1 Building Yu Lin Li, Office Room 406, 4th Floor, Youanmenwai. **CITS tours** are generally for package tourists, often incorporating a whole day's sightseeing. If you take one you may end up visiting places that you don't want to see, have already seen, or are capable of seeing on your own.

Where to stay

There are hundreds of hotels in Beijing, and it is possible only to list a very few of them here.

Lottery winners should head straight for the **Palace Hotel** (☎ 6512 8899), where the cheapest rooms start at US$260. A bar of chocolate from the foyer shop will set you back US$7.5. Just across the street are the **Peace Hotel** (☎ 6512 8833), with rooms from US$90, and the **Taiwan Hotel** (☎ 6513 6688), which has doubles for Y798. The **Beijing International Hotel** (☎ 6512 6688) charges from US$100 for a simple tourist room to US$1200 for a suite. The **Beijing Hotel** (☎ 6513 7766), which is the closest hotel to Tiananmen Square is in the same price range: US$110 for a room. The **Minzhu Hotel** (☎ 6606 1579), is slightly more reasonable, charging only US$85 for a single. All of the above, of course, will automatically add 10-15% service charge to your bill.

For slightly more modest standards a good option is the **Qian Men Hotel** (☎ 6301 6688) on Hufang Lu, at Y630 a double. Single occupancy reduces this to Y580. The **Bei Wei Hotel** (☎ 6301 2266) is still pretty central but much cheaper at Y242 a double. The **Long Tian Hotel** (☎ 6771 2244 ext 5888) charges much the same prices (Y298 for a standard room and Y366 for a superior room, but it is much less conveniently located. The former backpackers' haunt, the **Qiaoyuan Hotel** (☎ 6303 8861), is also a fair way out from the city centre. It has recently been refurbished and has double rooms for Y280.

Currently, there are only two choices for those on a tight budget. The **Jingtai Hotel** (☎ 6722 4675) is reasonable: doubles go for Y90 (Y120 with bathroom), and the place is clean and friendly. It's not too far from the city centre, and the market on Anlelin Lu at the top of the lane is particularly colourful. Otherwise go for the **Jing Hua Hotel** (☎ 6722 2211), which is cheaper

and consequently extremely popular with backpackers. Doubles with bathrooms are unspectacular at Y150 – it's the dormitories that count here: a bed in the 30-bed dorm is Y26; in a six-bed dorm Y28, and in a four-bed dorm Y35. Bikes are hired from the restaurant next door for Y10 per day; there's a Y400 deposit is required; there is a reasonable travel service on the second floor.

Where to eat

There are thousands of restaurants and food stalls in Beijing. It is as well to remember, however, that some close very early, although the larger places are more in tune with Western eating hours. The best way to decide where to eat is probably just to keep your eyes open as you wander around, and then come back later. Taxis are cheap, and are the easiest way to get from your hotel to the city centre in the evening.

Wherever you are staying, you will probably want to try the local speciality which is, of course, **Peking Duck**. There is no one predominant Peking Duck restaurant; what there are in abundance are restaurants whose name seems to imply that they are the original roast duck restaurant. Generally most of these are not bad at all. The **Bin Yi Fang Roast Duck Restaurant** on Chongwenmenwai Dajie, is as good as any and is only a 10-minute walk from the railway station. Another favourite is the **Qianmen Roast Duck Restaurant** (☎ 6701 1379) at 32 Qianmen Dajie. Other duck restaurants are marked on most tourist maps.

An unusual option for eating out, if you can afford it, is **Mr Lee's Restaurant** (☎ 6618 0107). He specialises in serving dishes cooked in the same traditional ways as food that was prepared for the last of the Imperial line, at the turn of the century. A number of stories about how the Imperial household used to function are likely to accompany your meal. The only problem with this place (apart from the price) is that he is often booked several weeks in advance.

A good area to find excellent **contemporary Chinese food** is along Dongzhimennei Dajie. Go to Dongzhimen underground station and walk west along Dongzhimennei Dajie; you will find the street lined with small, cheap restaurants, most of which will be packed. All of them are good, although most people seem to end up with a favourite.

Another great spot is the *Sichuan Restaurant*, which is on a back street just off Jianguomenwai Dajie. To get here, go down Jianhua Lu, which is the small street leading south off Jianguomenwai, opposite the Friendship Store. Bear left at the first junction and left again at the first opportunity; you'll find yourself in a quiet back street running parallel with Jianguomenwai. There are several excellent places here, and in the summer, with the trees strung with lights, it's a good spot for a long, relaxed dinner.

For **Western food** there is no end of choice, and listing restaurants is almost pointless, because more and more are

---

❑ What to do in the evening

Beijing is not renowned for its nightlife but it has opened up dramatically over the last year or two, so there are plenty of places to visit (if your budget will handle it). For traditional entertainment, every visitor ought to make a big effort to either go to the opera or see an acrobatics display.

Opera Forget what the historians tell you about Chinese opera; if you enjoy elaborate costumes and ear-wrenching wailing, this is for you. Most head for the Peking Opera Troupe at the Liyuan Theatre. The theatre is at the Qianmen Hotel (☎ 1935-2045), 175 Yong'anlu; performances take place 7.30-8.45 on most evenings. Another popular venue is the Beijing Hu Guang Guild Halls at No3, Hufangqiao, Xuanwu district. If you're Western, it's obligatory after sitting through an opera to comment on how wonderful the costumes were.

Acrobatics You are unlikely to see better acrobatic displays than in China: leaping through hoops, throwing small children around, spinning plates on sticks and more – how could anyone fail to enjoy it? The best way to find venues is by checking the *China Daily* but there are usually shows at the Chaoyang Theatre (☎ 6507 2421), 36 Dongsanhuan Beilu, Hujialou, at 7.15pm nightly. The travel service at the Jing Hua Hotel organises tickets and transport to see the acrobats, for Y60.

Other There are plenty of Western-style places to see everything from films to drama, and live music. The best source of information is the main expat news-sheet *Beijing Scene* copies of which can be picked up from their office behind the Silk Market (Rm 168 Kindly Commercial Development Centre, 9 Xiushui Nanjie), or at most of the places listed here. *Beijing This Month* and *Beijing Weekend* also have details as does the *China Daily*.

There are now innumerable Western bars and restaurants which are great for a night out, among the most established being *Mexican Wave* on Dongdaqiaou Lu, Jianguomenwai, *CD Café* (great jazz on Friday nights) on East Third Ring Rd, south of the Agriculture Centre, and the *Sunflower Club* on South Ritan Park Rd, Jianguomenwai. Big names such as *Hard Rock Café* and *TGIFriday's* are also to be found. The *Poachers' Inn* is the nightclub where most expats seem to go after everything else has closed – it has the atmosphere of a teenage disco, so you'll need to be in the right mood.

opening on a daily basis. For fast food fans there are now more than ten branches of **McDonald's**, and probably an equal number of **Kentucky Fried Chicken** places. The Friendship store is flanked by **Pizza Hut** on one side, and **Vie de France**, a French bakery with delicious pastries and freshly baked bread, on the other. If you fancy any sort of Western food, consult *Beijing Scene* (see 'What to do in the evening').

What to buy

If you're planning to fly home from Beijing, the obvious advantage of doing all your souvenir shopping here is that you won't have had to carry it all across China with you. The disadvantage, of course, is that you may end up paying more, and that some things may not be available. Unless you are shopping for ethnic exotica from Xinjiang, however, Beijing will have virtually everything.

Lazy shoppers tend to head straight for the large **Friendship Store** on Jianguo-menwai Dajie, where shopping is straightforward, numerous Western luxuries are available, including books and newspapers, and prices are high. Still, it's very convenient. A nice gift from here might be one of the fragile silk or paper kites you'll have seen people flying at the Temple of Heaven. The **CVIC** and **Lufthansa Centres** likewise offer up-market goods (including Western designer names) for relatively high prices. If you're after books, go to the **Foreign Languages Bookstore** on Wangfujing Dajie, where choices are limited but prices are low. Check out the CDs and tapes upstairs. The **Wangfujing area** generally is a good place to browse with a variety of high quality goods offered from the many stores here. Bargain hunters and shopping addicts favour the little streets to the south of Tiananmen Square in the **Qianmen District**, where almost anything seems to be available from small stalls and shops. The best bet for souvenirs is the **Pearl Market** (Hongqiao),

which is in a large multi-storey building opposite the north-east corner of Tiantan Park. There's a food market in the basement, and on the upper floors you'll find everything else, including 'antiques' (don't believe what they tell you), pearls and semi-precious stones. Bargain hard! Another great shopping spot is the **Silk Market** on Jianguo-menwai Dajie, where clothing is the main thing on offer. This may not be the cheapest place in China for silk but if you shop around it's got to be close. It's good for designer and outdoor clothing, too, as many of the big names (Ralph Lauren, North Face, Karrimor etc) have their clothing made in China, and you can get things at excellent prices.

For the very lazy, the main hotels have smart gift shops and the Beijing Hotel in particular has several.

Moving on

Booking tickets out of Beijing is straightforward but expensive.

By rail **Domestic tickets** must be bought from the railway station from which you will be departing: thus west-bound travellers (Luoyang, Xi'an, Lanzhou) should go to the huge new **West Station** (take bus No 1 all the way west to its terminal), and most other travellers will need to go to the **Central Station**. Alternatively CITS will book for you, saving you the queuing and hassle – all for Y50. Note that there is a Foreigners' Ticket Office in Beijing Central Station: to get there, go through the Soft Class Waiting Room.

To get a ticket for one of the **international trains** you will almost certainly need to go through CITS or a private ticket agency. Whoever you use in the end, try to book as early as possible. Most people book their tickets in advance and pick them up when they arrive in Beijing to avoid being faced with a long wait. CITS currently charge between Y1600 and Y1800 for a ticket on the Trans-Siberian to Moscow.

Otherwise, good people to contact are **Monkey Business** (see p18) who specialise in Trans-Siberian and Trans-Mongolian rail travel. For more information see *Trans-Siberian Handbook*, also from Trailblazer.

By air Numerous airlines offer flights to major cities worldwide. A good place to start looking is in the **SCITE Tower** (confusingly spelt CVIK on the building itself, and SCITE on city maps) opposite the Friendship Store on Jianguomenwai, where among others, you will find British Airways. Before paying for anything however, visit the **CITS Air Ticketing Centre** in the Beijing International Hotel, which can sometimes offer the cheapest tickets of all. Sample fares through CITS are: London Y5500, Berlin Y5500, Hong Kong Y2310, Paris Y5500, Singapore Y3780 and Tokyo Y4390. Flights within China booked here include Xi'an Y980, Lanzhou 1120, Shanghai Y1100, Guilin Y1720 and Chengdu Y1570.

Hong Kong
香 港

With the Chinese flag now flying over Hong Kong, it's an interesting time to visit this former British colony. Despite its small area (1091 square km), Hong Kong is literally packed with things to do and places to see. This section aims only to give a quick outline of what's on offer.

Quite apart from the sightseeing and shopping Hong Kong is a great place to sort yourself out for the next leg of your travels and get visas, cash advances and plane tickets.

HISTORY

Hong Kong's early history, unsurprisingly, is remarkably similar to that of Guangzhou (see p180). The area was settled in Neolithic times, and subsequently became home to a number of ethnic groups such as the Punti, Hoklo and Tanka. In the early years of the Empire, however, the population soon diversified. During periods of violence and famine in the north, large numbers fled south to the relative safety of the coast and the islands nearby. Hong Kong was not always a safe haven, however, for the area was often a target for Japanese pirates.

With the arrival of Western merchants who traded initially from a base on Macau, Hong Kong became an important staging post. Foreign ships would often call in to replenish water supplies on their way to Guangzhou. Mistaking the name of a nearby village for the name of the whole island, they called the island Hong Kong. It wasn't long before Hong Kong's potential was recognised. The British, who wanted to have a base of their own, noted that the bay between the island and the peninsula was an excellent natural harbour, providing both shelter and deep water. The Chuenpee Convention in January 1841 (a half-hearted attempt to settle the dispute that led to the First Opium War) gave the excuse that was needed. Although the treaty drawn up at the convention was never signed and was subsequently rejected by both sides, the arrangements were hazy enough to permit a liberal interpretation. On 26th January 1841 Commodore Bremmer landed and hoisted a flag at Possession Point.

The following year Hong Kong was formally ceded to Britain 'in perpetuity' under the terms of the Nanjing Treaty. The cession was merely a formality. Land had first been offered for sale by the British Government in June 1841, some 14 months beforehand. Large scale building followed the initial property sales and the island quickly developed as a major trading centre. The Treaty of Tianjin (June 1858) led to the cession of Kowloon Peninsula, and the Treaty of Beijing (1860) gave the British Stone Cutter's island. By 1881 Hong Kong had a population of over 160,000. In 1898, in order to allow the colony to become self-sufficient, a further stretch of territory was added. Under the terms of the Convention of Peking, The New Territories were leased to Britain for a period of 99 years. Despite the fact the Britain technically 'owned' the islands and peninsula, it was the lease on the New Territories which expired in 1997, which prompted Hong Kong's return to China.

During the early twentieth century, Hong Kong consolidated its position as an industrial and financial centre of South East Asia. Increasing pressure for space led to huge reclamation projects. Today, many of the

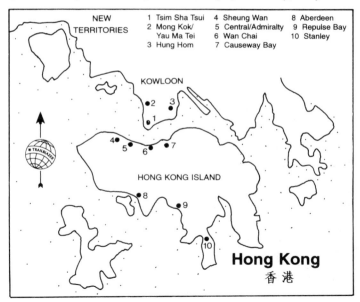

old colonial buildings in 'Central' district are to be found some distance from the harbour. It's hard for the visitor to imagine that many of them were on the waterfront originally. During the Second World War, Hong Kong surrendered to the Japanese on Christmas Day 1941. After enduring 3¹/₂ years of Japanese occupation, it was liberated in August 1945.

From 1949 onwards, Hong Kong has continued to develop but has been constantly affected by events across the border in China. After the Communists gained power, Hong Kong experienced an initial wave of immigrants. Large numbers followed in the early 1960's, in an attempt to escape the famine caused by the Great Leap Forward, and there was rioting in the late 1960's as the Cultural Revolution seeped across the border. Today, with a population of six million, crowded Hong Kong is one of the most industrially and economically powerful areas in the world.

WHAT TO SEE

Some of the main attractions are suggested below. Many visitors will want to get a separate guide book just for Hong Kong, or at the very least pick up a selection of the excellent brochures handed out by HKTA.

The Peak

Victoria Peak is the highest point of Hong Kong Island. For many years, the Peak was the preserve of the wealthy, as property up here with its marvellous views was at a premium. Although the area just below The Peak itself has been developed, with a large restaurant/tourist centre, you can avoid this easily, and there are a couple of attractive walks that you can take in order to see all the views. The Peak's popularity has almost been superseded by the method of getting there. The **Peak Tram**, a funicular railway, is a remarkable piece of engineering, particularly when you consider that it is over 100 years old and used to be the only way up to the top before the road was built. It takes about five minutes to climb the 373 metres up the frighteningly steep incline. The start of the tram is at The Lower Tram Station on Garden Rd, and a return ticket costs HK$21. Trams run every 10-15 minutes from 07.00-23.59.

Kowloon Park

It's really surprising to find this pretty and well laid out park right in the middle of crowded and dirty Kowloon. Near the centre of the park is an attractive aviary, with a large collection of birds. In the north of the park is a public **swimming pool** complex, just the place to come if you need a break from the summer heat. Entry to the pool is HK$18.

The **Hong Kong Museum of History** is near the centre of the park. The museum provides a fascinating insight into Hong Kong's past, and its present identity. It's open from 10.00-18.00 daily, except Fridays (closed all day) and Sundays and Public Holidays (13.00-18.00). Entry is HK$10 for adults and HK$5 for children.

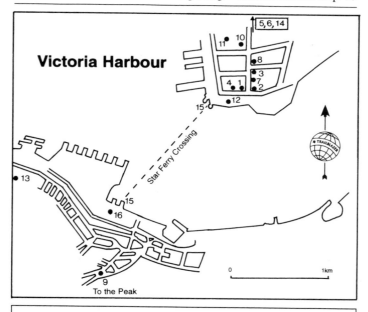

Victoria Harbour

Star Ferry Crossing

To the Peak

0   1km

VICTORIA HARBOUR (HONG KONG) – KEY

Where to stay

1 Peninsula Hotel 　　　　　　　　　1 半岛酒店
2 Hong Kong Sheraton 　　　　　　　2 香港喜来登酒店
3 Holiday Inn 　　　　　　　　　　　3 金域假日酒店
4 The YMCA/Salisbury 　　　　　　　4 基督教青年会
5 Shamrock Hotel 　　　　　　　　　5 新乐饭店
6 Bangkok Royal Hotel 　　　　　　　6 曼谷贵宾酒店
7 Chungking Mansions 　　　　　　　7 重庆招待所
8 Mirador Building 　　　　　　　　　8 蜜拉都大楼 (音译)

What to see

9 Tram Station for the Peak 　　　　　9 山顶缆车站
10 Kowloon Park 　　　　　　　　　　10 九龙公园
11 Hong Kong Museum of History 　　11 香港博物馆
12 Hong Kong Cultural Centre 　　　　12 香港文化中心
13 Western Market 　　　　　　　　　13 西港城
14 Jade Market 　　　　　　　　　　　14 玉器市场

Other

15 Star Ferry Terminals 　　　　　　　15 天皇码头
16 Post Office 　　　　　　　　　　　16 邮政总局

Hong Kong Cultural Centre

On the waterfront next to the ferry terminal at Tsim Sha Tsui, these impressive buildings include a theatre, concert hall and the **Hong Kong Museum of Art**. There are regular exhibitions, concerts and plays and a programme can be picked up inside. Next to the Cultural Centre is the **Hong Kong Space Museum**, one of the largest planetariums in the world.

❑ **Rates of exchange**
All prices quoted here are in Kong Kong dollars.

US$1	HK$7.75
UK£1	HK$12.31
Can$1	HK$5.59
Aus$1	HK$5.64
NZ$1	HK$4.93
DM1	HK$4.31

Ocean Park

On the south side of Hong Kong Island, Ocean Park is billed as South East Asia's largest entertainment and leisure centre, with facilities ranging from a huge water park to the world's largest reef aquarium. Bus No 629 goes there direct from the Lippo Centre in Central, and bus No 6X from Central also passes the park.

PRACTICAL INFORMATION
Orientation and services

(Hong Kong ☎ **area code** 852)

Hong Kong consists of a collection of islands and a peninsula. At the centre of the territory is Hong Kong Island itself. To the north, across Victoria Harbour, is Kowloon, and beyond that are the New Territories. To the south lies an archipelago of islands – some quite large (Lantau actually dwarfs Hong Kong Island), others tiny and uninhabited. The heart of the place is Hong Kong Island and the southern tip of the peninsula – Kowloon; on the prime real estate around the Victoria Harbour can be found the most crowded, expensive and exciting aspects of Hong Kong life.

The **Hong Kong Tourist Association (HKTA)** offices are a good starting point for any visitor. There are currently three: one by the Star Ferry terminal in Kowloon, another in the basement shopping centre of Jardine House, in Connaught Place, Central district, and a third at the airport. The offices give out excellent free maps.

There's a large **post office** near the Island Ferry Terminal in Central, and branches of most **banks** can be found in the Central district, too. Most banks will advance cash on a credit card. American Express has a large office here.

Visas are easy to obtain. Consulates include: Australia (☎ 2827 8881), UK (☎ 2523 0171), Canada (☎ 2810 4321), France (☎ 2529 4351), Germany (☎ 2529 8855), China (☎ 2585 1700), Japan (☎ 2522 1184), Vietnam (☎ 2591 4517), Singapore (☎ 2527 2212) and India (☎ 2528 4028). To take the sweat out of **getting visas** many travel services will do the work for you. I used Shoestring Travel (☎ 2723 2306), in Alpha House on Nathan Rd, opposite Chungking Mansions.

Local transport

Public transport in Hong Kong is excellent. **Buses** generally run from 06.00 - midnight and fares range from HK$1.3 - HK$32. If you catch an air-conditioned express bus the fare will be considerably higher than catching a slow non air-con bus. **Taxis** have a basic fare of HK$14 plus HK$1.20 for every 200 metres. Fees for going through any tunnels are extra; if you use either of the cross harbour tunnels you will pay HK$20 more. The **MTR** (Mass Transit Railway) is Hong Kong's metro/underground, and operates from 06.00-01.00 daily. Tickets cost HK$4-12.50, and the ticket machines accept HK$ 10,5,2,1, and 0.5 coins. There are also stored value tickets available for HK$70, 100 and 200. The **KCR** or **Kowloon to Canton Railway** serves various places in the New Territories before continuing to Guangzhou (Canton). The **trams** on Hong Kong Island are a good option too; they run east-west along the north side of the island from 06.00-23.59. The standard fare is HK$1.60.

Finally among Hong Kong's most famous means of transport is the **Star Ferries**, which have been running since 1898, and which operate between Kowloon (Tsim Sha Tsui) and Hong Kong Island (Central). These go approximately every 5 minutes between 06.30-23.30 and cost HK$2 on the upper deck, and HK$1.7 on the lower deck. Ferries also operate to Wanchai (07.30-22.50, HK$2) and from Central to Hung Hom/Whampoa Garden (07.00-19.20, HK$2 or HK$2.5). The Star Ferry company also operates boats to the other islands; look for details at the ferry terminals or enquire at the Tourist Association offices.

Tours

There are various tours on offer, possibly the most enjoyable of which are the evening harbour/island tours on a junk, with drinks and dinner on board. A good way to appreciate the layout of Hong Kong Island might be to take a short tour on an open top tram, which takes in many of the best sights, while saving your feet. The Tourist Association has brochures which give suggested itineraries around Hong Kong, so that you can explore by yourself.

Where to stay

Hong Kong isn't a cheap place to stay, and consequently budget travellers usually limit themselves to a few days only. For those with some spare cash, however, there are some of the smartest hotels

in the world. Undoubtedly one of the plushest of these is the **Peninsula Hotel** (☎ 2366 6251) where the tone is set by the fleet of identical Rolls Royces outside. The cheapest room here is HK$2600! The **Hong Kong Sheraton** (☎ 2369 1111), and the **Holiday Inn** (☎ 2369 8016) both of which are nearby, look positively cheap by comparison; rooms in the latter start at HK$1700. Coming down in price, the **YMCA/Salisbury** (☎ 2369 2211), is literally only metres from the Peninsula Hotel and is clean and friendly. Rooms here start at HK$800 for a single and HK$945 for a double, although they have dormitory beds for HK$180. Facilities include two swimming pools, so you're hardly roughing it.

Other mid-price hotels can be found further from the waterfront. A couple of km north at 223 Nathan Rd is the **Shamrock Hotel** (☎ 2735 2271) where a double room costs HK$800. Around the corner from this is the **Bangkok Royal Hotel** (☎ 2735 9181) which has an air of faded adequacy, and bills itself as the 'most affordable and comfortable hotel in Hong Kong'. Singles are HK$644, and doubles are HK$ 736.

For budget travellers there are two main places to try: Chungking Mansions and the Mirador building next door. Chungking Mansions, at 36-44 Nathan Rd, is only a few yards from the Sheraton but couldn't be more different. The five 16-storey high-rise towers contain a mass of small apartments where locals are willing to rent rooms. Most of the places to stay are in Block A, but there are others, so you might want just to take the lift to the top of each building and walk down looking around as you go. The following in Block A are worthy of note. The **Travellers Hostel** (☎ 2368 2505) on the 16th floor has some of the cheapest doubles available – from HK$140. This is the place to stay if you want to prove your cred as a low-budget traveller: it's like a scene from *Midnight Express*. On the 12th floor, the *Peking Guest House* (☎ 2723 8320) has air-conditioned single rooms from HK$160 and doubles from HK$240, and is clean and friendly. On the 11th floor the *Fortunate Guest House* (☎ 2366 5900) has singles for HK$150 and is also clean and friendly.

The Mirador Building a few metres north of Chungking Mansions is in the same mould, but is a bit cleaner, quieter, and generally more pleasant. A few places stand out here. On the 13th floor the *New Garden* has beds in a crowded dormitory for HK$60 or HK$80, and single rooms for HK$200. The *First Class Guesthouse* on the 16th floor has doubles for HK$300. The *Cosmic Hotel* on the 12th floor charges HK$180-220 for doubles has been recommended. On the 5th floor, the *Mei Lam Guesthouse* seems particularly friendly and reliable and has double rooms for HK$350.

Where to eat

Probably Hong Kong's most famous places for food are the floating restaurants in **Aberdeen Harbour**, on the south side of Hong Kong Island. To get to the restaurants, take a free motorboat from Aberdeen Praya (waterfront). If you're after a bit more excitement head for the **Lan Kwai Fong** area, to the south-west of Central MTR station, where there are large numbers of Western-style bars and restaurants.

What to buy

Hong Kong is a wonderful, if expensive, place to shop, particularly if you're coming from China. You can find everything from local markets to huge air-conditioned shopping centres crammed with designer names. Try any of the large shopping complexes in the Central district. For traditional Chinese arts and crafts visit the Western Market, near Sheung Wan MTR station. To the south-west of this, Hollywood Rd is

said to be good for antiques and curios. The stalls at the **Jade Market**, at the junction of Kansu St and Battery St, sell jade in every conceivable form. It's a fascinating place to browse.

Moving on

To Guangzhou   There are trains, buses and boats to Guangzhou, and tickets can be organised through any travel agent. CTS (☎ 23157188) provide a good service. One of their offices is in Alpha House, a couple of floors below Shoestring Travel. If you don't want to hang around for very long when you reach Guangzhou they can also arrange your rail ticket onwards from there (well worth while, considering how hard rail tickets can be to obtain in Guangzhou). The office is open Mon-Sat 09.00-17.00 and on Sundays and Public Holidays 09.00-12.30 and 14.00-17.00. If you're travelling to China and are considering taking the Trans-Siberian, Moonsky Star (☎ 2723 1376) specialise in getting tickets, and are at: E-Block, 4th floor, Flat 6, Chungking Mansions. If you book your place with them here, they can have your ticket waiting for you in Beijing.

To Macau   Ferries to Macau run from the terminal in Sheung Wan.

By air   Hong Kong is a good place to buy air tickets because it is well served by international airlines, and prices are relatively low. A new international airport is under construction but in the meantime all flights go from the airport to the north-east of Kowloon. Arrival at or departure from this airport is nothing if not exciting, as the flight path usually involves a very low approach over tower blocks or a swift take off from a runway that ends in the sea. A frequent airbus service runs out to the airport; HKTA can provide details.

(**Opposite**) The distinctive and high tech architecture of Hong Kong's Central District.

PART 5: THE EASTERN PROVINCES

Beijing to Hong Kong

The Eastern Provinces have been historically crucial to the Middle Kingdom. They control routes both for coastal trading and inland communications; the Yangtse River and the Grand Canal, China's two most important inland waterways, run through the Eastern Provinces and the farmland here is incredibly fertile. Almost all the provinces along the coastal plain could claim to have been the cradle of the Chinese nation, and the area has a colourful history. Nanjing, for example, was originally the Imperial Southern Capital and later became the scene of China's subjugation to the Western Powers during the Opium Wars. Later still it was the headquarters of Hong Xiuquan during the Taiping rebellion and it subsequently became the Nationalist capital in the 1920's. Likewise Shanghai has played a crucial part in China's history. Suzhou and Hangzhou are reputed by the Chinese to be two of the most beautiful places on earth, and Confucianism was born in Qufu.

From the tourist's point of view the Eastern Provinces are packed with fascinating sites that give an excellent insight into China's history and heritage. Some of these cities and tourist sights are among the most famous in China, which unfortunately also means that they can become crowded and prices in this part of China are comparatively high.

BEIJING TO TAI'AN   [568km, 8-9 hrs]

Km 0: Beijing Central Station Most trains running southwards depart from this station, a huge blockish construction, built during the period of Sino-Soviet entente.

Km c20: Fengtai Fengtai is the large junction to the south of Beijing where the trunk line running south towards Guangzhou separates from the trunk line running south-east along the coast towards Nanjing and, eventually, Shanghai. This was the scene of a major diplomatic incident in 1900. During the Boxer rebellion, as the siege of the foreign legations

---

(Opposite) Top: Tiananmen Square (see p77), in the centre of Beijing, is decked out with flowers for the impressive National Day celebrations on 1st October each year. **Bottom:** The Summer Palace (see p82) on the outskirts of Beijing

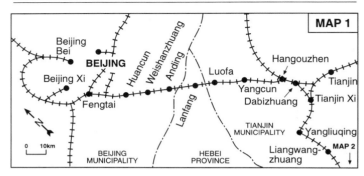

dragged on, joint Western forces were rushing to relieve their compatriots. Russia saw the confusion as a chance to gain control of Manchuria, and took over all of the railways as far as Tianjin. Control of Fengtai would have given the Russians a stranglehold on the main line to the south as well. On 18 September 1900 as they approached along the railway, they found that the station was defended by British soldiers who refused to move. In the end the problem was resolved on 4 October 1900 by letting the Germans operate the line instead.

Km 146: Tianjin Most southbound trains will actually go around the city, stopping perhaps at Tianjin north or west stations but not entering the metropolis itself. Tianjin is one of the three major cities in China granted the status of municipality – the equivalent of province. Following the Treaty of Tianjin in 1858, it was opened to foreigners and concessions soon sprang up. Chinese resentment at the foreign presence boiled over in 1870 when, during the incident which came to be known as the Tianjin Massacre, ten nuns, two priests and a French official were murdered. The Chinese mob that carried out the killings supposedly believed that the nuns were kidnapping the Chinese orphans that they took into their orphanage. Several Chinese were executed as a result.

From Tianjin west station, the km markers reset themselves to zero.

❑ Jing Hu line

You are now travelling on the Jing Hu line. After the Imperial government came round to the idea of building railways, this was one of the first to be approved. The report presented to the throne in 1880 stressed the potential value that railways could have to national defence and suggested that two lines should be built as a matter of priority. The first line, to connect Tianjin and Shanhaiguan with Beijing, was completed by the early 1890's. The second line, the Jing Hu line, which was designed to stretch all the way down the east coast, was not completed until some years later because of lack of funds.

Km 67: Tangguantun At this point the line enters Hebei province.

Km 116: Cangzhou Between Cangzhou and Dezhou keep an eye out to the right of the train for a glimpse of the Grand Canal. Northern sections of the canal are in very poor repair so it may be difficult to spot but the course of the ancient waterway parallels the railway for several km.

Km 230: Dezhou Shortly before arriving at Dezhou the line enters Shandong province.

Km 351: Jinan Just before Jinan, the railway crosses the Yellow River (see p306). Jinan is the junction for the line heading east towards Qingdao, a coastal town which was the centre of the German sphere of influence in the late 19th and early 20th century. It is said that the Kaiser was impatient to get his hands on a slice of China and earmarked Shandong province as Germany's territory at an early stage. Before finally making a move, he communicated his intentions to Tsar Nicholas to see if Russia would oppose him. When the Russians inferred that they would turn a blind eye, the German navy immediately landed on the coast.

Following the Treaty of Versailles (1919), in which it was agreed that all German holdings in China should pass to the Japanese, there were mass protests, still recalled now as the May 4th Movement. The Japanese occupied Qingdao but nonetheless wisely kept a low profile for many years. In the 1930's it was a bridgehead for their push into China. Today all that remains of this part of Shandong's past are some European-style buildings and the railway line which leads from Jinan to them (built in 1900). And of course, the Qingdao brewery, which produces Tsing Tao, the finest beer in China.

Km 422: Tai'an Tai'an is the home of sacred Mt Tai (Taishan, see p109).

MAP 3

Wangzizhuang
Queshan
Yancheng
Licheng
Sangzidian
Yellow River
Jinan
Dangjiazhuang
Chaomidian
Gushan
Zhangxia
Qingyang
Wande
Jieshou
TAI'AN
Honggou
Dawenkou
Beijipo
Ciyao
Wuchun
Yaocun
YANZHOU
Baijiadian
QUFU
Chengjiazhuang
Zouxian
Tengzhou
Nanshahe
Xuecheng
SHANDONG PROVINCE
Xuzhou
Gaojiaying
JIANGSU PROVINCE
Sanpu
Jiagou
Fuliji
Shilipu
Suxian
N
Lingjiaqiao
ANHUI PROVINCE
Xisipo
0   10km
Renqiao
MAP 4
Tangnanji

TAI'AN TO YANZHOU [85km, 1½ hrs]

It's only 85km to Yanzhou, a journey that can just as easily be done by bus.

Km 451: Dawenkou Important remains of a late Neolithic site were uncovered here in 1959. The find was significant enough to have led to the naming of Dawenkou culture. Shandong has proved rich for archaeologists: another famous neolithic site in the province has given its name to one of the Neolithic types – Longshan culture.

Km 507: Yanzhou All change for **Qufu** (see p117). Confucius' hometown is some 15km from the town of Yanzhou. Originally it was planned that the railway should run to Qufu itself, but Confucius' descendants, the powerful Kong family, lobbied against the move, arguing that it would alter permanently the *feng shui* of the hallowed site. They won the day. Keep your eyes open as the train approaches Yanzhou if you want to see steam trains in action; the sidings before the town itself can get extremely busy and there are usually at least two or three huge QJ's doing their stuff. On an early morning, with the steam rising around them, it can be very photogenic.

YANZHOU TO NANJING [509km, 9 hrs]

Km 601: Xuecheng An extremely ugly and polluted industrial area. Shortly after leaving Xuecheng the train enters Jiangsu province (briefly), before leaving it again for Anhui province.

Km 670: Xuzhou Xuzhou was the scene of an important battle in 1948-1949, which marked the turning point in the war between the Communists and the KMT. Having secured Manchuria in late 1948 the Red Army started to push south, with the enormous task of defeating the KMT in central

China. The battle here lasted 65 days and ended on 10 January 1949 in a decisive Communist victory. The Kuomintang lost 600,000 men, and suffered a defeat which marked the beginning of the end.

Km 695(L): To break the monotony of the incredibly flat coastal plains, there's at least the semblance of some hills here. It doesn't last for long, however, and the land soon goes back to being flat as far as the eye can see, with numerous canals and rivers. The area through which the train has been passing up to now is the North China Plain, and apart from some isolated hills, pretty much all of it lies below 200 metres. Geologically, it is made up of delta deposits of the Yellow River. The river has changed its course several times over the centuries and has been named 'China's Sorrow' because of its tendency to cause mass destruction when it breaks its banks. It has been suggested that the building of the Grand Canal (see p104) disrupted the natural drainage of the plain, and was responsible for the instability which has plagued the river ever since.

Km c830: Bengbu The river crossing just before the train arrives in this large city is evidence enough that the canals and waterways still form a vital part of China's transportation infrastructure. The water is crowded with barges and small ships. Recently there have been moves to dredge the entry to these canals from the Yangtse River in order to make them usable by even larger vessels. The whole of the coastal plain around here is laced with rivers and stretches of canal.

❏ Lower Yangtse region

As the train moves into south Anhui, and approaches the Yangtse River, so one enters the area known as the Lower Yangtse region. This area is one of the most crowded and prosperous in China. Despite having poor mineral resources, the transport links provided by the canals, the Yangtse itself and the coastal ports have favoured it as an area for industrial growth. Agriculturally, too, the area is blessed, with short winters, rich soils and plenty of rain. For centuries the surplus of grain produced in this part of the Empire was shipped up the Grand Canal to the north where it was needed. Nowadays, with huge urban populations to feed, the land has to be farmed intensively just to provide for the people who live here.

Km 990: Yong Ning Zhen This is the first stop as you cross back into Jiangsu province.

Km 1009-15: Yangtse River This is China's longest river (see p102). The bridge, measuring 6.7km including the extensions at either end, is the source of considerable pride to the Chinese. It was completed in 1968, and was built without Russian help, after the Soviet Union withdrew all aid in 1960. Before the bridge existed there was a train ferry.

Km 1016: Nanjing See p125.

The Yangtse River
In Chinese the river is known as Chang Jiang (Great River), and justly so; at 6300km it is the **longest river in China**, and the third longest in the world. Marco Polo, visiting Chengdu (in modern day Sichuan province) spoke of it with awe: '...the rivers reunite into one immense river which is henceforth called Kiang-sui, and this continues its course for a journey of eighty to a hundred days till it flows out into the Ocean...On its banks are innumerable cities and towns, and the amount of shipping it carries and the bulk of merchandise that merchants transport by it, upstream and down, is so inconceivable that no one in the world who had not seen it with his own eyes could possibly credit it. Its width is such that it is more like a sea than a river'.
     There are many frequently quoted statistics about just how large this river is, although the distances and figures don't necessarily convey the sense of scale. Early Western visitors tried to compare it to the rivers back home. John Francis Davis, who took part in Lord Amherst's embassy to Peking in 1816 recalls that: 'Taking the Thames as unit, Major Rennell estimated the proportions of the Yangtse-keang and Yellow River at fifteen and a half and thirteen and a half respectively'. Harold Rattenbury in *China-Burma Vagabond* meets an airline pilot who had travelled to meet Chiang Kaishek in Hankow, 700 miles upriver from Shanghai. 'The captain told me he had gone to Hankow on the aircraft-carrier *Hermes*...and had there transferred to the services of the Chinese General'. Hankow (Wuhan) is by no means the end of the line for river transport. Today it's the point where many passenger boats start their westward journey through the Three Gorges. The river remains navigable well beyond Chongqing, over 1500 miles upriver from Shanghai.

NANJING TO SUZHOU   [219km, 3¹/₂ hrs]

Km 303: Nanjing From Nanjing the km markers (on the right of the train) start to count backwards towards Shanghai which is 303km away. As befits one of the most prosperous regions in the country, the train services change beyond all recognition. Double decker air-conditioned carriages ply the routes at high speed between the major cities – luxury!

Km 241: Zhenjiang Zhenjiang is a large industrial city full of concrete high-rise buildings. In the past, however, it was renowned for its beauty and was a capital during the Three Kingdoms period. Situated next to an ancient ferry point across the Yangtse, it was a natural place for the Grand Canal to meet the Great River. Its position at the junction of the canal and river guaranteed trade for many years until the arrival of the railway.

     On the other side of the Yangtse, the first canal town that is reached is Yangzhou, the scene of one of the great historical mysteries that China has to offer. In 1951, a tombstone was found here commemorating the death of an Italian girl, Katerina Vilioni, in the city in 1342. Bearing in mind that Marco Polo visited only sometime between 1272 and 1295, what was she doing here?

Km 213(R): Danyang On the approach to Danyang station, the huge chemical plant on the right says it all about the direction in which China is moving. The area you have been travelling through has traditionally been one of paddy fields and canals – and has earned itself the nickname of the Land of Fish and Rice. The future lies in industry, however, and to achieve maximum potential, the environmental implications are being ignored. From here on in to Shanghai, although the paddy fields are shoe-horned into any space available, it is really one long industrial sprawl.

Km 150(R): By this stage the track is running parallel to one of the busy canal routes. Although it may not look like it, with the constant movement of barges full of industrial supplies, the canals themselves are ancient and are parts of the system which once comprised the Grand Canal (see p104).

Km 84: Suzhou The famous Garden City, renowned for its beautiful canals and gardens. As the train approaches the station you may be able to see, on the left, the leaning pagoda which stands atop Tiger Hill. For the city guide see p137. Beware of the rickshaw and taxi drivers when you get out of the station – they are nothing if not persistent.

SUZHOU TO SHANGHAI [84km, 1½ hrs]

The section of railway from Shanghai to Nanjing was built by British engineers. Work started in 1904, but took longer than expected. *The Times* correspondent in Shanghai wrote of the problems which were being encountered:

'Another source of difficulty lies in the removal of graves. This is a question which presents itself everywhere in China; but in the country between Shanghai and Wuxi it is unusually prominent, because the line runs through what might well be described as a continuous graveyard. Tombs and

family burying-grounds, frequently of great size are scattered haphazardly throughout the highly cultivated fields...for each grave's removal compensation has to be paid at rates varying between 10s and £1...the smallest remains will suffice to justify a claim, and unidentified ancestors are therefore in demand all along the line'.

The problem was one which foreign railway engineers had encountered elsewhere in China. When the Imperial court originally wanted to discourage railway building, one of the excuses was that the lines would have to cross ancient family burial grounds, which was unthinkable. The engineers, aware that it was a sensitive issue, took plenty of time to negotiate routes, and paid compensation for graves which had to be moved. As one American engineer noted, however, what sprang up was a thriving business. For a small amount of money an ancestor could be 'borrowed', and the remains placed in the route of the railway. Compensation would then be claimed, and the ancestor would be returned, together with a small sum, to the lender.

Km 0: Shanghai For the city guide to Shanghai see p146.

SHANGHAI TO HANGZHOU   [201km, 3½ hrs]

From Shanghai heading south-west, the km markers start counting from zero. Initially they appear to swap sides of the track randomly. The first half hour of the journey is simply a long haul through extended suburbs.

Km 82: Fengjing Here the line leaves Shanghai municipality and enters Zhejiang province. Zhejiang is a mountainous and densely populated region which is particularly important for its agricultural output, silk production and rapidly growing industries.

❏ **The Grand Canal**
This enormous feat of engineering was the longest canal ever built, stretching 1500 miles through eastern China. Although parts were built at different times the main work of joining all the sections into one continuous system from the Yangtse to Luoyang and Beijing was achieved in the Sui Dynasty (581-618). Further work was undertaken by the Yuan Dynasty who straightened the route, cutting it by nearly 400 miles. The Mongol historian Rashid-ud-deen, writing in 1307, described it thus:

'The canal extends from Khanbalik [Beijing] to Khinsai [Hangzhou]...ships can navigate it, and it is forty days' journey in length. When the ships arrive at the sluices, they are raised up, whatever be their size, by means of machines, and they are then let down on the other side into the water'.

Successive dynasties relied on the canal to move grain from the Lower Yangtse region to the cities of the north. Huge manpower was required for the upkeep of the canals, however, and during the Qing Dynasty they began to fall into disrepair.

Km 201: Hangzhou The famous Chinese city, renowned for its West Lake and Soul's Retreat Temple. See p158.

HANGZHOU TO NANCHANG [636km, 16-17 hrs]

Km 0: Hangzhou Once again, the km numbering resets itself, this time because the train is now on the Zhe Gan line. Leaving Hangzhou you cross the huge bridge over the Qiantang River. You should be able to see the 60m-high Six Harmonies Pagoda (see p164) on the north bank.

Km 347: Yushan The train has now crossed into Jiangxi province. For several years in the late 1920's and early 1930's the railway line from Shanghai never got further than Yushan. This was not so much because of technical difficulties as the fact that much of the territory to the south-west was made unstable by the ongoing battles between the KMT army and the Communists. When the Communist forces eventually moved northwards, building recommenced and the line was finally completed.

Km 380: The attractive scenery as the train approaches the large town of Shangrao, makes a wonderful change to the flat countryside of Jiangsu province and the Lower Yangtse Plain.

Km 398(L): If you're near a window which opens have a camera handy – there's a huge natural stone archway here, which can be seen from the train for a couple of km. Two or three km beyond the archway there's a great view to the left, looking down into a beautiful valley.

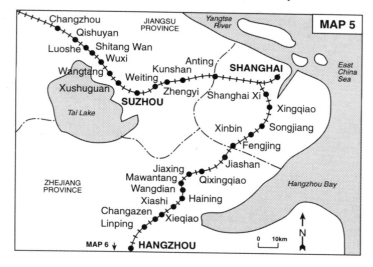

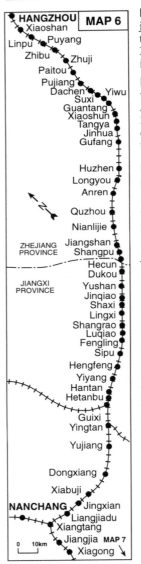

Km 487: Yingtan This major station is the junction where the branch line splits off towards the coastal cities of Fuzhou and Xiamen (formerly Amoy), the latter an important treaty port for the export of tea.

Km c609: Xiangtang This is the junction where the branch line to Nanchang and Jiujiang divides from the main line. It's 27km up the branch line to Nanchang – direct trains obviously take you straight there.

NANCHANG TO CHANGSHA
[417km, 9-10 hrs]

Km c900: Laoguan Shortly after leaving this station the line crosses into Hunan province.

Km c950: Zhuzhou This is the main rail junction where the Zhe Gan line (on which you have travelled so far from Shanghai), meets the Jing Guang line, China's main trunk line running north-south. If you're heading straight for Guangzhou the train will probably go through contortions here, heading off into sidings, stopping for an engine change and leaving the station in reverse.

On the Jing Guang line, which has km markers counting upwards from Beijing, Zhuzhou is at Km1617. From here it's approximately 50km north to **Changsha** (Km1568, see p175), with no particularly remarkable sights.

The remainder of this route guide follows the line southwards. The km markers are predominantly on the right.

ZHUZHOU TO GUANGZHOU
[655km, 12 hrs]

Km 1617: Zhuzhou

Km 1650 (R): The large river which has run parallel to the railway line to the west

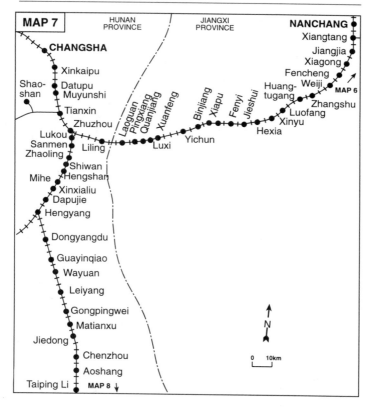

intermittently is the Xiang River which flows through Hengyang, Zhu-zhou and Changsha before ending up as a tributary of the Yangtse. It is quite large enough for commercial barges and is another example of the continued importance of the waterways in modern China.

Km 1752: Hengyang Hengyang is the junction for the lines leading south-west to Yunnan, Guangxi and Guizhou provinces.

Km 1965: Pingshi The range of hills through which the train is pass-ing effectively marks the border between Hunan and Guangdong provinces. Although at this stage there have already been a number of tunnels, the most impressive are yet to come. At nearly 14.5km in length the **Dayaoshan Tunnel**, which is just beyond Pingshi, takes nearly a quarter of an hour to get through.

MAP 8

↑ Jiedong
MAP 7

❏ Jing Guang line

The Jing Guang line, which stretches from Beijing to Guangzhou was given Imperial authority in 1889. From the start the line was to be built in two separate parts. North of the Yangtse would be the Hankow [Wuhan] to Beijing railway, and south of the river would be the Wuchang to Guangzhou line. The northern section was completed by November 1903, but the southern part was not finished until the early 1930's. A 1909 report suggests the problem:

'Construction is now proceeding as far as section 8, to a point at the north end of the 'Blind Boy' Gorge, 81 miles from Canton.

The line which up to section 5 presents few serious engineering difficulties, here enters a mountainous country, necessitating considerable tunnelling and deep cuttings in the rocky cliffs bordering the North River. As in some of the gorges through which the line must pass, the river has been known to rise as much as 65 feet, the difficulty of constructing a flood-proof permanent way can well be imagined.'

Km 2091 (R): Shakou With the river on the right and the peaks rising up next to it, the scenery here really is lovely. The North River, which continues parallel to the railway for many km, sometimes in sight and sometimes hidden, is one of the three major tributaries to the Pearl River, which flows into the sea through Guangzhou.

Km 2275: Guangzhou (See p180) The final approach to Guangzhou station is rather impressive, as the train travels through much of the city itself, with good views. If you've followed the route through the Eastern Provinces as described in this section, you've travelled 3423km by train between Beijing and Guangzhou.

GUANGZHOU TO HONG KONG

See p188-9.

Tai'an
泰安

Tai'an is an unattractive modern town but is an essential stop if you want to visit Taishan (Mt Tai), reputedly the most sacred mountain in the country. According to legend, Mt Tai was formed from the head of Pan Gu, China's creator, while his limbs formed four other holy mountains in the north, south and west and centre of the country; Mt Tai is the easterly one of the five sacred peaks. Over the course of the centuries successive emperors have come here on pilgrimages to commune with the deities.

The mountain is well worth a visit not only because it gives you a chance to take some real exercise (the climb is quite something) but also because it gives the foreign visitor an interesting insight into a part of Chinese culture. On Taishan you are surrounded by the remains of temples, gates and pavilions, ancient relics steeped in tradition, and, more noticeably, by hordes of Chinese who have come here for a holiday. Despite the crowds, Tai'an grows on you and you could easily spend a day on the mountain and a day or two exploring the sights around town.

HISTORY

According to Chinese folklore, Taishan has been a centre of worship for several thousand years, and even before China's unification in 221BC a stream of rulers, priests and intellectuals, including Confucius, had made the climb to be close to the gods. Even the mythical Yellow Emperor, one of Pan Gu's successors in the Chinese pantheon of deities, reputedly came here to offer sacrifices on the site of the Dai Temple. The temple itself, established in the Han Dynasty, subsequently became the focal point for offerings, and the start of the symbolic climb up the mountainside to heaven. As the temples grew in size and status, so the money lavished on them increased and it is reported that a Ming dynasty renovation of the Azure Cloud Temple at the summit cost over 150kg of gold.

Today, Taishan is a tourist sight more than anything else, although some elderly Chinese, and women praying for children, make the climb for religious reasons. The town itself has long benefited from the visitors but is now also an industrial centre in its own right.

TAISHAN

Route options

There are various options available to those wanting to walk up the mountain. Some go up at night when it's cooler, and reach the summit in time for sunrise, others climb during the day and stay the night at the top, and some avoid physical exertion altogether by getting a minibus halfway and taking the cable car up the remainder. You can, of course, combine these any way you want. There are also two other cable cars running from the top which allow you to descend to Peach Valley on the far side of the mountain and get a bus back from there (you'll need to check the bus timetables for this), or get a ride a short way down the other side of the mountain and walk on the lower slopes away from the town.

For those who want to walk, however, the obvious and recommended choice is to take the path straight up the mountain from Tai'an. It has the twin advantages of being the most direct route, and also of being unmissable – you *can't* get lost. If you have time on the way down you could go exploring the paths that criss-cross the mountainside, but since there are no decent maps available it's all guesswork, and you may end up walking a long way if you find that you've come down in the wrong place.

Perhaps the best option for those who intend to go up and down in the same day is to take the bus to the halfway point and walk the final stage to the summit in the morning, and then walk all the way back down to the town in the afternoon. It is quite possible to walk all the way up and down in a day but you'll need to be feeling energetic. The 1400-odd metre climb to the Jade Emperor Peak (1545 metres) covers a distance of 9km and there are over 6000 steps. The uphill climb takes nearly four hours of solid walking, and you should allow the same time for the downhill journey. Give yourself at least an hour on the top, as it's quite a large area, with lots of paths to wander around. If you intend to walk up at night take some warm gear and possibly a sleeping bag so that you won't freeze while you wait for the sunrise; even in summer the average temperature on the summit is some 8°C lower than the temperature in Tai'an below.

Walking the main path

Food and drinks stalls (along with walking sticks and all manner of tourist trivia) are available at stalls all the way up the path, so don't take too much with you.

Technically the path begins in front of the Yaocan Pavilion of the **Dai Temple** where sacrifices were initially offered. A straight road runs northwards through the centre of the temple and on through the town to the foot of the trail. The trail up the mountain was likened to the ascent to heaven, and thus a series of three gates remind you of the pilgrimage that you are making; at the base of the mountain is **Yitian Gate**, the First Gate to Heaven, mid-way up the climb is **Zhongtian Gate** (Middle Gate) and at the top finally you come to **Nantian Gate** – the South Gate to Heaven.

Most walkers ignore the temple bit, however, and, having passed through **Yitian Gate**, you find yourself at **Hongmen (Red Gate) Palace**, which is easily recognisable from its colour and from the fact that the ticket office is here. Foreigners pay Y20 to get on to the mountain. Starting the climb from here, you come first to the **Ten Thousand Immortals Tower**, which was built in 1620, during the Ming Dynasty, and which was used for the worship of the Mother Goddess, Wangmu. Beyond this is a much newer structure, the **Memorial to the Revolutionary Martyrs**. Off to one side of the trail is the **Doumo Palace** named after the Taoist deity, Doumo, although both Taoists and Buddhists worshipped here. No one is certain when the palace was originally built, but records show that it was renovated in 1542. Near the palace, if you have the time and energy, you can walk east from the main trail to visit the **Sutra Stone Valley**, an area of flat rock on which the **Diamond Sutra** has been carved.

Continuing up the main path you come to the **Feng'an Stele**, a recent addition to mark the burial of Sun Yatsen, whose body was brought via Mt Tai on the way down to his burial place in Nanjing. Above this, **Hutian (Sky in the Ewer) Tower** is an encouraging sight as it is only a short way below the halfway point. At 700 metres above sea level this spot, surrounded by hills, is supposed to resemble a ewer and therefore, according to Taoist theory, to be the residence of immortal spirits. At 850 metres, finally, you reach **Zhongtian Gate**, the halfway point of the climb. It takes most people about two hours to get here and everyone stops for a rest, a drink and a snack. The road which winds up the mountain via a west route ends here, so if you feel like catching a bus down you can do so. The cable car also starts from here on its way up to the summit (Y51 one way, Y102 return).

Above the middle gate there isn't too much to see, which is lucky because the climb is steep and most people are really not interested in sightseeing at this particular point. The upper half of the route does boast some of the more ridiculously-named sights: keep your eyes open for the **Welcoming Guest Pine**, so named because its branches droop as if bowing to those who approach it; just below it is the **Wusong Pavilion** where, according to legend Emperor Qin Shi Huangdi took shelter from the rain under a pine tree. He rewarded the tree by giving it a title and the status equivalent to that of a court official.

The summit

At the top of the final steep flight of steps you arrive at the south gate, which was originally built over 700 years ago in the Yuan Dynasty. Just inside the gate the devout make for the small temple to the god of Mt Tai, and everybody else makes for the drinks seller, and the nearest spot to sit down. To the west of the gate is the cable car station, and stretching to the east is the summit area and the buildings. In keeping with the theme of climbing up to heaven, the paved route leading to the north-east is called **Heaven Street**, and it is lined with places to eat, shops and small stalls.

The largest building on the summit, a short way along Heaven Street, is the **Azure Cloud Temple** (Bixia Temple). According to legend, Bixia was a young woman who was immortalised for her goodness, and the title of Bixia Yuanju (Goddess of Azure Clouds) was later conferred on her. The main hall of the temple is lined with bronze and there are statues of Bixia, and of Yuanguang Nainai (the goddess of eyesight) and Songsheng Niangniang (the goddess of fertility). By tradition, a woman who wants children should pray to the goddess of fertility here; on the way down the mountain, in order to convey her exact wishes, she should then place a number of stones in the forked branches of a pine tree, a stone for each child required. The temple was originally built in the Song Dynasty and has been renovated several times since. Entry is Y2.

A short distance to the east of the temple is the **Bridge of the Immortals** and a lookout point, which is near the **Cliff of Sacrifice**. In ancient days, it is said that young people, overcome with religious fervour, would leap off the cliff hoping that their self-sacrifice would bring their parents luck. A wall was built to prevent further loss of life, and the cliff was renamed Cliff of Treasuring Life. To the north is the highest point of the mountain, the **Jade Emperor Peak**, which is crowned by the **Jade Emperor Temple**. The Jade Emperor was considered by Taoists to be the greatest of the gods; inside the temple (entry Y1) is a bronze statue of the deity made in the Ming Dynasty. A short distance south-east of the peak is the Sunrise Watching Peak, where **Tanhai Rock**, a huge slab sticking out from the mountainside is a favourite spot to watch the dawn.

Alternative route
On the way down the mountain, at Zhongtian Gate you can leave the main path and follow an alternative route if you're feeling energetic. Much of it is along the road but apart from maniacal bus drivers who take the hairpin bends at full speed, it's fairly deserted and passes through some attractive scenery, and near some of Mt Tai's other famous spots including **Black Dragon Pool**. Various paths cut across the hillsides and could provide convenient shortcuts if you have the time to explore. Even if you walk straight along the road, this is definitely the long way back to Tai'an: it's about 12km from Zhongtian to the town.

OTHER THINGS TO SEE IN TAI'AN

Dai Temple
This is Tai'an's main attraction apart from Taishan itself. The temple was built as a gateway to the mountain and is symmetrically laid out along the axis leading north towards the Red Gate Palace. A temple was reputedly first built on this site in the Han Dynasty, and subsequent structures have been built and rebuilt many times since then culminating in the present temple which is said to have 813 rooms. This was where emperors would

come to offer sacrifices before their pilgrimage up the mountain.

Although several halls of the temple have now been turned into tourist shops a visit here is worth it just to see the famous **Tiankuang Hall**, which ranks with the Tiahe Hall in the Forbidden City, and the Dacheng Hall in the Confucius Temple as one of the three greatest halls in China. Built in the North Song Dynasty in AD 1009, the massive building contains a wonderful statue of emperor Dong Yue, the god of Mt Tai. Around the east, west and north walls of the hall is an amazing mural, 62m long, which depicts Dong Yue going on a tour of inspection. It's an incredible piece of artwork, and after all the tourist junk that surrounds the mountain itself, this is probably the only thing in the town which really gives the modern day visitor an idea of Taishan's history. Entry to the Yaocan Pavilion in front of the temple is Y1, and entry to the main temple is Y6.

Puzhao Temple

A 20-minute walk from the Taishan Guesthouse, the Puzhao Temple is signposted from the road as the Temple of Universal Illumination. It's set in a peaceful wooded area, that's ideal for a stroll and many locals wander up here for a picnic at the weekend. Still in use as a Buddhist temple, the main buildings were reputedly first put up in the Tang Dynasty and later rebuilt in the Jin Dynasty, since when they have been renovated several times. It's an attractive place, although a gift shop in the front courtyard detracts from its appearance somewhat.

In 1932 and 1937, General Feng Yuxiang came to stay here, and the rear halls of the temple house a display of photographs documenting his life. Entry to the temple is Y5, and the ticket also gets you into the **Memorial of the Revolutionary Martyrs of Luan Zhou Uprising**, which was built by Feng Yuxiang, a few hundred metres away. To get there, follow the paved road running north from the temple. The road forks, crossing a tiny bridge, and heads uphill for a short distance before reaching the memorial building. The place is rather neglected.

❏ **The Christian General**

Feng Yuxiang was a powerful northern warlord in the period after the collapse of the Qing Dynasty. Nicknamed the 'Christian General' for his new found faith, he famously baptised his soldiers with a fire hose. Having taken control of Peking in 1924, he started a long process of playing off one side against the other. He invited the Russians to re-equip his army, and at the same time started to negotiate with the KMT. When Sun Yatsen died, Feng along with one or two other of the main warlords effectively held the balance of power in China. He eventually sided with Chiang Kaishek but not before a considerable financial incentive had been used to gain his support. In the Anti-Japanese war he gained a reputation amongst the Chinese for his spirited defence against the invaders. He asked to be buried on the slopes of Taishan, and his tomb is a kilometre or so to the west of the Puzhao Temple.

PRACTICAL INFORMATION
Orientation and services
Tai'an is fairly large and the tourist facilities are all in different areas: the bus station in the west, the railway station in the south, and the best hotel and the start of the trail up the mountain are in the north. This is certainly one town where it's worth getting hold of a local street map as soon as possible on arrival so that you can see where the public bus routes are. Maps of the mountain are also on sale at the foot of the trail, or through CITS, who charge Y2. The Taishan Hotel has a free map available. Unfortunately while the maps of the mountain are useful, they do not have any English titles.

CITS (☎ 0538-8337020) have an office just south of the Taishan Guesthouse: from the guest-house gate walk south along the road 15-20 metres and turn left through a large vehicle gate into a courtyard. CITS are on the second floor of the building at the far end of the courtyard. They can be helpful if they feel like it, although if you drop in on a Friday afternoon you may not get much sense out of them. During the weekdays they will help to organise rail tickets. The **post office** is near the centre of the town, on the junction of Qingnian Lu and Dongyue Dajie. There is a **Bank of China** near the railway station, and another, smaller branch near the Taishan Guesthouse.

Local transport and tours
Buses run as shown on the city maps which are widely available. A useful bus/minibus is No3, which goes from the railway station past the Taishan

TAI'AN – KEY	
Where to stay	
1 Overseas Chinese Guesthouse	1 华侨大厦
2 Lao Dong Hotel	2 劳动宾馆
3 Taishan Guesthouse	3 泰山宾馆
4 Heping Yan Guesthouse	4 和平旅社
5 Dong Fang Guesthouse	5 东风旅社
6 Taishan Gong Yu Guesthouse	6 泰山公寓 (音译)
What to see	
7 Dai Temple	7 岱宗坊
8 Puzhao Temple	8 普照寺
9 Tiger Park	9 虎山公园
10 Food Market	10 泰山集货市场
Where to eat	
11 Taishan Shou Jou Dian Restaurant	11 泰山守旧店 (音译) 饭店
12 Uncle Sam	12 山姆大叔文物店
Other	
13 Railway Station	13 火车站
14 Long Distance Bus Station	14 长途汽车站
15 Bank of China	15 中国银行
16 Bank of China	16 中国银行
17 Post Office	17 邮局
18 PSB	18 公安局

Guesthouse and the foot of the trail. As far as tours are concerned, you certainly don't need a guide; it would be next to impossible to get lost on the mountain – all you have to do is climb the (many) steps. On the other hand, without a guide you'll miss out on much of the plethora of fairy tales and legends that are told about almost every part of the mountain: the trees, the pavilions and even the rocks themselves. CITS can provide guides (try to give them some advance warning) at a cost of about Y100 for the day.

Where to stay

At the top end of the market there are several places to stay in Tai'an but the choice thins out considerably in the case of budget hotels. The top hotel in Tai'an is the *Overseas Chinese Guest House*

(☎ 0538-8228112) which has doubles at a mere Y680 (although they promptly offered a 20% reduction). One traveller recommended its swimming pool which non-residents can use (for a price). The hotel also has three excellent restaurants and although a meal in the Chinese restaurant is likely to set you back at least Y150, this is probably the best place to come if you want to try local delicacies. The *Lao Dong Hotel*(☎ 0538-8331888), nearby, is also very smart but considerably cheaper: a single room costs Y320, and a double is Y350.

The travellers' favourite hotel in Tai'an is undoubtedly the *Taishan Guesthouse* (☎ 0538-8224678). The private rooms are fairly costly (a double is Y420) but there are dormitory beds available in clean modern triple rooms for Y50. The guest-house is ideally

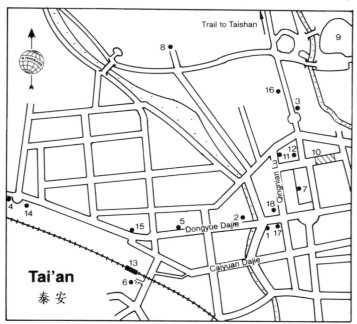

Tai'an
泰安

located at the foot of the trail, has good facilities and it's worth treating yourself to a little luxury after a full day's climbing/descending. Bus No3 from the railway station runs past the hotel.

There are many other places in town where foreigners can stay. The *Heping Yan Guesthouse* (☎ 0538-8222162) is near the bus station and consequently is the wrong side of town from just about everything but the staff are friendly and dormitory beds here are Y25. The *Dong Fang Guest-house* (☎ 0538-8336014) is near the railway station and is easy to recognise from the large sign on the front of the building, which confusingly says 'Dong Fang Music Wineshop'. The rooms are clean and a double here is Y120, while dormitory beds in triple rooms go for Y30. If you're really trying to economise, the *Taishan Gong Yu Guesthouse* has beds in extremely basic rooms for Y15. It's hard to find but it's actually very close to the station, in an alleyway just across the railway track from the station buildings.

Finally, many people like to stay a night at the top of the mountain in order to see the sunrise the next morning. The *Shenqi Guesthouse* (☎ 0538-8226877) on the summit was offering bunks in dormitory rooms for Y30. It's worth phoning in advance to check that they've still got these, as the single and double rooms are expensive, and it would be frustrating to get all the way to the top and find out there was nowhere in your price range to stay.

Where to eat
For an expensive meal you won't do better than the restaurants in the *Overseas Chinese Guesthouse*. For something a little easier on the pocket, try the restaurant at the Taishan Guesthouse, or explore the centre of town. For cheap food, a good spot is the *Taishan Shou Jou Dian Restaurant* – a tiny, friendly place which has tables out on the pavement during the summer.

Compared to other places in town the atmosphere is relaxed and unhurried. *Uncle Sam*, which is at the north end of the Dai Temple, is Tai'an's answer to fast food: their version of fried chicken is not great but is definitely edible. Finally there are plenty of cheap restaurants and snack stalls near the station.

What to buy
It may be useful to have a walking stick for the climb up the mountain, and there are various Mt Tai souvenirs, including T-shirts. If you're interested in herbal remedies, look into the **Herbal Remedy Centre** opposite the Taishan Guesthouse. CITS can sell you a small guidebook to Tai'an (Y15).

Moving on
By rail Tai'an is on the main line from Beijing to Nanjing/Shanghai so there are plenty of trains. Tai'an station isn't the easiest place to buy tickets, however, and if you encounter problems, you may prefer to get CITS to do it for you. At the ticket office, the window just to the left of the information point is where the sleeper reservations are issued. In a system which is unique among all the places I visited, you queue up at the sleeper window to collect a reservation slip and then take this to the ticket window in the main hall where you buy the ticket itself. Also unique to this station is the sale of sleeper tickets only in the morning before the day of travel, so get there at 8am if you can. One train worth trying if you're heading south is T161 which departs Tai'an at 06.10. A hard sleeper to Nanjing on this train costs Y95. For other train times see p367-75.

By bus There are regular public buses and minibuses to both Jin'an and Qufu. The minibuses congregate mainly outside the railway station.

By air The nearest airport is in Jin'an, 63km to the north of Tai'an

Qufu
曲阜

It is hard to imagine that Qufu, with its pleasant small town atmosphere, was once the capital of the state of Lu and the second most cultured city in China. Admittedly this was quite some time ago, mainly during the Zhou Dynasty (c1200-221BC) but it was during this time that Qufu really made it onto the historical map as the home town of Confucius. Actually, he was probably born in Zouyi to the south east of Qufu but he settled in the city first as a government official and later as a teacher and philosopher. As Confucianism grew in influence, emperors and statesmen made pilgrimages here and directed that the Sage's former residence should be expanded into a temple. Descendants of Confucius did pretty well out of it too, and the Kong family mansion came to imitate the imperial palace in size and layout. Patronage of the most powerful leaders in China persisted right up until 1935 when Chiang Kaishek granted the sage a new posthumous honour. The buildings were vacated only when the Communists came to power in 1949, and thus pretty much the whole of the Confucius Temple, mansions and cemetery are completely intact, if a little worn by tourists.

As far as the Confucius sights go, there's probably enough to fill a day here. Though initially you might be put off by the souvenir stalls the relaxed and sleepy atmosphere of the town grows on you, so you could easily stretch this to two days. For rail buffs, the junction just outside Yanzhou is one of the busiest in China and there are plenty of steam locomotives still in use in the marshalling yards. It's a pleasant bicycle ride from Yanzhou, through the countryside to the junction.

HISTORY

Legend has it that, in the Xia Dynasty (21st-16th century BC), the area of present day Qufu was the site of at least one capital city. Whether or not this is true, 20 or 30 Neolithic Period sites belonging to the Dawenkou and Longshan cultures have been discovered, proving that the area was settled at least 4000-5000 years ago. By the time the Zhou Dynasty arrived in the 11th century BC, the area was part of the State of Yan, and it was given by the new Zhou ruler to his brother, Ji Dan, in return for his help in conquering their enemies. Ji Dan, to whom a temple was subsequently built in Qufu, named his new acquisition the State of Lu and, being too busy to see to it himself, installed his eldest son as the Duke of Lu. For several hundred years Qufu, the capital, grew and prospered, for not only was it a period of relative peace, but the duke's descendants were exceptionally well connected at the Zhou court, and thus permission was granted to build extensively. The State of Lu maintained its autonomy for some 800 years and its expansion was continual and uninterrupted until 249BC when the Chu conquered it, before being overcome themselves by China's first emperor Qin Shi Huangdi. It is uncertain when the name of Qufu was adopted; the first reference to it is in the *Book of Rites*: 'To the south east of the Lu capital lies a hill ('fu'), winding ('qu') over 7 or 8 li.'

Although Qufu never became more than a seat of local government after 249BC, it played host to visits from 13 of China's emperors on 22 occasions and at their various commands the temples were enlarged while Confucian descendants were increasingly honoured. In 1522 the town was comprehensively rebuilt with the Temple of Confucius at its centre.

Today the Qufu district covers an area of 890 square km and has a population of 600,000 of whom one fifth have the surname Kong, and claim descent from Confucius. Apart from tourism, farming and light industry are important. Stone carving has traditionally been a local skill, and as you go up towards the Confucius Cemetery you will notice the stonemasons' yards on either side of the road; the raw materials come from Guanggou mountain, 10km south east of the town.

WHAT TO SEE

Temple of Confucius

The Temple of Confucius was originally established in the second year after the philosopher's death when his three-room former mansion was converted into a temple by the ruler of the State of Lu. In the period since its establishment, the temple has undergone 15 major reconstructions, and what you see today was built during the Ming and Qing Dynasties.

Laid out symmetrically on a north-south axis, it is over one km long. According to the tourist spiel it contains 466 palaces, pavilions, altars, halls and rooms, and if you really want to see it in detail, you'll be here for a week or more. Every arch, stone and tree in the place seems to have its own history and a name with numerous Chinese literary associations. In actual fact it really doesn't take too long to wander up the central axis of the temple and take in the main sights.

Entry is Y20. Leaving the ancient south gate of the city behind, you actually enter the complex through **Ling Xing Gate**, Ling Xing being by tradition a constellation representing literature, and thus the symbolism is of Confucius as a star come down to earth. At the far end of this court-yard you pass through **The Gate of the Timeliness of the Sage** and into a larger courtyard which is crossed by the Bi River; although the title 'river' is a misnomer, the channel filled with green stagnant water is unmistakable. Beyond the central bridge is the third gate of the temple, named **The Gate of Augmenting the Truth**. This structure was first built in the Song Dynasty and is named after a Confucian axiom in *The*

Analects: 'Man can augment the truth'. Beyond this is the **Gate of the Harmony of the Mean** which leads into the fourth courtyard, where the **Kuiwen Pavilion**, first constructed in 1018 and once used as the temple library, is found. The three-storey building is impressively solid despite its size; on the terrace outside it is a tablet telling of an earthquake which struck the area in the reign of Kang Xi (1654-1722). Most of the town was destroyed but the pavilion remained intact. Beyond it you enter the sixth courtyard of the temple where there are 13 stele pavilions to house the tablets presented to the temple.

Finally, in the seventh courtyard you come first to the Apricot Altar where Confucius reputedly used to teach, and then to the main building in the whole complex: **Dacheng Hall** (Hall of Great Achievements). The building is undeniably impressive: firstly it's huge and is usually considered to be one of the three great halls in China, the others being the Hall of Supreme Harmony in the Forbidden City, and the Tiankuang Hall in the Dai Temple in Tai'an; secondly the workmanship is awesome. The most striking features are the 28 stone pillars which support the building; each one is six metres in height, hewn from a single block of stone and carved with simply amazing dragon designs. The story goes that the workmanship on the pillars was so spectacular that when an Emperor came to pay his respects the pillars had to be covered with yellow silk to prevent him from being jealous. The original statues inside the hall were destroyed in the Cultural Revolution, and the ones you see today, depict-

---

❑ **Confucius and Confucianism**

Confucius, whose family name was Kong and given name was Qiu (but who also went by the name of 'Zhongni') is thought to have lived from 551-479 BC. His ancestors had served in the state of Song, but his great grandfather resigned his rank and title to settle as an ordinary citizen in Lu. His father died early, and to support his family, the boy entered the ranks of the Ru, the group of officials who mastered the knowledge of rituals. His quick learning and potential were recognised and he moved into an official career in the Lu State court. In his middle age, prompted by a strong belief in the value of formal education, he started his own school. Later, with some of his disciples, he spent three years travelling the country trying to get a ruler to accept and put into practice his ideas on education and administration. At 68 he returned to Qufu to teach and revise his works, which included the *Book of Changes*, the *Book of Rites*, and the *Spring and Autumn Annals*.

Confucianism has probably had so much appeal and been so openly supported by a succession of dynasties because it emphasises respect for the legitimate government and for elders. It's notable that, among others, the Dowager Empress Ci Xi looked favourably on the Kong family at a time when she was supervising the disintegration of the empire. Nor is it surprising that when, during the Cultural Revolution, Lin Biao declared that good citizens should strive against the 'Four Olds', Confucianism came in for a battering.

ing Confucius, his four companions and 12 disciples were made specially and put into the hall in 1984.

Behind the Dacheng Hall is **The Hall of Confucius' Wife**, and beyond that the northernmost building in the complex is **The Hall of Relics of the Sage**, where 120 carved stone plates, set into the walls, depict scenes from his life.

Passing through a doorway to the east of the Dacheng Hall, you come to the **Temple for Adoring the Sage**, and to the south of it, the well where Confucius was said to have drawn his water. Nearby stands **The Wall of Lu**, which was built to commemorate how his works were saved when Emperor Qin Shi Huangdi ordered that all books should be burnt. According to the legend, Kong Fu, the ninth generation descendant of the Sage, concealed copies of all the major Confucian classics inside the wall of his old residence, before fleeing the city. They were rediscovered several decades later. To the south of the wall is **The Hall of Poetry and Rites** and next to this, the eastern gate of the temple, which makes a convenient exit if you are going on to see the **Confucius Mansions**. Just inside this gate, which is known as **The Gate of the Former Dwelling of Confucius**, was the philosopher's old residence.

Confucius Mansions

The direct descendants of Confucius were well served by their forebear's fame. The Kong family lived next to the temple for nearly 2500 years, steadily accruing wealth, titles and privilege. In the Song Dynasty the eldest male descendant was granted the title, Master Yansheng, Yansheng meaning literally 'continuing the line of the sage'. The honours steadily piled up until the head of the Yansheng/Kong household came to have equivalent status to the prime minister, and even to be allowed, during the final years of the Qing Dynasty, to ride his horse into the Forbidden City. The last honour granted to the family was by Chiang Kaishek in 1935, who changed the title of the 77th generation descendant, Kong Decheng

---

❑ **The power of Kong**

At the height of the Kong family's power, they had over 1000 family guards, and owned more than 70,000 hectares of land with some 100,000 tenants. The Master of Yansheng held complete power in his area, including running his own court of law, with the authority to impose the death sentence. Rather in the manner of the Forbidden City, outsiders were forbidden by Imperial decree, and on threat of death to enter the living apartments in the mansion. Even the water carriers had to bring water to the walls of the inner apartments and empty it into troughs so that it could run through to the living quarters. The last remaining direct descendant in China, Kong Demao, recalls that fire broke out at one time in the inner apartments, and that only 12 of the mansion's 500 servants were permitted to (or dared to) enter the area to fight the flames. The fire raged for three days.

to State Master of Sacrifices of the Exalted Sage and First Teacher. The good times ended shortly afterwards with the arrival of the Communists; Kong Decheng fled with the Kuomintang to Taiwan where with certain circularity he became head of school examinations.

Construction on the site of the present mansions took place in the Song and Ming Dynasties, with large-scale reconstruction in the Qing Dynasty. Like the temple, the layout of the mansions is symmetrical along a north-south axis. Built on 16 hectares of land, the dwelling has nine courtyards, the first four of which contained offices and public rooms, while the other five contained the private residence of the family.

The first courtyard was devoted to administrative work, with offices on either side dealing with dispatches, and functions being modelled on the six ministries of the imperial government. The second courtyard is dominated by the **Great Hall** where the Master received officials, tried important cases and held ceremonies; the smaller hall just behind this was for the reception of top officials. To the north is the **Third Hall** (Hall of the Withdrawal) which was used for trying private cases or settling inter-clan disputes. Finally there are the inner apartments, complete with reception rooms, bedrooms and living quarters for the servants appointed to serve in the inner area. At the far north of the complex is a small garden. Entry to the complex is Y20

Forest of Confucius and Confucius' Tomb

Approximately 1km north of Qufu, the forest, also known as Confucius' Cemetery is the burial place of the great man himself and of most of his descendants. It was expanded on the orders of successive emperors, and now covers an area of two square km and is surrounded by a wall seven km long and four metres high. The **Divine Road** from Qufu to the cemetery runs directly north from the town's old north gate, passing through a ceremonial gate, the **Gateway of Eternal Spring**, halfway.

On arrival at the cemetery itself, and after the main gate, a wide paved route leads to a second inner gate. Just inside this, you come to a circular path which runs all the way round the forest. To get to the tomb of Confucius follow the path lined with souvenir stalls to the **Hall of Sacrifices**. The final approach is lined with huge stone guardians, and beyond the hall is the tomb itself.

To the east of Confucius' tomb is that of his son, Kong Li; to the south lies his grandson, Kong Ji. The sculptures of the tomb guardians and the ancient trees help to give the place a suitable atmosphere, and the forest is a restful place to wander around, or simply to picnic and read a book. Entry is Y10.

Yan Hui Temple

This temple, just to the south-east of the town's old north gate, is dedicated to Yan Hui, Confucius' most outstanding disciple who, despite being some 30 years younger, died before him. Yan Hui has been the subject of considerable veneration by visiting emperors and was granted the posthumous title of The Sage Returned and hence the temple is also known as The Temple of the Sage Returned. In the main building of the complex there is a statue of Yan Hui and probably the temple's most striking feature, the head of a dragon carved into the ceiling. A temple was first built here when the founder of the Han Dynasty, Liu Bang (256-191BC), visited to worship Confucius. Entry is Y3.

Temple of the Duke of Zhou

Situated a fair way to the north-east of the town centre, this temple is a peaceful place but there is little to see. The walk or cycle ride up here is pleasant, though. It was built in memory of the first ruler, Ji Dan, who granted the new State of Lu to his eldest son. **Yuansheng Hall** is the main building in the temple, and there is a portrait of the duke on the large piece of marble on the back wall, as well as a statue of him. Entry is Y2.

QUFU –KEY

Where to stay

1	Queli Hotel	1	阙里宾舍
2	Gold Mansions Hotel	2	金房子宾馆
3	Xingtan Hotel	3	杏潭宾馆 (音译)
4	Gua Shi Hotel	4	挂失宾馆
5	Luyou Hotel	5	旅游宾馆
6	Chang Cheng Guesthouse	6	长城招待所
7	Confucius Mansion Hotel	7	孔府饭店

What to see

8	Temple of Confucius	8	孔庙
9	Confucius Mansions	9	孔府
10	Forest of Confucius/Confucius' Tomb	10	孔墓/孔林
11	Yan Hui Temple	11	颜庙
12	Temple of the Duke of Zhou	12	周公庙
13	Drum Tower	13	鼓楼
14	Bell Tower	14	钟楼

Where to eat

15	Sage Bar	15	圣人吧
16	Overseas Chinese Restaurant	16	华侨餐厅

Other

17	Bus Station	17	汽车站
18	PSB	18	公安局
19	Post Office	19	邮局
20	Bank of China	20	中国银行
21	CITS	21	中国国际旅行社

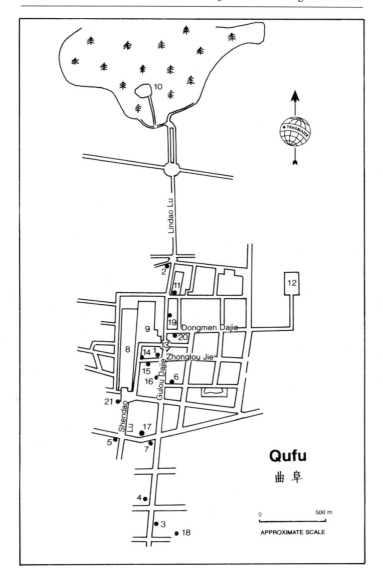

10

Lindao Lu

2

11

12

9

19

Dongmen Dajie

20

8

13

14

1

Zhonglou Jie

15

16

6

Gulou Dajie

21

Shendao Lu

17

5

7

4

3

18

Qufu

曲阜

0   500 m

APPROXIMATE SCALE

PRACTICAL INFORMATION
Orientation and services

The main railway station at Yanzhou is 15km west of Qufu, although there is another, much smaller station named Qufu on a branch line 4km east of town. Trains from Beijing and Nanjing/Shanghai stop at Yanzhou, and most visitors will want to depart from there, as it's on the main line. Minibuses run regularly from in front of Yanzhou station to the bus station at Qufu and the fare is Y2-3.

Qufu town itself is small enough to walk everywhere. The **CITS office** (☎ 0537-4412491), 1 Shendao Lu, is 50 metres south of the entrance to the Confucius Temple. The staff are friendly and helpful, and will arrange rail tickets if required. The **post office** is north of the Drum Tower on Gulou Dajie, and the **Bank of China** is a short distance away on Dongmen Dajie. The **PSB** is in the south of the town.

Local transport and tours

Hiring a bike is a good way to get up to the Confucius Cemetery, and there's a bike rental place just inside the front gate of the bus station; it's Y2 per hour, and you'll be asked to leave some form of ID. CITS are the people to see about arranging a tour, and they should be able to help to organise an English-speaking guide. Apart from the benefit of having someone explain the places in English there is little reason to take a tour; Qufu is small enough to get around easily by yourself, and there are even some explanations in English at the main sights.

Where to stay

The hotel situation in Qufu is excellent. While the top hotel in town offers good service, there are also plenty of small places that are willing to give foreigners a dormitory bed.

The best place in Qufu is the three-star *Queli Hotel* (☎ *0537-4411300*), which is right in the centre of the town,

just to the south of the Drum Tower. A double here is Y398. They will change money for non-residents, and there's a restaurant and shop.

The *Gold Mansions Hotel* (☎ 0537-4413469), next to the old North Gate is a new place, very smart but with little atmosphere. A double is Y240, and a triple is Y330. At the south end of town the *Xingtan Hotel* (☎ 0537-4412688) is the only one which is any distance away from the centre, about a 15-minute walk. It was obviously built to take tour groups, and despite the reasonable facilities, few independent travellers will want to stay here because of the extra walk to the town centre. A double is Y300, although they offered to drop it to Y200 almost immediately, so bargaining is definitely worth a try.

There are lots of cheap hotels in town. English is seldom spoken, and they cater mainly for Chinese travellers but most are relatively clean and friendly. The *Gua Shi Hotel* (☎ 0537-4416555) is one block north of the Xingtan Hotel and looks as though it was built for tour groups that have not yet materialised. The staff are friendly, and it even has a patch of garden. Doubles are Y100, but one person can stay for Y50. Opposite the bus station is the *Luyou Hotel* (☎ 0537-4411625), where they will start by showing you the expensive price list (Y234 for a double) but there are dormitory rooms in the run-down building at the back for as little as Y15. The rooms are fine and this is the cheapest price you'll find in town. The *Chang Cheng Guesthouse* (☎ 0537-4411319) which is on a side street off Gulou Dajie is excellent. Smart air-con doubles are Y100, while dormitory beds in clean triple rooms are Y18. The guest-house is signposted 'Chang Cheng Binguan' from the main road. Finally, directly opposite the bus station is the *Confucius Mansion Hotel* (☎ 0537-4412473) (look slightly to your left as you walk out of the bus station gate). A bed here is Y40.

There are plenty of other places in the town. Beware of overcharging and hotel touts. You're likely to be met by someone at the bus station who will insist on showing you to a hotel: the first place I was taken to was incredibly dingy and the price quoted was well above what the room should have cost.

Where to eat
Apart from the restaurant in the Queli Hotel there are a few other relatively up-market places to eat but nothing really special. About 20 metres east of the entry to the Confucius Mansions there is quite a good restaurant, and another can be found on Zhonglou Jie, just east of Gulou Dajie. The unpromising sounding *Sage Bar* which is opposite the Queli Hotel is cheap, friendly and serves good food, and *Overseas Chinese Restaurant* which is on the main street, a couple of hundred metres south of the Drum Tower is another good spot. The night market on Zhonglou Jie has a pleasant, relaxed atmosphere; some of the up-market street stalls have tables and chairs laid out on the pavement – a fun place to eat.

What to buy
This might be the place to buy a *chop* – a stone stamp engraved with your own personalised seal. Calligraphy, writing brushes and ink stones are also reasonable gifts to buy here. An unusual option is Kong Family Black Sesame Seed Cake (just like Confucius used to make), not exactly to everyone's taste but if you're tackling Taishan it might make a good snack. You may also come across 'Confucius Family Liquor' which is Mao Tai by any other name.

To find out more about the town get a copy of *A Visit to Confucius' Home Town*, the book that the CITS guides use. It costs Y10 from the Queli Hotel.

Moving on
By rail Yanzhou is on the main line from Beijing to Nanjing and Shanghai, so there is no shortage of trains running north or south to choose from. For train times see p367-75.

By bus Because the rail link is so convenient there are few long distance buses from Qufu. Buses to Jin'an (3 hrs) and Tai'an (2 hrs) depart every 1-2 hours from the bus station. Buses and minibuses operate a good shuttle service from Qufu bus station to Yanzhou railway station. The fare by public bus to Tai'an is Y7.5, and buses run daily, 07.00-17.00 approximately.

By air The nearest airport is in Jin'an, 80 km north of Qufu.

Nanjing
南京

Nanjing is a wonderful city: there are plenty of historic sites, a couple of excellent markets and one of the best museums in China. Somehow, although it's large and modern, Nanjing has retained a pleasant atmosphere, perhaps because the Purple Mountain and the Xuanwu Lake, both vast park areas, are so close to the city centre.

Despite the rapid development of the modern city, there is still plenty here to remind you of the long and fascinating history that Nanjing has experienced. You could happily spend two or three days here, if not more.

It loses some of its attraction in the midsummer, however; the hills surrounding the city stifle all wind and Nanjing can become fearfully hot.

HISTORY

The first recorded settlement in the area of present day Nanjing was the town of Wechen, under the control of the Wu state during the Spring and Autumn period. In 473BC the Wu were conquered by the Yue, who managed to establish their own city, Yuecheng, before being conquered themselves by the Chu, who named their new city Jinling. The name, at least, stuck (although the Chu had less success, being conquered themselves

---

NANJING – KEY

Where to stay

1	Jinling Hotel	1 金陵饭店
2	Nanjing Grand Hotel	2 南京饭店中心大酒店
3	Central Hotel/Fuchang Hotel	3 福昌饭店
4	Nanjing Hotel	4 南京饭店
5	Hong Qiao Hotel	5 虹桥饭店
6	Nanjing University Foreign Students' Accommodation	6 南京大学留学生招待所
7	Nanjing Normal University	7 南京师范大学
8	Shuang Men Lou Hotel	8 双门楼饭店宾馆

What to see

9	Drum Tower	9 鼓楼
10	Bell Pavilion	10 古亭晨钟
11	Xuanwu Lake Park	11 玄武湖公园
12	Jiming Temple	12 鸡鸣寺

Where to eat

13	Ninghai Lu	13 宁海路
14	Western Beer and Beefsteak City	14 西部啤酒牛排城
15	McDonald's	15 麦当劳
16	Kentucky Fried Chicken	16 肯塔基烤鸡店

Other

17	Main Railway Station	17 主火车站
18	PSB	18 公安局
19	Post Office	19 邮政局
20	Telecom Office	20 电报大楼
21	Passenger Station, Nanjing Port	21 南京港客运站
22	Foreign Language Bookstore	22 外文书店
23	CITS	23 国际旅行社
24	Advance Rail Booking Office	24 火车票预售处
25	Long Distance Bus Station	25 长途汽车站

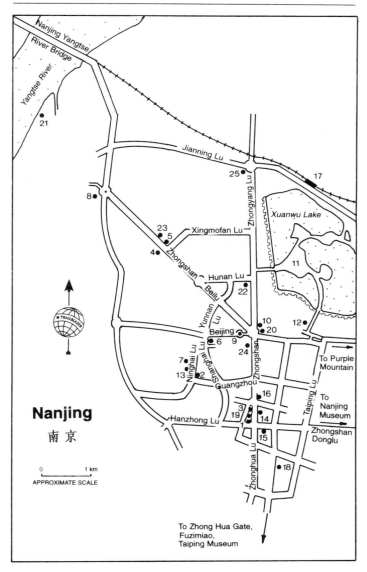

Nanjing Yangtse
River Bridge

Yangtse River

21

Jianning Lu

25

Zhongyang Lu

17

8

Xuanwu Lake

23
5

Xingmofan Lu

4

Zhongshan Beilu

11

Hunan Lu

22

Yunnan Lu

10
20

12

Beijing

6

9

Zhongshan

24

To Purple
Mountain

7

Ninghai Lu

13

2

Shanghai Lu

Guangzhou

To Nanjing
Museum

16

Taiping Lu

Nanjing

南京

3
19

14

Zhongshan
Donglu

Hanzhong Lu

15

0   1 km
APPROXIMATE SCALE

Zhonghua Lu

18

To Zhong Hua Gate,
Fuzimiao,
Taiping Museum

shortly afterwards) and the name Jinling is still sometimes used today. The city had its first taste of the big time during the Three Kingdoms period (220-280AD), when Sun Quan fortified it, renamed it Jianye, and made it his capital. Although southern dynasties came and went over the next 300 years, Nanjing remained a capital city until China's reunification by the Sui dynasty in 581. The first Sui emperor, who had his power base in the north, saw Nanjing as a potential threat, and the city was razed. By the 10th century it was a southern capital again, and finally, with the arrival of the Ming in 1368, it became the Imperial capital.

In 1421, however, Emperor Yongle moved his capital to Beijing and gave the city its current name, Nanjing, which literally means 'southern capital'. For centuries it continued as the great southern city of China, and as a seat of learning.

❑ In the early years of the nineteenth century, the Western writer of *The Description of the Empire of China* described Nanjing as follows: 'That which renders also this City famous is the great care it takes to cultivate the sciences: It singly furnishes more Doctors and great Mandarins than several Cities together; the libraries here are more numerous, the Book-sellers' shops better furnish'd, the Printing more beautiful and the Paper better than anywhere in the Empire besides...'

Well aware of the importance of the city, the Western powers chose to make a show of strength here in 1842 when, during the First Opium War, they sailed a fleet up the Yangtse. With Nanjing defenceless against the threat of Western firepower, the emperor agreed to sign the Treaty of Nanjing, which opened up five major 'treaty' ports to foreigners. The Western nations, with Nanjing in their grasp, had the power to make their own conditions, and the tone of condescension in the opening lines of the Treaty is clear: 'Her Majesty the Queen... and His Majesty the Emperor of China being desirous of putting an end to the misunderstanding and consequent hostilities which have arisen...'

Scarcely a decade later, in 1853, Nanjing was taken by the Taiping rebels and became the capital of The Kingdom of Heavenly Peace, until it was stormed by Chinese and foreign troops in 1864. In 1912, after the overthrow of the Qing, Nanjing was proclaimed capital by the Nationalists, although it was not until 1928 that it really became a seat of government.

The city suffered appallingly under the Japanese during WWII, when it is estimated that 300,000 Chinese were killed in the 'Rape of Nanjing'. Nanjing today is a busy, wealthy city and a major centre of foreign invest-

(Opposite) Eastern Provinces: Taishan (see p109), one of China's sacred mountains is climbed by a seemingly endless staircase of over 6000 stone steps.

ment. It has also retained its reputation as a university city; in addition to being a leading academic centre for Chinese students, there are also a large number of foreign students here.

WHAT TO SEE

The Drum Tower

In line with Ming practice, the Drum Tower was central to the walled city and was used both to announce the time at fixed hours and as a call to arms. Dating from 1382, it was built in the same decade as the city walls, during the spate of construction that took place after the first Ming emperor, Zhu Yuanzhang, adopted Nanjing as his capital. The three vaulted rooms at ground level now house two shops and a café, while on the upper terrace there is a huge bell and drum. The upper pavilion has what seemed to be a tea house which was under restoration when I visited. It should be a good place to stop for a break as you make your way around the city. The tower is open from 08.00-17.30.

The Bell Pavilion

A short way away from the Drum Tower, and just on the north side of the huge modern Telecom building, the Bell Pavilion isn't actually visible from the street at all. Walk down the lane on the north side of the Telecom building about five metres, and go up the steps on your left to find yourself in a small garden at roof top level of the shops on the street below. The bell itself is simply enormous and hangs in a tower that looks as though it couldn't possibly support the weight. Reputedly the bell dates from the 14th century, and was formerly housed near to the Drum Tower. The current pavilion dates from the end of the last century. There is also a 'yuppie' tea house here; although it's a reasonable place to stop for a drink, it's very expensive. There is no entrance fee to see the bell.

Xuanwu Lake Park

Right in the centre of Nanjing this has to be one of the best city parks in China, and it's a wonderful place to wander about in and relax. Entry is Y10 and you could easily spend an afternoon in here with a book and a picnic; there are plenty of teahouses, and even real grass! The park is constructed around a large lake with islands linked by causeways. Depending on whom you believe, the area is either named after the Northern God of Taoism, or was named following the appearance in 423AD of a black dragon in the waters – probably a large Yangtse alligator. You can get a pedal boat on the lake, take a boat tour, or just walk. Looking south from

---

(Opposite) Eastern Provinces: Opposite Chairman Mao's childhood home in Shaosan, Hunan province (see p176) the paddy fields are still planted and harvested in the same way as they always have been.

the islands across the lake, a section of the old Ming city wall, which is still in good repair, can be seen and it makes an interesting contrast with the modern high-rise buildings which are visible behind it. Looking south you can also see the pagodas of both the Jiming Temple and the Jiuhua Hill Park.

There is a zoo on one of the islands but the animals are absolutely miserable and it's not a particularly pleasant place to visit. The causeway south from the islands takes you out of the park on a road running through the old city wall, and thence past the entrance to the Jiming temple.

Jiming Temple

A visit here is easily combined with a trip to the park, and the temple is open to visitors from 07.00-18.00. It's a functioning temple, and if you arrive during a period of prayer, with bells ringing, worshippers chanting and incense smoke drifting around, it's hard to believe that you're so close to downtown Nanjing. The lower part of the temple is under renovation but the main hall, and upper part are lovely. Entry is Y2.

Nanjing Museum

Nanjing Museum is one of the best that you are likely to see in China, and you should allow at least a couple of hours here, as it is huge, the displays are excellent and there are good English explanations throughout. After a brief introductory spiel in which Nanjing and the surrounding area makes the claim to be the 'cradle of the Chinese nation', the exhibition is then split up into several parts: Jadeware, Bronzeware, Lacquerware, Ceramics, Transportation and Textiles. Not to be missed also is the display downstairs: 'The Archaeological Exhibition of Jiangsu Province', which has a particularly well laid out and well explained display of ancient burial sites.

After such an impressively balanced exhibition, the final caption at the end of the display on Buddhism and Taoism strikes a jarring note: '...since the class society the religion had been used to strengthen the class oppression. "The religion is the opium for the people". Generally, the religion is the negative value, negative force, and should be destroyed' (sic). Bus 9 runs past the museum. Entry is Y10.

Purple Mountain (Zijin Shan)

Purple Mountain is the name for the large wooded area of hills lying to the east of Nanjing. The woods are criss-crossed with paths, and this is a good spot just to stroll around, but there are also several interesting sites to visit on the hill sides.There is no fee for entry to the park area though each individual site has its own ticket office. Minibuses and public buses run regular shuttle services between the sights, and despite what the taxi drivers may tell you, it's almost always possible to get anywhere you want by minibus for Y1.

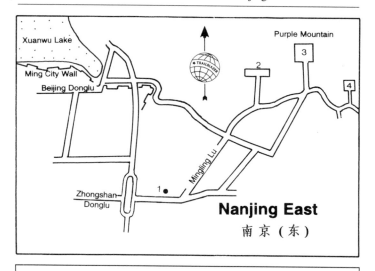

NANJING (EAST) – KEY

1	Nanjing Museum	1 南京博物馆
2	Ming Tomb (Tomb of the Emperor Hong Wu)	2 明孝陵 (洪武皇帝墓)
3	Sun Yatsen's Mausoleum	3 中山陵
4	Linggu Park	4 灵谷松风

Linggu Park is a good place to start a tour of the sights in the Purple Hills, as it is the furthest away from the city and from here you can slowly work your way westwards and back towards town. The park takes its name from the Linggu Temple, a small but beautiful place with massive statues (door guardians) just inside the entrance. The most prominent features of the park as you enter, however, are the huge Beamless Hall and the Linggu Pagoda, rather than the temple. The **Beamless Hall** is the first building you come to after entering the park. Built in 1381, it is noted for its huge vaulted ceilings (18 metres high in the middle), and, as the name suggests, it is made entirely of brick without the use of any beams. Its appearance is deceptive: the size and colour of the bricks, along with the fact that the hall has survived remarkably well, make it look rather modern, and it's hard to believe that it's 100, let alone 600, years old. The deception is reversed in the case of the massive **Linggu Pagoda** which stands behind the hall. Despite its impressive classical appearance from a distance, the 60-metre-high pagoda was built only in 1929, and is made for the most part of concrete. It's a fair climb to the top, but the view is good. In between the hall and the pagoda stands the Pine Wind Pavilion which was formerly dedicated to the Goddess of Mercy as part of the Linggu Temple, but now houses a rather tacky tourist shop. The **Linggu Temple** itself, which is probably the most attractive of the sights here, is tucked away in the trees to the east of the Beamless Hall. Entry to the park is Y5 and entry to the temple is a further Y2.

Sun Yatsen's Mausoleum is a huge construction covering some 80,000 square metres and dominating the area around it. Work began in January 1926 (Sun Yatsen had died in March 1925, and his body was initially entombed in Beijing) and took three years. From the statue which stands in front of the mausoleum by the road, the tomb avenue stretches back some 480 metres, and there are four massive flights of steps leading up to it. The memorial hall at the top of the steps is built of granite, and like all the buildings in the complex is tiled with blue tiles to represent the blue of the Kuomintang flag. Inside the front chamber of the hall there is a massive statue of Sun Yatsen, with scenes from his life carved in relief around the base. The walls of the front chamber are inscribed with his writings. The vault itself is in the rear chamber. Entry is Y12, and you will have to leave your bags at the entrance for Y0.5.

The **Tomb of Emperor Hong Wu**, the first Ming ruler, is probably the most interesting historical sight in the whole area. The tomb (known as Xiaoling) was built between 1381 and 1383, on the site of the original Linggu temple which was moved several km to the east to make room. Hong Wu's first empress Ma was buried here in 1382 and Hong Wu himself followed in 1398. The Stone Elephant Road, the sacred way to the tomb starts to the east of the tomb itself and is lined with pairs of stone lions, camels, elephants, unicorns and horses. The route then turns north and is flanked by stone figures: two pairs of generals and two pairs of ministers mark the way to the entrance. Once inside the outer wall, a 200-metre paved way leads to a massive inner gate which has a tunnel through it. On the far side, the burial mound covers the tomb itself, which is said to contain not only the bodies of the emperor and his first wife, but also those of the hundred or so concubines and ladies-in-waiting who were forced to commit suicide. Although the tomb hasn't been formally excavated, there are reports that it was plundered by Taiping rebels in the 1800's. Entry to the tomb is Y5.

Zhong Hua Gate

Back in Nanjing itself, the massive Zhong Hua gate is one of the best remaining sections of the old Ming fortifications. This was the Ming city's south gate. Even before Zhu Yuanzhang, otherwise known as Emperor Hong Wu, founded his dynasty in 1368, he started to fortify Nanjing. The city walls were built between 1366-86, and when complete

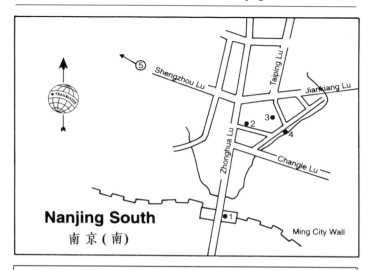

Nanjing South
南 京 (南)

Ming City Wall

NANJING (SOUTH) – KEY	
1 Zhong Hua Gate	1 中 华 门
2 Taiping Museum	2 太 平 天 国 历 史 博 物 馆
3 Fujimiao Market Area	3 夫 子 庙 市 场
4 Qin Huai Household Hotel	4 秦 淮 家 居 饭 店 (意 译)
5 Nanjing Massacre Memorial	5 南 京 大 屠 杀 纪 念 馆

they were reputedly over 33 km in length, 14.2 metres high and 14.5 metres thick. Zhu Yuanzhang's efforts to build such massive defences can possibly be attributed to his background. An orphan and former novice monk who became a bandit leader, he managed after several years of fighting to overcome his southern rivals and lead an uprising against the Yuan dynasty. Even established in power, his distrust of others led him to execute large numbers of potential rivals.

The south gate itself was built to be large enough to quarter up to 3000 soldiers in time of emergency, though it would have been quite a squeeze. Apart from the massive wooden gates, you can still see the slots in the walls where palisade-type inner gates could be dropped, either to fend off attackers, or to trap enemy troops who had managed to get in, thus allowing an ambush to be sprung. Entry is Y6, although the ticket sellers will probably try to charge you Y9, on the basis that you obviously want one of the 'information sheets', too.

Taiping Museum

Only a short distance from the Zhong Hua gate, the Taiping Museum is a fascinating place which charts the rise and fall of the Taiping Heavenly Kingdom. The museum is housed in the former palace of Yang Xiuqing, the Eastern King of the Taipings. Although the exhibits can be a bit confusing at times there are some titles in English, and the place really makes the history of the Rebellion come alive. An interesting twist to the story was the involvement of an Englishman who helped the Taipings. While Britain was formally allied with the Qing emperor against the rebels, Augustus Frederick Lindley is remembered as 'an Englishman friendly to the Taipings, [who] helped repulse the Qing water forces at Wuxi, with the armed steamer, *Firefly*, and captured a batch of steamers'. Lindley is honoured as a 'Friend of China. Enemy of Oppression'. This gives a clue to the care which has been taken over this museum. The Taiping cause has much mileage for China's Communist leaders; the final caption in the museum reads: 'The history of China has proved: without the Communist Party there would be no new China. Socialism is the inevitable selection of the Chinese people.' Entry is Y6, and the museum closes at 18.00.

Market area

Nanjing's market area in the district of Fujimiao is an excellent place to eat, stroll, shop, and just observe Chinese street life. The centre of the area is fairly modern and commercialised. Wander a short way, though, and you'll find yourself in a maze of alleys and market stalls selling everything from clothes to food to computers. Close to the centre of the market is the **Confucius Temple** which is a tourist trap, and certainly not worth the Y6 entry ticket.

Memorial Hall to the victims of the Nanjing Massacre

This memorial, built on the site where a mass grave was discovered, serves as a reminder of the atrocities that were inflicted on the people of Nanjing by the Japanese army. An estimated 300,000 people died and reputedly 10,000 bodies were discovered in this one grave alone. The hall houses a well presented photographic documentary of the events that took place. The memorial hall is approximately 5km west of the Fujimiao market area, on Chating Dongjie. Entry is Y12.

PRACTICAL INFORMATION
Orientation and services

Generally, Nanjing is an easy place to find your way around until you get into the back streets, at which point, if you're not careful you will easily get lost. This doesn't matter in the slightest, however, for the back alleys of the market areas are fascinating and a world in themselves. City maps in Chinese (for the bus routes) are for sale outside the railway station for Y2; a good tourist map with English titles (it's a bit old, and the bus routes aren't very accurate) is on sale in the book store of the Grand Hotel and at the Nanjing Museum.

If you are staying in the Nanjing University Foreign Students Dormitory, the Nanjing Grand Hotel is a good landmark to help you get your bearings: by day it's a dark brown high-rise building, and by night the neon sign on top of the hotel is unmistakable.

The main **CITS office** (☎ 025-3346444) is a fair way out from the city centre, on Zhongshan Beilu, and consequently they don't seem to get many individual foreign tourists. They are helpful, and offer both train and air ticket services as well as tours of the city. There is a small CITS office next to the Nanjing University Foreign Students Dormitory (20 metres further down the lane from the dormitory entrance, on the left), but they don't speak English. **CTS** also have an office slightly further up Zhongshan Beilu from CITS,which may be worth a try if CITS aren't being co-operative.

The main **post office** is on Zhongshan Lu, just south of the Central Hotel. The **PSB Foreign Affairs Department** (for visa extensions) is just off Zhonghua Lu (see map, p127). The **CAAC Office** is in the far south east of town. There's a large **Bank of China** east of the Jinling Hotel, on the far side of the roundabout but most of the large hotels will change money.

Local transport

City buses and minibuses are the best way of getting around Nanjing, although they are usually packed. Bus 13 gets you from the Foreign Students' Dormitory to the railway station. If you're en route to catch a train, allow lots of time for this journey as the traffic can be very bad. Bus 9 runs from the main roundabout by the Jinling Hotel to Sun Yatsen's mausoleum in the Purple Mountains. Bus 33 runs north – south through the city, along Zhongyang Lu and Zhongshang Lu, and is a good way of getting down to Fuzimiao, the Taiping Museum, and the south city gate. You could easily cycle to the Purple Mountains and elsewhere in the city, but bike hire places are hard to

find. There's reportedly one on Guangzhou Lu. Taxis are a good way of getting around if there are a few people to share the fare. From the Foreign Students' Dormitory to the Nanjing Museum costs about Y14, and to Fujimiao is about Y11.

Tours

CITS run half day and full day tours but they are ridiculously expensive (for a group of 4 people, it's Y292 per person for a half day tour!). All the sights in Nanjing are easy to reach by public transport, so you are probably best off going on your own.

Where to stay

There's no shortage of hotels in Nanjing, just a shortage of cheap ones. As befits a city which is very much a commercial centre, there are a lot of smart places to stay.

The most expensive hotel in the city is the *Jinling Hotel* (☎ 025-4455888), centrally located on Zhongshan Lu. Prices start at US$130 for a double. The *Nanjing Grand Hotel* (☎ 025-3311999) is slightly more reasonable with rooms from US$100 (although they rise to US$1900 a night for the Royal Suite). The *Central Hotel* (☎ 025-4400888), just around the corner from the Jinling Hotel has doubles from US$100, and the *Fuchang Hotel* (☎ 025-4400666) next door has doubles starting at US$80.

Coming down to earth slightly, the *Nanjing Hotel* (☎ 025-3411888) is slightly out from the centre of the city but has a certain old world style and is set in its own pleasant gardens. Doubles start at Y380, but with a bit of negotiating you can probably get this reduced. Across the road is the modern *Hong Qiao Hotel* (☎ 025-3400888) which has standard rooms for Y380. There are several others in this price range, but one that stands out is the *Qin Huai Household Hotel* (☎ 025-2211888) which is in a converted old house next to the Fuzimiao market in the south of the city. The market area has a great atmosphere, and this hotel, though relatively expensive (a double is Y390) is a wonderful change from all the stereotyped Western-style hotels elsewhere in the city. It's not easy to find, but it's at 128 Dashba Lu, which runs between Jiankang Lu and Changle Lu.

For budget travellers there are really only three places. Best of the lot is The *Nanjing University Foreign Students Accommodation* (☎ 025-6637651), although it's still not cheap: beds in a triple room cost Y60 each, and in a double room Y65. The rooms are clean and there's plenty of hot water, though. The sign on the outside of the building actually says 'International Scholars and Students Dept Nanjing University'. Accommodation is also available in *Nanjing Normal University*, which is a short distance away in the market area. Beds are available for about the same price in both but in the Normal University you are likely to be sharing a double room with a student who may already have strewn the entire place with their possessions. Finally, the *Shuang Men Lou Hotel* (☎ 025-8805961) is inconveniently located in the north west of the city but has doubles for Y180.

Where to eat

For local food there are simply hundreds of good places to eat. There are expensive restaurants all around the centre of the city and particularly in the market area of Fujimiao. For cheap places, two areas stand out: the market area on Ninghai Lu near the Grand Hotel, and the market area in Fujimiao. Although excellent food is on offer for low prices, do check the cost before you complete your order as some of the owners are not that scrupulous and you may end up paying over the odds. The local speciality is Pressed Salted Duck.

Nanjing is also a great place for street snacks; baotse and jaotse are widely available and there are also excellent varieties of bread, sweetbread and pancakes. For those hankering for Western food you could try the *Western Beer and Beefsteak City* which is near the Central Hotel, on the opposite side of the road. There are also at least three *McDonald's* and three *Kentucky Fried Chicken* places. Finally, in the area around the Foreign Students Dormitory there are a number of small places that cater for Western students and travellers: pasta, rice dishes and even pizza are available relatively cheaply, along with cold beer and groovy music.

What to buy

After a visit to Fujimiao you could come away with literally anything, but the most famous tourist souvenirs from Nanjing are Rainflower Pebbles, colourful lumps of rock which are displayed in bowls of water. The prices that are asked are absurd bearing in mind that they are just polished stone, so bargain hard. If you want to stock up on English books, you can find a reasonable selection in either the Foreign Languages Bookstore on Zhongyang Lu or the Century Bookstore which is further south on Zhongshan Lu.

Moving on

By rail Nanjing is exceptionally well connected by rail, both northwards to Beijing and south by inter-city services to Suzhou and Shanghai. The ticket office at the railway station is, however, absolutely chaotic, and only sells tickets for same day departures. For advance tickets the best place is the small ticket office in the centre of the city on Zhongshan Lu. It's 200 metres south of the traffic circle where the Telecom building stands, and next to the Gulou Binguan. It's open 08.00-12.00 and 13.30-17.00. For train times see p367.

By air The airport is to the south of the city and is probably easiest to get to by taxi. Going by public bus requires several changes (Bus 33 to Jinling Hotel, Bus 4 to CAAC office, then the CAAC bus to the airport).

The CITS ticketing service quoted the following prices: Beijing Y930, Shanghai Y320, Guangzhou Y1170.

By boat Boats east to Shanghai, and west to Wuhan run regularly. CITS quoted the following prices, (which include CITS booking fee and harbour fees) for the 17-hour boat journey to Shanghai: 2nd class (2 berth cabin) Y230, 3rd class (8 berth cabin) Y128, 4th class Y106.

To Wuhan, CITS quoted the following prices: 2nd class Y356, 3rd class Y179, 4th class Y143.

Suzhou
苏 州

A much quoted Chinese saying has it that 'there is paradise in heaven, and Suzhou-Hangzhou on earth'. Suzhou has long been considered by the Chinese to be one of their most beautiful cities, famous for its canals and classical gardens. Maintaining its reputation to the present day, Suzhou has become a major tourist destination, both for foreign and Chinese visitors. The reality is not quite as you might imagine; if you arrive expecting to find China's answer to Venice you're likely to be disappointed. Suzhou still has its unspoilt corners though, and is particularly worth a visit to see the famous gardens and to experience something of the silk industry for which the city, and indeed China, is renowned.

HISTORY

The first recorded town to be established on the current site was built by King Helu of Wu in 514BC. King Helu is also credited with building the first canals, which were probably more for drainage than transport. The Grand Canal dates from the seventh century, and thereafter the city's importance grew rapidly as a centre of the silk industry, a major canal city, and a centre of fashion. By the Song Dynasty, Pingjiang, as it was then called, was laid out with streets and canals much as we see it today. It was at this time that the residential gardens started to be built (although the earliest surviving garden, the Gentle Waves Pavilion, actually dates from the Tang Dynasty). Suzhou's star was in the ascendant, and throughout the Ming Dynasty the city's wealth and status continued to grow, making it one of the richest cities in the south of China.

The late 19th and early 20th centuries were not so kind, however. In the last hundred years or so, Suzhou has seen troops of the Taiping Rebellion, the Kuomintang, and the Japanese army passing through its streets. The gardens and buildings suffered their last beating at the hands of the Red Guards during the Cultural Revolution. You'd never know it though, for the gardens have been restored beautifully and are probably in better shape now than ever before.

Today the old city is at the centre of a sprawling new metropolis, with just as much grey concrete and ugly architecture as you'll see anywhere else in China. Surprisingly for such a relatively small city, Suzhou is turning into an important centre of foreign investment. Its position has recently been confirmed by plans to build a US$30 billion Chinese-Singaporean industrial park just outside the city limits.

Don't be put off, then, when you arrive at Suzhou station to find yourself in yet another large city, or set off down Renmin Lu and discover the usual selection of large department stores. At the centre of it all, the old moated city is still there with picturesque back streets and narrow waterways.

WHAT TO SEE

Despite initial appearances there are still some parts of Suzhou which are relatively unspoilt and are fun to explore. The old town around Shi Quan Jie is the obvious part but the canals are rather silted up around here, and the area is crowded anyway. A less visited bit is just to the west of the Silk Museum (ie the north-west corner of the old moated town). If you allow time to cut down a few of the alleys you can discover some wonderful canal-side streets. Be prepared to get lost; many of the lanes are tiny and half of them come to a dead end or the front door to someone's house. On the way around you may see the Chinese-style fishing nets that are raised and lowered from the water on bamboo frames; it takes a brave person to eat anything that comes out of these canals!

There are several museums. The **Museum of Silk** (see p139) is highly recommended. The **Municipal Museum**, however, has a limited display; if you've seen Nanjing Museum don't bother with this one. The **Folk Customs Museum** consists of several rooms full of dummies dressed in traditional costumes and is an utter waste of space.

The Temple of Mystery

A Taoist temple was first built on this spot in 276AD, but it had to be rebuilt in 1128AD having been burned down when the Jin invaded south China. The **Hall of the Three Purities**, built in 1184, is almost all that remains of the temple itself; it contains three huge statues and has a particularly ornate ceiling. The area around the hall contains various stone tablets, among which, to the east of the hall, is the Wordless Tablet. The story goes that when the third Ming emperor, Yong Le, usurped the throne from his nephew, he ordered an eminent man of letters, Fang Xiaoru, to write an imperial edict for him. Fang declined to do so and was consequently put to death with his family. A previous inscription which he had written on this tablet was ordered to be erased.

Originally, the area which is now covered by stalls in front of the temple, was the temple courtyard, and the side halls (which are now in many cases shops) were part of the complex too. The entrance hall still containing six massive and beautifully painted statues is now, sadly, a trinket shop, which opens onto Guanqian Jie. A poignant reminder of the China's new identity is the fact that the next premises on Guanqian Jie is a fast food outlet: this 12th century Taoist temple is next door to a Kentucky Fried Chicken joint. Entry to the temple is Y2.

North Temple Pagoda

The temple itself is no great shakes but the grounds are quite attractive. The 76-metre-high pagoda was built in the Ming Dynasty, and for Y5 you can climb to the top; it's hardly worth it as all you get is a view of modern Suzhou, ugly and polluted. There is, however, a small tea house under the eaves of the pagoda, which is a mellow spot to stop for a while. In the penultimate hall there's a display of musical instruments, but of more interest is the small picture gallery at the right end of the hall. Suzhou has traditionally been a home to artists: some of the original paintings, prints and woodcuts here are lovely and would make genuinely wonderful souvenirs or presents. If you're lucky and you get there when the old lady is tending the shop, have a chat; she speaks excellent English and is very interesting about Suzhou in the old days. To the east of the temple and included in the price of the entrance ticket is the small but attractive Garden of Plums. Entry to the temple area is Y6.

Museum of Silk

Not to be missed! Suzhou is famed for its silk industry and during the Ming Dynasty it was the centre of silk production in China. The museum starts unpromisingly with a well laid out but rather dry historical commentary, but further on you come to the practical section, which is excellent. The display starts with baskets of live silk worms being fed, and then follows through the natural progression of silk production by traditional methods. As you watch, skilled local workers spool the silk off the cocoon and dry and prepare the thread. Weaving is done on a series of traditional looms, and the cloth is finished with stone polishing. It really is a fascinating insight into one of China's most famous products. The museum is open 09.00-17.30 and entry is Y5.

The Gardens

In a guide of this type there isn't sufficient space to describe each garden in turn: what follows are simply the highlights. For more information, China City Guides edition on Suzhou (Y10 from CITS) is recommended. The guide goes into considerable detail about the layout of each garden, although after a few minutes of trying to work out which pavilion is which you may feel that it's altogether more relaxing just to ignore the names and form your own opinions.

The **Humble Administrator's Garden** is the most famous, the largest and probably the best garden in Suzhou. It's certainly the one that is most likely to appeal to Western tastes. The garden apparently took 16 years to build, and was the work of a Ming Dynasty official, Wang Xianchen, who retired to Suzhou having lost favour with the emperor. For comfort, he decided to turn to the simple life, believing that 'planting trees, watering gardens and growing vegetables...are the humble man's administration' – hence the name. Allow a couple of hours here at least, as it's a big place, and you'll also want to get your money's worth from the Y20 entrance ticket. It's open 07.30-17.30.

Near the Humble Administrator's Garden is **Lion Grove Garden**, which was originally laid out in the Yuan Dynasty. It's much smaller than the Humble Administrator's Garden and is a complete contrast in style, consisting mainly of grey weathered rocks in strange shapes, (the rocks were originally from Lake Taihu), and plants like bamboo in varying shades of green. To the Western eye it may seem an unusual concept of a garden and yet it has a beauty of its own. Entry is Y7.

In the south of the town, the **Master of the Nets Garden** is set back from the main road, down an alley running off Feng Huang Street. This is a much more recent affair, built about 200 years ago in the Qing Dynasty. Its name, originally Fisherman's Garden, was intended to imply aloofness from political power. It's small but pleasant, and entry is Y6.

Not far away is the **Surging Waves Pavilion**, which has the distinction of being the oldest classical garden in Suzhou, having been built in the late Tang Dynasty. The pavilion after which the garden has been named is not, as you might imagine, overlooking the water. It originally had a waterside position but was moved some 300 years ago and now stands at the top of the small hillock. This garden is not as popular as its neighbour, and consequently it's quite peaceful and a good place to sit and relax. Entry is Y3.

The Lingering Garden is in the north-west of the city. First laid out in the Ming Dynasty and called the East Garden, it formed a pair with the West Garden, which adjoins the nearby West Garden Monastery. In the late 19th century its name was changed to Lingering Garden, which was intended to suggest that it had endured through turbulent times. This may have been tempting fate, as it was comprehensively battered by the Japanese and Kuomintang, (and probably by the Red Guards, too), so that considerable restoration work has been needed. It's OK in a rocky sort of a way, but by this stage you may well have had your fill of twisted rocks and bamboo groves. Entry is Y9.

Tiger Park

Away in the north-west of the city, Tiger Park is one of the most famous places in Suzhou as far as the Chinese are concerned. In 550BC, King

Fuchai is reported to have buried his father here. According to the legend, three days after the burial a white tiger was seen crouched over the tomb, and the place subsequently became known as Tiger Hill. It's a pleasant public park with a central hill at the top of which is a wonderful crumbly old pagoda leaning at an alarming angle.

Almost every part of the park is the subject of some sort of myth and this is one place where the Chinese have really indulged themselves in inventing silly names for very ordinary features. There are several buildings which, by their titles, should really be palatial but are actually not much more than park benches with a roof over the top. Bus 5 gets you to the park and entry is Y12.

West Garden Monastery

This place ranks, for me, along with The Humble Administrator's Garden and The Silk Museum as a 'must see'.

The monastery was originally built in the Yuan Dynasty but in the Ming Dynasty it briefly became the private property of a government official, Xu Shitai, who renamed it West Garden as a pair for his East Garden (the present day Lingering Garden). In 1860, shortly before the Taiping army occupied Suzhou, the Qing troops torched the monastery before retreating from the city; it was rebuilt between 1869 and 1903. Although the monastery is only recently rebuilt it may be better for this, as the paintwork and silk are immaculate, and everything is beautifully restored.

The main building in the complex is the **Mahavira Hall.** This contains three massive wooden statues of the Buddha, which are flanked by two of Sakyamuni's disciples and two of the heavenly generals. To appreciate the intricate detail take a look at the carving on the pedestals. On the rear wall of the hall there is a statue of Guanyin, the Goddess of Mercy. She stands in the middle of a relief mural of scenes from Buddhist mythology. The Buddha is the grey figure near the top in the centre, where he is depicted meditating in the mountains before achieving enlightenment.

To the west side of the main courtyard is the **Hall of Arhats**. There are 500 individually crafted statues here. They stand along a series of galleries with paths which lead towards the centre of the hall, in a pattern known as the Eight Diagrams. Near the entrance to the hall is a wonderful statue of the Goddess of Mercy. The statue comprises four figures carved out of camphor wood, each having 250 hands in each of which is an eye, making this the 'thousand hand, thousand eye Goddess of Mercy'. Through a side door you come to the West Flower Garden, which is not particularly remarkable but very peaceful.

Entry to the monastery is Y4.5, and it is open 07.30-17.00.

PRACTICAL INFORMATION
Orientation and services

The railway station is at the north edge of the old moated town, and from just east of the station, Renmin Lu runs due south straight through the centre of the old city. Although the modern city of Suzhou is large and sprawling, the old city is fairly small; a taxi from one end to the other shouldn't cost more than about Y10-12, and you can easily walk to the Lexiang Hotel in about 20-25 minutes. As ever, try to get hold of a city map at the railway station, so that you can work out the bus routes.

CITS (☎ 0512-5223783 ext 2403), are based (with CTS) in the grounds of the Suzhou Hotel, and have an excellent map (Y3) with all the major tourist sites marked in English. The staff here are friendly, although they can get a bit pushy about trying to sell tickets for their tours. They can buy tickets for boats on the Grand Canal, but count your change carefully, and hold them to the price you agreed. Both the **post office** and the **Bank of China** are on Renmin Lu, near to the Lexiang Hotel.

Local transport

Although the town is not that big, buses 1 and 16 are useful as they run straight

---

SUZHOU – KEY

Where to stay

1	Bamboo Grove Hotel	1	竹 辉 饭 店
2	Aster Hotel	2	雅 都 大 酒 店
3	Suzhou Hotel	3	苏 州 饭 店
4	Shi Quan Hotel	4	十 全 饭 店
5	Dong Wu Hotel	5	东 吴 饭 店
6	Lexiang Hotel	6	乐 乡 饭 店

What to see

7	Temple of Mystery	7	玄 妙 观
8	North Temple Pagoda	8	北 寺 塔
9	Museum of Silk	9	丝 绸 博 物 馆
10	Municipal Museum	10	市 博 物 馆
11	Humble Administrator's Garden	11	拙 政 园
12	Lion Grove Garden	12	狮 子 林
13	Master of the Nets Garden	13	网 师 园
14	Surging Waves Pavilion	14	沧 浪 寺
15	Lingering Garden	15	留 园
16	Tiger Park	16	虎 丘
17	West Garden Monastery	17	西 园

Other

18	Railway Station	18	火 车 站
19	Bank of China	19	中 国 银 行
20	Long Distance Bus Station	20	长 途 汽 车 站
21	Boat Dock	21	轮 船 码 头
22	PSB	22	公 安 局
23	Post Office	23	邮 局

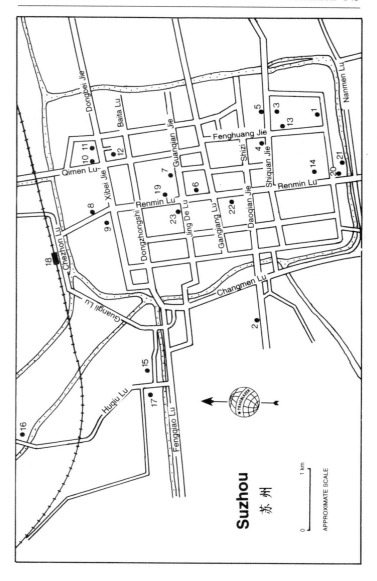

Suzhou

苏州

up and down Renmin Lu (to/from the railway station) and save considerable walking time. Bus 5 stops on Jing De Lu and runs out to a terminal at Tiger Hill, passing the Lingering Garden and the Temple of West Garden on the way. Taxis all have meters and are pretty good about using them.

Bikes are available for hire in several places and are a good way of getting about but you may have to shop around as some ridiculous prices are quoted. Bike hire at the Suzhou Hotel is Y30 per day. The guy on the alley running west from the gate of the Lexiang Hotel was asking Y15 per day, with a Y200 deposit.

Tours

CITS and the large hotels all offer tours. CITS operates a **Panda Bus**, which is an all-day tour costing Y260. This is not as bad as it sounds, bearing in mind that it includes all entry tickets, lunch, and an English-speaking guide. Having said that, though, you can see most places on the tour by yourself (with the exception of the Silk Mill, but you can go to the excellent Silk Museum instead), so for considerably less cash you can do the same sightseeing at your own pace. CITS also offer an **Evening Garden Entertainment** in the garden of the Master Of The Nets, which consists of two and a half hours of traditional music and other entertainments, with explanations by guides. This can be quite interesting but might be best avoided if you don't like being bundled together with large tour groups. Other tours such as a trip to West Hill Island in Lake Taihu are by arrangement only and are consequently expensive.

Where to stay

As you would expect of a major tourist spot such as Suzhou, there are lots of expensive hotels catering for group tours. There is, however, only one budget place in town. The *Bamboo Grove Hotel* (☎ 0512-5207601) is probably

the smartest place, and a standard room here is US$120. The *Aster Hotel* (☎ 0512-8291888) is in much the same league but is slightly further out and therefore less convenient; a standard room costs US$100, while a de luxe room costs US$128.

The *Suzhou Hotel* (☎ 0512-5204646) probably has the best location of all, right in the heart of the old quarter, and a double here costs US$70. Coming down the price range (though there are several others in the US$50-70 bracket), the *Shi Quan Hotel* (☎ 0512-5303652) is also very conveniently located and is much more reasonable at Y240 for a double.

Nearby, the *Dong Wu Hotel* (☎ 0512-5294360) is rather drab and depressing but a double here is only Y140, a fraction of the price of the Suzhou Hotel which stands opposite. The budget hotel in Suzhou is the *Lexiang Hotel* (☎ 0512-5222890) which is well away from the old quarter but is conveniently located in the market area. The rooms are clean and a bed in a four-bed room will cost Y50. Double rooms start at Y198. If you're travelling in peak season and want a dormitory bed, try to phone in advance, as this place can get booked up with Chinese tour groups.

Where to eat

Suzhou isn't a great place for food unless you've got plenty of spare cash. There are two main areas to go looking for restaurants: **Shi Quan Jie** in the south of the town has a lot of tourist-orientated restaurants, but because this is also the area where the expensive hotels are, even the homely places are pricey by budget traveller standards. The other area to eat is in the *market*, near the Lexiang hotel, where there are some very expensive restaurants but some cheap little places too. The problem here is that the cheap restaurants are all pretty uninspiring, and they tend to put up the price when they see a foreign face. The restaurants at the east end of the alley running past the front of the Lexiang Hotel are as good as any. If all else fails, **Kentucky Fried Chicken** is in the centre of the market area.

What to buy

Despite Suzhou's reputation for silk, it might be worth holding back until you get to Hangzhou, which is reputed to be the cheapest place in China for silk. If you're not planning a visit to Hangzhou, have a look at brocades, for which Suzhou is particularly famous.

Jade carvings can be found in the large tourist stores along Renmin Lu, and the paintings already mentioned on display at the North Temple Pagoda would make good souvenirs or gifts. Suzhou is also famous for tea, and jasmine tea is sold everywhere.

Moving on

By rail There are many trains going both to Shanghai and to Nanjing. CITS can help to book train tickets if required. For train times see p367-75.

By boat Some passenger services still operate on the Grand Canal. Probably the most useful of these is an **overnight boat to Hangzhou**, although there are also irregular services to **Wuxi** and beyond. The pricing of boat tickets is none too clear. I ended with a ticket which had the price Y55 printed on it, the same as the price the Chinese in my cabin paid. However I paid a commission to CITS to get hold of it for me, as they swore that a foreigner's price ticket would be far more expensive. It's probably worth having a go at buying your own ticket, before resorting to CITS. There is a ticket office near the boat dock itself.

According to CITS the following prices apply to the trip to Hangzhou:

	Chinese	Foreigner
Bunk in 4-berth cabin:	Y78	Y167
Bunk in 2-berth cabin:	Y109	Y217

❏ Boating on the Grand Canal

The trip along the Grand Canal certainly makes an interesting change from train travel. The canals around this part of the country are still heavily used for moving industrial goods, so it's more of an insight into modern China than a picturesque ancient sight. The barges are loaded right to the waterline with cargos such as bricks, sand and oil. Most of them are live-aboard boats, and in the evening you can see them moored up while supper's cooking and the kids are chasing each other up and down over the tarpaulins.

The boat I travelled on seemed typical of the other passenger boats on the canal. It was fairly smelly, with little space to wander around, (my idea of watching the sunset while lounging on the deck was a non-starter, as there was no deck to speak of), but perfectly adequate for a night. The standard of the two- and four-berth cabins was exactly the same, and bedding was provided in the form of a pillow and duvet. The boat was packed with Chinese, most of whom seemed to be using it as part of their business travel, rather than as a holiday trip. There was a small restaurant/bar area at the stern, with food available as long as you placed your order early. After supper the 'bar' turned into a karaoke hall briefly but they stopped at a reasonable hour.

Canal transport can be frustrated by the weather conditions. Movement can become impossible because of too much water, as well as too little. At 4am our journey came to an abrupt end when, because of the high level of water following heavy rain, the boat couldn't get under a low bridge. After a delay of five hours, we travelled the rest of the way to Hangzhou by bus!

Shanghai

上 海

Once known as the Paris of the East, Shanghai was, in its heyday, the epitome of exotic oriental lifestyle and excess. While millions sweated in appalling working conditions, members of the exclusive Shanghai Club sipped cocktails at the famous Long Bar, and gangsters like Big Eared Du lived in splendour. Businessmen, criminals and would-be revolutionaries all feature prominently in Shanghai's recent history. If only for its colourful past, most people will mark this place down for a fleeting visit at the very least.

Modern Shanghai may not be quite what you had visualised. The city is enjoying a rebirth as the powerhouse of Chinese industry and is the centre of an industrial zone that is expanding at a quite amazing rate. It is symbolised to the Chinese today by its most famous modern landmark, the Pearl Orient TV tower, a huge ultra-modern and fascinatingly ugly construction which towers above the new development area of Pudong.

Although some visitors are disappointed to discover a modern crowded city rather than a museum piece, others will feel that now is exactly the right time to visit. There is a distinct feeling here that history is coming full circle, and that Shanghai is going back to its old self. Foreign investment is high as multi-nationals pour in, and some of the former owners of the historic buildings along the Bund have even been invited to move back into their old premises. In place of the Shanghai Club, world class five-star hotels now have their own exclusive clubs, where wealthy industrialists go to relax and strike deals. Nanjing Lu, previously famous throughout South East Asia as *the* place to shop, now houses some of the biggest and smartest shopping centres you'll come across. Even the nightlife, for which the city was notorious, is making a comeback – although you'll need plenty of money to enjoy it. Amongst all this development there are still several historic sights to be seen. Shanghai warrants at least a couple of days of your time.

HISTORY

Shanghai is a relatively new city. In the Tang Dynasty the area was part of Huating county, and apart from a small fishing village there was little here. Sometime after this, the settlement began to grow and acquired the name Shanghai – literally meaning 'near the sea'. By the 16th century the town had grown large enough to merit a perimeter wall to protect it from marauding pirates and was trading in cotton and textiles. It was not until the Western nations arrived, however, that its development really started.

Following the signing of the Nanjing Treaty at the end of the First Opium War, Shanghai was one of five 'treaty ports' that were opened up to foreign trade. In 1843 the British accordingly landed, selected an area for the British Concession and started trading. They were quickly followed by the Americans and French, who carved out their own concessions, and in 1863 an International Settlement was established. Merchants from all over the world crowded in to make Shanghai one of the largest trading bases in South East Asia.

While the Westerners were keen to ensure their own privileges (private police forces were brought in from abroad, and the concessions were entirely outside Chinese jurisdiction) there also sprang up an extremely rich class of Chinese merchants. Protection rackets were rife, and gangsters, wielding power through the triads, became immensely powerful. Among those who fell under the influence of the gangsters were many of China's first generation of political leaders (an excellent account of both Shanghai in the early 1900's, and the political scene which was shaped here is given in Sterling Seagrave's *The Soong Dynasty*).

In keeping with its growing reputation as a centre of politics, Shanghai played a formative part in the history of the Chinese Communist Party when, in 1921, the first National Congress was held here, in secret. Six years later, in April 1927, the Communists met with disaster. Chiang Kaishek, supposedly an ally, engineered the Shanghai Coup in which hundreds of workers were slaughtered by hired gunmen. This single act of treachery paved the way for the struggle between the Communists and Nationalists, which finally led to the Kuomintang flight to Taiwan in 1949.

Today Shanghai is a political and commercial powerhouse. A municipality under direct control of the national government, it's destined to lead the world's fastest growing economy into the next century. Everywhere you go you'll see the signs of the future which the city has planned for itself – huge flyover systems are under construction, tunnelling under the river has begun for the new underground line, and office blocks are going up at an awesome rate. Shanghai has the largest harbour in China, capable of handling 100 million tons of cargo annually. Shanghai railway station has 120,000 passenger arrivals daily, and the airport sees around 10 million travellers passing through it each year. In addition to attracting foreign businesses, Shanghai has thriving industries of its own, among them chemicals, shipbuilding, electronics, and precision machine tools.

Although Shanghai seems set to be one of the major trade centres in South East Asia, there are some signs that the government may be going too fast. Sparkling new buildings are sitting empty because there is a surplus of office space at the moment. It seems certain, however, that Shanghai will continue to grow in importance.

WHAT TO SEE
The concession areas

For the majority of visitors, the most fascinating aspect of Shanghai is its history as a European 'colony'. An excellent historical background on how the Western nations came to establish and then administer their concession areas, is given in the Shanghai History Museum (see p149). There's quite a bit of the old order left in the modern city, however, from the buildings of the Bund, to some of the place names and shop signs. In outline, the **American Concession** was to the north of the Wusong River (which was called at the time, and still is often referred to as Suzhou Creek). To the south of the Creek, stretching down the Bund as far as the present day Yan'an Lu was the large **British Concession**, and to the south of this was the **French Concession**.

The buildings along the Bund are the most obvious remains. They are pretty much unchanged, and recently there has been talk of some of the old owners leasing them back from the government. Among the most notable buildings, the two which now make up the Peace Hotel were originally the **Cathay** and **Palace** hotels. The Tung Feng Hotel, which now shares its lobby with a Kentucky Fried Chicken outlet, was originally the exclusive **Shanghai Club**; though it's hard to imagine the atmosphere now, some of the fittings such as the incredibly ancient lift give a clue as to what it might have been like. The old **Town Hall** was, at the time of writing, locked up and seemingly awaiting a new function but the **Customs House** is still in use. If you poke your head through the door you can see that the lobby has the original light fittings, lifts and mosaic ceiling. The **Hong Kong and Shanghai Bank** was in the large domed building and originally had two huge bronze lions outside the doors. Today the lions can be found in the Shanghai History Museum. The main shopping street was, and still is, **Nanjing Lu**, and if you walk down it today you can still see some of the old shop signs. Finally, the large open area which today is Renmin Park was formerly the **racecourse**.

❏ **Boat Trip on Huangpu River**

Boats depart three times a day (twice a day in winter) from a boat dock just south of the Diamond Restaurant, on this four-hour tour up the Huangpu River. It's another way to see the city, and gives you an idea of the size and industrial importance of Shanghai, as well as a view of the impressive Yangpu Bridge, reportedly the world's longest cable stayed suspension bridge, with a central span of 602 metres. (If you're interested in seeing the world's third longest suspension bridge you'll find it in Shanghai too – it's a short distance south from the Bund). Four hours is a long time to stare at docks and container ships, however, so bring a book and some snacks.

Tickets vary from Y30 for a seat outside on the lower deck to Y100 for a place on the top deck, but the Y30 seat is perfectly adequate.

The old Chinese city

The old Chinese city is in the area bounded by Zhongua Lu and Renmin Lu, south of what used to be the British Concession. The city wall was demolished in 1912, making way for the two roads which now encircle the area. Famous in those days for being a warren of tiny alleys and narrow backstreets, the district has retained some of this atmosphere, and is an intriguing place to wander around, particularly if you've become tired of the big city feel of the rest of Shanghai.

In the centre of the old town is the **Yu Yuan Garden**, a classical Chinese garden which was first built in 1559, and in 1853 served as a headquarters for a branch of the Taiping rebels. Unfortunately it has become something of a tourist trap. If you've been, or are going to Suzhou don't bother with this, as it's rather faded and the Y15 entry fee is more than it's worth. Next to the garden is a pedestrian area, which is being redeveloped. Small tourist-orientated shops are being built in traditional styles and, whatever your feelings about avoiding the tourist hordes, it's a reasonable place to shop and eat. In the centre of the area is the *Huxinting Teahouse*, which is a famous spot; just the place to sit with a pot of tea and watch the world go by.

Once you get out of this central tourist zone, however, you are likely to have a much more interesting time. It's best to allow at least a couple of hours, forget about the map and just wander, trying to keep away from the main roads as far as possible. In many ways the streets of the old town are just one continuous market, and there are lots of places to buy a snack and eat cheaply. Take a camera!

Shanghai Museum

Literally millions of dollars have been spent creating the new Shanghai Museum which is in a glistening circular building in Renmin Square. Like everything else in the city, the museum is intended to be the biggest and the best, and indeed it is probably the best museum in China. There is a fantastic range of exhibits, which are beautifully lit and presented, with clear explanations in Chinese and English. Although parts of the museum were still being completed at the time of writing, there were three excellent exhibition halls open showing ancient Chinese bronzes, sculpture and ceramics.

It's open 09.00-18.00 daily (09.00-20.00 on Saturday). Entry is Y35 (which includes a cassette audio tour), or Y5 if you can produce some student ID. If you get in as a student, the audio tour will cost you Y30 extra but since the written explanations are so good, you really don't need it.

Shanghai History Museum

In some ways this place is even more interesting than the main Shanghai Museum; although you will have seen ancient Chinese bronzes before, you are unlikely to have seen any of the exhibits here, which relate to the history of the city itself. The museum is well laid out, has English labels and even has sound effects. Among the many interesting pieces are the original maps on which plans to divide up Shanghai into the concession areas were drafted, and a facsimile of part of the Treaty of Nanjing which precipitated the carve-up. There are excellent photographs which give an insight into Shanghai life at the turn of the century.

The museum is at 1286 Hongqiao Lu, not far from the airport, and it isn't very easy to get to. You could take the subway to Shanghai Stadium and catch a taxi from in front of the Sheraton Huating Hotel; alternatively bus 505 passes close by. It's open from 09.00-15.30 daily; entry is Y15.

Jade Buddha Temple

Despite being one of Shanghai's major tourist sights, the Jade Buddha Temple is actually fairly modern. It was built in the classical style between 1911 and 1918, to house two jade statues which had been brought from Burma by a monk named Huigen, in the 1880s. The main statue is undeniably impressive; housed in its own separate room near the rear of the temple, it is carved from white jade, is 1.9 metres high and is of a seated Buddha, dressed in a robe embroidered with precious stones. In a separate room there is a second smaller statue of a reclining Buddha.

For all its relative modernity, the temple has a peaceful ancient feel to it and is still in use as a place of worship. The main hall contains three large Buddhas, and 7000 block printed Buddhist sutras dating from the Qing Dynasty. The temple had a narrow escape during the Cultural Revolution. Though there are different stories about this, one has it that the Red Guards arrived to find the gates locked and pictures of Chairman Mao plastered over them. Since it would have been unthinkable to have ripped the pictures, the temple was left alone. Entry is Y15

Zhou Enlai's former residence

This house is one of a number of buildings in the suburbs to the south-west of the city centre which underline Shanghai's importance in recent Chinese history. After the end of WWII, the Kuomintang and the Communists made moves towards negotiation. The Communist delegation led by Zhou Enlai opened an office in this house, the Kuomintang agents were based in the house across the road in order to keep a close eye on what the Communists were up to, and General Marshall, the US mediator, lived a short distance away in a house that is now a hotel (see p155). It was hardly an auspicious or cordial arrangement. Not surprisingly the talks broke down, Zhou Enlai's delegation was ordered to leave, and the house was vacated in 1947.

Although the rooms are still furnished there's really not a lot to see but it's an interesting place to mull over the power struggle that happened such a relatively short time ago. Entry is Y4, and the house, at 73 Sinan Lu, is closed on Monday and Thursday mornings.

PRACTICAL INFORMATION
Orientation and services

Although Shanghai is huge, it is probably easiest to consider the area of the Bund and the streets running west from it towards Renmin Square as the centre of the city; since this area contains the main shopping streets and covers the ground of the old foreign concessions, this is where many of the most famous tourist sights are to be found. To the north-west of the centre is the main railway station, and to the west of the city is the airport.

Two landmarks that will help you navigate your way around the city are the Pearl Orient TV Tower in Pudong to the east of the city centre, and the huge TV station tower which is to the west of the city centre.

CITS (☎ 021-6321 7200) have an office on the Bund, on the ground floor of the building which houses the Industrial and Commercial Bank of China; this is directly opposite the unmistakable Diamond Restaurant. The office is open 08.30-11.30 and 13.00-16.45, daily (although you may not get much response out of them at weekends). The staff here handle international air tickets and boat tickets, hydrofoil tickets to Putuoshan and Ningbo, domestic air tickets, and rail tickets, as well as tours. There is also a **CITS office** in the soft class waiting room at the railway station, although they're not much use, particularly when their one English-speaking member of staff is out of the office.

An excellent initiative which Shanghai is so far alone in taking is in starting up a tourist information service. There are now three **Travel Information Desks**, which have been set up by the Municipal Tourism Bureau: one at the airport, another at the main railway station, and the third just inside the northern entrance to the Renmin Square subway station. The helpful staff speak English and distribute free tourist maps and information sheets, as well as selling the *Shanghai Star*, the city's English-language newspaper.

The main **post office** is just north of the Bund, and a five-minute walk from the Pujiang Hotel; poste restante is held upstairs. There is also a smaller post office next to the Bund itself, about 30 metres down Jiu Jiang Lu, and another

---

❑ **Consulates**
Australia 17 Fuxing Road (☎ 021-6433 4604)
Austria Rm 514, West Tower, Shanghai Centre, 1376 Nanjing Road
  (☎ 021-6279 7196)
Belgium 1375 Huaihai Road (☎ 021-6433 4466)
Canada Suite 604, West Tower, Shanghai Centre, 1376 Nanjing Road
  (☎ 021-6279 8400)
Denmark 6A, Qihua Building, 1375 Huaihai Rd (☎ 021-6431 4301)
France 1431 Huaihai Road (☎ 021-6433 2639)
Germany 151 Yongfu Road (☎ 021-6433 6953)
Israel 6/F, 16 Hennan Road (☎ 021-63740220)
Italy 127 Wuyi Rd (☎ 021-6252 4373)
Netherlands Rm 1403, Hilton Int'l Hotel, 250 Huashan Road
  (☎ 021-6248 0000)
New Zealand F/15, Qihua Building, 1375 Huaihai Road (☎ 021-6433 2230)
UK 244 Yongfu Road (☎ 021-6433 0508)
USA 1469 Huaihai Road (☎ 021-6433 6880)

SHANGHAI– KEY

Where to stay

1	Shanghai Hilton	1	上海希尔顿饭店
2	International Equatorial Hotel	2	国际贵都大饭店
3	Sofitel Hyland	3	上海海仑宾馆
4	Peace Hotel	4	和平饭店
5	Pacific Hotel	5	太平洋饭店
6	Tung Feng Hotel	6	东风饭店
7	Tai Yuan Villa	7	太原饭店
8	Yangtse Hotel	8	杨子饭店
9	Asia Hotel	9	亚洲饭店
10	Pujiang Hotel	10	浦江饭店

What to see

11	The Bund	11	外滩
12	Old Chinese City	12	城隍庙
13	Shanghai Museum	13	上海博物馆
14	Shanghai History Museum	14	上海历史博物馆
15	Jade Buddha Temple	15	玉佛寺
16	Zhou Enlai's Former Residence	16	周恩来故居
17	Shanghai Centre	17	上海商城 (波特曼·香格里拉饭店内)
18	Lyceum Theatre	18	兰心大戏院
19	Jin Jiang Hotel	19	锦江饭店

Where to eat

20	Shanghai Old Restaurant	20	上海老饭店
21	Zapu Lu	21	乍浦路美食店
22	Diamond Restaurant	22	钻石饭店

Other

23	Main Railway Station	23	主要火车站
24	Main Post Office	24	主要邮政局
25	Bank of China	25	中国银行
26	Advance Rail Booking Office	26	火车票预售处
27	CITS	27	国际旅行社
28	PSB	28	公安局
29	Pearl Orient Tower	29	东方明珠电视塔
30	Renmin Square	30	人民广场
31	Friendship Store	31	友谊商店
32	Foreign Languages Bookstore	32	外文书店

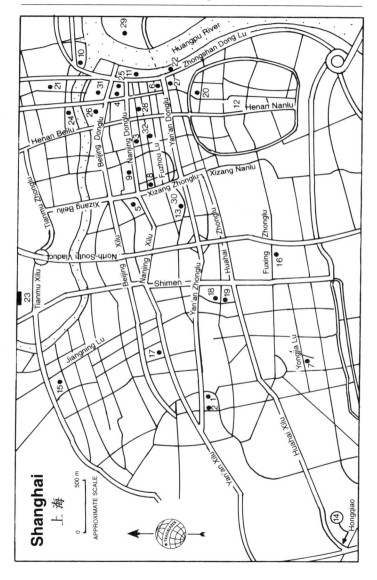

Shanghai
上海

post office at the main railway station. The **PSB** is on Hankou Lu, about 150 metres west of the Bund. There is a **Bank of China** next to the Peace Hotel. Most hotels will change money and travellers' cheques.

Local transport

Subway The subway in Shanghai is excellent: it is clean, cheap (Y2), relatively uncrowded and beats the traffic jams; best of all, in summer it's wonderfully cool compared to the humid heat above ground. At the moment it's slightly limited because it has only one line, although this will get you near to many places of interest, and a second line is under construction. Keep hold of your ticket: unlike the subway in Beijing they sometimes ask you to show your ticket on leaving the system.

Bus Buses are not so convenient in Shanghai as in other cities because the routes are complicated to follow, the buses are ridiculously crowded, and the traffic is often at a standstill anyway.

Bus 64 runs from the main railway station to the junction of Beijing Donglu and Henan Beilu, from where you can walk to the Pujiang Hotel.

Bus 20 runs straight along Nanjing Road and is useful to get to the Shanghai Centre. **Bus 65** runs from north to south and vice-versa straight along the Bund.

Bus 505 runs from near the Shanghai Museum (Renmin Square) to just north of the Shanghai History Museum.

Taxi The taxis waiting in front of the railway station are generally unwilling to use a meter and will quote you two or three times the going rate automatically. If this happens, walk to the main road a short distance away (a couple of hundred metres at most), and hail a cab; away from the station, you shouldn't have any difficulty persuading the driver to use the meter. Bear in mind that if the traffic is heavy you're going to have a slow and expensive ride.

Tours

CITS organise some tours including full- and half-day tours of the city, and trips to Suzhou and Hangzhou. You can pick up details of what's on offer at their office on the Bund.

Where to stay

By now the story will be getting familiar: there are numerous excellent top range hotels but really only one budget hotel.

Among the best hotels in the city are the **Shanghai Hilton** (☎ 021-62480000) where the cheapest single room is US$230, and the **International Equatorial Hotel** (☎ 021-62481688) where singles start at Y1650. Nearer the river is the **Sofitel Hyland** (☎ 021-63515888) with double rooms at US$200, and although you may not stay here it's worth noting where it is, as it's a good landmark if you're in the area, and it also has an outstanding cake shop next door.

If you're going to pay top money to stay in Shanghai, you may as well stay somewhere with some atmosphere. Several of the old hotels that operated in the 1920's and 30's are still going, and the most famous of these is the **Peace Hotel** (☎ 021-63216888) on Nanjing Lu, near to the Bund. The hotel has buildings on both the north and south sides of the street which are equally impressive – wood panelling, marble and old fittings; the prices, too, are the same: a double starts at Y720. The **Pacific Hotel** (☎ 021-63276226) on Nanjing Xilu is in a beautiful old building and the reception area, at least, has been carefully preserved; single rooms here start at US$55, while doubles are US$75-90 and upwards.

A cheaper place with some history is the **Tung Feng Hotel** (☎ 021-63218060) which is right on the Bund, and is immediately recognisable because it now shares its entrance lobby with a Kentucky Fried Chicken outlet. The lobby area seems to be a thoroughfare for everyone else, but presumably the rooms are quieter, and at Y300 for a single and Y450 for a double it's not too bad by Shanghai standards.

A hotel that has been highly recommended is the *Tai Yuan Villa* (☎ 021-64716688), situated in the quiet streets near the former residences of Zhou Enlai and Sun Yatsen. The house was built in the 1920's as the private residence of an English lady, Mrs Marcus. From 1945-1949, however, it was occupied by General Marshall, the chief mediator between Chiang Kaishek and Mao Zedong. From 1949 the house was the residence of Madam Jiang Qing (Mao's wife). It's a lovely old place with its own gardens but was under renovation at the time of writing, so the very reasonable Y300 charge for a double room may be about to rise.

Much less inspiring but about as central as you get, the *Yangtse Hotel* (☎ 021-63517880) is on Hankou Lu, a side street off Renmin Square, and has singles for Y360 and doubles for Y440. A short distance away, the old *Asia Hotel* (☎ 021-63223226) is right in the middle of Nanjing Lu. Unfortunately it appears to have little of its original décor left, and now has a shopping centre on its ground floor; walk through the stalls and up the stairs to get to the reception. A standard room here is Y352.

Finally, the backpackers' hotel is the *Pujiang Hotel* (☎ 021-63246388) which was formerly the Astor House Hotel, opened in 1860. It's just across Suzhou Creek from the north end of the Bund. A bed in a seven- or eight-person dormitory room is Y55, and a double room is Y300-330.

Where to eat

There are hundreds of places to eat in Shanghai, and a variety of both local and foreign food is on offer, but unfortunately many of the restaurants are quite expensive. At the top end of the scale you really will find it hard to beat the restaurants in the best hotels: try the Jin Jiang Hotel, Portman Shangri La, or the Sheraton for a start. The information sheets distributed by the Tourism Bureau or CITS have extensive listings, too. You could also head straight down to the area around the Yu Yuan Garden in the old Chinese quarter, where there are several good places, among them the *Shanghai Old Restaurant*, which is one of the oldest and most famous of Chinese restaurants in the city.

For excellent cheap Chinese food head for Zapu Lu, which is only five minutes' walk west of the Pujiang Hotel. You can't go wrong here: the street is lined with tiny family-run restaurants serving excellent local food. Don't expect an English menu. Huanghe Lu is the other good street for cheap food.

For snacks in the centre of town try any of the side streets off Nanjing or Fuzhou Lu, where you will find numerous food stalls. On the Bund itself, you can't miss the *Diamond Restaurant*; it's the very ugly wedge-shaped building. Though it has absolutely no atmosphere, it's not a bad place for a snack, and in some ways is a traveller's dream: it serves cheap Chinese food at fixed prices in a cafeteria style setting; just pile your tray with anything which looks good and head for the cashier.

If you're after Western-style food, you can have a breakfast binge at the Peace Hotel, where their all-you-can-eat breakfast buffet costs Y96. For other meals here, try to get into the 8th floor restaurant, where the setting is exactly as it was in the hotel's glory days – right down to the chinaware. See if they'll let you go up to the roof too – the view along the Bund is spectacular.

There are lots of smartish foreign-style restaurants and cafés. The *Fest Brew House* which is just off the Bund on Hankou Lu, beside the old Customs House, is cashing in on the Chinese fad

❏ SHANGHAI – WHAT TO DO IN THE EVENING

Shanghai has an active nightlife and is really the only city in China, apart from Beijing, where visitors have a choice of entertainment in the evenings. In order to get an update of what's on, the best place to look is in the *Shanghai Star* which has a listings guide, or in *Culture and Recreation*, a broadsheet which is produced fortnightly and is often available in hotel reception areas. A few regular options are listed below.

Acrobats

Everyone should see the Chinese acrobats at some stage during their visit to China. The Shanghai Acrobatic Troupe are one of the best groups in the country. Unfortunately they lost their own venue recently, and at the time of writing were performing nightly at the Shanghai Centre, which is a part of the ultra modern Portman Shangri La hotel complex.

Tickets range from Y30-60, and can be bought at the ticket office outside the Centre on the day of the performance, but try to get them in the morning as they can sell out. Don't let the touts who hang around near the ticket kiosk persuade you that all the official tickets are sold out before you've tried for yourself.

Jazz at the Peace Hotel

This is something of an institution and is well attended every night. The band performed at the Hotel before the Cultural Revolution and have been brought back together recently. They're getting on a bit and the music can sound slightly tired but it's not a bad way to spend an evening, – or it wouldn't be if it wasn't so ridiculously expensive. A pint of Tsing Tao is Y46 to which they add a Y6 service charge. Just when you think that you've successfully nursed a single drink for long enough the bill shows that there's a cover charge of Y42 for the music. In all, then a single beer has set you back Y94! You could argue that it gets better value the more you drink, of course.

Lyceum Theatre

It's actually no longer the Lyceum theatre, but this was its original name in the good old days, and it still functions as a theatre. Check with CITS, or the Shanghai Star to see what's on.

Jin Jiang Chamber Music Concerts

The Jin Jiang Hotel hosts these excellent concerts in a small auditorium in its grounds, every Friday evening at 8 pm. Entry is only Y10, and the performances are by members of the Shanghai Symphony Orchestra, reputed to be the best orchestra in the country. The programme for the forthcoming Friday is available either by asking at the hotel, or by checking the *Shanghai Star*.

for German-style brewhouse/restaurants; it's a nice enough place to eat with food in the Y30-70 bracket. *Pasta Fresca Da Salvatore*, just south of the Hilton Hotel on Changshu Lu, is really worthwhile and not too expensive: Y100 per head is a realistic price. For fast food, Shanghai is littered with *McDonald's* and *Kentucky Fried Chicken* places too. Finally special mention should go to the *Hai Hai Bakery*, in the side street behind the Sofitel Hyland Hotel – their chocolate éclairs are second to none!

What to buy

Shanghai is shopping paradise: just wander along Nanjing Lu and check out any of the huge department stores. Even the area under Renmin Square has been turned into an exclusive arcade: the Hong Kong Shopping Centre. For authentic souvenirs, however, the best place to look is probably around the central area of the old town; although it's aimed at tourists it's still a pleasant place to wander and contains many small curio shops. The Friendship Store is just a few metres west of the Bund, on Beijing Beilu, and the Foreign Languages Bookstore is on Fuzhou Lu, just east of the junction with Fujian Lu.

Moving on

By rail Although tickets are readily available in Shanghai, it can be a frustrating place for foreigners to buy them. **CITS** will book tickets for you, and if you have time, and don't mind spending a bit more cash, this is by far the easiest option. They need seven days' notice for hard sleeper tickets, and more like three days for soft sleepers – so unless you're spending a week in Shanghai they'll twist your arm to take a soft sleeper. There's a **Foreigners' Booking Office** inside the soft class waiting room at the main station but they will only book tickets on the day of departure, which is not much good if you want to guarantee getting a sleeper on a particular day. They're open from 08.00-11.30 and 12.30-17.00. Another place to try is the travel office in the **Longmen Hotel**, which is just next to the main station, but they will book tickets only for trains leaving that day or before 14.00 the next day. They will also tell you that they deal only in hard seat and soft sleeper tickets. Finally, the **ticket office** at the station itself sells only same day tickets and is chaotic in the extreme.

Worth a try before any of the above, however, is the **advance booking office** in town. For long distance trains (ie north of the Yangtse River and south of Hangzhou), tickets are sold at 230 East Beijing Road (Beijing Dong Lu), just west of the junction with Sichuan Zhong Lu, on the north side of the street. Have your requirement written in Chinese; and if your first choice doesn't work try for a sleeper on a slow train, as tickets for the express and fast trains always sell out first. There are advance booking offices for short distance trains, but since you're unlikely to want a sleeper,and the services are good, you'd be better off getting your ticket on the day of departure at the Foreigners' Booking Office.

Finally, note that there are two major stations in Shanghai, and although most trains seem to depart from the main station; double check when you buy your ticket. If you are leaving from the main station, just being a foreigner is enough to get you into the soft class waiting room, where they even have departure announcements in English.

For train times see p367-75.

By air Hongqiao airport is 15km west of the Bund area and is well connected with both domestic and international flights. Some sample fares (quoted by Shanghai Airlines) are as follows: Guangzhou Y1220, Beijing Y1100, Chongqing Y1420, and Xi'an Y1260.

By boat Shanghai is a good place to start any boat journeys: there are departures to Japan, Hong Kong, to the island of Putuoshan, and west up the Yangtse River, among others. CITS is the easiest place to obtain tickets and information about sailings but, if you want to book tickets for yourself, the central boat booking office is on Jinling Donglu opposite the CITS office. The Foreigners' Booking Office is on the second floor: have your requirement written down in Chinese and be prepared to be referred elsewhere; I was constantly told to try other places. A trip up the Yangtse all the way to Chongqing costs about Y700 and takes seven and a half days.

Hangzhou
杭州

Hangzhou, with its leafy walks and boat trips around the West Lake, is for the Chinese about as close to heaven on earth as it's possible to get. Foreigner visitors may have slightly different concepts of paradise but Hangzhou is still worth a visit of at least a couple of days. It's pleasant just to stroll around the lake, and the other sights include a very good museum and the awesome Lingyin Temple. Hangzhou is also reputed to be the best place in China to buy silk.

For budget travellers, however, this city can prove expensive – cheap hotels here are off-limits to non-Chinese. You should also note that as a major Chinese tourist destination, Hangzhou is best avoided at weekends and on public holidays: the train back to Shanghai on a Sunday evening is definitely one to miss.

HISTORY

Like many places in China, Zhejiang province, of which Hangzhou is the capital, claims to be the birthplace of the Chinese nation. Unlike rival claims, however, this one has an element of verifiable truth. Between 1973 and 1977, archaeologists working on a site near the village of Hemudu, in Yuyao County, about 120km south east of Hangzhou, unearthed the remains of culture some 7000 years old (carbon dating makes this reasonably reliable). Many of the items they found can now be seen in the Zhejiang Provincial Museum (see below), and the findings have led to the naming of the Hemudu Culture.

Hangzhou itself didn't make an appearance until much later. In the Qin Dynasty (221BC-207BC) the area was first referred to as the County of Qiantang. At the time there were settlements around the foot of Lingyin Hill but most of the area where the city stands today was covered by the tidal waters of the Qiantang River. For the next 600 years, as the river gradually silted up, leaving a natural lagoon (West Lake), the area consisted of little more than fishing villages. In 406AD the first city walls were built and the city was given its present name, which literally means 'city across the river'. In the 6th century, Hangzhou finally made it onto the map, with the arrival of the Grand Canal, and development started in earnest.

In 1138 under the name of Lin'an ('temporal peace') Hangzhou became the capital of the Southern Song, who had been evicted from their northern capital by the Chin. This was the city's golden age; the population rose from half a million to well over one million, and although Marco

Polo visited shortly after this, he still recalled that it was 'The finest and most splendid city in the world'. With the departure of the Southern Song, finally conquered by the Mongols, Hangzhou's fortunes waned slightly, although the city remained a centre of wealth and fashion. Silk became a major product, as did tea. In the 1860's Hangzhou was twice occupied by the Taiping rebels and over the course of two years much of the city was destroyed, both by the Taipings as they fought to occupy it, and the French troops who subsequently fought to liberate it. The Kuomintang had a headquarters here briefly during the Northern Campaign. By 1949 the population was 400,000.

Today the city is the capital of Zhejiang province and is home to approximately one and a half million people. It is not only a tourist destination: industries include silk, cotton, paper and electronics. Considerable effort has been made to keep the industrial side of the city away from the tourist attractions; the area of the lake is largely unspoiled, and the countryside to the west of the lake, where tea is one of the main crops, is easily accessible.

❏ Marco Polo

Marco Polo's journey overland to the court of Kubilai Khan, was one of the great events of the thirteenth century. The account of his travels (co-written with Rusticello, a romance writer of the time) is thought to have been penned in 1298. Proclaimed, in the prologue, as a 'Description of the World' it gave a firsthand account of the geography of the East, by a European who had travelled more widely than any before him. The 'Description' fired the imagination of generations of European readers. Columbus kept a private copy with notes scribbled in the margin. Centuries later, Coleridge immortalised the scene at the Mongol summer palace: 'In Xanadu did Kubla Khan, A Stately pleasure-dome decree'.

In line with the current trend in questioning the writings and claims of famous personalities, the spotlight has fallen on Marco Polo. One suggestion is that Marco, who was nicknamed 'Il Milione' – apparently for his expansive descriptions of the huge wealth of the Mongol court, may not actually have been to China at all. Why, for instance, did a man supposedly of such noted powers of observation fail to mention tea – a feature of Chinese life remarked upon by earlier Arab visitors? Equally one might have thought that the custom of foot binding would be worthy of comment, or he might have noted the existence of the Great Wall. Moreover, when historians started trying to trace the Venetian's steps, at the beginning of this century, they found that there were glaring errors in his itineraries, and notable features which could not be located.

It is more than possible, some argue, that like other travel books published in the 14th and 15th centuries, Marco Polo's account could have been cobbled together from the accounts of other travellers whom he had met as a merchant trading to Central Asia. Frances Wood's book *Did Marco Polo go to China?*, gives an excellent exposition of the cases for and against.

WHAT TO SEE

Lingyin (Soul's Retreat) Temple

Approximately nine kilometres west of the city centre, the Lingyin Temple was originally built in 326AD, although it has been restored or rebuilt several times, and the current buildings are only about 300 years old. At its peak the temple housed more than 3000 monks. Although it's packed with tourists these days rather than monks, the huge halls and statues, the carvings on the cliff face, and the wonderful setting still make for a unique atmosphere.

Two of the temple's old halls remain, and a third, rear hall has been built to replace one that burned down some years ago. In the **Front Hall**, seated within a pagoda-like structure, there is a large statue of a laughing Buddha which appears to be welcoming visitors to the temple. On either side are huge statues of the four Heavenly Generals. The hall itself is wonderful, and the detail of the painting on the ceiling panels is particularly impressive.

The second hall, known as the **Main Buddha Hall**, is the place which most people will remember about a visit here. The building is vast (33.6 metres high to be exact) and the enormous pillars are spectacular in themselves. It's difficult, however, to concentrate on anything other than the centre-piece: a breathtaking 19.6-metre-high sculpture of Sakyamuni. The sculpture was completed in 1956 (to replace three large statues that had stood here previously but which had suffered from neglect). Its relative newness doesn't detract from the splendour of the thing. Carved from 24 pieces of camphor wood and gilded with 104 ounces of gold, the Buddha is sitting on a lotus flower, which symbolises purity. Around the walls of the hall are a number of sculptures of disciples and mythical characters. At the back of the hall is a relief mural similar to that in the West Garden temple in Suzhou.

Opposite the temple, across the stream, 300 or so rock carvings can be found on the face of the **Peak Flying From Afar**. There are two accounts of how the peak attained its unusual name. In one, the temple's founder, an Indian monk named Hui Li, thought that he recognised the peak as one from his native country and wondered aloud how it could have flown there. In another, the peak was actually a native of Sichuan Province, given to flying around the country at random; after it dropped to the ground near Hangzhou, it was immobilised by the local villagers who carved 500 arhats in its rock, in order to keep it on the ground and thus prevent further damage. Although most of the carvings on the rock face date from the Yuan Dynasty, the most famous, the Laughing Buddha,

---

(Opposite) Eastern Provinces: Nanjing Lu (see p146), the busiest shopping street in Shanghai, is as crowded and fashionable today as it was in the heyday of the concessions.

was carved about 1000 years ago. The temple and rock carvings were reputedly saved from the violence of the Red Guards on the personal instructions of Zhou Enlai; after his decree to preserve the place, it was bricked up until 1971 to keep it from damage.

Bus 7 runs from the city centre to the temple. Entry into the park area (where you can see the rock carvings only) is Y10.5, and entry into the temple itself costs a further Y10.

Tomb of Yue Fei

The tomb is hardly one of Hangzhou's highlights although it seems to have found its way on to most tourist itineraries. Yue Fei was a brave and talented general, who, over a series of campaigns almost succeeded in winning back the old Song capital of Kaifeng and defeating the Chin. He was the victim of court intrigue, however; the prime minister, Qin Hui, favoured appeasement of the Chin and persuaded the emperor to order Yue to withdraw when he was on the verge of success. Back in Hangzhou, Yue was executed on false charges.

Yue's innocence and loyalty became clear some time later, and since then, his name has been synonymous with sacrifice and patriotism. One of the more notable items in the tomb area is a picture of Yue preparing to leave home, on his way to join the army. Full of patriotic fervour, he is reputed to have persuaded his mother to tattoo the words, 'Be Loyal to the Motherland' across his back! Qin Hui, conversely has become one of the arch villains of Chinese history, and along with his wife he is still reviled today. According to one local story, the statues of the two were once thrown into the lake to get rid of them; the lake started to stink so badly that the former prime minister's nickname became 'stinking Qin Hui'. Entry to the mausoleum is Y9.

West Lake

Yet again, local stories offer different explanations of how the lake got its name. The most obvious explanation is that it's to the west of the city, but another popular tale has it that it was named after a beautiful local girl about whom a poem was written in the Song Dynasty:

> 'Men say no jewels or robes enhanced
> The beauty of Xi Zi;
> And West Lake decked or unadorned,
> May well compare with her'.

The lake consists of three parts, divided up by causeways. The largest island, named **Solitary Hill**, houses a small park and a number of tea houses, as well as the exclusive *Louwailou Restaurant* and the **Provincial Museum**. It's a pleasant place to wander around and you can

---

(Opposite) Eastern Provinces – Top: Even by Chinese standards, Guangzhou (see p180) is one of the most crowded cities in the country. Try to avoid the rush hour. **Bottom:** The Pearl River runs through the heart of Guangzhou.

HANGZHOU – KEY

Where to stay

1	Shangri-La Hotel	1	香格里拉饭店
2	Zhejiang Hotel	2	浙江宾馆
3	Wanghu Hotel	3	望湖饭店
4	Overseas Chinese Hotel	4	华侨饭店
5	Huanhu Hotel	5	环湖宾馆
6	Xin Xin Hotel	6	新新饭店
7	Zhehua Hotel	7	浙华饭店
8	Xihu Hotel	8	西湖国宾馆

What to see

9	Lingyin Temple	9	灵隐寺
10	Tomb of Yue Fei	10	岳坟
11	Solitary Hill	11	孤山
12	Three Pools Mirroring the Moon	12	三潭印月
13	Zhejiang Provincial Museum	13	浙江博物馆
14	Baochu Pagoda	14	保淑塔
15	Six Harmonies Pagoda	15	六和塔

Where to eat

16	Louwailou Restaurant	16	楼外楼
17	Wusan Lu	17	吴山路 (拼音)
18	Kentucky Fried Chicken	18	肯塔基烤鸡店
19	Croissants De France	19	法国牛角面包店

Other

20	Railway Station	20	火车站
21	Post Office	21	邮局
22	Friendship Store	22	友谊商店
23	Bank of China	23	中国银行
24	CITS	24	中国国际旅行社
25	Boat Dock	25	客运轮船码头
26	Foreign Language Bookstore	26	外文书店

catch boats from the south shore of the island to **Xiaoyingzhou Island** (Island of the Fairies). This tiny islet was built in the Ming Dynasty with mud dredged from the lake, and is considered to be one of the most beautiful places in Hangzhou, encompassing as it does separate pools of water, leading to a famous sight Three Pools Mirroring the Moon.

Zhejiang Provincial Museum

The museum is extensive, well laid out and it has English labels throughout. Although the sections relating to the Hemudu culture are interesting, other parts of the museum are a bit thin on the ground for exhibits; maybe

they're planning to expand in the future. Two halls that contain things you are unlikely to have seen before are the numismatics display, which shows the development of various forms of money in China, and the Arts and Crafts Hall, which has some furniture with amazing workmanship and carving. The museum is open 08.15-16.45; entry is Y15.

Baochu Pagoda

This elegant, crumbly-looking pagoda is likely to be one of the first really notable things you see in Hangzhou, as it's perched on the hill just to the north of the lake (north-west of the CITS building). The original pagoda was built in 968AD, when the local ruler was summoned to the Song court at Kaifeng. His courtiers, worried for their king's safety, built the structure as a lucky charm for his safe return. History relates that it worked the first time he went to Kaifeng, although he wasn't so lucky the second time he visited. Last rebuilt in 1933, the brick-built pagoda is not nearly as old it looks from a distance.

There's nothing to see around its base and no stairs to climb but if you want to get a closer look, about 400 metres west of the Baidi Causeway there's a sloping driveway with a sign for 'West Lake Health Club'. Go straight up the drive and then climb the steps to the top of the hill.

Six Harmonies Pagoda

The pagoda stands a few kilometres south of West Lake, on the north bank of the Qiantang River. Originally built in 970AD, it owes its name to the Buddhist belief in Six Harmonies: harmonies of body, mind, speech, opinion, wealth, and abstinence from temptation. After it was built, the 60-metre-high pagoda was used as a night navigation aid for boatmen on the river, with lamps being hung near the top. The pagoda has had several reconstructions, including two since 1949.

PRACTICAL INFORMATION
Orientation and services

CITS (☎ 0571-5152888) are based in an old building on the corner of Beishan Lu and Baochu Lu. They are helpful, and are open 08.30-17.00. The main **post office** is on the other side of the city, at the east end of Jiefang Lu, near the railway station. The main **Bank of China** is a block east of the Wanghu Hotel.

Local transport

Local buses are good, and city maps with bus routes marked can be bought outside the train station. A Y1 bus fare will get you almost anywhere in town.

Tours

CITS are not happy for individual travellers to join in with tour groups, and predictably individually organised tours will be very expensive, so unless you can muster a large group, it's best to go it alone. Public transport is good, and you should be able to get hold of an English guide book in the Foreign Language Bookstore.

Where to stay

The smartest hotel in Hangzhou is the *Shangri-La Hotel* (☎ 0571-7977951), which has a fine location on the peaceful north shore of the lake. Prices for a hillview room (ie facing away from the lake) start at Y1360 for a single, and Y1575 for a double. You pay about Y400 more for a room facing the lake.

A really peaceful place to stay is the *Zhejiang Hotel* (☎ 0571-7977988). It's a fair way out of town on the west side of the lake and has the atmosphere of a country club rather than a hotel. A single room here is Y320, while a double room starts at Y500.

The *Wanghu Hotel* (☎ 0571-7071942) on the north-east corner of the lake wins a prize for having the largest entrance lobby of any hotel in China – you could get lost here. Single rooms start at US$50 and doubles at US$75. Just to the south, the *Overseas Chinese Hotel* (☎ 0571-707441) is nothing special; staff quoted prices of Y498 for a single room and Y598 for a double but dropped these by Y100 almost immediately.

To the south again, the *Huanhu Hotel* (☎ 0571-7065491) is better value, and occupies a prime site on the eastern lakeside. Relatively smart and glitzy, it has double rooms from Y260.

Close to the Shangri-La Hotel but much cheaper even though it shares the same peaceful bit of lakeside is the *Xin Xin Hotel* (☎ 0571-7987101). The cheapest twin room is Y202. If you don't mind staying on the 'wrong' side of town, the *Zhehua Hotel* (☎ 0571-7802366) is convenient for the railway station and is probably the cheapest place in Hangzhou if there are two of you: a double room here is Y135, or Y175 with a private bathroom.

The best value if you're travelling alone is the *Xihu Hotel* which is right on the corner of the street north of the Huanhu Hotel. A single room here is Y90. It's not too easy to spot, so ask around, and don't believe the taxi drivers if they tell you that it's closed.

Where to eat

Undoubtedly the classiest place to eat is the *Louwailou Restaurant* on Solitary Hill where you can try fish caught from the lake, or other local dishes such as 'Perch from Qiantang River'. The best area for small cheap eating places, however, is in the side streets just off the waterfront on the east side of the lake: the area around Wusan Lu, almost directly east of the Xihu Hotel has been particularly recommended. There are several Western style fast food places – *CFC*, the Chinese equivalent of KFC is on the waterfront, just north of the Xihu Hotel. *Croissants de France* is a reasonable place for a snack and a coffee – it's next to the Friendship Store.

What to buy

Hangzhou is reportedly the best place in China to buy silk, with prices lower even than the Silk Market in Beijing. You will have to bargain hard to get really low prices. Other local specialities include Longjing Green Tea, and sandalwood fans. If you want to know more about the city and the sights, you may be able to get hold of a copy of the English guidebook *An Incomplete Guide to Hangzhou*, in the Foreign Languages Bookstore, which is almost opposite the Friendship Store on the north-east corner of the lake.

Moving on

By rail Shanghai is only 3-4 hours away and there are plenty of excellent intercity trains, although you should try to avoid the last train on Sunday night. Hard Seat to Shanghai costs Y33 and booking is easy as there's a Foreigners' Ticket Office to the right of the main ticket hall which is to the right of the main station itself. The Soft Seat waiting room seems to be open to foreigners generally, regardless of whether you have a soft class ticket. For train times see p367-75.

By bus There's not much point in taking the local buses from Hangzhou, as the train service is so good, but one bus that might be of interest is the service to Mt Huangshan, which runs from the west bus station in summer only. There is a daily bus, and the journey takes approximately eight hours.

By boat Boats to Suzhou leave daily at 18.00 from the boat dock in the north of the city.

Nanchang
南昌

Nanchang is one of the uglier cities in China, and if you can avoid spending a night here you should. It is, however, the nearest main railway station (on this route) to Lushan, an interesting hill resort which is definitely worth a visit, and hence some basic details are included here. Apart from a couple of museums there is little to see in Nanchang.

Despite the discovery of neolithic remains in the area, little is known about Nanchang itself before the Han Dynasty (206BC-220AD) when it started to grow prosperous as a farming and trading town. Although the city apparently continued to enjoy reasonable affluence, little of note took place there until this century when, in August 1927, the Communists struck the first symbolic blow against the Nationalist army. Embittered by Chiang Kaishek's treachery (the Shanghai Coup had taken place in April), Communist leaders including Zhou Enlai and Zhu De organised an uprising in Nanchang. They held the city for only a few days before they were driven out by Nationalist troops.

Despite the apparent military failure, the Nanchang Uprising was important for two reasons. Firstly the remnants of the 30,000 strong force which took the city became the core of the Red Army which was formed soon afterwards. Secondly, the failure gave the lie to the Soviet model of urban revolution. From this point, Mao's theories of making revolution in the countryside by mobilising the peasants, began to gain credence.

Today Nanchang is the capital of Jiangxi Province, and a large industrial city with a population of roughly one million.

PRACTICAL INFORMATION
Orientation and services
CITS (☎ 0791-6224396) are based in a building behind the Jiangxi Hotel (north), and call themselves Jiangxi Travel Service. Try not to get hijacked by any of the other departments: the English/American office is very helpful, and will assist with ticket bookings if you give them at least four days notice. They are open from 08.30-18.00.

The **post office** is on the junction of Bayi Dadao and Ruzi Lu, on the southwest corner of Renmin Square. The **Bank of China** is just west of the Poyanghu Hotel.

Local transport
The public buses are good and the following might be of use during a brief stay in Nanchang:

Bus 5 runs from the station to the Xiangshan Hotel

Bus 2 runs from the station to the roundabout by the Nanchang hotel, and then north past both Jiangxi hotels, passing, en route, the long distance bus station.

Bus 1 runs directly north-south along the central road through the city.

Where to stay
Despite the fact that almost all the hotels in Nanchang have seen better days, accommodation is not particularly cheap. Slightly confusingly there are two Jiangxi Hotels within a few hundred metres of each other (I've added 'north' and 'south' to the name to distinguish them). The *Jiangxi Hotel (North)* (☎ 0791-6221131) is quite a pleasant place but it is also the most expensive hotel in town, – the cheapest rooms are Y600. Just a few hundred metres south on the main street is the *Jiangxi Hotel (South)* (☎ 0791-6212123), which though not as smart as its namesake, is OK and has doubles at Y180.

On the main roundabout west of the railway station, the *Nanchang Hotel* (☎ 0791-6271281) is probably the best budget hotel in town, with doubles for Y120. Across the road from it is the *Poyanghu Hotel* (☎ 0791-6229688) which is overpriced with doubles starting at Y186.

The cheapest place that's open to foreigners is the *Xiangshan Hotel* (☎ 0791-6781402). Unfortunately it's a fair way from the railway station and as

NANCHANG – KEY

Where to stay

1	Jiangxi Hotel (North)	1	江 西 宾 馆 (北)
2	Jiangxi Hotel (South)	2	江 西 饭 店 (南)
3	Nanchang Hotel	3	南 昌 宾 馆
4	Poyanghu Hotel	4	鄱 阳 湖 大 酒 店
5	Xiangshan Hotel	5	象 山 宾 馆

Other

6	Central Roundabout/Flyover	6	中 心 转 盘 处 (高 架 桥)
7	Railway Station	7	火 车 站
8	Renmin Square	8	人 民 广 场
9	Post Office	9	邮 局
10	Long Distance Bus Station	10	长 途 汽 车 客 运 站
11	Bank of China	11	中 国 银 行
12	CITS	12	中 国 国 际 旅 行 社
13	Advance Rail Booking Office	13	火 车 票 预 售 处

Nanchang

南 昌

0   500 m
APPROXIMATE SCALE

they may say that they've got no vacancies anyway, it could prove a frustrating trip. Dormitory beds (if you can get them) are Y30 in a four-bed room and Y60 in a three-bed room.

Where to eat

To the north-west of the central roundabout and flyover there are some small, cheap restaurants. Otherwise there's a small night market area on the street running east opposite the Jiangxi Hotel (north).

To the north of the central roundabout and flyover, along the main drag you can find fast food at the *Joint Venture Hunky Dorg Food Company* (sic) – not very joint, I think...

Moving on

By rail Although Lushan is a good place to visit, there is one drawback: Nanchang can be a difficult place to obtain rail tickets. This is because Nanchang is not actually on the main line at all but on a branch line. The easiest way to get around the problem is to catch an early morning train down the branch line to the junction at Xiantang and then jump on the next main line train that passes through.

To Guangzhou there is only one direct train every other day and tickets are in great demand. If you want to go there direct it would be a good idea to get CITS or even the business centre in the Jiangxi Hotel (north) to organise a ticket for you. CITS need at least four days' notice, and the business centre need five days' notice, so you could go and have a long relaxing time in Lushan and come back in time for your train. Another possibility is to take a train to Zhuzhou, or a bus to Changsha. As both of these are on the main Beijing-Guangzhou line, getting a train onwards from there should be no problem.

If you want to book your own ticket and have no luck at the train station ticket office, try the advance booking

offices in the town – one of them is about 300 metres north of the Jiangxi Hotel (north). To get to the other, catch Bus 1 south and get off four stops beyond Nanchang Hotel. The ticket office is about 50 metres north of the bus stop, on the east side of the road, (you should just be able to see the railway symbol on the front of the building). The entrance is around the back – go through the arch and up the stairs. It's open from 08.00-12.00 and 13.00-17.00.

If things get really desperate, try the ticket touts who hang around in the southern ticket office, but bargain hard and check the ticket when you get it to make sure it's what you want.

If you end up with a Hard Seat ticket to Guangzhou, prepare yourself. Because the train goes only every other day, it gets unbelievably crowded. It departs Nanchang at 12.30 every other day.

Trains to Jiujiang, in the' other direction up the branch line, are much easier. This is the best way to get to Lushan in the winter months, as you can get a minibus from Jiujiang up to Lushan. There are at least four trains a day:

Train No	Departure
T582	06.42
T82	07.58
T84	14.30
T376	18.14

By bus The best way to get to Lushan during the summer months is by bus from the long distance bus station. There are four or five of these a day, the journey takes about three hours, and costs Y35.5.

Buses also run to Changsha every day. It's a nine-hour journey, and the night buses should cost about Y64.

By air A flight to Guangzhou will cost Y660 and is easily obtainable.

Lushan
庐山

Lushan is one of the relatively few places along this east coast route where you can escape the big modern cities and the bustle of Chinese life. It's a peaceful spot, and although there's not a lot to do here apart from walk in the hills, that may be just what you need after a few weeks of travelling in China. A combination of fresh air, quiet, and (in the summer) pleasantly cool climate makes it an ideal place for a two- or three-day break from any itinerary.

HISTORY

Lushan is first referred to by name in the *Historical Records* by Sima Qian (145-90BC). In the fourth century the Dongling Monastery was set up and subsequently became the centre of the Pure Land Sect of Buddhism, and from this time onwards, the mountain was visited by a number of famous figures. In the eighth century the famous Tang poet Li Bai is reputed to have built a study near the Five Elders Peaks, and the Song Dynasty poet Su Shi (1037-1101) was another famous visitor. In the twelfth century, scholar Zhu Xi set up a centre at Bailudong House where, with his disciples, he pondered a fresh interpretation of Confucianism, the product being Neo-Confucianism, which went by the name of *The School of Universal Principles*.

Mount Lushan was 'discovered' towards the end of the last century by Western missionaries. One of them, Edward Selby Little, persuaded officials to lease him property on the ridge, and Guling was opened to Westerners in 1895. It became a fashionable resort to which the foreign community could retreat in the height of summer, and during the 1930's it was nicknamed the Summer Capital. Over 600 villas were put up, in a variety of styles, according to the wealth and country of origin of their owners. This variety can still be seen today, with an unusual selection of English country houses, European-style villas and squat farmhouses.

After WWII, with the original owners gone, the officials moved in: Chiang Kaishek and his wife had a villa here, and it was in Lushan that he met General Marshall to negotiate the future of China. Shortly afterwards, with the Communists' victory, Mao and his wife moved in, taking over the Chiangs' former residence. In 1959 and 1970 Lushan was the scene of two crucial Communist Party conferences, in which Mao fought bitterly to maintain his control. In the 1959 conference, Peng Dehuai spoke out against the folly of the Great Leap Forward and was rewarded for his honesty and insight by being removed from office.

Today, Lushan still draws a few visitors because of its Communist history, (it was designated as a site of special interest during the years of the Cultural Revolution), but for most people it's a pleasant and picturesque holiday spot. Like Beidahe in the north, Lushan has become a resort where departments can send their workers for a much-needed break. Thus the hill sides are dotted with large buildings and guest-houses which belong to departments and remain empty until the next batch of holiday-makers arrive.

WHAT TO SEE

Meilu Villa
Built in 1903 for an English lady, Mrs Winifred J Barrie, the villa later became the property of Chiang Kaishek and his wife during the 1930's and 40's. Mao Zedong took it over in the 1950's, and it is the villa which Jung Chang and her brother inadvertently photographed in *Wild Swans*:

'On our way down, we passed a two-story villa, hidden in a thicket of Chinese parasol trees, magnolia, and pines....It struck me as an unusually lovely place, and I snapped my last shot. Suddenly a man materialized out of nowhere and asked me in a low but commanding voice to hand over my camera. He wore civilian clothes, but I noticed he had a pistol....Some tourists standing next to me whispered that this was one of Mao's summer villas.'

The villa has a small photo display but otherwise is pretty bare. You can have a Coke on Mao's old rooftop patio, though. It's open 07.30-18.00.

Meeting Hall
Built in 1937 as a meeting hall for Chiang Kaishek's Lushan Officers' Training Regiment, the building was the scene of crucial meetings of the Chinese Communist Party in 1959 and 1970. Today the hall is laid as though for a conference, and is vaguely reminiscent of a school theatre, with rows of folding seats set out in front of the stage. On display are some photos taken during the conferences but it's not the most gripping of places to visit. Entry is Y4, and there are a couple of other buildings around the square which you can also go into.

Floral Path Park
Surrounding Ruqin Lake, Floral Path Park is described on the sign by the entrance as 'A pearl among Mount Lushan's scenic spots'. The lakeside setting gives it a certain charm; it's a pleasant place but nothing out of the ordinary. Entry is only Y4 so it's not going to break the bank.

Brocade Valley
This seems to be a highlight of a visit to Lushan for Chinese tourists so you may well find that it's fairly crowded, but it's still not a bad place to visit as the path along the side of the steep glacial valley has spectacular views. Although there's a string of spots with suitably grand names, only

two are of real historical interest. The **Negotiation Platform** has a small, locked building which looks rather like a closed tea shop but was in fact the spot at which General Marshall, the US special mediator, met Chiang Kaishek to negotiate the future of China, between July and September 1946. Further along the 1500 metre path is the **Immortals' Cave** which houses a small temple in a natural cave.

Hanpo Pass

This is basically a vantage point, which reputedly has excellent views, although unfortunately the whole area was fog-bound when I visited. From the Pass you should be able to see **Five Old Men Peak** to the left of the Hanpo Ridge, and **Taiyi Peak** and **The Plough Tip Peaks** to the right of it. Although most people seem only to walk up the steps as far as the first pavilion, try following the path down on the other side, and along the rather melodramatically named **Knife Edge Crest** to the final pavilion, which is a bit more peaceful. From here, if you are on foot, you can cut down to the road leading to Five Old Men Peaks.

Just below the Hanpo Pass car park is a **chairlift**, which takes you down the hillside. A return ticket on the chairlift costs Y40.

Five Old Men Peaks

The hill received its name because it has five separate peaks which supposedly resemble a group of old men seated in various postures. It's fun walking over the peaks, and the views should be great (again the visibility was poor when I visited), but be prepared for an energetic climb. It takes about half an hour of scaling staircases to get to the first peak, after which I counted peaks two, four and five, so peak number three remained, for me, a mystery. The highest point is peak four at 1357 metres.

Rather than turn back after the last peak, most people choose to walk down to the area of the small hamlet above the **Three Cascades Waterfall**. To do this, return from the pavilion on the fifth peak to the small green wooden hut and take the path down hill that runs from beside it. The total time from starting your climb up the first peak to arriving back down at the road will be at least one hour, even if you are walking quickly.

Three Cascades Waterfall

To get to the waterfall from the road you can either walk or take the small railway (Y20 for the trip down, and Y30 for the trip up). Although the railway saves you the first half hour of walking, (actually it's a very attractive section of path, alongside a river), it doesn't get you to the waterfall itself. From the lower station you must then walk down a formidable flight of steps. Quite apart from the attractive waterfall, the entire walk is very pretty, so if you've got time, go for it. Be warned, however: if you choose to do the whole thing on foot, it will take you at least two hours to get from the top, down to the waterfall and back up.

❏ Lushan on foot

It is quite possible to get everywhere in Lushan on foot and you can make a circuit of Hanpo Pass, Five Old Men Peaks and Three Cascades Waterfall, starting and ending in Guling. The whole excursion involves eight and a half hours of walking (excluding time sightseeing, resting etc). It left me pretty weary at the end but it was very enjoyable. If you want to cut this down slightly you could take a taxi out to the far end of the circuit, (the waterfall) and just do the walk back; or if you arrive at the waterfall at a reasonable hour (ie mid-afternoon) there's a fair chance that you'll be able to get a minibus back. Finally you could, of course, just miss one bit out.

One possible route is as follows: take the road running south-west out of Guling towards Lulin Lake and then cut uphill to join the path that runs above the museum – unlike some other paths in the area, this one is clearly marked, as well as being attractive and peaceful. The path brings you out near **Hanpo Pass** from where you can walk along **Knife Edge Crest** and, just before the final pavilion, go down the long flight of steps to your left. In effect this cuts a corner, and saves you walking back from the Pass and turning right at the road junction. At the bottom of the steps you find yourself back on the road near the entry to the **Lushan Botanical Garden** (entry Y5). Turn right and walk along the road to the start of the climb up **Five Old Men Peaks**. Coming down on the other side of the peaks you arrive at the start of the railway above the waterfall. After your visit to the waterfall you can walk back along the road to Guling (several kilometres).

If you are thinking of short-cutting by using the local footpaths, it's worth having a compass and a healthy distrust of the accuracy of the local maps. The obvious path that should take you straight south from Guling to the area of the waterfall (it follows a stream to a small reservoir, and then appears to cut across to the waterfall) is overgrown at first and then disappears completely.

PRACTICAL INFORMATION
Orientation and services

Lushan is centred on the small town of **Guling**, and the main places of interest are scattered around the surrounding hills. There is an **entrance** to Lushan, on the main road up the mountain, where all minibuses must stop, and visitors must pay an entrance fee – foreigners pay Y30. **Maps** of the area are available for Y2, either at the entrance gate, or in the small shops in the town. They give a fair idea of the layout and main places of interest but are not great – failing to show any difference between roads, pedestrian streets and footpaths for a start. The **Bank of China** and the **post office** are both within 100 metres of the Guling Hotel, up the narrow pedestrian street opposite the hotel. **CITS** (☎ 0792 282427) have their office about 400 metres down the hill from here, on the right as you walk down the main road. The staff are friendly and helpful and several languages are spoken.

Local transport

The ideal way to get around Lushan and the surrounding area would be by bike, but according to CITS, bikes are not allowed in Lushan. There are plenty of taxis, though, and these might be worth while for a few of the longer trips.

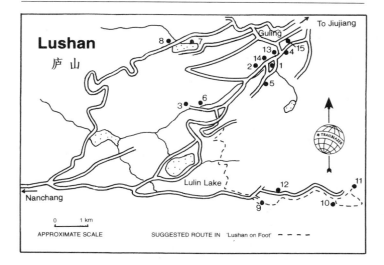

APPROXIMATE SCALE

SUGGESTED ROUTE IN 'Lushan on Foot' – – – –

LUSHAN – KEY

Where to stay

1	Meilu Villa Hotel	1	别墅村宾馆
2	Lushan Hotel	2	庐山宾馆
3	Lushan Dasha	3	庐山大厦
4	Guling Hotel	4	牯岭饭店

What to see

5	Meilu Villa	5	美庐别墅
6	Meeting Hall	6	人民剧场 (庐山会议旧址)
7	Floral Path Park	7	花径
8	Brocade Valley	8	锦绣谷
9	Hanpo Pass	9	含鄱口
10	Five Old Men Peaks	10	五老峰
11	Three Cascades Waterfall	11	三叠泉
12	Botanical Gardens	12	植物园

Other

13	Bank of China/Post Office	13	中国银行 / 邮局
14	CITS	14	中国国际旅行社
15	Bus Station	15	汽车站

There are also a few minibuses that go out to the main tourist sites. You *can* do everything on foot in Lushan (see p172), and if you're a keen walker this is definitely the best option, as it's a rare chance to get away from the crowds. Some of the places of interest are a fair distance away, however.

Tours

CITS will tell you that there are three main sights in Lushan: Hanpo Pass, Five Old Men Peaks, and the Three Cascades Waterfall. Tour buses operate daily, providing transport to these three spots; when you get to the Pass there is time to look around, and in the case of the Peaks and the Waterfall, buses wait while visitors walk the fairly lengthy routes to see each sight. Buses start early in the morning from the centre of town and because of the time allowed for passengers to walk to the sights, take most of the day, returning at 3 or 4pm.

Where to stay

The most expensive place in Lushan is the *Meilu Villa Hotel* (☎ 0792-8282927) which has rooms and even separate villas on its area of wooded hill side. A double here is Y400. Just as good but with more atmosphere is the *Lushan Hotel* (☎ 0792-8282060), a three-star hotel which is like an English country house, set back from the road up its own driveway. Double rooms start at Y210 and triple rooms at Y280.

A fair way down the hill from the centre of town and next to the hall where the famous Lushan Conferences took place is the *Lushan Dasha* which was originally a study house for the training of Kuomintang officers. A double here is advertised as Y280, but I was offered one at Y200. It's a bit of a hike from everywhere else, though, and rather dark and dreary.

The cheapest place to stay is the *Guling Hotel* (☎ 0792-8282435) which is near the town centre and has beds in three-bedded dormitories for Y30. The building which these triples are in is wonderful – like an old, large and rather neglected cricket pavilion. There are also double rooms for Y80, and far smarter rooms in the modern building for Y200 and upwards.

Where to eat

There are several small restaurants around Guling, none of which particularly stand out.

If you're staying at the Guling Hotel, the small restaurant on the corner opposite is adequate, and you could try the *Sichuan Restaurant* which is in front of the hotel. On the main road about 150 metres downhill from the Lushan Hotel, is a reasonable small place but watch them for overpricing, as they are obviously of the opinion that foreigners will pay whatever bill is put in front of them.

Near the centre of Guling there is a largish restaurant with its own courtyard area, set down below the level of the road, which is another good place to try, provided you get there before they start the evening's karaoke.

What to buy

There are plenty of shops selling tourist goods but since there are few Westerners here it's mostly aimed at the Chinese. A walking stick might be a useful if you're going to go hiking. Tea is another gift which seems to sell well here. The shops also have an amazing variety of dried foods on offer, which they will let you try if you ask. Stock up for your next long train journey.

Moving on

Buses to Nanchang depart regularly from the bus station a few metres uphill from the Guling Hotel. There are also regular buses to Jinjiang, which is one and a half hours away, and the fare is about Y15.

Changsha
长 沙

Very few Western travellers stay long in Changsha, the large, grey, dirty capital of Hunan province, but there are a couple of sights nearby that are definitely worth seeing. The most famous of these is Chairman Mao's birthplace in the village of Shaoshan, while the provincial museum in Changsha has an interesting display of artefacts from the excavation of the Han Tomb at nearby Mawangdui.

Since Changsha is well connected by rail to pretty much everywhere, it makes a reasonable base for a day or two while you collect your onward rail tickets and do a bit of sightseeing.

HISTORY

Changsha had long been in existence as a major city of the State of Chu, before China was unified by Qin Shi Huangdi in 221BC. Despite its subjugation to the Imperial court in the north, it continued to maintain an element of independence during the Han Dynasty. The tombs which have been discovered at the Mawangdui site show that not only was the city substantial in size by the middle of the Han Dynasty but also that there was considerable wealth and culture here.

Changsha remained a major city throughout the centuries, and finally was opened up as a treaty port around 1900. Both Mao and Liu Shaoqi were born nearby, and Mao subsequently studied at the teacher training college here. During WWII, the city was devastated by the Chinese themselves, as they attempted to slow the enemy advance by using a scorched earth policy. In Changsha, the plan ended in disaster. For whatever reason, officials failed to warn the inhabitants that they were about to set fire to the petrol and oil cans already in position and thousands of citizens died. Even Harold Rattenbury (*China-Burma Vagabond*), who had just visited Shenyang as it recovered from Japanese fire bombing, was astounded, recalling that 'the desolation of Ch'angsha reminded me of Pompeii or a town through which a tidal wave has swept'.

WHAT TO SEE
Hunan Provincial Museum

The museum is somewhat confusing in its layout; displays are housed in three separate areas, two of which are rather disappointing. The third, however, (which fronts on to the tarmac car park/basketball area) contains the main exhibition of the finds from the Mawangdui excavation.

Since all three areas charge separate entry fees, it's probably only worth visiting the main exhibition, where the entry ticket costs Y10.

The **Mawangdui site** just outside the city was excavated in the early 1970's, to reveal three undisturbed Han Dynasty tombs. The tombs belonged to Li Chang, the Marquis of Dai and prime minister of Changsha state, who died in around 186BC, and to his wife, Xin Zui, and their son, both of whom died sometime around 168BC. Each body was contained in a set of coffins, one within another, the outsides of which were painted with intricate designs of real and mythical creatures. The coffins were placed at the bottom of tomb shafts 16 metres deep and the incredible preservation of the body on display, which is that of Xin Zui, is attributed to the deep burial and the fact that the tomb was sealed with a thick layer of white clay which provided a constant temperature and humidity. Most people will find that the sight of a 2000 year old corpse in a truly remarkable state of preservation is the thing they remember most clearly about this exhibition but it shouldn't detract from the other items in the hall upstairs. The tombs yielded a vast amount of material which gives an insight into culture and development in the Han Dynasty. Included among the burial objects were weapons, funerary money, musical instruments, books, clothes and lots of food. Even the recipes were put in – recorded on bamboo strips.

The museum is open from 08.00-12.00 (last tickets 11.15) and 14.30-17.20 (last tickets 16.45).

Other things to see in Changsha

To the south of the Provincial Museum, the **park** is not a particularly remarkable place but is much better than many city parks in China: it's large and leafy, and generally a good place for a stroll. Entry is Y2, and a ticket to get into the small **zoo** in the centre costs a further Y5.

Yu Lue Mountain has been recommended as a particularly attractive spot and a good place to escape the dust and noise of Changsha. It's outside the city centre in the area of the Hunan University, west of the river.

EXCURSION TO SHAOSHAN

The small farming village of Shaoshan where Mao was born has, predictably, been transformed by tourism and even when you get to the Mao house itself there's not a great deal to see. It's an interesting place, though, to mull over the personality and origins of the man who changed China forever, and whose influence persists even today.

It's perfectly possible to stay in Shaoshan, and since it's set in very attractive countryside this could be enjoyable; otherwise, day trips are possible, and organised day tours are available, too (see p179). Shaoshan itself is split into several areas. The new village has the rail and bus sta-

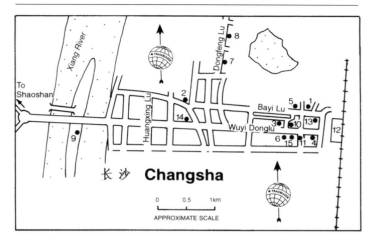

长沙 **Changsha**

CHANGSHA – KEY

Where to stay

1 Hunan Furama Hotel
2 Xiang Jiang Hotel
3 Lotus Hotel
4 Xin Xing Hotel
5 Nanhai Hotel
6 Dong Fang Hotel

What to see

7 Hunan Provincial Museum
8 Park

Where to eat

9 Riverside Cafés
10 Kiddies Restaurant
11 Chaoyang Lu

Other

12 Railway Station
13 Long Distance Bus Station
14 Post Office
15 Bank of China

1 湖南富饶码宾馆(音译)
2 湘江宾馆
3 芙蓉宾馆
4 新星宾馆(拼音)
5 南海宾馆
6 东方宾馆(音译)

7 湖南省博物馆
8 烈士公园

9 江边咖啡馆
10 汉堡包快餐店
11 朝阳路

12 火车站
13 长途汽车站
14 邮局
15 中国银行

tions, while the old village, a few kilometres away, contains **Mao's house**, a museum and the *Shaoshan Hotel* (☎ 0732-5685127) where double rooms cost Y120 and triples cost Y135. The other main place of interest is **Dripping Water Cave** which again is a few kilometres away but since minibuses constantly shuttle backwards and forwards between all the areas, transport should not be a problem.

Dripping Water Cave is the only place which needs any explanation. It's really not a cave at all but a set of buildings which were put up so that Mao could use Shaoshan as a retreat while carrying out his duties. Facilities include meeting rooms, recreation areas and even a large complex of bombproof shelters. If anything, the modern visitor here will find it a poignant contrast to the traditional and attractive farmhouse down the road in which the young Mao grew up. By the time he returned here after decades on the move, he was able to put up this concrete eyesore in the prime spot, and in a style utterly alien to anything the villagers would have seen before. The young local boy had now become 'The Great Helmsman' who wielded almost imperial power.

If you're planning to make your own way to Shaoshan you can get there either by train (three hours) or bus. The train departs at 06.40 and starts back from Shaoshan at 16.00. Alternatively there is one bus a day (08.30) from the public bus station which is just to the north-west of the train station. Tickets are sold at the booth in the centre of the ticket hall.

PRACTICAL INFORMATION
Orientation and information

The railway station is on the east side of the city, and the city centre is bounded to the west by the Xiang River (although the suburbs continue for a couple of kilometres at least). The road running due west from the station to the river, Wuyi Lu, is Changsha's main avenue; the commercial and shopping area is towards the west end of Wuyi Lu, and most of the hotels are at the east end, near the station.

Facilities are similarly split: in the city 'centre' (west), the **post office** is on the junction of Wuyi Xilu and Cai'e Zhonglu, and there are branches of the **Bank of China** on Cai'e Lu and in the grounds of the Xiang Jiang Hotel. Near the railway station (east), the main branch of the Bank of China is on the corner of Chaoyang Lu and Wuyi Donglu, just east of the Dong Fang Hotel. **CITS** (☎ 0731-4467867) go under the name of Hunan Tourism, and

have a ticket centre in the grounds of the Lotus Hotel. They are helpful and can assist with both air and rail tickets. Next door to the CITS office (on the right as you face their door) is a private **travel service** who can sometimes get rail tickets if CITS have used up their quota. The **CAAC** have an office near the railway station ticket hall.

Maps of the city are available for Y2 outside the railway station. Not all bus routes are featured on them, though.

Local transport

Local minibuses and buses are good. **Bus 12** and **118** run from the station straight down Wuyi Lu and across the bridge to the west side of the river.

Bus 113 runs down Wuyi Lu before turning north to go up past the provincial museum. **Minibus 3** goes from the station along Bayi Lu and then north past the museum.

Tours

CITS tours to Shaoshan are prohibitively expensive but the travel service next door to their office runs a day tour costing Y80. The price includes all entrance tickets, and the tour takes in the house of Liu Shaoqi (Mao's right-hand man) and then continues to Shaoshan. If you're lucky the guide may speak a little English, although this is primarily a Chinese tour. It does take the hassle out of getting to and from Shaoshan.

Where to stay

For foreigners the choice of middle to top class hotels is reasonable in Changsha but the lower end is very limited indeed. The most expensive hotel is the **Hunan Furama Hotel** (☎ 0731-2298888) which is just around the corner from the station, at 72 Ba Yi Xilu. All Western luxuries are on offer here and rooms start at Y500. The next best place is the **Xiang Jiang Hotel** which is a fair way from the station, in the city centre. Prices start at US$48 for a double. The **Lotus Hotel** (☎ 0731-4401749), which is just down Wuyi Donglu from the station, is friendly and is slightly more reasonable; double rooms here cost Y242. The **Xin Xing Hotel** (☎ 0731-2297288) is almost opposite the station and is most easily recognisable by the neon sign which says 'Xu Xing International Club'. A double room costs Y298.

Probably the best bet, however, if there are two of you is the **Nanhai Hotel** (☎ 0731-2297888), which is next door to the Hunan Furama Hotel;it has clean air-conditioned doubles with private bathroom from Y198. Another place you could try in the same price bracket is the **Dong Fang Hotel** (☎ 0731-4428888) which quotes a single room as Y168, but it's not a very inspiring place. Although this seems a lot if you're on a tight budget, there are few alternatives. Opposite the station there are two or three small guest-houses which are really for Chinese only, but which might take you. A single room in one of these will cost Y65-80. You'll have to look carefully for them – just inside the shop fronts they have a board with prices advertised, and a small reception booth next to the stairs.

Where to eat

A good option for eating out, if the weather is fine at least, is to catch a bus down Bayi Lu and over the bridge to the island in the middle of the river. The riverside cafés along the east shore are visible from the bridge if you walk the last bit, and they make a fine place to sit and watch river life going on: fishermen, bathers, barges etc. The food is good and the atmosphere is relaxed.

Near the railway station there are lots of cheap places to eat, and there are two friendly cafés opposite the Nanhai Hotel on Xiao Yuan Lu. Just down Wuyi Lu, near the Lotus Hotel, is Changsha's own fast food joint, **Kiddies Restaurant**, which is a good spot for a snack and to escape the midsummer heat. Finally an excellent place to eat cheaply (particularly in summer) is Chaoyang Lu, just east of the Dong Fang Hotel. There are pavement stalls all along here, mostly with chairs and tables laid out. The uncooked food is displayed on barrows in front of the stall: just point out what you want and they'll fry it up for you.

Moving on

By rail Changsha is a good place to buy tickets, although the ticket office, which is to the right of the station, is huge and chaotic. Either CITS or the private travel service next door to them will help you to get tickets; the going rate for commission is Y40-50. A Hard Sleeper to Guangzhou should cost in the region of Y180, and to Guilin about Y100. For train times, see p367-75.

By air Some sample fares are: Guangzhou Y620, Guilin Y480, Shanghai Y920, Beijing Y1340.

Guangzhou
广州

Guangzhou, or Canton to use the English name, is the major city in the south of China, and is a huge industrial and financial centre. Having been open to foreigners for longer than any other city in China, Guangzhou has a distinctive atmosphere to it: a long history of foreign trade, proximity to Hong Kong, and the establishment of the Special Economic Zone in Shenzhen have all shaped the modern city. Guangzhou's collective consciousness is firmly set on trade and making money. 'Vibrant, energetic and ambitious' might be one chosen description; 'pushy, greedy and over-crowded' is the alternative way of looking at it.

Most people find the noise and dirt here very unpleasant, even by Chinese standards, and as there aren't many spectacular things to see, do not linger. Guangzhou has excellent travel connections, however, particularly to Hong Kong and Macau, and so most travellers end up here for at least a day or two, which is ample time to see the main sights.

HISTORY

Although there is evidence of settlement in the area well before even the Qin Dynasty, the city received its current name only during the Han Dynasty, by which time it was already a major port. Guangzhou's prosperity was assured by its excellent location: the Pearl River estuary provided shelter from the monsoons, and the tributaries of the main river allowed excellent navigable communications inland. By the end of the Han Dynasty trade was established with both Arab and Roman merchants.

Over the succeeding centuries, Guangzhou's status fluctuated according to the fortunes of the Imperial court in the north. During periods of weak government and fragmentation there was little Imperial control, whereas under the major dynasties, the Tang, Song, Ming and Qing, the city reverted to its position within the Empire. The population of Guangzhou and the surrounding area grew vastly in times of trouble, as thousands fled south to escape the violence that engulfed the northern provinces. The Hakka people, for example, migrated south from Shanxi province from the 11th century onwards and are now mainly found in Guandong and Guangxi provinces.

Arriving in 1517, Portuguese merchants were the first Europeans in Guangzhou. Initially the Chinese refused them permission to land, but they were finally granted a small trading base on Macau. Other Western merchants followed and trade flourished. Tea, silk and spices were all major exports and, from the late 18th century onwards, opium was the main import. By the 1830's China's trade deficit was alarming, and the Emperor dictated that the import of opium should stop. The resulting First Opium War ended with Hong Kong being ceded to Britain and Canton being formally opened to foreign trade.

A foreign concession was established in the city on today's Shamian Island, and trade continued until the Arrow Incident in 1856. In response to a dispute over customs procedures and a supposed 'slight' to the British flag, the city was 'softened up' with a preliminary bombardment before a joint Anglo-French force occupied it. Although trade was resumed afterwards, the foreigners' actions were not easily forgiven. Nationalist feelings ran high in the south and it is no coincidence that the Taiping Rebellion started in this part of China, or that Sun Yatsen chose Guangzhou for his several attempts at insurrection.

In the early years of the Republic, with Yuan Shikai and the warlords effectively ruling the country, Guangzhou was at the heart of the Nationalist movement. Through a series of alliances with the local warlords, Sun Yatsen established a base here. With the help of Russian adviser Michael Borodin, the Kuomintang opened the Whampoa military academy in 1924. The cadets of the academy (many of whom were triad members loyal to Chiang Kaishek) were later used to massacre opponents in Guangzhou. The move effectively ended support for the Nationalist cause, but since Chiang Kaishek was about to start the Northern Expedition, the city had become less important to him by this time.

Today, Guangzhou is the capital of Guandong Province and is the largest city in southern China. The city itself holds some 3.7 million people, although the municipality contains more like 6.2 million.

WHAT TO SEE

The Six Banyan Trees Temple

The temple was originally founded in 537AD to house some of Buddha's remains that had reputedly been brought to China. Although the temple is sometimes referred to by the name of the pagoda, either as the Flower Pagoda or the Thousand Buddha Pagoda, the name Six Banyan Trees originated with six large trees which once stood here. The poet Su Dongpo visited the temple in the Song Dynasty and inscribed the two characters, thus ensuring that the name stuck.

Although the temple is not particularly exciting, the pagoda is impressive. The original was burnt down in the 10th century and the pagoda that now stands here was built in 1097. The 57-metre high structure has nine storeys on the outside but actually has 17 levels inside. A climb to the top probably once upon a time revealed an excellent view of the surrounding area; all you now see are roofs and high-rise buildings. Entry is Y6.

Guangxiao Temple

This is the oldest temple in Guangzhou and is a huge place. Originally it was the site of an official's residence, which was converted into a temple in the fourth century AD. Although the buildings have been comprehensively restored during the 19th and 20th centuries, the place has retained its atmosphere. It's still in use as a temple. Entry is Y1 and it's open to the public 06.00-17.00.

Museum of the Western Han Tomb of the Nanyue King

The tomb of the Nanyue king was one of the most important archaeological discoveries of the 1980's and this museum is cleverly laid out on the actual site. The tomb itself is shown as though it had just been excavated: visitors descend to the entrance and can walk around the underground chambers. The king was buried here in a jade suit with jade ornaments and weapons piled around him. Also buried with him were numerous supplies for the next world: animals, food and 15 unfortunate individuals, whom archaeologists think were cooks, concubines and possibly a musician. Inside the main museum building the many artefacts that were recovered from the tomb are on display. Generally, they are well-preserved, and the museum is excellently laid out with English explanations throughout. The museum is open from 09.30-17.30 (last tickets 16.45). Entry is Y30, but it's money well spent.

Parks and gardens

Guangzhou is well off for parks, and it's a relief in this crowded, dirty city to be able to escape into them for a while. The largest is **Yuexiu Park** which is just to the south-east of the railway station. Probably the most famous sight here is the **Five Storey Tower**, also known as Conquering the Sea Tower, which was built in 1380 at the start of the Ming Dynasty. Although this was under renovation at the time of writing it should reopen soon; previously it has housed one of the city museums. The large ugly stone tower on top of the central hill in the park is the Sun Yatsen Monument. Looking south from the park you should also be able to see the Sun Yatsen Memorial Hall, which is spectacularly large. Towards the west side of the park, for an extra Y2 you can get into the Celestial Rams Courtyard although it's pretty uninspiring. The central sculpture commemorates an ancient legend, in which five gods riding on rams came down to Guangzhou and presented the people with corn as a symbol that they should be protected against famine. Entry to Yuexiu Park is Y2.

Opposite Yuexiu Park, on the west side of Jiefang Lu, is the **Orchid Garden**, where allegedly there are 200 varieties of orchids in over 10,000 pots. It's a wonderfully peaceful place to come to unwind; the Y8 entry ticket includes a free pot of tea at the central pavilion, where you can lounge for an hour or two.

Huanghuagang Park, also known as the Tomb of the 72 Martyrs is towards the north-east of the city, and was constructed in 1918 to commemorate those who fell in an armed uprising in Guangzhou on 27 April 1911. The attempt failed because of poor organisation and the fact that the authorities got wind of the plans well in advance. Having fought their way into the grounds of the governor's residence, the revolutionaries found that the officials had long since fled, and that they were surrounded by Imperial troops. Few escaped. The main point of interest in the park is the central monument. Entry to the park is Y5.

Near Shamian Island is the **Culture Park**, which looks fairly promising as the sign by the entrance says that it has 'a focus on exhibitions, open air tickets including centre acting theatre, BaiHua Theatre...Storytelling platform...' It probably is a good place to come if you can discover a programme of events. Otherwise it's just a rather decaying Chinese amusement park. Entry is Y2.

❏ The tea trade

For nearly two centuries, China's trade with the West was dominated by two major products: silk and tea. By the mid 17th century tea was starting to become fashionable in England. Samuel Pepys records in his diary that on the 25th Sept 1660 'I did send for a cup of tee, a China drink, of which I had never drunk before'. Merchants soon realised that there was money to be made, and rapid transport became important. Specially designed ships – tea clippers – were built, and competition sprang up to see who could move the cargoes back to London fastest. In 1866 nine ships sailed simultaneously from Foochow (a treaty port to the east of Guangzhou). After completing the 16,000 mile sea voyage in 90 days, less than two hours separated the first three competitors as they docked in London.

The opening of the Suez canal and the advent of steam ships cut the time it took to complete the journey but in no way lessened the competition. In 1882 the SS *Stirling Castle* made a record time of 28 days from Woosung to London. Overland trading to Russia, partly using camels, was revolutionised by the arrival of the Trans-Siberian railway at the turn of the century. Christina Dodwell, in *A Traveller in China* records that there was a mixed reaction to the new method of transport.

'...there were immediate complaints about the flavour. It transpired that when sent by camel and packed in hessian bags, the tea absorbed some of the camel sweat which contributed to its distinctive flavour. By the Russians, the camel-free flavour was found inferior. So later consignments were packed with camel hairs in the wrapping'.

Although there were enquiries about whether tea couldn't be grown in India, it was not realised until 1834 that there were wild tea bushes in Assam. It was many years, however, before the tea-drinking public could be educated into the taste of Indian tea. China continued to hold the majority of the market until the end of the 19th century.

GUANGZHOU – KEY

Where to stay

1	Guandong International Hotel	1	国际大厦
2	Holiday Inn	2	文化假日酒店
3	Garden Hotel	3	花园酒店
4	Cathay Hotel	4	国泰宾馆
5	Bai Yun Hotel	5	白云宾馆
6	Liu Hua Hotel	6	流花宾馆
7	Hong Mian Hotel	7	红棉大酒店
8	Friendship Hotel	8	友谊宾馆
9	White Swan Hotel	9	白天鹅宾馆
10	Victory Hotel	10	胜利宾馆
11	Shamian Hotel	11	沙面宾馆
12	Guangzhou Youth Hostel	12	广州青年招待所

What to see

13	Six Banyan Trees Temple	13	六榕寺
14	Guangxiao Temple	14	光孝寺
15	Museum of the Tomb of the Nanyue King	15	南越王墓
16	Yuexiu Park	16	越秀公园
17	Orchid Garden	17	兰圃公园
18	Huanghuagang Park	18	黄花岗公园
19	Culture Park	19	文化公园
20	Qingping Lu	20	清平路

Where to eat

21	Beiyuan Restaurant	21	北园酒家
22	Timmy's	22	添美食
23	Hasty Tasty	23	中国大酒店底层快餐店
24	McDonald's	24	麦当劳

Other

25	Main Railway Station	25	主火车站
26	Post Office	26	邮局
27	Bank of China	27	中国银行
28	Advance Rail Booking Office	28	火车票预售处
29	CITS	29	国际旅行社
30	Friendship Store	30	友谊商店
31	Passenger Terminal - ferries to Hong Kong/Macau	31	客运码头 (去港/澳)
32	PSB	32	公安局

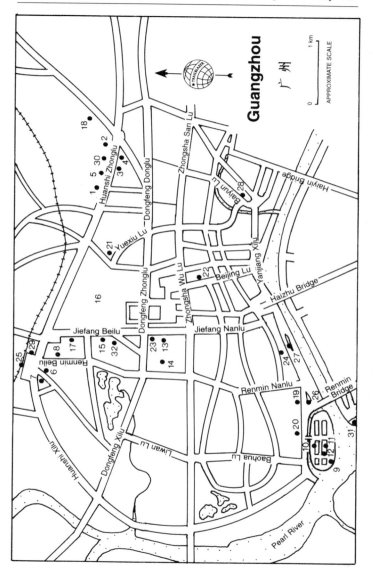

❏ Colin Thubron, in *Behind the Wall* records his visit to a Guangzhou food market thus:

'Then I arrived at the owls. They were chained to their cages in a bedraggled row...on a cage beside a brute faced entrepreneur, perched a barn-owl..In its quaint face the eyes gleamed defiantly. It was beautiful.

...The man perhaps knew that foreigners did not buy in the market, and he greeted my questions with boredom. He would have no trouble selling it, he said. (Some peasants believed that to devour a whole owl – feathers and all -was a cure for epilepsy.) Then he saw that I was fingering money. So he tugged out one of the bird's wings, pinched its chest and shoved his fingers into its mouth. 'That's the best part.'

For its beauty and its fierceness – and perhaps as a penance for eating wildcat – I paid over the equivalent of £4.'

Markets

The backstreets of Guangzhou are fascinating, and you can easily lose yourself in a maze of alleyways. On market stalls and in the tiny shops there are sackfuls of interesting stuff for sale, including dried seahorses and jellyfish. The largest free market for agricultural products takes place in and around Qingping Lu, opposite Shamian Island.

The main part, on Qingping Lu itself, is more like a witches' market – dried reptiles, roots, and reindeer antlers are all on offer, along with other things you won't even recognise. The street which crosses it halfway up contains the live food market. Stay away from here if you're an animal lover: even cats and dogs are for sale here.

White Cloud Mountain

White Cloud Mountain is the nearest bit of relatively uneven ground to Guangzhou and lies to the north-east of the city. The park covers an area of 21 square km, and contains several small peaks. It's a pleasant place to walk, and you can spend at least a morning, if not a day, just exploring. It's quite possible, too, to walk from one side to the other, as buses run to both the north and south entrances of the park, so there are no problems getting out there or back.

To get to the north entrance of the park take Bus 265 from the western end of Yuehua Lu, at the north-east corner of the People's Park. The journey takes about half an hour and costs Y8, which includes the Y5 entrance fee.

If you decide to walk over the top of the hill to the south entrance, the route will take you past **Star Scraping Peak**, the highest point, where, conveniently there is a drinks shop. On the way down from the peak you pass a couple of 'attractions' (a Forest of Steles, and the Minchun Valley Bird Reserve) before arriving at a car park area. Buses run down the hill and can drop you at the start of the route of Bus 24, which takes you back into the city.

PRACTICAL INFORMATION
Orientation and information
Chinese maps showing bus routes are available outside the train station, and an excellent English language map can be bought for Y2 from the Guangzhou Youth Hostel.

There's a **Bank of China** near Shamian Island, on Changdi Lu; they will advance money on a credit card here, at the desk of the 2nd floor.

There are two large **post offices**, both of which hold poste restante: the post office next to the railway station holds letters, while the large post office on Liuersan Lu, opposite the entrance to the Cultural Park (near Shamian Island) holds parcels. If you fail to collect your parcel within a week of its arrival you have to pay Y1.5 per day, which is added to the standing charge of Y8.

The **PSB** have a visa office a short distance south of the Museum of the Tomb of the Nanyue King; it's open 08.00-11.30 and 14.30-17.00, but closed on Saturday and public holidays.

Local transport
City buses are good, some particularly useful ones being:

Bus 5 runs from its start point just west of the railway station, most of the way down Jiefang Lu and across to Shamian Island.

Bus 57 runs past Shamian Island to its terminal which is conveniently close to the advance rail ticket booking office.

Bus 265 runs from near the People's Park to the north entrance of the White Cloud Hills.

Bus 24 runs back to the People's Park from the south side of the White Cloud Hills.

An **underground railway** system is being built, the first section of which is due for completion in 1997.

Tours
CITS are extremely unhelpful towards individual travellers, so they are not the best people to ask. All tourist sights in Guangzhou are easy to get to by yourself but if you really want to take a tour, try the travel services in any of the major hotels. Alternatively you could try the **Riverside Travel Service** (☎ 020-83839888) which is on the ground floor of the GITIC Riverside Hotel, at 298 Yan Jiang Lu, not far from the terminal of bus 57. Their tours cover most of the major sights but are expensive.

Where to stay
There are literally dozens of top range places to stay but, as usual, very few cheap hotels.

City centre Many of the best hotels are concentrated in the city centre, and these include the **Guandong International Hotel** (☎ 020-28656363) which forms part of a huge international business complex and has standard doubles starting at US$130.

Slightly further up the road the **Holiday Inn** (☎ 020-87766999) also charges US$130 for its cheapest rooms, as does the **Garden Hotel** (☎ 020-83338989). There are others in the same league around here, as well as some slightly cheaper places. The **Cathay Hotel** (☎ 020-83862888) has doubles from Y500, and the **Bai Yun Hotel** (☎ 020-83333998) has cheaper rooms in its east building: doubles are Y300, and triples Y330.

Near the railway station there are several mid-range hotels. The **Liu Hua Hotel** (☎ 020-86668800) opposite the station has double rooms for Y317, and the **Hong Mian Hotel** (☎ 020-86663989) next to it has doubles from Y295.

The **Friendship Hotel** (☎ 020-86679898) a couple of blocks away from the station, is a bit quieter, and one of the better places to stay, particularly if there are three of you. A double room here is Y168 and a triple is Y198; the rooms are clean, pleasant and wonderfully cool.

Shamian Island Possibly the best place for accommodation in Guangzhou, however, is on Shamian Island, which was formerly the foreign concession area, and consequently has some lovely old buildings. The most expensive place here is the *White Swan Hotel* (☎ 020-81886968) which has double rooms from US$120 but if you don't mind doing without a swimming pool, the *Victory Hotel* (☎ 020-88862622) has more atmosphere, and doubles here are a more reasonable Y398.

Almost opposite the White Swan Hotel is the *Shamian Hotel* (☎ 020-81912288) where doubles are Y275 and triples are Y405, although one traveller I met had stayed here for Y160 after a bit of bargaining.

Just around the corner is the only real budget accommodation in Guangzhou, the *Guangzhou Youth Hostel* (☎ 020-81884298) which has one eight-bed dormitory room with beds for Y40-50 (as soon as there's a extra demand, the price goes up). A bed in a triple costs Y80, and it's Y90 for a bed in a double room, although for the same price you can get a single room without air-conditioning. In the peak season the dormitory in particular can be hard to get into, so phone in advance if possible. This is one of two places I came across in China which advertised on their literature that they required a man and woman who wanted to share a room to show their marriage certificate (though I doubt whether they ever enforced it).

Where to eat
Guangzhou is famous for its seafood and there are plenty of restaurants around to choose from. A good place to splash out in is the *Beiyuan Restaurant*

on Xiaobei Lu at the junction with Yuexia Beilu. Established in the 1930's and restarted in 1957, it's constructed in classical type pavilions around a pond; despite appearances, prices are actually not as high as you might think.

On Shamian Island, the *Victory Hotel* has very good seafood, although a meal here will set you back about Y100 per person. There are also two less expensive places opposite.

For a taste of traditional dim sum, a good place to try is literally just around the corner from the Guangzhou Youth Hostel. The restaurant with the art deco interior has a good atmosphere, and the food is great – just pick what you want as the trolley comes past the table.

Also on Shamian Island are various other places worth a visit. There are a couple of good and inexpensive small restaurants along the same road as the Guangzhou Youth Hostel, and the *Shamian Coffee House*, which is directly across from the Youth Hostel and looks a bit like a trucker's cafe, has excellent cheap food.

Fast food has also hit Guangzhou: the two home-grown outlets being *Timmy's* which can be found on Beijing Lu, and *Hasty Tasty* which is beneath the China Hotel. *McDonald's* and *Kentucky Fried Chicken* have each got several outlets.

Snacks and fruit are widely available and excellent.

What to buy
Guangzhou is famous for its jade and ivory carvings, but they don't come cheap. A good place to start your search for a souvenir, at least to see what's on offer, would be the Friendship Store on Huanshi Donglu, just near the Baiyun Hotel.

Moving on – Hong Kong
The lines are already in place for a direct **train service** from Hong Kong to Guangzhou, and this will undoubtedly

be the quickest method of travel (apart from private jet, of course). It is likely to be reasonably expensive, though, so it would be worth investigating the slower local trains, rather than the showpiece intercity service.

There are also a number of **direct buses** which do the trip in about 3-4 hours, picking up from the larger hotels in Guangzhou and depositing you near Kowloon Tong KCR station. Tickets cost around Y180, and are on sale, among other places, at the CTS office on Haizhu Square, or the reception desks of the China Hotel, Holiday Inn, White Swan Hotel or Guangzhou Youth Hostel.

It's possible, also, to get an **overnight boat**, departing at 21.00. The cheapest tickets are about Y200, and you should be able to buy these yourself at the Passenger Terminal.

Boats also go to **Macau**, departing at 20.30 and cost about Y80 in third class. The passenger terminal is to the south of the river (see the map on p184).

Moving on – elsewhere

Guangzhou is a frustrating place to buy a train ticket. The ticket office in the railway station sells tickets only for the next day, and CITS will only help with tickets to Beijing (Hard Sleeper Y486, Soft Sleeper Y734) although if you try really hard you might persuade them to get you a ticket to another major city. The travel service in the Guangzhou Youth Hostel will do the donkey work for you but will charge a hefty commission, and the ticket touts who hang around near the station quote ludicrous prices.

Before you try any of the above, it's well worth a visit to the **advance booking office** on Baiyun Lu. They don't seem to see too many foreigners here, and it's a tiny place but, after hours of trying in and around the station, I got my ticket here within a few minutes. To get here take bus 57 from in front of Shamian Island to its eastern terminal. From there it's a short walk up Baiyun Lu. The ticket office is just before the roundabout on the right – look for the railway symbol on the front. Tickets are on sale here for Changsha, Guilin and Shanghai as well as other locations.

By bus The long distance bus station is just west of the railway station and buses run from here to Guilin. A variety of private buses also go from near the railway station, and unless you speak Chinese it can get extremely confusing trying to work out where you should be buying a ticket. Probably the easiest thing to do is to try the public bus station first. Alternatively, head for the CITS office and you will be grabbed by one or more of the ticket touts as you approach. Bargaining is advisable; the going rate seems to be about Y165 for the 14-hour journey, and buses depart at 18.00.

Travelling by bus to Guilin certainly cuts down a lot of the hassle of getting hold of a train ticket.

By air CITS have an air ticketing centre (☎ 020-86662708) with their office next to the railway station, and quoted the following prices: Beijing Y1790, Shanghai Y1220, Xi'an Y1410.

PART 6: THE WESTERN PROVINCES

Hong Kong to Beijing

The Western Provinces are the area to make for if you want to see some of the most stunning scenery that China has to offer. Whereas most of east and north-east China is categorised as 'plains' (North China Plain, Lower Yangtse Plain), the South-West and Western Provinces are on the next topographical 'step' up towards Tibet.

This mountainous area has a character of its own. Quite apart from the unforgettable scenery, the sheer inaccessibility (compared to the rest of China, at least) has formed a distinctive way of life. The south-west was, for a long time, not even a part of the Central Kingdom because of the difficulties of trying to conquer the mountain tribesmen. In effect many of the tribes here were persuaded to pay lip service to the Emperor, on the agreement that they would be left to carry on their own lives. To some extent this continues today in the Guangxi Autonomous Region.

The contrast with central and eastern China is striking. Although there are a few large cities and smart hotels, the south-west is somehow more relaxed. There is more colour and individuality here, quite apart from the fact that there is much, much more space. Unlike the overcrowded coastal cities and intensively farmed Lower Yangtse Plain, this area has the lowest population density in China. In summer, the plateau has a further advantage: unlike the rest of China, it's cool. Kunming, nicknamed 'The Spring City', is the ideal place if you want to escape the sweaty heat of the lowlands.

Many travellers come to western China en route to somewhere else. There are air connections to Tibet (and thence some take an overland route to Kathmandu), or land connections to Vietnam, Laos and Burma (Myanmar). The famous Three Gorges boat journey down the Yangtse starts in Chongqing, and also there are bus trips high into the mountains to Dali and Lijiang or to the almost untouched Jiuzhaigou National Park.

If you want to see temples and major historical sites relating to the history of the Central Kingdom itself, you are probably best off staying in central and eastern China. To enjoy some magnificent scenery, and experience China at a slower pace, go west.

HONG KONG TO GUANGZHOU
See p96.

GUANGZHOU TO GUILIN
[877km, 17 hrs]

Km 2275: Guangzhou Thankfully Guangzhou's station is rather less chaotic once you get inside the building. Since plenty of trains originate in Guangzhou, many of which are prestigious express services, you may well be pleasantly surprised when you get to the train itself.

During the initial part of this journey the kilometre markers are difficult to follow: they seem to swap sides randomly.

Km 2152: Liangjiangkou The river to the left of the train is the North River, which continues parallel to the track for many km. It is one of the major tributaries of the Pearl River (which flows through Guangzhou), and the barge traffic that still plies the river today is continued proof of Guangzhou's status as a great port. How many coastal cities, after all, can claim not only to have sheltered harbour facilities but also to have three major rivers allowing easy transport inland?

Km 2015 The first of the tunnels start here. For a description of the problems that they encountered when building this stretch of line, see p108.

Km c1980 Shortly after passing Lechang station, the railway enters the longest tunnel of all. The **Dayaoshan Tunnel** is nearly 14.5km and takes about quarter of an hour to get through. Shortly after leaving the tunnel, the line crosses into Hunan province.

Km 1752: Hengyang Hengyang is the junction for lines leading south-west to Yunnan, Guangxi and Guizhou provinces. Although the line to Nanning was not completed until 1951, Harold Rattenbury *(China-*

MAP 9

Jiedong
MAP 10
Chenzhou
Aoshang
Taiping Lu — HUNAN PROVINCE
Baishidu
Pingshi — GUANGDONG PROVINCE
Dayaoshan Tunnel
Lechang
Ankou
Meicun
Huangang
Shaoguan
Maba
Wushi
Dakengkou
Shakou
Hetou
Liangjiangkou — Yingde
Jiuhengshi
Pajiangkou
Yuantan
Juntian
Xinjie — Jianggaozhen
GUANGZHOU
Xiancun
Shitan — Shilong
Hengli
Changping
Zhangmutou
Tangtouxia
Pinghu
Buji
Shenzhen
0   10km
HONG KONG — Kowloon

MAP 10

Xinxialiu
Dongyangdu
Hengyang
Guayinqiao
Sanjang
Wayuan
Tanzi-
shan
Leiyang
Gong-
Jilongjie
ping-
wei
Baihepu
Matianxu
Qidong
Jiedong
Xinqiaopu
Nanheling   MAP 8/9
Qiyang
Huangyangsi
Lengshuitan
Lanjiacun
Dong'an
HUNAN
PROVINCE
Miaotou
Huangshahe
Yongsui   GUANGXI
PROVINCE
Xintanping
Quanzhou
Caiwan
Xianshui
Nantang
Xing'an
Juntiancun
Darongjiang
Sanjie
GUILIN
Daxihe
0   10km   Tangbao
Yongfu
Putao
Daduahe
Huangmian
Youlan
Luzhai
Dijing
Luobu   MAP 11
Liuzhou

Burma Vagabond), gives an interesting account of its earliest origins. When he visited Hengyang, late in 1939, the city was recovering from a Japanese fire bomb attack. Nonetheless it was continuing to play an important part in the withdrawal of the Chinese to the south-west.

'Hengyang is a large city and a junction on the Canton-Wuchang Railway. What I was not prepared for was to find that it was the terminus also of a new wartime railway to Kueilin [Guilin] in Kwangsi and beyond...Here was a new railway completely moved from Honan and the north as the Japanese invaded the country. Rails, sleepers, wagons, engines had been moved hundreds of miles in the face of the Japanese advance.'

Km 0 As the train is now on a new line (the Xiang Gui line) the km markers reset themselves again. This time they are numbering upwards from Hengyang towards Nanning, and the marker posts are on the left.

Km 38: Tanzishan Even this close to central Hunan the scenery appears to be changing as you head south-west towards Guilin. The hills are slightly larger, the valleys are terraced to use every inch of cultivable space, and the countryside is bright green.

Km 140: Lengshuitan This is the place that Harold Rattenbury was heading for (in case you were wondering). He recalls that

'We left the train at a river mart called Lenhsuit'an – "Cold Water Rapids"...from a fishing village and a ferry, Lengsuit'an had become an important junction of river, rail and road traffic. The place swarmed with refugees, coming, going and staying. Soldiers, too, were always passing through.'

Km 190 This is how most people imagine China to be: the views from the train are spectacularly beautiful, consisting of densely wooded hills, terraced hillsides and intensively farmed valley floors. In mid summer, the paddy fields are scenes of constant activity, with water buffalo ploughing while whole families harvest in the next paddy. Sheaves of harvested rice stalks are laid on the sides of the fields to dry in the sun.

Km 206(L) About four km past the small station of Miaotou there is an outstanding view to the left. The small village, set against a backdrop of cliffs and fields is definitely worth a photo if you're quick enough.

Km309: Juntiancun By this stage of the trip, with only 50 km to go until Guilin, you will have noticed that the famous Guilin scenery has already started to appear on both sides of the train. The hills are made of resilient rock, which has survived the erosion of everything else around it, leaving a series of sharp peaks.

Km 352: Guilin Bei (North) Don't get out at this station, or you'll have a long walk into town.

Km 356: Guilin One of China's most famous beauty spots. Most budget travellers head for the minibuses outside the station without so much as a glance at Guilin itself: Yangshuo holds more attractions. See p210.

GUILIN TO NANNING   [433km, 7-8 hrs]

Although this route has, over the last year or two, only really been of interest to those heading to or from Vietnam, things may be about to change. With the completion (in 1997) of the new railway from Nanning to Kunming, this may become the obvious way to get from Guilin to Kunming. Km markers are on the left throughout the journey.

Km 400: Again, as the train heads south-west from Guilin, the countryside is incredibly verdant and lush. This entire journey is through the Guangxi Autonomous Region, an area granted a degree of self administration due to its large population of ethnic minorities including the Zhuang and Miao, among others. The capital of the province is Nanning.

Km 532: Liuzhou Liuzhou is the junction where the lines divide for Nanning to the south-west, and Guiyang, Chengdu and Kunming further west. The line from Liuzhou to Nanning was completed in 1951. From Liuzhou onwards, the scenery is similar to that of Guilin for several km.

Km 725(L): The large waterway which appears on the left of the train here is the Yong River. The railway runs parallel to the river almost all the way to Nanning from here. There are usually a large number of barges of the river, and the navigation markers can be seen at each bend.

Km 789: Nanning Nanning is the terminus for most trains on the Xiang Gui line, so unless you've managed to get a train which takes you beyond it, you'll have to get off here and buy another ticket for the train to the border. For a route guide to the line from Nanning to the border, see p196.

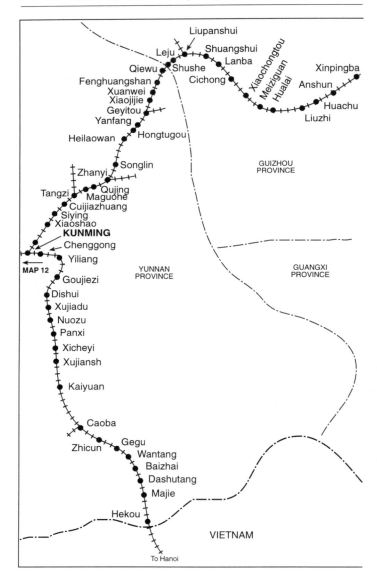

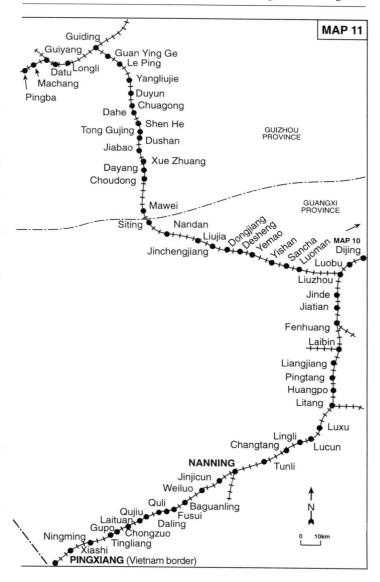

MAP 11

Guiding
Guiyang
Guan Ying Ge
Longli
Le Ping
Datu
Machang
Yangliujie
Pingba
Duyun
Chuagong
Dahe
Shen He
Tong Gujing
Dushan
Jiabao
Xue Zhuang
Dayang
Choudong

GUIZHOU
PROVINCE

Mawei

GUANGXI
PROVINCE

Siting
Nandan
Liujia
Dongjiang
Desheng
Yemao
Jinchengjiang
Yishan
Sancha
Luoman
MAP 10
Dijing
Luobu
Liuzhou
Jinde
Jiatian
Fenhuang
Laibin
Liangjiang
Pingtang
Huangpo
Litang
Luxu
Lingli
Lucun
Changtang
Tunli
NANNING
Jinjicun
Weiluo
Baguanling
Quli
Qujiu
Fusui
Laituan
Daling
Gupo
Chongzuo
Ningming
Tingliang
Xiashi
PINGXIANG (Vietnam border)

N

0   10km

NANNING TO PINGXIANG   **[220km, 4hrs]**

The route from Nanning to the border passes through some beautiful and unspoilt countryside. The kilometre numbering continues from Km 789 at Nanning itself and the marker posts are on the left side of the train.

Km 800: Nanning Nan (south)

Km c810 (R): Jinjicun If you've caught the early morning train keep an eye out to the right of the track after leaving Nanning. The large river which runs beside the railway for a short distance can be quite a sight, wreathed in mist and with small local boats navigating it.

Km 863: From this point onwards the scenery starts to resemble Guilin's distinctive limestone peaks again.

Km 964 (L): The large river to the left after leaving Ningming is the Zuo River which flows across the border near Pingxiang and reaches the sea at Haiphong.

Km 1008: Pingxiang Pingxiang is about as sleepy a town as you're likely to come across. From the station you can negotiate with a rickshaw driver to get you to the border. If you've got a little time, stop for something to eat at any of the stalls on the road outside the station. The food is great and in this little frontier town the hassle you may have come to associate with China simply doesn't exist.

NANNING TO KUNMING   [1449km]*

* (Via Liuzhou). The trip from Nanning to Kunming should soon become considerably easier with the opening of the direct line (some time in 1997). In the meantime, however, the only way to get to Kunming from Nanning is to backtrack to Liuzhou and turn left, towards Guiyang. From Nanning to Kunming is 1499km but there are currently no direct trains, so you have to change. Most people break their journey at Guilin, Liuzhou or Guiyang.

Km 532: Liuzhou The train turns off the Xiang Gui line at this point and heads west on the Qian Gui line (completed in 1940) towards Guiyang. The km markers again reset themselves to zero, counting upwards towards Guiyang.

Km c313: Mawei Shortly before arriving at Mawei station, the line crosses into Guizhou province. The scenery around here is spectacularly beautiful. From the vantage point of the train you can see thatched huts and tiled houses. The steep hillsides are terraced and paddy fields line the valley bottoms.

As the train passes from valley to valley, each one of which has only a few houses and a patch of intensively farmed valley floor, it's not hard to imagine that with the exception of the railway and the telephone lines, little has changed here in centuries. Who after all would go to the incredible effort of conquering a mountainous area where an attack on each tiny hamlet would involve a trek over high mountains – possibly to find that the people had moved on before you got there? John Francis Davis, writing in the 1830's, confirms this view.

'North of Kuang-sy lies Kuei-chow, a small mountainous province, of which the south boundary has always been independent. It is peopled by a race of mountaineers called Meaou-tse, who thus deny the Chinese in the midst of their empire. They gave the government much trouble in 1832, and are said to have been 'soothed' rather than 'controlled', to use favourite Chinese expressions...The men do not shave their hair like the Tartars and Chinese, but wear it tied up...The Chinese, in affected contempt, give them the names Yaou-jin and Lang-jin, dog men and wolf men...As soon as their children can walk the Chinese say that the soles of their feet are seared with a hot iron, to enable them to tread on thorns and stones without pain, but this perhaps deserves little more credit than the grave assertion at Canton that the people have tails...'

Today the Miao minority still live in Guizhou, as do several others including the Zhuang, Hui and Bai.

Km 398(L): On the left are some small tomb-like structures in the middle of the fields. There are several such groups of buildings along this stretch of line. They call to mind the problems which the railway builders encountered in trying to avoid crossing ancient burial grounds.

Km 605: Guiyang Guiyang is the capital of Guizhou province, and although there's nothing of great interest here, a few travellers stop to change trains, or simply to break their journey. Despite the modern face of Guiyang, the city has the attraction of place that's not much visited by tourists. If you are stopping here, you could try the ***Tongda Hotel*** (☎ 0851-5790484) which is opposite the station building. The cheapest place that accepts foreigners is the ***Jinqiao Hotel*** (☎ 0851-5829958) which is a fair way from the station but where dormitory beds go for Y35. Bus 1 from the station stops directly outside the hotel. There is a great area to eat just to the north-west of the junction of Zhongshan Xilu and Zhonghua Zhonglu.

Km 0: Guiyang Once again the km markers reset themselves, as the remainder of this journey takes place on the Gui Kun line, which runs (as the name suggests) from Guiyang to Kunming. The line was completed in 1966. Kilometre markers are on the right for the first 77km.

Km 77: The scenery, as you leave Guizhou behind, starts to change. The train is climbing from the mountainous scenery of Guizhou province (Guiyang is at an altitude of 1070m) to the Yunnan plateau (Kunming is at an altitude of 1893m). As the scenery changes, so does the temperature. For travellers coming from Guilin or Guangzhou in mid summer, this will be a wonderful feeling. Slowly the stifling heat and humidity of the plains changes to cool European style summer weather.

The km markers change to the left side of the track here.

Km 160: From here onwards the track runs through a spectacular series of tunnels which clearly demonstrate why this particular line took so long to build.

Km 302: Have your camera ready. Up to this point, the line has passed along the sides of some huge valleys and all the views have been to the left of the train. Here the line crosses a saddle and there are really **spectacular views** on either side. It's quite amazing to see that the mountainsides are still terraced at this point. The angle of the slope on which the terraces are built allows each plot of land to be only a foot or two wide, before the edge of the plot drops away sharply to the next piece of land.

It is at this point that the line crosses into Yunnan province, the most south-westerly province in China. Looking out of the train window, it's not hard to understand why this was, for a long time, the most inaccessible part of the Empire. It was reached only by taking a boat down the Yangtse and then undertaking several days' trekking through the mountains. Until the arrival of the French railway to Kunming in 1910, most supplies had to be carried over the mountains by long lines of coolies.

It was here too, that China's own opium was grown for export to the West and for resale to the Chinese people themselves. The opium trade was controlled by the triads and during Chiang Kaishek's time lined the pockets of the government. Opium addiction was a huge problem in Yunnan, where there was a saying that 'Out of ten men, eleven smoke opium'.

Km 480: Qujing Although the Gui Kun line wasn't completed until 1966, work started during the Anti Japanese War, when south-west China suddenly became all important. Harold Rattenbury (*China-Burma Vagabond*), travelling in late 1939, came across the engineers starting work on the line.

'The largest place en route was Ch'uhching, where the main road turned off to Kueiyang, centre of the road system for south and south-west China, and three days' journey from Kunming. Ch'uhching had become a construction centre for both road and rail, and was quite up-to-date. On a later journey I found a Shanghai restaurant there, foreign food and a foreign menu, with a Shanghai chef in charge. He was meeting the needs of East Coast Chinese engineers, but what a jolt for backwoods China to have such strangely progressive citizens suddenly projected into its midst. It was a little bit like finding the Ritz Hotel in the west of Ireland'.

Km 639: Kunming The capital of Yunnan province and the ideal starting point for travel to some of the most fascinating and beautiful parts of south-west China. See p218.

❏ The narrow gauge line to Vietnam

Kunming is also the starting point for the old French narrow gauge railway into Vietnam, via Hekou. The line was built to extend French influence into China and to exploit the mineral resources which Yunnan was reputed to have. It took much longer to complete than had been imagined because of the appalling terrain which had to be crossed. The preliminary surveys were completed in 1899 but because of the bad feeling locally, and the disruption of the Boxer Rebellion, nothing further was done until 1901 when work started on the French side of the border. The main problem, as one commentator wrote at the time, 'was how to climb the wall-like ascent of 5000 feet from the Red River on to the plateau'. Even when this technical problem was solved the climate took a terrible toll. PH Kent (*Railway Enterprise in China*), writing at pretty much the same time as the line was being built, recorded the difficulties: 'Shut in between two walls of mountains, the air in the Namti Valley is stagnant, and under the tropical sun generates malaria of a most deadly kind...when the work was commenced the death rate was appalling. In one year, it is said, five thousand coolies, representing roughly seventy per cent of all those engaged on the work, lost their lives...'

Work was finally completed in 1910 and one of the most inaccessible cities in the world was suddenly on the railway. Harold Rattenbury (*China-Burma Vagabond*), writing in 1939, recalled: 'I'd travelled by the narrow-gauge railway from Hanoi to Kunming five years before, four days and three nights, amidst marvellous mountain scenery...Because of frequent landslides there was no travelling at night. I'd looked down and seen the winding track by which I'd travelled hundreds of feet below. I'd come over a steel bridge, which crossed an almost bottomless chasm, and wondered what would happen if that bridge were destroyed. The Chinese answered that conundrum in 1942. They destroyed the bridge and removed all fear of an attack on Kunming and the Burma Road up those step mountains and over that chasm'.

Despite having been closed for nearly 17 years after the war against Vietnam, the line is open today. Much of the old track is parallelled by a new one (also of 1000mm gauge). Just to the north of the main railway station in Kunming, too, there's a short section of disused narrow gauge track which crosses Beijing Lu.

KUNMING TO CHENGDU   [1100km, 24hrs]

From Kunming to Chengdu, passing near Emeishan and Leshan en route, is a distance of 1100km, and takes about 24 hours.

Km 1100: Kunming Km markers along the logically named Cheng-Kun line count backwards towards Chengdu and are to the right of the track. The line was initially surveyed in 1953, and was completed in 1970. Any question about why it took so long to build will doubtless be answered within an hour or two of setting off. Impressive simply isn't the word – in some places this line is just one long tunnel with the occasional flash of daylight, as it carves its way through the mountains. This also

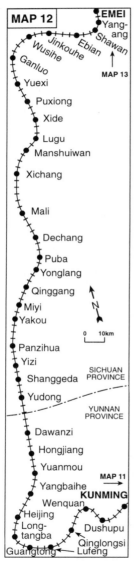

unfortunately means that, although there are tantalising glimpses of superb scenery, you may as well bring a good book. For much of the journey you hardly get long enough to adjust your eyes to the daylight before you're back in a tunnel again.

Bear in mind as you travel down the line, and perhaps catch a glimpse of the date of construction painted near the entrance of each tunnel, that this line was being built in the same period as the Great Leap Forward, and was completed during the Cultural Revolution. It was a period when hundreds of thousands of people were carted off to do forced labour. Huge numbers never returned, and it seems certain that many of them died building public projects such as the railways.

Km 800: The line passes into Sichuan province. Almost as it does so it passes over the Jinsha River, which is the main tributary to the Yangtse. At this stage in its journey down from the Tibetan highlands, the river starts to become navigable.

This part of the mountains is peopled almost entirely by minority tribes who retain some of their old way of life.

Km 557: Xichang Nearby in the mountains is China's satellite launching centre. In recent years, China has been trying to capture a share of the world's commercial satellite launches by offering considerably lower prices than anyone else: half the price asked by the Americans and quarter that of the Japanese. In February 1996, however, a Long March 38 rocket exploded shortly after leaving the ground. Western experts believe that the Chinese industry may take a while to recover its credibility on the commercial market.

Km 232: Ebian The river of the right here is the Dadu River, a tributary of the Yangtse. It joins the Min River in Leshan and flows on to meet the main river at Yibin.

Km 156: Emei Get out here if you're planning to visit the holy mountain – see p227.

Km 0: Chengdu The capital of Sichuan province, see p240.

CHENGDU TO TAIYUAN
[1493km, 30 hrs]

The initial section of the journey along the Bao-Cheng line to Baoji is 669km through mountainous terrain. This line was completed in 1955 and was one of the first to be electrified: the tunnels were so long that the crews of the steam locomotives were half smothered by the time they got to the other end. Km markers are on the right and count backwards towards Baoji.

Km 631: Guanghan Near Guanghan, at Sanxingdui, is the site of what has been called 'The single most remarkable Chinese archaeological find of the last decade'. In 1986, archaeologists excavated two large pits, which were part of a Shang Dynasty (16th century BC-11th century BC) site. The pits offered up literally hundreds of unique items, including a bronze sculpture of human head with gold leaf on it, a bronze bird's head, and a huge bronze standing figure. The finds have altered perception of early Chinese history, because they show that an advanced culture existed in what is now Sichuan, apparently having had no contact with the cultures of the northern plains.

Km 271: Yangpingguan Shortly before Yangpingguan the train leaves Sichuan province. It now passes through Shaanxi, apart from a very brief detour into Gansu.

Km 0/1247: Baoji If you're trying to follow the km markers, this is where things begin to get complicated. The train has now reached the junction with the Lung Hai line, and starts travelling east towards Xi'an,

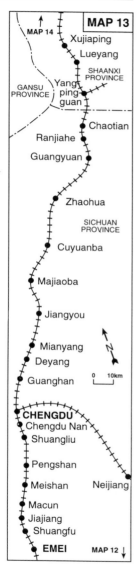

MAP 13

MAP 14

Xujiaping
Lueyang

SHAANXI PROVINCE

GANSU PROVINCE

Yangpingguan

Chaotian

Ranjiahe

Guangyuan

Zhaohua

SICHUAN PROVINCE

Cuyuanba

Majiaoba

Jiangyou

Mianyang
Deyang

0   10km

Guanghan

CHENGDU
Chengdu Nan
Shuangliu

Pengshan

Meishan   Neijiang

Macun
Jiajiang
Shuangfu

EMEI   MAP 12

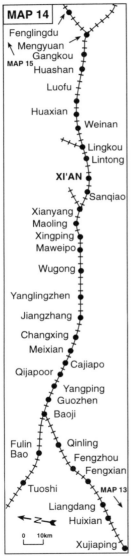

MAP 14

Fenglingdu
Mengyuan
Gangkou
MAP 15
Huashan
Luofu

Huaxian
Weinan
Lingkou
Lintong
XI'AN
Sanqiao
Xianyang
Maoling
Xingping
Maweipo
Wugong
Yanglingzhen
Jiangzhang
Changxing
Meixian
Cajiapo
Qijapoor
Yangping
Guozhen
Baoji
Fulin   Qinling
Bao   Fengzhou
          Fengxian
Tuoshi   MAP 13
          Liangdang
          Huixian
0   10km
          Xujiaping

beyond which it heads off northwards to Taiyuan. The km markers at this point reflect the distance to the sea (the end of the Lung Hai line) rather than to Taiyuan.

For the section of the journey covering Bao Ji, Xi'an and Mengyuan (Hua Xian), see p302.

Km 799/528: Mengyuan Mengyuan is the junction where services to the north for Taiyuan leave the Lung Hai line. On the trunk line Mengyuan is at Km 799, whereas on the Nan Tongpu line leading north, Mengyuan is at Km 528; the markers are now counting backwards to Taiyuan, which is 528km away.

Km 512: Gangkou Shortly after passing through Gangkou, the line crosses the Yellow river into Shanxi province.

Km 108: Pingyao The Shuanglin temple, which is just outside Pingyao town, is one of the main attractions in the area (see p251). You can either get to it by bus from Taiyuan, or hop off the train here and catch another train onwards later.

Km 0: Taiyuan The Shuanglin Temple and the Jin Temple, make Taiyuan well worth a visit. See p249.

TAIYUAN TO DATONG [355km, 7-8hrs]

Kilometre marking along the Bei Tongpu line is confusing at first but settles down eventually, with the markers on the right hand side of the track, counting backwards towards Datong.

Km 194: Xuanggang After the monotony of the plains in the early part of this journey, the large hills on this stretch of the line come as something of a relief. In the evening light the countryside can actually look quite beautiful, until you catch a glimpse, across the embankment, of one of Shanxi's mining towns – all concrete and coal dust.

Keep an eye out to the right around here, as you can occasionally catch glimpses of the Han Dynasty watch-towers which still dot the countryside. Although they're pretty overgrown they are unmistakable and are witness to the fact that this part of the country has been a frontier region for as long as the Chinese have been here. Those who take the CITS tour to the Hanging Temple outside Datong will probably get the chance to have a closer look at one of these watch-towers en route.

Km 166: Ningwu Just to the north of this station, the railway passes through what used to be the line of the Great Wall. There's not much to see any more but you may still be able to distinguish some of the old fortification if you look hard.

Km 0: Datong China's coal capital, and the site of the famous Yungang Grottoes. See p256.

DATONG TO BEIJING   [428km, 8hrs]

There are two possible routes from Datong to Beijing. The **Jing Bao line** stretches northwards towards Zhangjiakou (formerly called Kalgan) before curling back towards Beijing. This was the earliest line in China to be built entirely by Chinese engineers; the Beijing to Kalgan section was started in 1905 and once complete it was extended to Datong. The newer **Da-Qin line** runs much more directly eastwards, passing Beijing to the north, and continuing to the coast at Qinhuangdao.

A brief summary is given here of the newer line, which is used by at least two of the major passenger trains. Km post numbering starts at zero and counts up towards Beijing, although it gets confused near the end of the journey as the train effectively

passes to the north of the capital and then approaches from the east.

Km 104: Yangyuan This station is the first stop after the train crosses out of Shanxi province into Hebei.

Km 138(R): To the right of the train you can see one of the old mud watch-towers which are common in this part of northern China.

Km 225(R): To the right of the train is the large Guanting Reservoir. It is fed primarily by the Sanggan River, alongside which the railway has been travelling.

Km 274: The line enters the **Jundushan Tunnel**, at 8.5km one of the longest in China.

Km c368/0: Somewhere just beyond Chawu station, the train starts looping southwards towards Beijing. The km numbering begins to count down from here – markers remain on the right.

Km 5: Beijing Dong (east): Don't let this one catch you out. Train No 335 terminates at Beijing east station, a tiny, badly lit place just inside the fourth ring road. This is no particular hassle, except of course that the east station isn't on the underground, so you'll probably have to take a taxi.

Guilin
桂 林

Guilin is considered by the Chinese, along with towns such as Hangzhou and Suzhou, to be one of the most beautiful places in the country. Most people will have already seen pictures of its famous limestone peaks, as they feature widely on Chinese tourist literature. Scores of poets, politicians and others have written about the magnificent scenery around here, and according to the CITS brochures, 'The mountains and waters of Guilin are the finest under heaven'. If you have already visited one or two places in China, all this may set a few alarm bells ringing, as you visualise a town that will be both expensive and overdeveloped. Broadly speaking you'd be right. Nothing, however, can detract from the extraordinary natural scenery, and Guilin's smaller neighbour, Yangshuo, is peaceful, pretty and cheap.

All in all, Guilin should be on your itinerary, even if you plan to get a bus straight from the railway station to Yangshuo. If you can afford a night in a hotel here, or if you have to wait for a train, it's certainly worth having a look around.

HISTORY

Guilin became established in the Qin Dynasty (221-207BC) when canal building started near here to link the area to the Yangtse River. With the canal complete, the town's importance as a trading centre was assured, and it became the provincial capital – a position it held until the start of this century. During the Second World War large numbers of refugees fled to Guilin and the city was badly damaged by Japanese bombing.

Today Guilin is a large town which thrives on tourism. It's definitely not the idyll that the Chinese would have you believe but it does have some lovely countryside around it and a busy though relaxed atmosphere.

WHAT TO SEE

There are really only a couple of places worth visiting in Guilin.

Reed Flute Cave

Entry to the cave is an extortionate Y44, and you may well prefer to save your time and money, and visit a cave near Yangshuo instead. There is no denying, however, that this cave complex is amazing and, unusually for a tourist sight in China, it is very well presented. The big difference between visiting this place and, say, the Water Cave in Yangshuo is that this one is well lit, and so you can appreciate its scale and beauty. As usual, almost every part has been given a name. Some of the titles are surprisingly apt: for example, the Stage Curtain really resembles a stage curtain. I defy anyone, however, to make the massive imaginative leap required to see how Centipede Frightened By a Magic Mirror got its name. Bus 3 from the railway station gets you to the cave, but a better way to get there would be by bicycle, as the countryside is lovely once you're clear of the town.

Seven Stars Park and Cave

Although not particularly spectacular, Seven Stars Park is a good place for a stroll, and you can climb one or two of the peaks to get a fine view of the town and river. Entry is Y12, and the entrance to the Seven Star Cave inside the park is a hefty Y25 extra.

PRACTICAL INFORMATION
Orientation and services

Despite being a large town, Guilin is easy to get to grips with because most of the places of interest to visitors are around a small stretch of central road. The railway station is towards the south end of this road (Zhongshan Nanlu) and most of the hotels are either on the road or just off to the side.

The main **post office** is next to the railway station, and the Bank of China is just off Zhongshan Lu, about a kilometre north of the station. CITS (☎ 0773-2827254) are on Ronghu Lu but aren't much help unless you want to book a plane ticket or take one of their tours; they don't book train tickets. The town is bounded to the east by the Li river.

One thing to **beware** of is the number of 'students' who approach you wanting to 'practise their English'. Some are certainly bona fide but others are hard to get rid of. Sooner or later they will start trying to sell you boat tickets, invite you to their cousin's art shop, or into some ridiculously expensive 'traditional tea house'.

Local transport

Guilin isn't a particularly big place, but the public **buses** are still useful. **Bus 1** runs from the railway station north along Zhongshan Lu. **Bus 11** runs up Zhongshan Lu and off along Jiefang Lu to terminate at the Seven Stars Park. **Bus 3** goes from near the station to Reed Flute Cave, which is to the north-west of the town. **Bikes** are also widely available for hire, and two places to try are next to the railway station (on the pavement just to the south-east of the station entrance), and outside the Overseas Chinese Guesthouse.

Tours

CITS offer full- and half-day bus tours. Like everyone else in Guilin they will also suggest that you buy a boat ticket from them for a trip down the Li River. This tour has become something of an institution, and consists of five hours on a boat going down river in the morning (lunch is included), and then getting a tour bus back to Guilin with a couple of stops for photos on the way. Some people rave about it but for most, two or three hours on the water is quite long enough, and you can take a similar trip from Yangshuo for Y30 rather than the ridiculously expensive Y380-400 they charge for this one.

Where to stay

Guilin boasts a range of hotels from top class to basic. Unfortunately none have dormitories, which tends to mean that

---

GUILIN – KEY

Where to stay

1	Sheraton Guilin	1	文 华 大 酒 店
2	Tai Lian Hotel	2	泰 联 饭 店 (拼 音)
3	Guilin Osmanthus Hotel	3	丹 桂 大 酒 店
4	Taihe Hotel	4	泰 河 饭 店
5	Jinggui Hotel	5	京 桂 宾 馆
6	Hidden Hill Hotel	6	隐 山 饭 店
7	South Stream Hotel	7	南 溪 饭 店
8	Guilin New City Hotel	8	新 城 市 酒 店
9	Overseas Chinese Mansion	9	华 侨 大 厦

What to see

10	Reed Flute Cave	10	芦 笛 岩
11	Seven Stars Park	11	七 星 公 园

Where to eat

12	Yiren Lu	12	依 仁 路
13	Food Market	13	小 吃 街

Other

14	Railway Station	14	火 车 站
15	Post Office	15	邮 局
16	Bank of China	16	中 国 银 行
17	CITS	17	中 国 国 际 旅 行 社

---

backpackers high-tail it straight to Yangshuo, where accommodation is very cheap.

At the top of the pile in Guilin is the **Sheraton Guilin** (☎ 0773-2825588) which faces on to the river, and has rooms starting from US$105. Slightly more reasonable is the **Tai Lian Hotel** (☎ 0773-2822888) which is on the main street and has single rooms for US$50 and doubles for US$80. Probably better value is the **Guilin Osmanthus Hotel** (☎ 0773-3834300) which has double rooms in the cheaper east wing for Y294, although there are plenty of more expensive rooms available too.

The **Taihe Hotel** (☎ 0773-3834801) is pleasant enough and has 'ordinary' double rooms for Y150; to the south, again on Zhongshan Lu, the **Jinggui Hotel** (☎ 0773-3834328) has the cheapest double rooms you're likely to find,

starting at Y80. The **Hidden Hill Hotel** (☎ 0773-3833540) next door to the Jinggui and just north of the station has double rooms from Y100 and triple rooms for Y120.

Opposite the railway station the **South Stream Hotel** (☎ 0773-3834943) is a tiny building which has cheap rooms advertised, although the cheapest they would offer me was Y100. Next door is the **Guilin New City Hotel** (☎ 0773-3832511), which is the large place directly opposite the station. It's nothing to write home about, with rooms starting at Y200.

There is just a chance that the **Overseas Chinese Mansion** (☎ 0773-3835753) which is about a 15-minute walk south of the station, will allow you a single bed in a four-bed room for Y50, if business is really slow. It's a pleasant place to stay but it can be very frustrat-

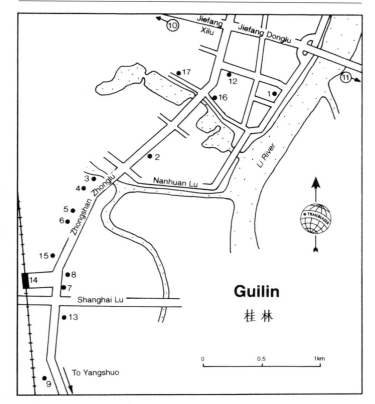

Guilin

桂林

0   0.5   1km

To Yangshuo

ing, as they seem to make up the prices as they go along. Ring a day or two in advance and ask if you can reserve a dormitory bed, and that way they can't spring the 'dormitory full' card, or raise the prices as you walk through the door.

Where to eat

The best food in town is to be found in the restaurants of the large hotels but, apart from this, a good place to start looking for food is along Yiren Lu, a small side street just off the northern end of Zhongshan Lu. For relatively cheap food in a quiet, hassle-free and air-conditioned atmosphere the *Taihe Hotel Restaurant* (next to the entrance of the hotel itself) has an English menu and good food.

There is an excellent *food market*, which is both cheap and a fun place to eat. It's near the south-east corner of the Shanghai Lu and Zhongshan Lu crossroads.

What to buy

Paintings, stone and wood carvings, and ceramics are all listed in the tourist literature as examples of local handicrafts but whether you can believe this or not is debatable. Guilin attracts thousands of foreign tourists each year so the shops are likely to sell what the visitors want, whether or not it's local.

If you're going on to Yangshuo save your money for the shops there.

Moving on

By rail If you're staying in Yangshuo, the easiest way to organise a rail ticket is through any of the travel services there, although of course you will have to pay a commission. Some hotels in Guilin operate similar services but the **ticket office** at the station is actually not bad. The Foreigners' Window (which naturally is labelled in Chinese) is Window 8, and some English is spoken: it's open from 07.30-11.30 and 15.00-18.00. Sleeper tickets go on sale three days before the day of departure and sell out quickly. Tickets for the Guilin-Kunming train can be difficult to obtain unless you get in there early; tickets to Guangzhou can also be elusive. For train times see p367-75.

By bus The bus to Guangzhou is a real option if train tickets are hard to come by. CITS quote Y180 for a bus leaving at 15.00 and arriving at 08.00.

Transport to Yangshuo couldn't be easier – minibuses go regularly from outside the railway station and the one-hour journey will cost you Y5-10 depending on how hard you bargain.

By air There are no shortage of places that will organise air tickets for you – CITS are probably as good as any other. Some sample prices are:Beijing Y1750, Xi'an Y1060, Guangzhou Y490, Shanghai Y1320, Kunming Y850 and Hong Kong Y1450.

Yangshuo
阳 朔

Along with Dali and Xiahe, Yangshuo is one of the major travellers' haunts in China. People spend days here, weeks even, and it's easy to see why: the town is cheap, the surrounding countryside is beautiful, and there's a thriving social scene. Most visitors will tire of Yangshuo after a few days but it's a great place for a rest, and there's enough to see to keep you here for two or three days at least. Best of all, you can enjoy better scenery than at Guilin for a fraction of the price.

WHAT TO SEE

The river and the natural scenery are really the main attractions in Yangshuo, and the best way to get a good view of them is to take a boat trip. There are various options available. One tour takes you by bus to the village of Qingping, and then upstream on what is supposed to be the most beautiful stretch of the river to **Crown Cave**. Entry to the cave is Y40 and although it's been developed as a tourist attraction, it's still reputed to be impressive. The return journey is by boat and bus in the afternoon. Another popular option is to get a boat from Yangshuo to Qingping, and then bicycle back along the country lanes. It's a full day's excursion (approximately three and a half hours upriver, and then about the same time cycling back), and the cycle ride takes you through some wonderful scenery. In the evenings you can join boats going to watch the cormorant fishing, where the local fishermen use tame cormorants to catch the fish for them. Take lots of fast film.

Realistically, two to three hours on the river is plenty for most people, as by that time you will have seen a fair cross section of its scenery: bamboo groves, water buffalo, cormorants and lots of huge hills. Practically all the places in Yangshuo will sell you tickets for the boats (typically Y40 to Qingping) but it's cheaper still to buy them yourself at the boat dock just before departure, – Y30 for a ride to Qingping is more like it if you haggle a bit.

Moon Hill

While most of the peaks around Yangshuo are just good for looking at, Moon Hill, one of the highest, with a large natural stone archway near the top, is fun to climb and provides excellent views of the surrounding countryside. Some people make a point of climbing it to watch the sunrise or sunset.

The hill is about a 50-minute cycle ride south-west of Yangshuo. Take the main road out of Yangshuo, forking right before you leave the town and then left at the next small junction. After 45-50 minutes you'll see Moon Hill on your right: it's unmistakable, being the only one with a huge hole in it. If you have some spare time you can also stop off en route to see the **Great Banyan Tree**, reputedly 1300 years old, which is just west of the small river bridge you cross some half an hour after leaving Yangshuo.

Caves

Limestone formations can provide just as spectacular sights below the ground as they do above it. Several large cave complexes in the area are accessible.

Some of the caves are commercialised (electric lighting, proper steps, entrance tickets etc), whereas to get into others requires scrambling, wading and generally getting filthy. **Reed Flute Cave** and **Crown Cave** fall into the first category, while **Black Buddha Cave** and even more so the **Water Cave** fall into the second.

The best advice is to check the advertisements in the cafés to see what's available. The trip to the Water Cave is organised from the Café De Paris, and is highly recommended. Four hours of wading, rafting and scrambling through underground caverns, with only the light of a few head torches, culminate in arrival at a massive underground waterfall and crystal clear rock pools. It is an awe-inspiring and thoroughly enjoyable way to spend a morning and will set you back about Y60-70 per person.

Other Activities

If you have some time and the desire to study a Chinese discipline, give a thought to doing it in Yangshuo. You can take courses here in, among other things, Kung Fu, Taichi, massage, and Mandarin.

YANGSHUO – KEY

Where to stay

1	Yangshuo Resort Hotel	1	阳朔饭店
2	Yangshuo Youth Hostel	2	阳朔青年旅舍
3	Golden Leaves Hotel	3	金叶饭店
4	Good Companion Holiday Inn	4	良友假日酒店
5	Zhu Yang Hotel	5	驻阳饭店 (音译)
6	Si Hai Hotel	6	四海饭店
7	Xilang Hill Hotel	7	西郎山饭店

Other

8	Bus Station	8	汽车站 (停车场)
9	Post Office	9	县邮电局
10	Boat Docks	10	阳朔码头
11	CITS/CAAC	11	中国国际旅行社
12	Bank of China	12	中国银行

PRACTICAL INFORMATION
Orientation and services

Yangshuo is a tiny place. Even if you walk all the way around the town (including the bits that are of little interest to visitors) it won't take you more than an hour, and you can stroll round the main part in more like twenty minutes. There are two main streets that are of interest: Pantao Lu and Xi Jie, which have most of the hotels and restaurants on them. The **post office** is at the junction of these two streets, and there is a branch of the **Bank of China** near the waterfront; walk along Xi Jie towards the river and turn left on the river front road (Bin Jiang Lu).

CITS seem to have two offices, the more useful of which is in the Good Companion Holiday Inn, while the other is side by side with the **CAAC** office up the side street from the bus station. A good map of Yangshuo is available at the Yangshuo Youth Hostel (among other places) for Y2.

Local transport

Bicycles are available for hire everywhere, usually for Y5 per day. Many of these machines have taken a pounding, however, so do check the bike carefully before you accept it.

Tours

The travel services in the cafés and hotels will offer any sort of tour that you want, from trips to local villages to full day tours, river trips, caving expeditions etc. Look around at what's on offer when you arrive, and ask others what they've done.

Where to stay

When it comes to accommodation, Yangshuo is a budget traveller's dream come true: there is only one hotel that is upmarket, and lots of cheap, friendly places. The top hotel in town is the **Yangshuo Resort Hotel** (☎ 0773-8823208) where all rooms have air-conditioning, and the cheapest start at US$29. Apart from this place, the other hotels in Yangshuo compete for the 'cheapest and best' award, and there's not a lot in it. The **Yangshuo Youth Hostel** (☎ 0773-8822347) has nothing to do with the YHA but is popular mainly because it's the first place most people see as they step off the bus. It's a good place to stay: clean, friendly, and some of the staff speak English; a bed in a dorm is Y10 (or Y15 in a dorm with a private bathroom), and a single room is Y30. If you've got some time on your hands the manager here gives Mandarin lessons, and this has to be one of the cheapest, most relaxed places in China to learn the language.

The **Golden Leaves Hotel** (☎ 0773-8822860) is next door to the Youth Hostel, and is slightly more upmarket, although it also has dormitory beds for Y15-20. The **Good Companion Holiday Inn** (☎ 0773-8822766) has nothing to do with the Holiday Inn chain, as the prices show: private rooms start at Y30, and the dormitory is Y10. Air-conditioned doubles cost Y50.

A short way to the east, the **Zhu Yang Hotel** (☎ 0773-8821601) is slightly more expensive, with rooms from Y100, but there's a dormitory here too, with beds for Y20. The slightly higher prices and location just away from the central junction seem to mean that this hotel loses out on business – so for somewhere reasonably quiet to stay, it's worth a try. Down Xi Jie is the **Si Hai Hotel** (☎ 0773-8822013) which is a popular place with travellers. Private rooms here start at Y30 and a bed in the dormitory costs Y15-20. The cheapest place, by a whisker, and one of the most peaceful, is the **Xilang Hill Hotel** (☎ 0773-8822312) which has doubles with private washing facilities for Y40, or Y20 without. The rooms are in old buildings around a pleasant courtyard, just the place to spend an afternoon with a book.

Where to eat

A restaurant listing is useless in Yangshuo as the streets are lined with good places to eat, most serving a variety of Chinese and Western food.

Many of the places also offer 'interest' food (the sort of thing that you can say that you tried once) – snake, dog and other such delicacies. This is also a good place to try out local alcohols because, whereas most restaurants in China sell booze only by the bottle, here it's often sold by the glass, so you've nothing to lose if you don't like it.

What to buy

As you might expect, Yangshuo is an excellent spot to catch up on some shopping. There is a fair range of good quality stuff available and, just as important, the atmosphere is relaxed enough to allow visitors to browse. Among the most popular items are chops (stone seals, engraved with your own name/birthsign/emblem), calligraphy, paintings and clothing. Colourful hand-painted T-shirts are good value at under US$2.

Moving on

For most people, getting away from Yangshuo simply involves hopping on a local **minibus** back to Guilin to catch the train but there are other options. The travel services in the hotels and cafés can tell you what's on offer, but the popular routes include getting a bus to Guangzhou, and taking a bus/train combination to Kunming, as both of these avoid a potentially long wait to get a sleeper ticket on the train.

The nearest **airport** is in Guilin.

Nanning
南宁

There is little reason to come to Nanning unless you're either going to or from Vietnam. If you're leaving China, your visit here will be brief as train tickets to the border are easily obtainable. Coming into China you may find yourself staying here a day or two if you have to wait for a train ticket, although Hard Seat tickets to Guilin are in plentiful supply.

Nanning is the capital of the Guangxi Autonomous Region and is a large, busy and rather jaded looking place; despite its nickname of 'Garden City' there is little here to attract tourists.

WHAT TO SEE

This is clutching at straws, as there really isn't too much to see in Nanning.

The **Guangxi Provincial Museum**, on Minzu Dadao, is rather depressing, and barely worth the Y3 entry fee. Apart from several locked rooms, there's a small collection of ethnic clothing, a display of bronze drums and a photo display on the life of a famous Chinese educationalist. The pictures even included X-rays from the poor guy's visit to hospital!

Renmin Park (Y1) is a nice place for a wander. The inner garden (which costs a further Y1 to get into) is pretty. You could also take a stroll along the **river front** near Jiangbin Lu for an interesting insight into another side of life in Nanning. The barges are moored up in long lines, and in the evening, people fly kites on the river wall.

Qing Xiu Shan Park is the best place in Nanning to spend a spare afternoon. Built on the highest spot in the area, a few km to the south-east of the city centre, the park is still being landscaped and extended but consists of a large area of hillside with extensive lawns and wooded walks. Near the highest point there's a **pagoda** from the top of which you get a good view of the city and surrounding area. There is, of course, the ubiquitous boating pond but it's quite tastefully done, and the whole place is big enough to be able to escape the crowds. To get to the park catch a bus (no number: ask local people) from the north side of Chaoyang Square. The trip costs Y3, and entry to the park is Y2.

If you haven't had your fill of caves already you could visit the **Yiling Caves**, which are a short distance to the north of Nanning. Buses go from Chaoyang Square and take about an hour to get there.

PRACTICAL INFORMATION
Orientation and services

The parts of the city that are of interest to travellers are all to the north of the Yong River. The station is at the north end of Chaoyang Lu, which is the central road that most visitors will be interested in. **CITS** (☎ 0771-2833402) are just up Xinmin Lu from the large five star Mingyuan Xindu Hotel. They don't book rail tickets, and have little that's of interest to travellers but the staff are friendly and speak good English, so this is the place to come if you need help or information. They say that they can organise **Vietnamese visas**, but since this involves sending your passport back to Guangzhou, with a resulting wait of 10 days, it would be quicker and safer to go to Guangzhou yourself. Next door to the CITS office is the **Nanning Air Service Company**, who offer fairly competitive rates on air tickets. The main branch of the **Bank of China** is on Minshang Lu, but there's a sub-branch in front of the Xiang Yun Hotel. There's a large **post office** on Suzhou Lu which has all services including customs.

Local transport

The city centre is pretty much all walkable but the bus services are good and easy to understand with the help of a local map. **Bus 6** runs past the station, south-east along Chaoyang Lu and then east along Minzu Dadao past the provincial museum. If you're staying near the station catch this bus right opposite the station building, as the next stop is a fair hike down the road. Going north from the station, bus 6 takes you to the northwest corner of Renmin Park, from where you can walk south along Renmin Lu to the park entrance. **Bus 7** runs from the railway station south-east to Renmin Lu and then up Minzu Lu, passing in front of the Mingyuan Xindu Hotel and near the CITS office.

Tours

CITS offer a two-day tour to the rock paintings at Huashan and thence to a minority area. The tour costs Y400 per person (minimum two people), which includes a guide, accommodation and transport, and the itinerary takes you south towards the Vietnam border by train, and then by boat to the 'Ethnic Holiday Village'. After a visit to the rock paintings, a night is spent in the village, before visiting a nature reserve the next morning.

NANNING – KEY

Where to stay

1	Mingyuan Xindu Hotel	1	明园新都饭店
2	Xiang Yun Hotel	2	湘云饭店 (拼音)
3	Jin Yue Hotel	3	金月饭店 (拼音)
4	Fuxing Hotel	4	福星饭店 (拼音)
5	Milky Way Hotel	5	银河大厦
6	Phoenix Hotel	6	凤凰宾馆
7	Yingbin Hotel	7	迎宾饭店

What to see

8	Guangxi Provincial Museum	8	广西省博物馆
9	Renmin Park	9	人民公园

Where to eat

10	Hangzhou Lu	10	杭州路
11	American Fried Chicken	11	美国炸鸡 (华越美)

Other

12	Railway Station	12	火车站
13	CITS	13	中国国际旅行社
14	Bank of China	14	中国银行
15	Bank of China	15	中国银行
16	Post Office	16	邮局
17	Foreign Language Bookstore	17	外文书店

Where to stay

The *Mingyuan Xindu Hotel* (☎ 0771-2830808) is extremely luxurious and has rooms from Y800. Just up the road the *Xiang Yun Hotel* (☎ 0771-2822888) has double rooms from Y380, and next door the *Jin Yue Hotel* (☎ 0771-2802338) has double rooms for Y230. Better value than either of these is the *Fuxing Hotel* (☎ 0771-2828298) which is right in the centre of the city and has twin rooms for Y268. Although it's slightly more expensive, it's a much more comfortable place and facilities even include a swimming pool. Near the station, the *Milky Way Hotel* (☎ 0771-2828223) has pleasant air-conditioned single rooms for Y140, while on the other side of the road, the *Phoenix Hotel* (☎ 0771-2829833) has air-con doubles for Y80, but is slightly run down. The cheapest accommodation

you'll find in Nanning is the *Yingbin Hotel*, a friendly place on the corner directly opposite the station. A single room is Y50, and a bed in a three-bed dorm is Y18.

Where to eat

Probably the most enjoyable (and cheapest) place to eat in Nanning is near the station, on Hangzhou Lu. The north end of the street is taken up by a covered fruit market (which is great to wander around anyway) but to the south of this the street has many small restaurants with excellent food. In the summer, with the tables out on the pavement and the restaurants packed with locals, there's a lively friendly atmosphere. Apart from this there aren't many places that stand out. There are a couple of cheap restaurants on the west side of Chaoyang Lu, just to the north of the

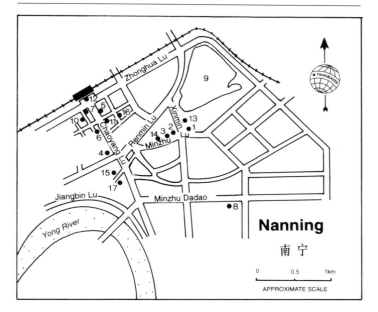

junction with Renmin Lu. Nanning's own, home-grown fast food restaurant is *American Fried Chicken*, a short way down Chaoyang Lu from the station; it has reasonable food and prices.

Moving on

By rail There are lots of trains out of Nanning but tickets can be hard to come by. If you're going north (ie into China) the easiest thing might be to get a Hard Seat ticket to Guilin, and enjoy yourself there while you wait for a ticket onwards. Currently there is no direct train to Kunming, so you must either go to Guilin or Guiyang and change. A new line from Nanning to Kunming is under construction, however, and is due for completion in 1997; this should ease the ticket situation considerably.

Going south to **Pinxiang** on the Vietnam border is easy. There are two trains operating: T317 is a daily service departing Nanning at 07.30 and arriving at Pinxiang at 11.52. The same train (now called T318) returns in the afternoon, leaving Pinxiang at 13.58, and arriving at Nanning at 18.19. A Hard Seat ticket costs Y29, and the train is a double deck air-con, intercity-style service. T511 is a slow service which departs Nanning at 11.00 and arrives in Pinxiang at 17.55; it returns the next day, as T512, departing Pinxiang at 08.35 and arriving in Nanning at 15.08.

By bus There are also buses to Pinxiang, which take about the same time as the fast train, and the journey costs Y23. The bus station is at the corner of Chaoyang Lu and Huadong Lu.

By air Nanning Air Service Company quote the following prices: Kunming Y660, Chengdu Y960, Guangzhou Y710, Beijing Y2040.

Kunming
昆明

Kunming is known as the Spring City because of its perennial mild weather: in January temperatures seldom fall much below eight degrees centigrade and the midsummer average is only 20 degrees. Despite the fact that it's a large city with the usual high-rise blocks and big hotels, Kunming has a relaxed atmosphere, which some attribute to the fact that it is so far from the central control of Beijing. It's a natural focal point for travellers arriving from or departing to some of the most interesting parts of south-west China, and it's also the jumping-off point to one of the most popular travellers' haunts of South East Asia – Dali. With a couple of sights that are worth seeing in the city itself, most people seem to spend at least two days here.

HISTORY

The city of Kunming has been in existence for at least two thousand years. During the Qin Dynasty (221-207BC), when China was first unified, it became nominally part of the Chinese Empire. Protected by its remoteness and political in-fighting in the north, however, the distinction was largely theoretical. For several hundred years, despite its subject status it continued to operate pretty much independently, enjoying good trading connections with the countries to the south and south-west. In the Tang Dynasty (618-907AD), however, a local tribe became powerful enough to break away from Imperial control. The Nanchao kingdom defeated the Tang army sent to suppress it, and made Kunming their second city (the main capital was near Dali).

The region came back under central control with the arrival of the Mongols and it was at this time that Marco Polo is supposed to have visited the city. In his account he notes the diversity which the traveller finds there: 'At the end of the five days he reaches the capital of the kingdom, which is called Yachi, a large and splendid city. Here there are traders and craftsmen in plenty. The inhabitants are of several sorts: there are some who worship Mahomet, some idolaters, and a few Nestorian Christians'.

With the demise of the Mongols, the Ming Dynasty set about consolidating its grip on the empire. In the far south-west this included settling large numbers of Han Chinese in minority areas, to make them easier to govern. In addition, the Ming renamed the city 'Yunnan-fu' a name which was still being used in the early years of this century. At the end of the dynasty, Yunnan-fu was the final retreat for the last Ming prince, who was hunted down by the Manchus. He is reputed to have been strangled to death by a Chinese general. Feelings against the Qing ran high, and the Muslim population (there is still a considerable Muslim minority in Kunming today) staged a rebellion in the 1860's, which was harshly suppressed.

The way of life in Kunming changed for ever in 1910, with the arrival of the French-built railway which stretched north from Hanoi. The railway started Kunming's transformation into a modern city and the Second World War, during which Kunming became a refuge for those fleeing westwards, continued the process. The Americans and British, keen to support the Chinese resistance against the Japanese, shipped supplies along the famous Burma Road – over 1000km of dirt track that was hastily built by 160,000 coolies. When the Japanese captured a central section of the road, supplies had to be flown in instead. Harold Rattenbury (*China-Burma Vagabond*) noted the transformation first hand:

'Between 1934 when I'd last been there and 1939 very great changes had come over Kunming. It wasn't only the airfield and planes overhead all day long. It wasn't merely the hundreds of trucks that crowded the roads and streets or were gathered in great car parks. It wasn't just the refugees, the dust and the soldiers. Kunming, from being an old world town on the borders of China, tinged, since the opening of the Indo-China railway, with French influences, had become in two years of war one of the key places in China. The city was not the back gate, but the main gate into China at that time...'

In the period since Liberation, Kunming has been joined to the outside world by rail lines to Guiyang and Chengdu, and a new line direct to Nanning is being built at the moment. The original railway south across the border has been replaced in stretches with a modern line, although the route is pretty much the same. During the war with Vietnam the line was closed, and it was reopened only in 1996.

Today, Kunming is a modern city with a population of approximately two million. It is the capital of Yunnan Province.

WHAT TO SEE

Yuantong Buddhist Temple

The temple, which is in the north of the city, was built in the Tang Dynasty (618-907AD), and was originally called the Putuoluo Temple. It was enlarged and renamed in the Yuan Dynasty, and despite the fact that it was subsequently rebuilt much more recently, some of the Yuan Dynasty statues have survived. This temple is definitely worth a visit.

The main buildings include the Octagonal Pavilion, which sits in the centre of a pond, in front of the Great Hall. Around the sides of the pond run cloisters, and to get to the hall you can either walk through these or across the bridges that give access to the pavilion. The Great Hall itself has three enormous statues of Buddha, and the pillars in front of the statues are wrapped in the coils of two huge blue dragons which are roaring at each other; these were added in the Ming Dynasty. Behind the Great Hall is a further shrine to house a magnificent bronze Buddha. In the cloister just to the side of the Great Hall is a restaurant and tea shop, which is a mellow place to sit and watch the world go by. Entry for foreigners is Y10.

Bamboo Temple

Originally built in 1280, the Qiongzhu (Bamboo) Temple belonged to the Chan Sect of Buddhism which had spread from central China to Yunnan. It's a magnificent place. The entrance courtyard sets the tone, with a large incense burner, flanked by two enormous trees; through the second gate, the main courtyard is leafy and beautiful. The temple's main attraction, however, is in the rooms immediately to the left and right of the second gate. These two small halls are crammed with 500 life-size sculptures of the Arhats, each statue having been individually crafted with its own features, expression and actions. The sculptures were executed by Sichuan sculptor Li Guangxin, between the years 1883-1890. Free of much of the conventional stylisation of Buddhist sculpture, they are remarkably life-like. They look so real in fact, that despite an element of caricature in their portrayal, you half expect one of them to tap you on the shoulder when you turn away. The sculptures continue around the walls of the Great Hall, where more monks are portrayed in a seascape with mythical creatures. The main statues in the Great Hall are reputed to date from the Yuan Dynasty.

The craftsmanship around the whole temple is immaculate. In particular spare a minute to look at the tracery in the woodwork. The doors around the courtyard in front of the third hall are superb. The temple is still very much in use, although it's also an attraction for locals from Kunming who come here at the weekend to play cards, chat and drink tea.

Entry is Y10. It's about 12 km from the city centre, and minibuses run out to the temple from the area in front of the Yunnan Hotel. Although you'll have to ask around for the right bus on the way out, getting back is easy, as minibuses wait outside the temple until they're full.

The Stone Forest

The Stone Forest (Shilin) is billed as one of Kunming's main tourist attractions. The 'forest', which is a karst (limestone) formation of rocks weathered into weird and wonderful shapes, is actually interesting enough but, unfortunately, it's over-touristed. With an entry fee of Y33, it's also overpriced. Since it's 126 km south-east of Kunming, a visit will take the best part of a day.

Getting there is easy: dozens of tour buses ply the route. The bus ride from Kunming takes two and a half hours. The best thing to do is simply to wander away from the crowds and explore by yourself: you can't get lost as there's a paved ring road running around the outside of the formation which will take you straight back to the entrance.

Rail enthusiasts might prefer an alternative way to get to the Stone Forest. Take a train from the north station (T501 departing at 07.35 is suitable) to Yiliang. This runs along the route of the old French railway which was built at the beginning of the century to extend their trade across the border. The line runs through the original cuttings and over the old bridges, alongside the more modern line to Hekou. The gauge on this line is narrower than on the mainlines (1000mm), although the train itself looks pretty normal; it's just like a modern Chinese train but with one less seat abreast in the Hard Seat carriage. The trip takes two and a half hours and costs Y4. From Yiliang you can catch a bus to Shilin (if you're lucky), or to Lunan from where you should be able to catch a minibus to Shilin. In all it will take you considerably longer than catching a tour bus and won't cost you much less.

Yunnan Provincial Museum

The museum is not very impressive but you might want to have a quick browse if you're in the area. Just inside the compound (you won't need to buy a museum ticket for this) is the Boyiyuan Art Gallery, which is definitely worth seeing.

Entry to the museum is Y10. There are exhibits on Yunnan minority groups, looms and weaving techniques, local excavations and revolutionary history. They hold little interest for foreign visitors, who are likely to have seen the better displays elsewhere, and certainly the minorities clothing and customs are much better covered in the Sichuan University Museum, in Chengdu.

The **Boyiyuan Art Gallery** is just to the right of the front door of the museum and contains some lovely, if fairly expensive paintings, and woodcuts that would make fantastic souvenirs.

West and East Pagodas

Just to the south of the city centre, these two pagodas were built in the Tang Dynasty. The west pagoda is just off a side street from the market area and sits in its own courtyard where a large number of mainly elderly locals gather to play mahjong and while away the afternoons. Entry to the courtyard is Y2.

Mosque

A interesting place to look into, mainly because it presents such an unexpected contrast to everything else in Kunming. The mosque is down a small side alley just off Jinbi Lu. Having stepped off the busy main road, the paved courtyard and ancient buildings on either side feel rather like an undiscovered part of old Kunming.

West Hills

Much better than any of the parks in Kunming, the West Hills are a good place to combine walking with (more) temple viewing. The hills overlook Dai Lake, and for centuries pavilions and temples have been built here where they can command the view.

At the highest point is the main tourist attraction: a series of **caves** and walkways carved into the side of a sheer cliff face. The carving is inter-

---

KUNMING – KEY

Where to stay

1	Holiday Inn	1	假日酒店
2	Kunming Hotel	2	昆明饭店
3	Green Lake Hotel	3	翠湖饭店
4	King World Hotel	4	世界王宾馆
5	Golden Dragon Hotel	5	金龙饭店
6	Three Leaves Hotel	6	三叶饭店
7	Chuncheng Hotel	7	春城饭店
8	Camellia Hotel	8	茶话宾馆
9	Yunnan Hotel	9	云南饭店

What to see

10	Yuantong Buddhist Temple	10	圆通寺
11	Bamboo Temple	11	筇竹寺
12	Provincial Museum	12	省博物馆
13	West Pagoda	13	西寺塔
14	East Pagoda	14	东寺塔
15	Mosque	15	清真古寺
16	West Hills	16	西山
17	Green Lake Park	17	翠湖公园

Where to eat

18	Yunnan Typical Local Food Restaurant	18	云南特色风味饭店
19	Cafés	19	咖啡馆 (南杂盛)
20	Wei's Place	20	哈哈餐厅
21	Journey To The East	21	东方之旅

Other

22	Main Railway Station	22	中心火车站
23	North Railway Station	23	火车北站
24	CITS	24	中国国际旅行社
25	Post Office for Poste Restante	25	候领邮件邮局
26	Post Office	26	邮局
27	Bank of China	27	中国银行
28	Foreign Languages Bookstore	28	外文书店

esting but this is not the place to come if you dislike crowds. The walkways and steps are very narrow, and the Chinese tend to stop and pose for photos in the most inconvenient spots, so very quickly the whole cliff face turns into one big 'people-jam'. Entry to the caves and the summit area costs Y20, and there are various other minor attractions, although generally they're not worth much. At the top of the hill is the **Sanqing Temple**, and a miniature **Stone Forest** (ie an area of grey boulders). If you're feeling lazy, you can get a chairlift up the last part of the hill (the lift costs Y25 each way) and then walk down.

It's possible to ignore the summit altogether, and simply walk downhill from near the chairlift station to the car park at the bottom of the hill. The walk takes about an hour, you can either walk down the road past the **Taihua** and **Huating** temples, or go exploring on the hillside.

The easiest way to get to the West Hills is by public bus: take Bus 5 west from outside the Camellia Hotel to its terminal stop, and change to Bus 6, which has its final stop at Gaoyao at the bottom of the hill (from here minibuses run uphill). The trip takes an hour, and costs about Y2.

Kunming

昆 明

0   0.5   1km

APPROXIMATE SCALE

PRACTICAL INFORMATION
Orientation and services
The main railway station is in the south of the city, at the southern end of Beijing Lu. The north station (for trains to Hekou on the Vietnamese border) is at the north end of Beijing Lu. Approximately half way between the two stations, Dongfeng Lu cuts Beijing Lu at right angles and the city centre is just to the west of this intersection. The **Bank of China** has its main branch in a massive building one block north of the intersection, and getting money on credit card is relatively easy here. The bank is open from 09.00-11.45 and 14.30-17.30. There is a large **post office** on the north-east corner of the Dongfeng Lu/Beijing Lu intersection. Most services are available here, although to send international parcels and to collect poste restante, you'll have to go to the post office one and a half blocks south on Beijing Lu.

CITS have an office on Huancheng Lu, and another next to the King World Hotel. Neither of these is really much use unless you want an air ticket or one of their tours. There's a CITS ticket office, too, just west of the Kunming Hotel but again this is only for air tickets. Decent maps of Kunming are easily available; the Foreign Languages Bookstore sells one for Y1 which has bus routes and some English titles.

The area next to the West Pagoda has a large **street market**, and just east of Beijing Lu and north of Wei's Place is a very lively **food market**.

Local transport
Although many people enjoy the freedom of hiring a bike and getting themselves around a new city, Kunming has a good and relatively uncrowded bus service. **Bus 23** runs directly north-south along Beijing Lu, connecting the north and south (main) tations. **Bus 5** runs east-west along Dongfeng Lu.

Tours
Kunming is a good starting point for visits to various places in Yunnan Province, and CITS have capitalised on this to produce several expensive tours. Destinations include Dali, Lijiang (3-day/2-night tour for Y2100) and Xi Shuang Ban Na (4-day/3-night for Y2300). Closer to home, there is also a day tour to see West Hill and the Ethnic Cultural Villages (Y180).

Tours to the Stone Forest are widely available (most simply offer to get you there and back on a tour bus). The Camellia Hotel bus is as good as any: for Y30 the bus will pick you up and drop you off at the hotel, saving all the hassle of dealing with public transport. Generally, if you're thinking about taking a tour, shop around. Most of the hotels seem to offer them, so there is no shortage of options.

Where to stay
The *Holiday Inn* (☎ 0871-3165888) has rooms for US$110 upwards, and although these may be too pricey for you, the restaurant has some good offers: the all-you-can-eat breakfast buffet is served from 06.30-10.00 and costs Y85. Opposite the Holiday Inn is the *Kunming Hotel* (☎ 0871-3162063) which has rooms from US$100 upwards. A lovely place to stay, if you're feeling wealthy, is the *Green Lake Hotel* (☎ 0871-5158888) which is on the south-east edge of Green Lake Park, and is a lot quieter than the hotels in the city centre. The cheapest rooms here are US$90.

(Opposite) Top: Guilin (see p206) and Yangshuo (see p210) are famous for their limestone scenery. Boat trips along the Li River are an excellent way to see the area at its best. **Bottom:** Bathing water buffalo, Yangshuo.

Near the south (main) railway station there are several places. The *King World Hotel* (☎ 0871-3138888) is large and flashy, and has rooms from US$88; the *Golden Dragon Hotel* (☎ 0871-3133015), opposite, has reasonable facilities but seems rather overpriced at US$80 and upwards.

The *Three Leaves Hotel* (☎ 0871-3512542) is the nearest place to the railway station and is pleasant, with double rooms from Y238.

Budget travellers have a far more limited choice. The *Chuncheng Hotel* (☎ 0871-3163071) is a fair way from the station but was recommended by those who were staying there. The cheapest double room here is Y82, while a standard double with a private bathroom is Y154, and a triple room is Y221.

Best value of all is the *Camellia Hotel* (☎ 0871-3163000), where a dormitory bed in a clean, modern room is Y30. There are also double rooms from Y140. Bike hire is available here for Y1 per hour, although a Y400 deposit is required.

Where to eat

Kunming has loads of trendy travellers' restaurants that serve both Western and Chinese food. If you're catching up after being away in some remote corner of Yunnan you'll find that these places serve the usual range of pancakes, French toast etc, while most of them serve good local food too. Other places to try Yunnan cuisine include the *Yunnan Typical Local Food Restaurant* which is on the corner of Dongfeng Lu and Beijing Lu. The staff here are none too friendly but the food is good and reasonably priced.

For more expensive local food try the enormous restaurant next to the Camellia Hotel, or the very glitzy place in front of the Yunnan Hotel.

Cheaper local food can be found in the two modern restaurants at the south end of Green Lake Park; the modern place on the corner of Cuihu Nanlu and Cuihu Xilu is worth a visit. Also try the area around the mosque on Jinbi Lu, and there are, predictably, lots of very cheap places to eat around the main railway station.

When it comes to travellers' cafés there is quite a choice. Near the Camellia Hotel there are several to choose from, including the *Aloha Café, Bluebird Café* and *Golden Triangle Café*. Nearer the railway station, *Wei's Place* on Huancheng Nanlu, has great food (both Chinese and Western) and the coldest beer around; they also have a book exchange, and can help out with travel advice if needed.

Much further out but definitely worth a visit is a small street of cafés in the north of the city, near the university. Tian Jun Dian Lane is just off Yi Er Yi Dajie (also known as the North Ring Road), and it has several Western-style and Chinese places serving everything from traditional food to carrot cake. *Journey to the East* has good music, a lively atmosphere and a book exchange, and is a hang-out for many of the foreign students at the university. To get to Tian Jun Dian lane, go to the northwest end of Dongfeng Xilu, turn right (east) at the junction with Yi Er Yi Dajie, and it's the first lane on your right. Bus 22 stops near the lane, and continues on to the north railway station.

What to buy

There is little that is of specific interest in Kunming, although you might like to look into the Yunnan Antique Store in the centre of the city. The Foreign

---

(Opposite) Top: The entrance to the Bamboo Temple (see p220) in Kunming. The 13th century temple houses a collection of 500 near-lifesize figures by the sculptor Li Guangxin. **Bottom:** Market area in Kunming.

❑ Buying a railway ticket in Kunming

At quarter to eight the queue is already well established and stretches all the way across the large ticket hall. In front of me people stand patiently, – who knows what time the front runners arrived? Behind me against a pillar, a mother and children are smiling. They're probably waiting to take shifts from whoever's standing in the queue at the moment.

The old man in front of me must be at least 70. He's on two crude wooden crutches, and is shaking uncontrollably. He speaks English. He is going to see his son in Chengdu. He has two visible teeth, one of which is more a sort of tusk, protruding from his upper jaw; the rest is gummy smile. He says the desk will open at eight o'clock. The sign above the window says eight thirty. I hope resignedly that I'm in the right queue.

At five minutes past eight there's a movement in the line, and everyone starts to crane their necks to see if the window has opened. Others come from around the ticket office to stare at our window for two or three minutes and then, when there is no movement, they drift away. At eight thirty five the window opens. Suddenly all the people near the front of the queue are very popular, and all those who have arrived late are charming ('Would you mind getting this ticket for me?', 'Could I just step in front, I only want to ask a quick question...')

Ticket office staff, like school prefects, sit on the counter and push the queue back, and a roving force of uniformed police try half-heartedly to sort out angry disputes. Nothing, however, can stop the determined and the desperate. Around the hall and particularly around the ticket windows, tempers run high. The professional ticket touts feign a sense of humour and laugh when they are pushed out of the queue where they have attempted to squeeze in. They move nonchalantly to one side, smoke a cigarette with studied cool, and then subtly try again. As soon as the window opened, the old man in front of me seized his chance, hobbled to the front of the queue and pleaded infirmity. It worked, and now that he has got his ticket he comes back to say goodbye.

By nine thirty I'm beginning to lose hope. The queue isn't moving, mainly, I realise, because the touts have been successful, and each of the young men in front of me is queuing to buy a handful of tickets. There'll probably be nothing left by the time I get to the window. Mentally I plan my visit to the ticket agency. I glance across to the next queue and another tourist catches my eye and grins. We are the only two foreigners in the ticket hall, and after a couple of hours I'm barely five metres further forward. You have to smile.

I stretch my arms above my head and yawn. And then an amazing thing happens. The female railway employee who has been co-supervising our queue sees me and, leaving the counter, walks along the queue.

'Where are you going?' I show her my piece of paper with my destination written in Chinese.

'One?'. 'Yes, one'.

'Come with me'. She drags me to the front of the queue, tells the others to let me in front of them, and tells the girl who's selling the tickets to serve me next. The ticket costs me Y150, – Y250 less than the ticket agency wanted. I am elated and amazed. I take the ticket and my bag to the back of the hall and check the details disbelievingly...

Languages Bookstore, just around the corner is a good place to stock up on reading material. The paintings at the Boyiyuan Art Gallery (see p221) really are worth a look, too.

Moving on

By rail Kunming has a reputation for being a terrible place to get rail tickets but, wherever you are in China, it's always worth trying to buy your own rail ticket, before resorting to the travel services. Tickets in Kunming are first offered for sale at 08.30, three days before the day of departure (eg 10th of August for a 12th August departure). In order to stand a reasonable chance you should be in the queue by 07.00. Ensure that you have your passport with you, as there is a notice in the ticket office saying that it is required (although you may not actually have to produce it).

If you have no luck in the ticket office, there are a couple of travel services which may be able to help you, although their commission is likely to be Y80 or more. The travel service in the Camellia Hotel may tell you that they can get soft sleeper tickets only; a better place to try at first attempt, is a small ticket agency, which operates from a booth on Dongfeng Donglu about 150 metres west of the Camellia Hotel. Their mark-up seemed to be in the region of Y150, but unlike the

Camellia Hotel, they claimed that they could get Hard Sleeper tickets. For train times, see p367-75.

Tickets for trains south to the Vietnamese border are easy to get hold of and you can probably buy a Hard Sleeper ticket to Hekou (Y86) on the day of departure. Trains leave from the north railway station, although not all go all the way to Hekou. T313 is one that does, and it departs at 14.45.

By bus The **ticket agency** west of the Camellia Hotel (see above), quoted what seem to be fairly typical prices: Stone Forest Y35, Dali Y80, Lijiang Y130.

There is another ticket agency, the **Tourist Bus Booking Office**, just west of the Chuncheng Hotel. Alternatively shop around for the best prices by haggling with the drivers of the private buses by the main railway station, from where most seem to set out. The Y80 fare to Dali is fairly standard, however, and gets you a space on a sleeper bus for the overnight trip.

By air Kunming United Airlines, next to the Chuncheng Hotel, quoted the following prices: Guilin Y730, Beijing Y1850, Shanghai Y1860, Guangzhou Y1000 and Chengdu Y700. Also try the CITS ticketing office on Dongfeng Donglu.

Emeishan

Mt Emei, situated 160 km south-west of Chengdu, is the westernmost of China's four Buddhist holy mountains. Comparatively few Western tourists make the time to come here and walk the old pilgrims' path to the summit, but those who do are rewarded by finding that it's one of the most peaceful and pretty areas that are easily accessible in western China. Don't be put off by the distinctly touristy appearance of Baoguo village at the foot of the mountain; once you start climbing, the scenery's lovely, and a night or two in one of the monasteries high on the slopes of Mt Emei may well prove to be a highlight of your trip. The only caveat to this is that walking up Emeishan is really a summer activity. You can still get up it in winter but be prepared for bitter conditions.

Mount Emei first became a focus for religious activity nearly 2000 years ago. Originally a centre for Taoism, the Buddhist presence began to make itself felt during the Jin Dynasty (265-420AD), with the building of the Wannian Temple, which is still the principal temple on the mountain today. The complex was added to during the Ming Dynasty and still houses a statue of the Buddhist deity of the mountain, Samantabhadra. Over the centuries there has been a stream of famous visitors, including various emperors, and the temples have amassed a wealth of history (and property, some of which can still be seen). Unfortunately many of the temples have also been victims of various misfortunes, including a number of fires.

Because slopes of the mountain rise through several temperature variations, there is a wide variety of indigenous rare plants and animals. Whether the mountain's holy status had anything to do with the preservation of these over the years is open to debate but much of Emeishan is now designated a nature reserve. Among the most unusual residents here are the dove tree and the withered leaf butterfly.

Although Emeishan is a tourist attraction today, the monasteries are still in use. Unlike temples which have been opened to the public in large cities, these institutions are peaceful places, each with a character of its own. The administration is by the monks; if you stay in any of the monasteries you will pay for your bed and arrange your meal with them.

THE MOUNTAIN

Planning your route

At 3099 metres, Emeishan is bigger than you might imagine, and along with fond memories and great photographs, your most immediate remembrance of the place is likely to be legs that ache for several days afterwards. It really is a wonderful walk, though, and there are several options available so that you can tailor your walking to your own time limit and energy levels.

At the most basic level, you don't have to walk at all. There are minibuses from Baoguo to Jieyin Hall, from where the cable car runs to the summit. On the other hand, if you do this you will see only the most touristy bits of the mountain, and you will miss out entirely on the beautiful, quiet walks which Emeishan has to offer. For the slightly more energetic, a good option is to get a minibus and cable car to the summit, and then walk down. Alternatively, some people just avoid the summit altogether, and enjoy a day or so walking on the lower slopes of the mountain, where it's easier to stay away from the crowds.

Assuming that you want to walk up or down Emeishan, there are three good points to start or finish your hike: Wannian, Qingyin and Baoguo, as all three are accessible by road, and, in the case of the first two, there are bus services which can get you back to Baoguo, where you are likely to be staying. Do bear in mind, however, that buses may be scarce in the late afternoon and early evening, so if you're relying on catching transport back to Baoguo, try to get to either Wannian or Qingyin in good time.

Effectively, if you ignore the web of paths on the lower slopes, there are two routes up the mountain which join about three quarters of the way up. The shortest route from the bottom to the top starts from Wannian; although there is just about the same amount of climbing involved, the path is fairly direct and is a constant ascent nearly all the way. The other route to the top, from Qingyin Pavilion via Hongchun Terrace and Xianfeng Temple, climbs and falls through some spectacular scenery, and will take you a considerably longer time. If you plan to walk up the mountain and back down, therefore, it's worth considering ascending from Wannian, and descending via Qingyin.

The path from Baoguo to Qingyin runs along the lower slopes, and is not part of the ascent at all but a long extension of the lower path. Although starting your walk from Baoguo seems very convenient, you may be better off saving this part for the trip down; when you get to Qingyin you can decide whether to get a bus or complete the last 12 kilometres on foot.

It *is* possible to walk up the mountain in a day and back down the next day although this does not allow you time to enjoy the route properly. It's pretty much constant walking if you want to get it done in a couple of days; I was extremely tired by the time I got back to Baoguo, and was hobbling for about three days afterwards. If you have three or four days to spare you will enjoy yourself more. Leave as much as possible in a hotel in Baoguo before you start walking; the steps are quite steep enough without your having to haul all your belongings up, too.

Don't expect that the walk up Emeishan is going to take you into the wilderness. There are **food and drinks stalls** most of the way up the path, and although they put a slight mark-up on items to cover the porters' costs, you can get all you need along the way.

The ascent

If you are going to start walking from Wannian, it makes sense to get as early a start as possible. Minibuses leave from Baoguo at any time from about 06.30 onwards (although you can wait for ages while they try to fill each bus with passengers). The driver is likely to drop you on the road at **Jingshui**, from where you can walk up the slip road to the large car park and chairlift. The lift runs up to Wannian Temple (Y30 for the ride up) and might be useful if you want to save a little time. Entry onto the mountain whether you're walking or catching the chairlift is Y30.

After about half an hour's walk from the car park, you come to **Wannian (Ten Thousand Year) Temple**. This is the most important of the temples on Mt Emei and was originally built in the Jin Dynasty, although it was substantially rebuilt after being destroyed by fire in 1945. At the far end of the main courtyard is a unique brick-built hall, with a domed ceiling. Inside is an gigantic copper statue of the Boddhisattva Samantabhadra riding on a white elephant. The statue was cast in 979AD, during the Northern Song Dynasty, and weighs 62 tons. Around the walls of the hall in niches are 24 iron Arhats, and above them, lining the upper walls are 282 small bronze Buddhas.

From Wannian Temple, it's approximately a two-hour walk up to **Chu Hall** (Chudian). This temple is small and rather plain but a welcome sight and a good place for a rest. Food and water are on sale, and there is *accommodation* a quarter of an hour further up the path at **Huayan Peak**, where the small monastery commands excellent views. From Huayan Peak the path descends for a short way, and after about 25 minutes' walk, it crosses a saddle, where there is a large thriving food stall. Here the route is joined by the other path up from Qingyin, and if you want to descend Emeishan via a different route, this is where you will make the turning. The saddle may also be the first place where you come across the famous Emeishan monkeys.

From the saddle the path climbs again, and after half an hour you find yourself at **Xixiang (Elephant Bath Pond) Monastery**, the most beautiful monastery on the mountain, with wonderful views and a secluded feel to it. The monastery got its name from a story that Samantabhadra (who is depicted in the statue in Wannian Temple), once rode his elephant to the Golden Summit, and stopped here to wash the animal in a pond. There is plenty of *accommodation* at Xixiang, and it would make a good place to

---

❏ **Emeishan monkeys**
The monkeys on Emeishan are seasoned veterans in the art of getting food from tourists. They know the best places to wait and are bold enough to scare many walkers into giving them something. The problem is made worse by the reaction of some Chinese tourists. Chinese women tend to scream as soon as a monkey gets too close, and throw bag-loads of food at them. Chinese men on the other hand seem to see the confrontation as a chance to prove their manhood and antagonise the animals, even giving them a quick whack with a walking stick, which provokes understandable violence from the monkey concerned.

The porters on the mountain have the right idea: they simply hurry past the animals, shouting at them to get out of the way. It can, however, be rather daunting when you are confronted by two or three large monkeys sitting in the middle of the path. Walk past the animals quietly and without exciting them; don't ask for trouble by openly carrying food or, even worse, eating as you go.

spend the night if you're making the ascent over a couple of days. The path passes through the monastery itself, so you will have to pay the Y1 entrance fee.

Approximately an hour and a quarter beyond Xixiang is **Jieyin Hall**, an unattractive built-up area at the foot of the cable car, and the end of the road up from the base of the mountain. There's a small temple but it's not worth stopping for. From Jieyin Hall, the final steep ascent to the summit takes about an hour and a half and is something of a slog. Just below the top the path starts to level out and there are several places to stay but having come this far you may as well get all the way to the top itself.

There is a monastery next to the **Golden Temple** on the summit, which has *accommodation*: beds in triple rooms for Y40. It's a fantastic old place with loads of atmosphere. You can eat here in the evening, but make sure you order your food in advance and get to the dining room early, or you'll be lucky to get anything. If you don't fancy the noodles on offer here, there are several restaurants just below the summit. Although the **Golden Summit** is not actually the highest point on the mountain (the Golden Temple is at 3077 metres, whereas further along, the peak reaches 3099 metres), most people never bother to go further than the temple, watching the sunrise from the terrace of the temple itself. Being some 2548 metres higher than Baoguo, the top of Emeishan gets distinctly cool at night, even in the summer (the temperature here is reckoned to be 15 degrees centigrade lower than in Baoguo). The monastery rents old PLA greatcoats for a yuan or two, with the result that everyone wanders round looking like clones.

The descent

Having seen the sunrise, it's wise to set off as quickly as possible, as the path down to Jieyin Hall can get tremendously crowded. Once past Jieyin Hall the crowds should diminish slightly because many people will be going down by minibus.

Two and a half hours' walking should get you back down to Xixiang, and a further half-hour will take you to the saddle where the path divides. Initially the new path leads down very steep steps and after an hour and a quarter you arrive at **Xianfeng Temple**, a suitably ancient but rather plain-looking set of stone buildings. The scenery around this part of the mountain is superb, with enormous cliffs, thick forest and tiny winding paths. It's possible to stay at Xianfeng, and it would make a good place to break the ascent if going up this way. An hour and a half's walking further down the mountain you can expect to be at **Hongchun Pavilion**, outside the front gate of which is the Hongchun Tree which is said to have been there for over 1500 years. *Accommodation* is available.

Beyond the Hongchun Pavilion the path, which has been crossing and recrossing the river until now, starts to run alongside the river, down to Qingyin Pavilion, an hour further on. In comparison to the temples above it, Qingyin is a small metropolis, with snack sellers and tea houses. Central to Qingyin is **Jiewang (Receiving the Princes) Pavilion** where, according to tradition, two princes, entrusted by Emperor Kangxi with bringing gifts to the temples, were received by the monks.

You can catch a bus back to Baoguo from Qingyin, or walk back – it should take you about two and a half hours. If you're walking, bear in mind that the path is in a poor state of repair, and that it is not nearly so well marked as those you will have been used to. (This is another good reason not to start your walk up the mountain from Baoguo: I met one traveller who had abandoned his first attempt to walk up Emeishan, because he got lost on the small tracks out of Baoguo). The walk is very attractive, however, and thoroughly recommended if you have the time. From Qingyin the path goes up a short flight of steps and through a small hamlet. It stops being paved for about 100 metres, and then there is a small paved staircase going uphill to the right, while the earthen path continues around to the left. Although the steps to the right appear to be in poor condition, this is the route you need to take. From here the path is relatively easy to follow, and it takes an interesting route through villages, and even people's courtyards. On the way you pass **Chunyang Hall**, **Leiyin Monastery** and finally **Fuhu Monastery**, the largest monastery on Mt Emei, before arriving in Baoguo.

PRACTICAL INFORMATION
Orientation and services
The nearest large town to the mountain is **Emei** itself, which has a railway station on the Kunming-Chengdu line and bus connections to Leshan and Chengdu among other places. Although Emei is neat and has a showcase feel to it, there's nothing here of interest, and most visitors head straight for the village of **Baoguo** which is at the foot of the mountain and is only a short taxi ride from Emei. Emei station is about 8km from Baoguo, at the foot of the mountain.

Baoguo is tiny, and almost entirely devoted to tourism, with hotels and cafés on both sides of the only street. There are no services (bank/post office/CITS) available here, although if you need information the staff at the Teddy Bear Café will probably be able to help you, as will the staff in the Hong Zhu Shan Hotel.

There are two maps which are widely available and show the routes up the mountain. Both are artist's impressions, and are not particularly reliable in their ability to represent distance or detail. Following the route described above, it would, however, be difficult to get lost on the mountain, as the main paths are paved and unmistakable. The small black-bordered map is probably the better of the two, because it gives a 'plan' view, rather than an oblique view of the mountain.

Local transport
To get to Baoguo from the railway station take one of the blue taxi vans. They normally hold six or seven passengers, and the proper price for this is about Y3-5 per person for the ride to Baoguo. From Baoguo back to Emei the usual fare is more like Y1 or Y2, as the taxis have problems finding customers once they get to the village.

From Baoguo, there are minibus services operating around the base of

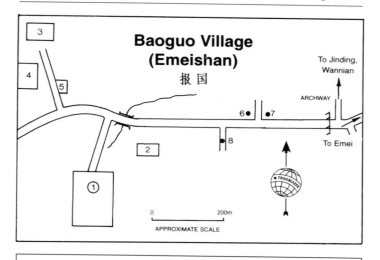

Baoguo Village (Emeishan)
报国

To Jinding, Wannian

ARCHWAY

To Emei

0   200m

APPROXIMATE SCALE

BAOGUO – KEY

Where to stay
1 Hong Zhu Shan Hotel
2 Jin Ye Hotel
3 Emeishan Forestry Hotel

Other
4 Baoguo Temple
5 Buses for Emei/Jinding/Wannian
6 Tintin Restaurant
7 Teddy Bear Café
8 Market

1 红珠山宾馆
2 金叶宾馆
3 峨嵋山森林宾馆

4 报国寺
5 去峨嵋／金顶／万年寺汽车站
6 亭亭饭馆
7 小狗熊饭馆
8 市场

the mountain. Local buses and minibuses will take you around to either Qingyin or Wannian, both of which are possible places to start or end your walk; you can also walk directly from or to Baoguo. Minibuses run directly to the foot of the cable car, near the top of the mountain. The earliest of these leaves at about 4 am to get passengers to the top in time to see the sunrise.

Tours are not needed, and none is available anyway.

Where to stay
In Baoguo there are three main places to stay, although a little rooting around may reveal others. The ***Hong Zhu Shan Hotel*** (☎ 08426-525888) is the most up-market of the hotels, and has eight buildings set in a large area of wooded hillside. One of these buildings was reputedly used by Chiang Kaishek. Rooms start at Y198. The smartest place to eat in Baoguo is here, in the restaurant in building No 8.

The *Jin Ye Hotel* (☎ 08426-523666) is a fairly smart, modern place in the centre of the village where rooms start at Y220. The backpackers' haunt is the *Emeishan Forestry Hotel* (☎ 08426-590050) near the Baoguo monastery. A bed in a double room here is Y30, and apart from hungry mosquitoes, the place is fine. Some foreigners have managed to stay in the *Baoguo Monastery* before, and it's definitely worth a try though you may meet with blank looks and a straight refusal.

Where to eat

Back down in Baoguo, there are lots of places to eat along the single village street, but the travellers' favourite is the *Teddy Bear Café* where there is great food and cold beer. The friendly owners will help out with travel and other advice, and if required they may also be

able to get train tickets for you. Next door is the *Tintin Café* which is obviously trying to capture the same market, but hasn't managed to do so yet. If you want to stock up on snacks and fruit for your walk, there is a small fruit market half way up the village street.

Moving on

By rail Trains from Emei run to both Kunming and Chengdu. With several trains originating there, Chengdu will be a much easier place to get hold of long distance rail tickets than Emei. Take a bus to Chengdu and buy rail tickets there. For train times see p367.

By bus Buses and minibuses run regularly from Emei (town) to Leshan and to Chengdu. The staff in the Teddy Bear Café will help you to arrange your bus tickets but you can easily do it yourself.

Leshan
乐 山

Leshan, only three quarters of an hour by bus from Emei, and 4 hours from Chengdu, is home to the largest carved stone Buddha in the world. 71 metres in height, the sculpture is set back into the west cliff of Lingyun Hill, where it overlooks the confluence of three fast-flowing rivers, and stares out towards Mt Emei. The tourist brochures claim that 200 people can stand on the feet of the statue alone. When you descend to the base of the cliff to find yourself dwarfed by the Buddha's toes, this isn't hard to believe.

In addition to the Giant Buddha the area has a number of other worthwhile sights, and since the town is a fairly relaxed place, it's a good spot to stay for a day or so. You may even consider that it's worth longer than a day, for Leshan has a further claim to your time: Mr Yang. A retired interpreter and English teacher, Mr Yang is one of the few people you will meet on your travels who speaks English well enough, and who has enough time, to sit and chat about China. A visit to his restaurant may open up all sorts of opportunities; he can organise trips in the area, or give you a personal tour of Leshan. If, by this stage in your travels, you are feeling frustrated at not being able to ask all those interesting questions that have occurred to you, make some time in Leshan.

HISTORY

The fact that Sichuan province is still occasionally known as Shu is a testimony to Chinese depth of tradition. In the distant past this area was part of the Shu state, of which Leshan became the capital in the 5th century BC. When China was first unified in 221BC, the First Emperor initiated a policy of resettling his loyal subjects into newly conquered areas. Intentionally or otherwise, the mass influx of Qin families laid the foundations for Leshan's prosperity. The newcomers brought with them advanced culture, and this, coupled with the natural resources in the area (namely salt and iron), and the town's convenient communications on the Min, Qingyi and Dadu rivers led to the establishment of a comparatively rich society. This wealth is reflected in the ornate tombs which have been found in the area (see the Mahao Cave Tombs Display, below). The city's name at this time was Jiazhou, meaning 'auspicious place'. The name Leshan was adopted in 1734.

Today Leshan is a large town which has a pleasant enough atmosphere, particularly along the riverside. Like most Chinese towns there are a number of small industries, but in Leshan tourism has become a major source of income. Unfortunately this spoils the visit here for some people, who feel that the constant succession of entrance fees is prohibitive. You just have to accept that almost every gate has a ticket office next to it, and be selective about what you visit. There's even a chance that by the time you read this the government's unpopular system, currently under review, of charging higher prices for foreigners may have been abolished.

WUYOU HILL AND THE GIANT BUDDHA

Getting to Wuyou Hill

Ferries to Wuyou Hill depart from the dock opposite the Taoyuan Hotel; the trip costs Y10, and the boats go as soon as they're full. You see the Giant Buddha from the best angle, as the ferries take you straight past it, even pausing for photographs. Having arrived at the dock south of the Buddha and below the Wuyou Monastery, the boat will be met by a horde of taxi-drivers who will offer to drive you to the Giant Buddha, swearing blind that the path has been closed and you can't get around on foot. Don't believe a word of it. The best way to see most of the sights in the area is to walk between them: from the ferry dock, the path takes you via the Wuyou Monastery, the Mogao Cave Tombs Display, the Buddha itself and the Lingyun Temple. Entrance to the monastery (the ticket office is at the bottom of the steps) is Y2.

Wuyou Monastery

At the top of the first flight of steps you arrive at the gate of the **Wuyou Monastery**. Also known as Zhengjue Monastery, this place was originally built by Monk Huijing between 766 and 779, in the Tang Dynasty. The main halls are rather more recent, having been built in the Qing Dynasty, although some of the sculptures here are hundreds of years old, and the place feels wonderfully ancient. To the west of the temple doors is the Hall of the Arhats, which houses 500 individual statues.

Continuing the walk northwards, from the temple entrance the path goes over the brow of the hill, and then down a long flight of steps. (If you're recovering from climbing Emeishan, you'll particularly enjoy these...). At the bottom of the steps is the stone bridge connecting Wuyou Hill to the mainland. According to legend, Wuyou Hill was not always an island but was once part of Lingyun Mountain. The separation was the work of magistrate Li Bin, who sought to calm the river waters by digging a new channel.

Mahao Cave Tombs Display

On the far side of the bridge the path goes left along the waterfront and passes the entrance to the **Mahao Cave Tombs Display**. Entry is only Y2, and the display is worth seeing. The tombs date from the Han, Tang and Song Dynasties, and what you see here is only a fraction of the large number of such cave tombs in the area. The method of burial is distinctive from contemporary interment elsewhere in China (the Han tomb at Mawangdui near Changsha was buried 16 metres below the ground, and in northern China brick-built tombs were being adopted). There are, however, many similarities including the symbolic imagery on the outside of the coffins.

Further along the path, you arrive at a collection of buildings which represent the layout of an **old fishing village**. Although there is little here which is of interest, the path goes straight through the 'village', so you have no option other than to pay the Y2 entrance fee.

The Giant Buddha

Beyond the old fishing village is the **entrance** to the enclosure around the Giant Buddha and the Lingyun Temple, and the entrance ticket is Y31. Although there are several more separate entrance fees which you can choose to pay inside, this is the last one you *have* to pay. To get to the **viewing area** above the Buddha's head, follow the path straight through the garden area. You'll know if you're about to go off track, as someone will demand more money from you to go into a side temple/path/stairway. There's no doubt that the Buddha is impressive when seen from above: the spectators' area is about level with the top of the statue's head and you suddenly realise the scale of the thing.

The Giant Buddha (Dafo), was the brainchild of the abbot of the Lingyun Temple, Master Haitong. Seeing that the lives of local boatmen were frequently being lost in the turbulent waters below the cliff, he had the idea of carving a massive stone Buddha to try to calm them. The statue was started in 713 and took 90 years to carve, with work being completed well after Haitong's death. According to the stories, Haitong's scheme was jeopardised at one stage by a jealous official who threatened to take the funds that had been raised for the statue's construction. In order to demonstrate his determination not to hand over the money, Master Haitong declared that he would rather gouge out his own eyes first. When this failed to deter the official, Haitong resolved to prove his point, and, digging out his own eyes, offered them to the official on a tray. On the clifftop near the Giant Buddha stands a statue of Haitong with his tray.

By the right hand side of the statue's head, the **Cliff Road** is a steep set of steps leading down the cliff to the statue's feet, a good angle for photographers but it will cost you a further Y10 to get down there. Once at the base of the statue, rather than try to battle against the crowds to get back up the steps you can go through a tunnel starting by the statue's left heel and winding through the cliff. It leads past two lookout points and would be a reasonably pleasant place to linger, except that it seems to have a dual function as a urinal.

Back up by the right hand side of the statue's head, there is no charge for entry to the **Lingyun Temple**. Built between 618 and 626, in the Tang Dynasty, it was rebuilt in 1667. The three magnificent statues in the first hall date from the Qing Dynasty. To the north-west of the temple, it's possible to get to the Linbao pagoda, the 38-metre-high Tang Dynasty pagoda that you can see from the waterfront in Leshan.

From the Lingyun Temple, the steps downhill take you out of the park area and back to the main road. From the gate, walk along the river bank a short distance to catch the ferry back to Leshan. The boat costs Y1, and you are expected to keep the ferry ticket for collection on the other side.

PRACTICAL INFORMATION
Orientation and services
Leshan is fairly easy to find your way around, as most of the places of interest are on or near the riverside. There is obviously more to the town than this, but once away from the river it's not especially attractive. The main shopping street is Dong Dajie, which changes name three times along its length: at the east end it's Dong Dajie, in the centre it's Yutang Jie, and towards the west it becomes Xian Jie. The **post and telecom office** is in the centre of this on Yutang Jie. Across the road is the main **bookstore** which sells good street maps of Leshan, with bus routes marked on them. Vendors on the ferry dock sell another map that's adequate

for getting around. If you've come from Emeishan, however, you may find that your Emeishan map has a plan of Leshan on the back. Finally, if you need any information or directions, the staff in the Taoyuan Hotel are helpful, and Mr Yang will assist.

Local transport
Leshan is small enough to be able to walk everywhere and the place is swarming with bicycle rickshaws, should you want one.

Tours
Mr Yang is your man for getting a tour organised. Apart from giving guided

---

LESHAN – KEY

Where to stay
1 Jiazhou Hotel
2 Taoyuan Hotel

What to see
3 Wuyou Monastery
4 Mahao Cave Tombs Display
5 Giant Buddha
6 Lingyun Temple

Where to eat
7 Mr Yang's Restaurant
8 Hudao Jie
9 Riverside Restaurants

Other
10 Boat Dock
11 Bank of China
12 Post/Telecom Office
13 Central Department Store
14 Book/Map Store

1 嘉州宾馆
2 桃源宾馆

3 乌尤寺
4 麻浩崖墓
5 乐山大佛
6 凌云禅院

7 杨家餐厅
8 乎道街 (音译)
9 江边饭店

10 轮船码头
11 中国银行
12 邮政电信大楼
13 北货大楼
14 书店 (地图店)

---

tours of the area around the Giant Buddha, he has also, in the past arranged tours to local schools, and to small villages in the surrounding countryside.

Where to stay

Two places in Leshan stand out. At the upper end of the scale, the *Jiazhou Hotel* (☎ 0833-2139888) is fairly smart and has double rooms from Y360. If nothing else they have a useful bookshop with some guide books in it. A good place for backpackers is the *Taoyuan Hotel* (☎ 0833-2134796) which is directly opposite the ferry pier. The staff are friendly, and although they say that individual travellers must pay the full price of the double room (Y60), with some friendly persuasion you will probably be able to get a single bed for Y30. Slightly confusing is the fact that the same people own the hotel next door to the Taoyuan, which is much smarter,

and where rooms start at Y240. The expensive wing (☎ 0833-2127758) has a Chinese name over the door, whereas the cheaper part has 'Taoyuan' written in English.

Where to eat

Along the river front by the Taoyuan Hotel there are lots of small restaurants with reasonably priced food.

If you have made contact with the owner, however, you will probably prefer the friendly atmosphere of *Mr Yang's Restaurant* which is at 49 Basta Lu, just west of the Jiazhou Hotel; – keep walking west along the road and the restaurant is a tiny place opposite the hospital (look for the large red cross).

Alternatively the market area around Hudao Jie has lots of small places to eat, and is a good place to try a Sichuan speciality. You buy skewers of uncooked vegetables and meats (for

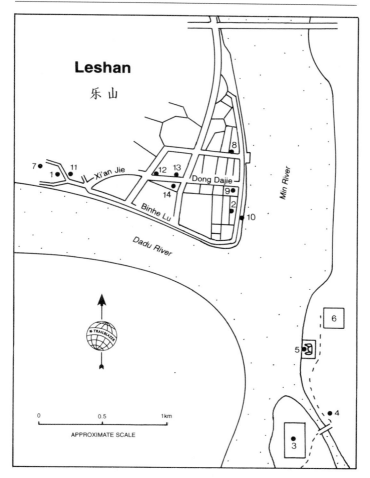

Leshan

乐山

1 jiao-5 jiao each, depending on what's on the skewer) from the stall holder, and cook them yourself in the pot of boiling spices in the centre of the table. You will probably also be charged Y2-3 for the cost of the ingredients in the pot, and the small dish of oil into which you can dip your cooked food, to cool it down before eating it.

Moving on

By rail The nearest railway station to Leshan is in Emei. Even if you're going to Kunming it's probably easiest to get a bus to Chengdu and buy your ticket there.

By bus There are public buses and minibuses going both to Emei and to

Chengdu. The fastest (and most comfortable) way to get to Chengdu is on one of the twice daily air-conditioned coaches which offer an express service, departing Leshan at 08.40 and 15.50 daily. The trip takes three hours and costs Y25. You can buy tickets from the kiosk near the ferry dock, although you should get them as early as possible the day before. Public buses, too, go regularly throughout the day, and again tickets can be bought by the ferry dock. Minibuses are always available, taking 4-5 hours and costing Y20. You'll probably be dragged into one of these anyway.

Chengdu
成都

Chengdu is one of those places, rather like Kunming, where most travellers seem to end up at some time. It's a good place to organise onward travel into Tibet and also the starting point for excursions to the national parks in the west of Sichuan province. Since many travellers want to visit both Xi'an and Kunming, Chengdu makes a welcome break in the middle of a long journey. It's also conveniently close to a number of other attractions, notably Emeishan, Leshan, and Chongqing (the start of the Three Gorges Cruise). The city itself ostensibly has plenty to see but actually many of the sights which are marked on tourist maps are rather disappointing. Nevertheless Chengdu is a good place for souvenir shopping.

HISTORY

Chengdu has a long and colourful history. It was founded during the Warring States Period (475-221BC), when the King of Shu moved his capital here from Leshan. It is said that, on founding the new capital, the king declared his intention to build it into a thriving city within three years and within a short period the city was well established. During the Qin and Han Dynasties, the Shu Kingdom was brought into the empire and Chengdu was relegated to the status of a regional capital. During the latter period (206BC-220AD) the city became famous for its production of brocade, leading to its nickname the Brocade City. Another, later nickname, Hibiscus City refers to Chengdu's mild climate; visitors today still find the street markets filled with flowers and an abundance of fruit.

With the collapse of the Han Dynasty, Chengdu became a capital city once again – this time under Liu Bei, who proclaimed himself emperor here in 220AD. Although he died two years later, the Shu state continued for some years under the direction of his son and grandson. Their reigns are recorded in the city's Wuhou Temple. Much later, in the period of turmoil following the end of the Tang Dynasty in 907, Wang Jian, who had risen to prominence as a captain in the Emperor's bodyguard, proclaimed himself emperor. Although his son succeeded him in 918, their state, the Former Shu, lasted only until 925.

With the arrival of the Mongols, Chengdu was badly damaged. It seems to have recovered fairly quickly, for during the reign of Kubilai Khan, Marco Polo visited, and was impressed by the city's opulence: 'The branch-streams within the city are crossed by stone bridges of great size and beauty. They are eight paces in width, and in length up to half-a-mile according to the width of the stream. Along the bridges on either side are fine columns of marble that support the roof; for all the bridges are covered with handsome wooden roofs richly decorated and painted in red...' Not long afterwards, in the Ming Dynasty, Chengdu was made the provincial capital. City walls and a viceroy's palace were built, although the ravages of the Cultural Revolution and of the city planners have now seen these demolished.

Chengdu today is a busy provincial capital with a surprisingly wealthy air. Like other large Chinese cities, it has the usual big hotels and city centre developments but there are still some small back streets to wander in. Among its other industrial enterprises, Chengdu is rapidly becoming known for its manufacture of furniture.

WHAT TO SEE

Baoguang Temple

Also known as the Divine Light Monastery, the temple is actually not in Chengdu at all but about 40 minutes' minibus ride outside the city. It really is worth a visit, though, for the superb sculptures. The best way to get there is to catch a minibus from in front of the station; the ride costs Y3-5, and you should ask either for the temple itself ('Baoguang Si'), or the town ('Xindu'). Entry to the temple is Y2.

The temple is thought to have been founded in the Han Dynasty, although most of the buildings you see today are much more recent – the complex was comprehensively renovated in the 17th century. In the main part of the temple the roofs are particularly ornate: on the roof of the second hall there are dragons coiled along the ridge. On the hall furthest from the entrance, statues of mythical animals are actually chained to the tiles, like tethered guard dogs. The eaves of all the buildings are exaggeratedly upturned and ornate. The real attraction, however, is off to the right hand side of the main area, where in a huge room there are 500 life-size statues of the arhats. There are other temples in China which have similar collections of sculptures: the Bamboo Temple in Kunming, and the West Garden Temple in Suzhou for instance, but that doesn't make these any less spectacular. Each statue is individually crafted of clay and stone, and covered in gold leaf. The story goes that you can discover something of your own future by finding your particular statue and reading the characteristics which are written above it. To find your statue, start anywhere you like and count along the figures the number of your age. You'll then probably have to get someone to interpret what's written on the wooden plaque. In the centre of the hall is a magnificent 100-armed Buddha. No pictures are allowed, and the strips of film hung prominently by the entrance are evidence of what happens if you try to sneak a quick snapshot. The monastery also has a pleasantly shady tea house and vegetarian restaurant.

Wenshu Temple

This place is less spectacular than Baoguang but it's an active and interesting temple in the north of the city. It's on Wenshuyuan Jie, a small side street off Renmin Beilu; there isn't a street sign but the lane is easily recognisable from the colourful stalls which line it, selling everything from incense sticks to Mahjong sets. Entry is Y1 and the place has a peaceful atmosphere, which you can enjoy to the full from the comfort of a wicker chair in the temple teahouse. Food is available here too.

Qingyang Temple

The last of the temples I'd recommend in Chengdu, Qingyang Temple is interesting because it's Taoist, rather than Buddhist. Although the temple was reputedly founded in the Tang Dynasty, the buildings that remain today date from the Qing Dynasty. In comparison with, for example, the Wenshu Temple, the halls here are extremely sparsely furnished but in the centre of the main hall there are three magnificent gold statues. The Taoist Yin/Yang symbol is seen in various places around the temple.

❑ **Taoism**

Taoism, one of the three great Chinese systems of thought, had its origins almost at the same time as Confucianism – in the 6th century BC. Sima Qian, the first great Chinese historian, records that Lao Tzu, the founder of Taoism, was an archivist at the Zhou court who instructed Confucius. According to Sima Qian's account, Lao Tzu, seeing the collapse of the dynasty to be imminent, travelled away to the west leaving behind him, on two scrolls, the great text of Taoism – the *Tao Te Ching* or *Book of the Virtuous Way*.

Taoism has it that the Way (Tao) is indescribable and is a matter of the individual finding perfect harmony with life. This harmony is actually man's natural state which has been lost over the centuries; it can only be rediscovered through intuition, rather than through intellectual pursuits. Thus there is no religious dogma, because life is unknowable. Sin does not feature in Taoism; bad behaviour is simply a sign of stupidity and ignorance, for no one would knowingly violate the natural way.

Sometime in the early history of Taoism, opinion became divided as to the proper approach to discovering the Way. One major branch of Taoism developed the principle of non action – by retreating from the world to a life of contemplation. Another branch favoured more active pursuits, with a concentration on alchemy and the search for an elixir of life.

The Tomb of Wang Jian

The tomb of this Former Shu emperor, who died in 918, is a genuinely interesting archaeological site, with only one drawback: the entrance fee. A Y2 ticket gets you into the compound but you must then pay a further Y15 to see the tomb itself (what else did you come for?).

Excavated in 1942, the tomb consists of one large chamber with six-metre thick walls, which was buried under a huge mound. In the centre of the chamber is a coffin platform, on which the emperor's remains were placed. The platform is guarded by 12 strong men, whose upper bodies only are shown, as though they are about to pick up the platform and carry it away with them. The relief sculptures around the edge of the platform depict 24 female musicians. At the far end of the chamber is a platform which represents the emperor's bed.

Sichuan University Museum

The museum was founded in 1914, and has a collection of over 40,000 artefacts. It's one of the better museums you'll see in the China, because of the thought that has obviously been put into constructing the exhibitions. Also useful are the English explanations at the beginning of each section. Four sections were open at the time of writing: Stone Carvings and Inscriptions, Ethnology, Painting and Calligraphy, and Folklore.

To get to the museum, go south-west from Jiuyianqiao Bridge, along Taiping Jie. It's about a 10 minute walk to the university entrance, and you pass 'No 12 Middle School' on your left after about five minutes. Go through the university gate (on the left of the road) and walk straight down the avenue to the small ornamental lake on the left. The museum is in the large building just behind the lake. Entry is Y10.

Sichuan Opera

Chengdu is an ideal place to experience a Sichuan Opera, and the travel service in the Traffic Hotel offers an afternoon trip to the opera for Y50. While you can easily get there yourself for considerably less, it's worth considering taking the tour for two main reasons: firstly the tour lets you go back stage (not as tacky as it sounds – it's good fun), and secondly the guide will interpret what's going on in the plot, without which the opera soon becomes three hours of colourful wailing. If you do feel like going independently, Bus 7 runs straight past the theatre, which can be found on the second floor of the building, above a furniture shop.

Panda Breeding Centre

Sichuan has the highest population of giant pandas anywhere in the world. Wolong Panda Reserve, however, is a day's bus journey away and some people are extremely disappointed when they get there; Chengdu Zoo is just plain depressing. A better option is to head for the Breeding and Research Centre just outside Chengdu. There is a tour available which costs about Y80. You can easily get to the Centre by yourself, but in the end you won't do it much more cheaply unless you choose to cycle. Take a public bus as far as the entrance to the zoo (to the north-east of the railway station) and then a moped rickshaw to the Centre, which will cost Y10-15 each way, as it's a fair way out. Entry is Y30.

In order to get the pandas to behave naturally, an environment has been created in which they can hide away. Since pandas are shy creatures, you may just visit on a day when they don't want to play. If all else fails, try looking in the Giant Panda House where they may have two or three of the animals confined. On the other hand, if you strike lucky your photographs should be excellent. One visitor found herself so close to the pandas that she thought she'd strayed into the enclosure by mistake.

Other things to see
Wuhou Temple (Temple of the Marquis of Wu) lies to the south-west of the city centre and is dedicated to Zhuge Liang, a prime minister in the Three Kingdom period. After Liu Bei seized power in 220AD, Zhuge Liang was one of several leading figures who supported the new emperor and fought for him on many occasions. All of these figures who are commemorated in the temple have become national heroes, and their exploits are recorded in the 14th century Chinese novel *The Romance of Three Kingdoms*. Zhuge Liang, who was not only prime minister but also the emperor's chief strategist, is probably the most famous of them all. The buildings you see today date from the 17th century and are no longer in use as a temple. At Y10 this is a rather overpriced tourist attraction.

The **Zhaojue Temple**, is not especially inspiring either but is an enormous and largely empty place next to Chengdu Zoo (the easiest way to get into it is through the zoo; entry to the zoo is Y3, and entry to the temple is a further Y1). It's worth a visit if you're up this way, simply because its size is impressive.

Wangjiang Park, which is to the south of Jiuyianqiao bridge, is a large place running along the side of the river, and it's dedicated to...bamboo. Entry is Y3. **Nanjiao Park** is, if anything, even less inspiring and nearby, **Du Fu's Thatched Cottage** has to be one of the biggest rip-offs in China – Y30 to see the place where this famous poet might have built his cottage 1200 years ago. By far the best of the parks in Chengdu is **Renmin Park** in the city centre. If you want to lounge with a cup of tea and a book, there's a good teahouse just inside the east gate, off Jinhe Lu. The monument to the martyrs of the Railway Protection Movement Uprising in 1911 is just inside the west gate of the park.

The **provincial museum** was undergoing work when I visited. At the time, there was only a rather disappointing display of 'Han Dynasty Pottery and Stone Carvings in Sichuan'; entry was Y2. It's worth poking your head in here to see if there have been any new developments.

PRACTICAL INFORMATION
Orientation and services

Chengdu has one of the more confusing systems of street names that you are likely to come across in China, with name changes every three or four blocks. To make matters worse there seems to be a fatal lack of communication between the people who put up the street signs and the people who make the city maps. Some of the newer maps are pretty much up to date, but if you're getting confused it can be easier simply to navigate by the street layout, rather than by the names on the signs. An excellent map (dated 1996) with English titles is available from some street vendors but it doesn't have bus routes on it, so you'll probably have to buy a Chinese map as well.

The **post office** is on the corner of Xinglong Jie and Shuwa Jie. The poste restante service (which is in the tiny 'EMS' room) is definitely not one of the better ones in China: letters are left in a cardboard box from which anyone can remove them without proof of identity. There's a **Bank of China** in front of the Jin Jiang Hotel, and **CITS** have a booking office just opposite.

Local transport

Bike hire is probably easiest to arrange at the Traffic Hotel, where they charge Y10 per day, with a Y300 deposit required. The buses are easy to work out if you have a city map; a key service is Bus 16, which runs south from the main railway station straight along Renmin Lu, passing not far from the Traffic Hotel.

Tours

As befits a major travellers' haunt, there's no end of tours on offer. You can find out what's going on from the travel agencies in and around the Traffic Hotel. Not all travellers have been happy with the tours so check with someone who's been on one before making a booking. There are also a number of private operators hanging around outside the hotel, particularly around the long distance bus station, who are trying to cash in by undercutting the travel services inside the hotel. Be careful with these guys, too, although most of them are probably bona fide.

Within the city, there are tours to the **Panda Breeding Centre**, and the **Sichuan Opera**. Further afield, you can get tickets organised for a cruise through the **Three Gorges**, -although it would be cheaper to do it yourself. Buses to Chongqing go from the long distance bus station, which is next door to the Traffic Hotel. **Jiuzhaigou National Park** is the subject of a 7-day tour, and **Wolong Panda Reserve** is also a popular destination.

For tours to Tibet see p248.

Where to stay

By the time this book appears the new *Holiday Inn* on Zongfu Lu will be open. It is unlikely, however, to displace the *Yinhe Dynasty Hotel* (☎ 028-6618888) as Chengdu's most expensive place to stay: the cheapest room here is US$118. Almost as exclusive is the *Jin Jiang Hotel* (☎ 028-5582222), which is in an older building on Renmin Nanlu; the cheapest single here is Y690, and the cheapest double is Y800.

Opposite the Jin Jiang is the *Minshan Hotel* (☎ 028-5583333), a smart four-star hotel with rooms from Y800. Next to the Holiday Inn is the *Shudu Mansion* (☎ 028-6753888), which obviously aspires to be in the league of top hotels but somehow just misses the mark. It's comparatively good value though, with doubles from Y380.

Right out on the ring road to the west, the *Jin Chuan Hotel* (☎ 028-7784938) can at least be said to be peaceful, but with the cheapest single room at Y360, there's no reason to

CHENGDU – KEY

Where to stay

1	Holiday Inn	假日酒店
2	Yinhe Dynasty Hotel	银河王朝酒店（音译）
3	Jin Jiang Hotel	锦江宾馆
4	Minshan Hotel	岷山饭店
5	Shudu Mansion	蜀都大厦
6	Jin Chuan Hotel	京川宾馆
7	Jinhe Hotel	金河大酒店
8	Chengdu Grand Hotel	成都大酒店
9	Traffic Hotel	交通饭店

What to see

10	Wenshu Temple	文殊院
11	Qingyang Temple	青羊宫
12	Tomb of Wang Jian	王建墓
13	Sichuan University Museum	四川大学博物馆
14	Wuhou Temple	武侯祠
15	Zhaojue Temple	昭觉寺
16	Chengdu Zoo	成都动物园
17	Baoguang Temple	宝光寺
18	Panda Breeding Centre	熊猫饲养中心
19	Wangjiang Park	望江公园
20	Nanjiao Park	南郊公园
21	Du Fu's Thatched Cottage	杜甫草堂
22	Culture Park	文化公园
23	Renmin Park	人民公园
24	Provincial Museum	省博物馆

Where to eat

25	Restaurants	饭馆
26	'Smart' Restaurant	高级饭馆
27	Kentucky Fried Chicken	肯塔基烤鸡店

Other

28	Main Railway Station	中心火车站
29	Sichuan Opera Theatre	川剧院
30	Post Office	邮局
31	Bank of China	中国银行

come out this far unless things are getting really desperate. Just opposite Renmin Park the *Jinhe Hotel* (☎ 028-6642888) is a vast three-star affair which was being renovated at the time of writing but which seemed reasonable value with economy rooms at Y150, and standard rooms starting at Y260. Another big hotel with prices in the same bracket is the *Chengdu Grand Hotel* (☎ 028-3333888) which is opposite the station, in the north of the city. The cheapest double rooms here are definitely worth considering, at Y188.

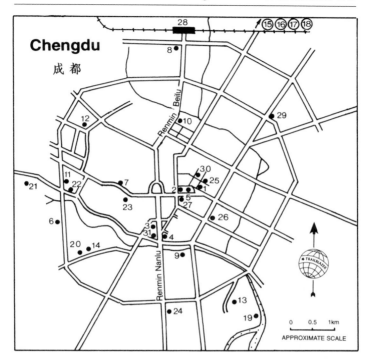

Chengdu

成都

The location is poor from a tourist's point of view, but if you're just stopping over and catching a train onwards, it couldn't be better.

By far the most popular travellers' hotel in Chengdu is the *Traffic Hotel* (or in Chinese, *Jiaotong Hotel*) (☎ 028-5551017). A bed in a very clean three-bed dormitory is Y50, and the hotel literally has everything you could ask for: English-speaking staff, currency exchange, bike hire, international phone call facilities, four travel services, and its own traveller-friendly restaurant. The only drawback about this place, in fact, is that it will shatter your illusions that you have travelled anywhere in the least bit remote: – it's a heaving mass of foreigners. Conversely of course, it's a lively place to be.

Where to eat

Sichuan food is famous for being particularly hot and spicy so take care. A good place to try local food cheaply is along the road running east-south-east from the post office, where there are a number of small restaurants. Gong Bao Ji Ding (chicken cooked with chilli and peanuts), although available all over the country, is excellent here. Chengdu is also a great place for trying street snacks (the area west of the Shudu Mansion Hotel has several snack sellers), and for fruit. For a smart meal in a local restaurant, there's a good place on the corner at the junction of Hongxin Lu and Dongda Jie.

Many travellers don't get much further than the *Flower Garden Café*, which is just outside the Traffic Hotel, and which seems to share the same kitchen with the restaurant just inside the hotel compound. The food here is good and cheap, and there's a selection of Western dishes, as well as Chinese food. There are several Kentucky Fried Chicken restaurants in the city centre. An interesting variation to normal KFC fare, is that in Sichuan they give you an extra sachet of chilli powder to go with your meal; I guess the habit of eating spicy food dies hard.

There are a couple of bars on the small road leading east from the Minshan Hotel. The *Reggae Bar* is unmistakable, as it has a large neon Eiffel Tower on the front of it, and slightly further down the road is the *Feelings Bar* which turns into a 'Boney M' sort of nightclub after about 9pm.

What to buy

If you have been despairing of ever finding a suitable souvenir, or gift for someone at home, Chengdu is the place to catch up with your shopping. There are two excellent street markets that take place in the evenings in the area of the Jin Jiang and Minshan Hotels. Along the pavement in front of the Jin Jiang Hotel, there is a large art market selling everything from calligraphy, to watercolours, fans and charcoal sketches. Opposite this, on the street around the entrance of the Minshan Hotel, there is an antiques market. It's fun for a

---

❏ **Visiting Tibet**

If Chengdu is a meeting point for travellers in Western China it is so, in large part, because it provides one of the two main access points from Central China into the autonomous region of Tibet. Sadly, the roads which run due west from Chengdu through the mountains into Tibet, are still off limits to foreigners. Although there are repeated tales of travellers who've managed to hitch lifts on trucks going this way, if you're keeping to any sort of itinerary forget about this one.

Tibet was occupied by Chinese forces in the 1950's and for some 30 years following the flight of the Dalai Lama, his retinue and several hundred thousands of other Tibetans to India, it remained closed to the outside world. Western curiosity has been fuelled, particularly in recent years, by the high profile that the Dalai Lama has taken on the world political stage. Consequently, since the Chinese started to relax travel restrictions in the mid 1980's, it has become an increasingly popular destination.

The only land route open in Tibet (from China that is), is via Xining and Golmud in Qinghai province. It's possible to get as far as Golmud on the train, after which you need to catch a bus to Lhasa. The bus journey takes 24-36 hours. Once in Tibet, Lhasa contains the most important tourist sights but there are numerous possibilities for trekking and touring elsewhere. A popular option is to head west from Lhasa, crossing the border into Nepal.

Travel to Tibet can be organised easily from Chengdu, either as a tour or as a 'budget entrance' to Lhasa, in which case you pay for the travel permit and the flight only. Two days' notice is required to get the permit organised, and the minimum price (for the permit and flight only) is Y2300. If you want to organise your onward travel into Tibet before you arrive in Chengdu, you could contact the Chengdu Tianfu International Travel Service (☎/fax 028-5543869) which is based in the courtyard of the Traffic Hotel.

browse if nothing else, but do watch your bag/wallet in the crowds. If you're going to buy anything in the markets, be hard-nosed about the bargaining, as you can probably get at least 50% off the asking price. Near the Traffic Hotel several vendors sell ethnic woven cloth and embroidery. It's uncertain how genuinely 'local' this is, and how much it's put together to meet travellers' tastes for colourful shoulder bags, but it's very attractive. Finally, Chengdu is still famous for its brocade, although you'll probably have to go to the large stores or a hotel shop to see this.

Moving on

By rail The ticket office at the railway station is huge, and despite having a window selling tickets one or two days in advance, there is no foreigners' ticket window. If you can predict your requirements three days in advance, you should put in an early appearance at the advance booking office on Dongyu Jie, in the centre of the city. Tickets go on sale here, as in other cities, three days before the day of departure, and this office is much less crowded than the ticket hall at the station. Or you can get one of the travel services in the Traffic Hotel to book your ticket. They claim their commission is Y50, but, having obtained a quote from them and then bought my own ticket, a more realistic figure seems to be Y80-90. For train times see p367-75.

By bus The long distance bus station is next to the Traffic Hotel.

By air The office in the entrance of the Traffic Hotel will quote prices but you should also try the Chengdu Coach Ticket and Air Ticket Booking Centre, just opposite the Jin Jiang Hotel.

Taiyuan
太原

Two outstanding sights, the Shuanglin Temple and the Jin Temple (100 km and 25 km outside Taiyuan, respectively), make a stop in this extremely ugly, modern city worthwhile. Since Taiyuan is expensive and there's no other reason to come here, budget travellers may choose to avoid it. If you have the time, money and stamina, however, make the effort to get to here. Who knows, after a day or two the city may even start to grow on you.

HISTORY

Although Chinese tourist literature claims that this area was first settled some one million years ago, archaeologists tend instead to point to evidence of settlement in Neolithic times (c4000-5000BC). By the Zhou Dynasty (c1100-221BC) the area belonged to the State of Jin, and remarkably, even today, Shanxi province is still sometimes known as Jin for short. The principal city, Jinyang, was founded in the area of today's Taiyuan, sometime in the Spring and Autumn Period (722-481BC). With the arrival of the Qin in 221BC the city was renamed Taiyuan, although since then it has also gone by the names of Bingzhou and Bafu. Even at this early stage the city was of considerable importance, for military reasons as much as anything else. Its prime position near the northern defences of the Empire also made it extremely vulnerable. Over the course of the following centuries the city was taken and retaken both by northern invaders and Chinese armies.

During the Sui Dynasty (581-618), Taiyuan was instrumental in the armed uprising of Li Yuan, who subsequently established the Tang Dynasty. Along with the first Tang Emperor, several subsequent emperors came from Taiyuan, so that it came to be known as the City of Dragons. During the Song Dynasty, in 979, the city was completely destroyed by fire, although accounts vary in apportioning the blame. According to some, the emperor, mindful of Taiyuan's propensity for producing new rulers, ordered the city to be burnt down. Others say the destruction was caused by yet another invasion from the north. At all events, the final blow came the following year when the ruins were flooded, washing away all trace of the city.

Despite this commendable thoroughness on someone's part, a new city was soon springing up a short distance from the old site. During the Ming Dynasty, Taiyuan prospered as a centre of trade and a strategic city. In the Qing Dynasty there was considerable anti-Manchu feeling, and the Boxer Uprising succeeded in translating this into anti-Western sentiment. On July 9 1900, Taiyuan was the scene of a particularly foul crime, as 45 Westerners, missionaries, their wives and young children, were publicly beheaded by the Boxers.

In the period after the fall of the Qing Dynasty, Taiyuan was the headquarters of the powerful northern warlord Yan Xishan. Today, it is the provincial capital and a large industrial city. Shanxi province is known as the 'Home of Coal and Iron' and the Taiyuan Iron and Steel Complex is one of the biggest in China. The province is also a centre for the chemical industry and electricity generation, providing much of the power used in Beijing. The city is laid out along the central axis of a six-lane main road, with a grey and uninspiring square as its centrepiece. The city centre is clean; but as you get further from the centre, the backstreets are drab and filthy. There is life beyond all this though, and a trip to the night market suddenly brings back the colour. As in many other places which are not really on the tourist map the people are friendly, too.

WHAT TO SEE

Shuanglin Temple

The Shuanglin Temple is approximately 100km south of Taiyuan, and it will take you at least half a day to get there and back; it shouldn't be missed, however, as it really is unique. The temple was built approximately 1400 years ago; it is now no longer functioning, but is preserved as a museum. Within the perimeter wall are 10-20 ancient buildings which are crammed with over 2000 statues made of wood and clay, many of which are from Song, Yuan, Ming and Qing Dynasties. If this sounds a bit like other places you've already seen, believe me, it isn't. The sheer number of sculptures, the detail of the work, and the setting make this the sort of place which is arresting as soon as you walk through the first gate. The halls are all wonderful, but the **Hall of the Boddhisatva** is outstanding, with a beautiful multi-armed central statue, and literally hundreds of sculptures around the walls. In other rooms the larger, life-size, statues complete with glass eyes are eerily lifelike.

The temple is near the town of Pingyao, which is on the railway line south of Taiyuan, so you could get there as an excursion from Taiyuan by train, or alternatively stop off on your way to or from Taiyuan. It's just as easy, however, to go by bus from Taiyuan long distance bus station. If you're making an early start, take the 07.20 bus (Y7.5). The journey takes just over two hours and you are likely to be dropped on the main road outside Pingyao, near a rank of motorbike/sidecar taxis. If you can bargain with these guys you're doing well, as you're something of a captive audience. The correct fare for the ten-minute ride is probably about Y5 but unless you're insistent they'll almost certainly get more out of you.

You can walk, but it's a fair way, and you'll have to keep asking for directions. Should you decide to walk, continue up the main road and after a mile or so take a farm track off to the left. The track cuts across some fields, under a railway bridge, and then down an avenue of trees, at the end of which is the temple. Entry to the temple is Y10. To catch a bus back to Taiyuan, go back to where you were dropped off and flag down the first bus or minibus to come past.

Jin Temple

This is the other place that really stands out in Taiyuan, and again it is breathtaking. The Jin Temple is situated near the source of the Jinshui River, approximately 25km southwest of Taiyuan. Work on the temple began 1500 years ago, although there have been many additions and renovations since then. What sets it apart from other similar places you will have seen is the amazing workmanship and the fact that it is all so well preserved. Unlike other famous sites, there are few signs of scuffed paint and modern additions for tourists, and the original workmanship is stunning. Every inch of the old buildings' roofs, eaves and rafters is carved or painted, and the statues inside the buildings are imposing and beautiful. Even the trees are spectacular: there are a number of huge trees here which are hundreds of years old.

The first building inside the front gate is the **Mirror Hall**, which is notable for its carved and painted eaves. The hall, which was designed to be used as a stage, is tremendously ornate. Directly behind the Mirror Hall, and having passed over the **Bridge of the Immortals**, the visitor comes to four iron warrior figures, which were cast in the 11th century. Behind them stands the **Hall of Offerings** in which offerings to the Goddess could be placed. Beyond this is the **Feiliang (Flying) Bridge**, and on the far side of the bridge (actually it's more like a terrace) stands the beautiful **Goddess Palace**. The hall, which has dragons coiled up the pillars, houses a large central statue of the Goddess and a number of smaller statues of her maid servants. To the right of the Goddess Palace is the **Zhou Cypress**, a huge old tree growing at an angle, and reputedly planted in the 12th century.

The best thing to do is simply wander around the complex – it's not too big, so you can take your time seeing everything. Try to come here in good light (ie not in the late afternoon) as it's a wonderful place to take photographs, and some of the pillared areas get quite dark later in the day. Bus No 8 runs out to the temple from the central square; the trip takes about 50 minutes and costs Y1. This bus stops by the entrance to a park, and the Y5 ticket allows you to walk through the park to the temple entrance which is on the far side. Entry to the temple itself costs Y18.

Chongshan Monastery

This old monastery is just a few streets back from Taiyuan railway station, and the peacefulness and attractiveness of the place make a wonderful change from the ugliness of modern Taiyuan. The monastery was founded in the Tang Dynasty, and was originally much larger than it is today, but many of the buildings were destroyed by fire. What remains dates from the Ming Dynasty.

The temple is tiny, and the only parts that are open to the public appear to be a small courtyard, and the main hall. The hall itself is impressive, with a high ceiling and three huge gold figures. Guanyin, the Goddess of Mercy, is in the centre with a thousand gold arms arranged in circles behind her. On either side of the hall there are display cabinets with old books, manuscripts and illustrations on show. On your way out, take a look at the huge bell and drum over the entrance: the drum in a tower on the left of the gate, and the bell in a tower on the right.

Twin Pagoda Monastery

The twin pagodas, which are in the area to the south-east of the railway station have become the symbol of Taiyuan city. The monastery was built in the Wanli Period of the Ming Dynasty (1573-1620), and the pagodas, each 13 storeys high and octagonal, are built of bricks but made to look as though they are wooden; the stonework even has carved brackets and beam ends to keep the illusion alive.

The pagodas are currently under renovation, although you can climb one of them to get a view of dirty, smoky Taiyuan. To get to the pagodas, walk south from the station along Jianshe Nanlu, and after a short distance turn left up Chaoyang Jie. After crossing a railway bridge you take the first turning on the right and walk along this road for approximately 10 minutes. Now you should be able to catch a glimpse of the pagodas to the left, and you must take a left side street, and then turn right again to get to the entrance. Entry is Y6.

Renmin Park

The park is rather plain but very extensive, so if you feel like a solitary walk, there is plenty of room. The main amusements area is to the left of the lake as you enter the park; for peace and quiet, head off to the right hand side. Entry is Y6.

Provincial Museum

Based in an old temple on the west side of the central square, the policy here seems to have been to put anything in the rooms, just as long as they were filled up somehow. The museum really isn't worth a visit.

There are four separate rooms with papercuts glued to the wallpaper, two rooms with stuffed birds and another two with boring photographs. It's a shame because in the back rooms, covered in dust, there are a few interesting statues and sculptures but they're dreadfully neglected. Entry is Y10.

PRACTICAL INFORMATION
Orientation and services

Taiyuan is an easy city to get around, mainly because it's centred on a huge road, Yingze Dajie, which runs from east to west through the middle, and which is bisected by several streets running north-south. The railway station is at the east end of Yingze Dajie, and all the hotels are spaced out along the road, as it runs westwards towards the river. The central square is about 600 metres west of the railway station and sports a single, rather plain, white statue in the middle of an otherwise bleak paved area.

The **post office** is on the corner of Yingze Dajie opposite the station, and the telecom office is on the corner of Yingze Dajie and Jiefang Lu. There is a relatively small branch of the **Bank of China** next to the large shopping centre on the corner of Yingze Dajie and Xinjian Lu. Another absolutely huge Bank of China building stands on the corner opposite. **CTS** (☎ 0351-4079165) have an office at 8 South Xinjian Rd, opposite the Shanxi Grand Hotel. The staff here are extremely co-operative and may even be able to help you get a reasonably priced room in Taiyuan. The **PSB** have offices just to the north-east of the central square, on the back street leading to the Chong-shan Monastery.

Finally, keep your eyes open for the extraordinary Gold Coast Amusements Centre which is just west of the junction of Xinjian Nanlu and Yingze Dajie. In a city full of grey high-rise blocks, this really makes you look twice. It's a replica of an ocean liner, moored up next to the pavement; the detail is there even down to the navigation lights. The city planners must have been in a mellow mood when they let this one through.

Local transport

Most of the centre of Taiyuan is walkable but the buses and minibuses are easy to get the hang of with the use of the local map. CTS may be able to think up a tour or two, but there's little point as you can easily do it all yourself.

Where to stay

If you're travelling on a low budget, prepare yourself for a frustrating time. Taiyuan simply doesn't cater for budget travellers, and the one place I found which was suitably priced was so depressing that I opted not to stay there anyway. Just accept that you're going to have to pay over the odds, and enjoy the comfort. A visit to CTS may help you to get reasonably priced room, if they 'fix' it with their friends.

At the top of the pile, the best place in town is the *Shanxi Grand Hotel* (☎ 0351-4043901), on Xinjian Nanlu. It's pleasant and smart without being deliberately flash, the staff are charming and the restaurant looks great, too. A single room here is US$70, and a double room is US$80. Slightly flashier, but cheaper, is the *Yingze Hotel* (☎ 0351-4043211), on Yingze Dajie. Rooms in the smart west building start at Y480, although there are double rooms available from Y300 in the east building.

Opposite the central square, the *Binzhou Hotel* (☎ 0351-442111), has potentially the cheapest accommodation in town. The double rooms in the basement are only Y44, and are not really for foreigners, but a little wheedling will get you in. The facilities are awful, however; a single toilet and one dirty wash basin in an unlit room are all that's provided for a complete floor. You'd be far better off paying a bit more and getting one of the pleasant double rooms upstairs, for Y140 or Y170. For any of these rooms, go to the door west of the main entrance and prepare to be persistent: they are likely to tell you there's nothing free. Once you've got past the initially stony reception, they're reasonably friendly.

Near the station there are a couple of places which may be possible. The *Jiaotong Dasha* is next to the long distance bus station, and will turn away all foreigners immediately, but with help from CTS you should be able get an adequate double room here for Y80.

East of the Jiaotong Dasha is the *Tielu Hotel* (☎ 0351-4041522) which will accept foreigners but may ask you to pay a ridiculous price just to see how you react.

Just to the north-east of the Binzhou Hotel, on the other side of Yingze Dajie, is the *Yun Shan Hotel* (☎ 0351-4041351), which claimed to have rooms from Y198, although the receptionist seemed quite willing to bargain. There are other hotels in Taiyuan, but most have starting prices in the region of Y300.

Where to eat

Noodles, I was told by the CTS staff, are Taiyuan's local speciality, and this about sets the tone for eating out in this city: you'll get food, but don't expect it to be exciting. If you plan a splurge, consider the *Shanxi Grand Hotel*, as the menu alone makes your mouth water, and the service is excellent. Apart from this, however, the next best place is probably the expensive-looking *Yingze Restaurant* on the junction of Xinjian Nanlu and Yingze Dajie. There are two cheap and friendly places just to the east of the Jiaotong Dasha (and yes, the noodles were great).

Alternatively, for the main market and snack area, go north up Jiefang Lu from where it meets Yingze Dajie. There are lots of places to eat around here including *California Beef Noodle King*, which may leave you wondering when beef noodles became so popular in California. The snack stalls are plentiful, and the local fad seems to be instant fry food: you pick your favourite snack (fish, sausage, chicken) and have it deep fried and spiced to order. If you're after nightlife, you're going to be disappointed, although there are a couple of Western bars near the front of the Yingze Hotel.

Moving on

By rail There are regular trains running both north and south from Taiyuan,

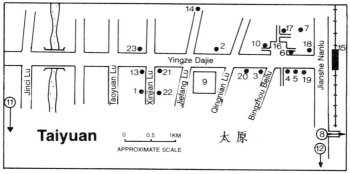

TAIYUAN – KEY

Where to stay

1	Shanxi Grand Hotel	1	山西大酒店
2	Yingze Hotel	2	迎泽宾馆
3	Binzhou Hotel	3	并州饭店
4	Jiaotong Dasha	4	交通大厦
5	Tielu Hotel	5	铁路宾馆
6	Yun Shan Hotel	6	云山饭店

What to see

7	Chongshan Monastery	7	崇善寺
8	Twin Pagoda Monastery	8	双塔寺烈士陵园
9	Renmin Park	9	人民公园
10	Provincial Museum	10	省博物馆
11	Jin Temple	11	金寺
12	Shuanglin Temple	12	双林寺

Where to eat

13	Yingze Restaurant	13	迎泽餐厅
14	Market Area	14	小吃街

Other

15	Railway Station	15	火车站
16	Central Square	16	五一广场
17	PSB	17	公安局
18	Post Office	18	邮局
19	Long Distance Bus Station	19	长途汽车客运站
20	Friendship Store	20	友谊商店
21	Bank of China	21	中国银行
22	CTS	22	中国国际旅行社
23	Bank of China/Shopping Centre	23	中国银行/购物中心

and even though there isn't a foreigners' ticket window you should have no difficulty in getting a ticket for an onward journey. Taiyuan, surprisingly, has one of the smartest station concourses you're likely to see in China, complete with little restaurants and an unusually trendy shopping area. For train times see p367-75.

By bus The long distance bus station is the place for most local connections but a private operation which might be of interest is the luxury coach service from Taiyuan to Beijing. The modern air-conditioned coaches depart from a special office on the west side of the Jiaotong Hotel, and the eight-hour trip costs Y102.

By air The airport is approximately 15km south of the city, and there are various air booking offices along Yingze Dajie.

Datong
大 同

Datong, at the centre of the major coal producing area in China, is even less prepossessing than Taiyuan but there are several impressive sights in or near the city – and a good cheap place to stay.

The most famous of the sights is the collection of Buddhist sculptures in the Yungang Caves, a set of carvings and paintings which are acknowledged as being among the finest in China. Equally worth seeing are the nearby Hanging Monastery, and the Huayan Monastery, which is to be found in the city itself.

Datong is, if possible, best visited as an excursion from, or en route to, Beijing, because sleeper tickets for the trains onwards can be hard to obtain.

HISTORY

For centuries the area in which Datong stands today has been of strategic importance. During the Han Dynasty, Pincheng, as the city was known, was used as a garrison, guarding against incursions from the north. The relics of this period, nearly two thousand years ago, can still be seen by visitors today: the Great Wall runs past Datong to the north, and the surrounding countryside is dotted with Han Dynasty watchtowers. The situation on the northern border of the Empire was volatile. In 200BC the first Han Emperor, Gaozu, led a force of 320,000 troops against the northern tribes. The expedition almost met with disaster when they found themselves surrounded, in an area only five km from present day Datong.

(Opposite) Top: The Giant Buddha at Leshan (see p236) is the largest carved stone Buddha in the world. **Bottom:** The scenic route up Emeishan (see p227), from Qingyin Pavilion via Xianfeng Temple passes through some spectacular scenery.

Following the Battle of Baideng Mountain, however, they finally managed to break out, and thereafter attempted a policy of negotiation and appeasement.

Pincheng's glory days occurred between 398-494 when the Northern Wei Dynasty adopted the city as its capital. During this period the Yungang Caves were constructed, and Pincheng became the most prosperous city in China, with a population of up to one million. Following the removal of the capital to Luoyang, however, the city descended to the level of a county seat. In the Liao and Jin Dynasties it was renamed Datong, and was awarded the status of secondary capital. It had lost none of its strategic importance; with the renewed interest in the Great Wall during the Ming Dynasty, Emperor Taizu sent one of his own sons to be the military commander. The Nine Dragon Wall which still exists in Datong was part of his palace.

Today Datong sits on the largest coalfield in China, producing one third of all the country's coal, and the area has been dubbed the Sea of Coal. This explains the drab, dirty appearance of just about everything in and around the city. You will probably notice this most if you take a public bus out to the Yungang Caves; everything you touch is covered with coal dust. Once you get outside the city limits, however, Datong is surrounded by surprisingly beautiful countryside. The city is some 1000 metres above sea level and is pleasantly cool in summer (compared to Beijing) but can get bone-chillingly cold in winter.

WHAT TO SEE

The Yungang Caves

Yungang is considered to be one the three best preserved Buddhist cave sites in China (the Mogao caves in Dunhuang, and Longmen Caves in Luoyang are often cited as being of the same magnitude). In all there are 53 carved grottoes, stretched out along nearly a kilometre of the southern face of Wuyou Hill; contained within them, according to the literature, there are 51,000 statues.

Work on the caves started under the supervision of monk Tan Yao sometime in the fifth century, after the Northern Wei adopted Datong as their capital. According to accounts of the time, the project went on over 50 years and employed some 40,000 labourers. The major effort ceased when the Northern Wei moved their capital to Luoyang (where work immediately started on the Longmen Caves). Some carving continued, however, and the statues in Cave 3 are thought to date from Sui or Tang Dynasty. Surprisingly, although the majority of the caves were carved

---

(**Opposite**) **Top:** The spectacular Yungang Caves (see opposite) where the largest of the thousands of statues is 17 metres high. **Bottom:** The Hanging Monastery (see p259) near Datong, was built on a sheer cliff to avoid being washed away by floods.

over a fairly short period, you can clearly see the development of styles between the earlier and later caves. The earlier ones have often huge but very plain carved images, whereas work in the later caves gets increasingly detailed and intricate.

The entrance to the complex is near the centre of the cliff face. The caves here are better preserved than elsewhere on the site, because of the protection afforded by the temple which stands in front of them. The first cave you come to is **Cave 6**, which is awesome. Inside the large cave, a central pillar has been sculpted to look like a wooden structure, with four pagodas sitting on top of it. Literally every square inch of wall space is carved and painted, including a series of relief carvings which run around the walls showing scenes from Buddha's life. **Cave 5**, next door, forms a pair with this; a seated buddha 17 metres high dominates the scene, with other figures in niches around the walls. To the east of these two are **Caves 1-4**, which have suffered with time and are rather worn, although **Cave 3** is impressive, and would have been the largest in the complex, had work not stopped mid-way through when the capital was moved from Datong.

To the west of Cave 6 are some more memorable sights. **Caves 7 & 8** form a pair, and although some of the statues are fairly weathered, much of the detail is still there. Particularly interesting are the ceilings, which have been carved with 'sunk panels' to make them look as though they're made of wood. Other notable features in **Cave 8** are the figures of Shiva and Vishnu riding a bull and peacock respectively, which are carved on either side of the inner archway: such evidence of Indian influence is rare.

Caves 9 & 10, again form a pair, and are notable for the wonderful painted designs on the outside of the second chamber. Although access to the inner chambers is barred, what you can see of the work inside is also well preserved. **Cave 11** has beautifully preserved paintings, and is significant for having yielded an accurate way of dating the caves; an inscription inside gives the earliest date in the whole complex – AD 483.

As you go west from here the caves get progressively earlier, and **Caves 16-20** are the earliest in the complex, having been constructed under the direct supervision of Tan Yao in the reign of He Ping (AD 460-465). The detail of these early carvings is less intricate, but the scale is huge: the main statue in **Cave 16** is a 13.5-metre-high Sakyamuni Buddha.

The caves are 16 km to the west of Datong. To get there (unless you're with a tour), take bus 7 from the area of the Yungang Guesthouse, (or Bus 2 from the railway station) to the terminal stop, and change to Bus 3. The journey from the city to the caves on this bus takes about half an hour and costs Y1; the bus will drop you outside the entrance to the cave complex. Entry to the caves is Y25.

The Hanging Monastery

Situated 75km south-east of Datong, near the small market town of **Hunyuan**, the Hanging Monastery is actually only one of several temples built on Hengshan Mountain. It is easily the best known, however, because of its precarious position. Yet again, a mad Chinese monk decided to built a place of worship in the most difficult spot he could find. Consequently we have a temple which is not so much hanging from, as clinging to, a sheer cliff face. The reasoning behind its vertigo-inspiring position is not implausible in that it's built at the top of a narrow valley prone to terrible flooding. Only by putting it so far up the cliff face could they guarantee that it wasn't going to get ruined at the next heavy rains.

The temple was built in the Northern Wei Dynasty, approximately 1400 years ago, to serve a dual purpose. Situated in a valley which frequently flooded, the temple was built to allow monks to pray on behalf of the farmers for their land to be protected. It also aimed to promote unity among China's people by symbolically combining the three main religions/philosophies: Buddhism, Confucianism and Taoism. Thus the deities portrayed inside the temple are from all three religions, and the highest hall in the structure has all three side by side on the altar: Buddha in the centre, a Taoist deity on the left and Confucius on the right.

The temple in its spectacular setting is unique and highly photogenic, a natural magnet for tourists. Entry (not included in the CITS tour price) is Y20. If you want to come out here independently you'll have to get a public bus or minibus to Hunyuan, and get a taxi to take you the last three and a half kilometres.

Wooden Pagoda

This very impressive pagoda is in the small town of **Yingxian**, which is 75km south of Datong, and only about an hour by road from the Hanging Monastery. Sixty-seven metres in height, it's the oldest and highest wooden pagoda in China, having been built in 1056. The octagonal edifice is said to have survived seven earthquakes, and a glance inside reveals why. Huge timbers have been carefully jointed to create an amazingly resilient structure, and the workmanship is impressive even to the untrained eye. There are five levels in the pagoda, three of which are open to the public. On each of these three levels there are Buddhist statues. At ground level, as you enter the pagoda there's a huge, 11-metre-high, seated statue of Sakyamuni, which is impressive in itself. Entry to the pagoda is Y12.

Minibuses (and the occasional public bus) do run between Hunyuan and Yingxian, and Datong and Yingxian. If you're planning to use public transport around here, however, do try to start as early as possible, because getting stranded in Yingxian or Hunyuan would probably mean a rather uncomfortable night. The journey back to Datong by minibus costs about Y10 and takes two and a half hours.

❑ Datong is nicknamed the **Phoenix City** because of an old legend. The people of Datong were originally very ugly. One day a hunter from the city saw a phoenix and, overcome by its beauty, decided to catch the bird. He winged it with an arrow, but when it fell to earth it turned into a beautiful woman. The huntsman married the woman, and their handsome offspring now populate Datong.

The tale of the phoenix is commemorated by the sculpture of the Phoenix which stands in the centre of the main square.

Huayan Monastery

This monastery, which belongs to the Huayan Sect of Buddhism, really shouldn't be missed.

Originally built in the middle of the eleventh century, most of the monastery buildings were destroyed soon after completion, during a war in 1122. Rebuilding commenced in 1140, and the enormous **Main Buddha Hall**, dates from this period. In the Ming Dynasty the monastery was divided into upper and lower halves, and this still applies today, unfortunately leading to two separate entrance fees. The temple is at the end of Shangshi Beixiang, a tiny lane leading south off Da Xijie.

As you come into the courtyard, the gate to the Upper Monastery is on your right. The huge Main Buddha Hall is the furthest building from the entrance. Reputed to be one of the two biggest Buddhist halls in China, it's raised on a high stone platform; the ancient weather-beaten exterior, and enormous studded wooden doors set the scene before the visitor even enters. Inside, the flag-stoned hall is literally a treasure trove. Five huge seated buddhas face the doors (which unusually for a Buddhist temple are facing east), and on either side of the hall are 10 standing attendants, leaning forward with their palms pressed together. Around the walls is a huge fresco, repainted in the Qing Dynasty, which covers some 887 square metres. Although the light is too dim to see it in detail, the parts nearest the door are the most visible and are spectacular. The ceiling is tremendously ornate and beautiful, with carved and painted panels.

In the Lower Monastery, the gate to which is across on the other side of the entrance courtyard, the main building of interest is the **Bhagavan Stack-Hall,** which is where the Buddhist sutras were kept. The hall was built in 1038 and was one of the few which survived the mass destruction in 1122. The whole place is incredibly dusty but the sculptures make the visit worthwhile. 29 golden figures fill the front of the hall: three large seated Buddhas and a number of attendants standing and seated around them. Around the walls, the scripture storage cabinets can still be seen. Entry to each half of the monastery is Y8.

Shanhua Monastery

The Shanhua Monastery, commonly known as the Southern Monastery, is less interesting than the Huayan Monastery but is worth a visit if you have time. Originally built in the Tang Dynasty, it was destroyed, along with pretty much everything else in 1122. It was rebuilt under the direction of monk Yuanman in the years that followed, and was subsequently renovated during the Ming Dynasty. Situated just off Nanmen Jie, at the south edge of the old city, the entrance gate faces towards some relatively intact remnants of the old city walls.

Inside the monastery, the front hall contains massive statues of the four generals. Behind that, the **Sansheng (Three Saints) Hall** has three huge seated statues, of Losana, Manjusri and Samantabhadra: the centre statue being gold coloured, and the ones on either side, painted. On the left inside the hall is a stone tablet 800 years old; the inscription, written by Song Dynasty scholar Zhu Bian, records the history of the monastery. The main hall was under renovation at the time of writing but is reputed to contain some wonderful statues. To the left (west) of the central area of the temple is a rather overgrown garden, where there is a smaller version of the famous Nine Dragon Screen. This one has only five dragons but otherwise it looks identical. Entry to the temple is Y12.

> ❏ **The Datong locomotive factory and steam engine museum**
> The factory was the last place in China to make steam locomotives. Between its foundation in 1959 and the end of 1988 when production of steam engines was stopped, the factory turned out 5572 steam locomotives. It now produces electric and diesel engines, and although steam is slowly being phased out on China's railways, many of the steam engines built here are still in operation in freight yards around the country. The most notable engine built here was the **QJ**, and most travellers touring China by train are likely to see at least a couple of these enormous locomotives at work somewhere along the way.
>
> There's plenty to look at, from watching axles being hammered out in the foundry, through seeing large sections being pieced together, and finally the production of the engines themselves. Part of the interest is just seeing how a Chinese factory works: pay incentive schemes are chalked up for the team that proves to be the most productive over the course of the month. The foundry area is good for photographs if you have fast film in your camera.
>
> The **Steam Engine Museum** is actually rather sad; there are some historic locomotives here but they are neglected and all rather rusty and peeling. Among the engines on show is the Type 0, reputedly the first steam engine to be imported into China, in 1882. There have been suggestions that this British-made engine was used to pull Empress Dowager CiXi's state carriage (which is on display here) although this seems unlikely. There are also examples of the engines made in Datong.
>
> You'll have to arrange a tour here through CITS giving them at least a day's notice. At about Y100 it's not too costly, however, if you can get a group of people together, and the English-speaking guide is invaluable.

The Nine Dragon Screen
The screen, originally built in 1392, is all that remains of the palace that was put up for Prince Zhu Guidai. It is, according to the tourist literature, 'The oldest and largest of its kind in China', and as such it has become

one of Datong's recognised tourist sights. To the uninitiated it really isn't worth the time or money, however. You are likely to see ceramic tiles in designs elsewhere (inside the Shanhua Temple, for one place), and realistically that's all you get here: a longish stretch of wall with some tiled dragons on it. Entry is Y6.

Datong Park
Datong Park is nothing special, but in comparison to the rest of Datong, it actually seems quite pretty. If nothing else it's a pleasant place to have a walk and watch the locals crashing the pedal boats on the boating pond. Entry is Y0.5.

DATONG – KEY

Where to stay
1 Datong Guesthouse	1 大同宾馆
2 Yungang Guesthouse	2 云冈宾馆
3 Feitian Hotel	3 飞天宾馆
4 Police Hotel	4 武警宾馆 (意译)

What to see
5 Yungang Caves	5 云冈石窟
6 Hanging Monastery	6 悬空寺
7 Wooden Pagoda	7 释迦寺
8 Huayan Monastery	8 华严寺
9 Shanhua Monastery	9 善化寺
10 Nine Dragon Screen	10 九龙壁
11 Datong Park	11 大同公园
12 Drum Tower	12 古楼

Where to eat
| 13 Tianhe Guesthouse | 13 天河宾馆 (音译) |

Other
14 Railway Station	14 火车站
15 Main Post/Telecom Office	15 邮电大楼
16 Central Square	16 红旗广场
17 Bank of China	17 中国银行

PRACTICAL INFORMATION
Orientation and services
The old city of Datong was square in shape and surrounded by large earthen fortifications. There was a main gate in the centre of each wall, and a road leading from each gate to a crossroads at the centre of the city. This layout (including sections of the old mud walls) is still clearly visible today, and the shape of the old city is marked on most tourist maps.

The railway station lies outside the old city walls to the north, and the main street in Datong, Caochangcheng Jie, runs straight north-south from the sta-

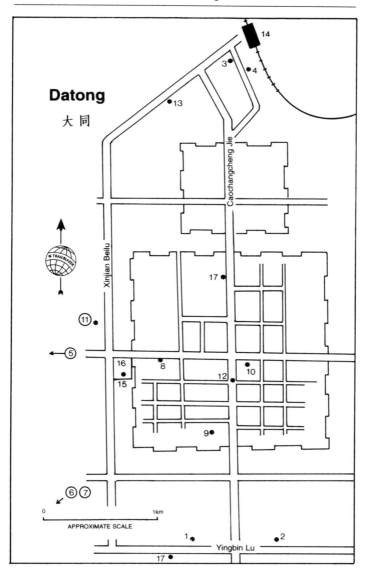

Datong

大同

Caochangcheng Jie

Xinjian Beilu

● 14

3 ● ●4

● 13

17 ●

⑪ ●

◄─⑤

16
●
15

● 8

12 ● ● 10

9 ●

⑥⑦

0   1km

APPROXIMATE SCALE

1 ●   ● 2

Yingbin Lu

17 ●

tion through the centre of the old city. On its way southwards, the street changes names, becoming Nanmen Jie and then Nanguan Jie, in the south. The two main tourist hotels in the city, the Yungang Guesthouse and Datong Guesthouse, are in this area. Mid-way through the old city Caochangcheng Jie is cut by Da Xijie, which runs straight east-west. Most of the tourist sights within the city are around the area of this central junction. The focal point of the modern city, the main square is to the west of the junction.

The main **post and telecom office** is in a huge building on the south side of the main square, and there is a sub branch near the railway station. The **Bank of China** has its main branch in the south of the city opposite the Datong Guesthouse, and there is another large branch under construction just to the north of the central junction.

CITS have two offices: their headquarters is in the grounds of the Yungang Guesthouse but they also have a more convenient office at the station (☎ 0352-5024176). Datong is the only city in China where the CITS will actively come and find you. From the office at the station you can collect an excellent free map of Datong, with all the tourist sights marked, and the staff here will also help you to get accommodation.

Local transport
The public buses around the city are good. Bus 15 runs from the station to the area of the Datong and Yungang guest-houses.

Tours
CITS have the tour business tied up, and no matter how independent you like to be, it really is worth considering one or more of their tours. The ideal would be a one-day tour to include the Hanging Monastery and the Wooden Pagoda since both are difficult to get to

by public transport. They tend, however, to run a daily tour to the Hanging Monastery in the morning and the Caves in the afternoon at a cost of Y100 per person. The guides speak good English and a huge lunch is thrown in, so most people feel that they've got their money's worth.

If you want to combine the monastery and the pagoda you could offer to pay half-price for a ride out to the monastery only. If the CITS minibus drops you at the local bus station in Hunyuan on the way back from the monastery, it's possible to make your own way back to Datong via the pagoda. The only problem with this is that you are at the mercy of the local bus services, and although you should have plenty of time to get back to Datong, you might just find yourself spending the night in Yingxian.

Other tours which CITS offer include trips to the Great Wall in the north, and to Mount Wutaishan, a holy mountain approximately a day's bus journey south of Datong. Their tour of the Datong Locomotive Factory and Steam Locomotive Museum costs about Y100 each for three people (see p261).

Where to stay
The choice of places to stay in Datong is limited, but all budgets are catered for.

The two largest hotels which take foreigners are in the south of the city. The *Datong Guesthouse* (☎ 0352-2032476) is a large but rather characterless place with double rooms from Y308, and beds in a four-bedded dormitory for Y80 each. Although this is expensive for dormitory accommodation, the rooms are very smart with private bathrooms and plenty of space.

A short distance down the road, the *Yungang Guesthouse* (☎ 0352-5021601) has more of a buzz to it and is more popular with foreign tourists. The double rooms are more expensive, starting at Y400, but the three-bedded dormitory rooms in the building by the front gate are excellent, and a bed here is only Y40.

The other two places that are open to tourists are near to the railway station. The **Feitian Hotel** is the large white-tiled building directly on the left as you exit the station itself. CITS will get you a double room here for Y180, and claim that without their help the same room would cost Y220; you can check this out yourself.

The other place near the station is not acknowledged by CITS, and the name isn't clear. It appears to be called something like the **Police Hotel** (☎ 0352-6033892) and was highly recommended by those who were staying there. As you leave the station building, turn left, walk past the ticket office and along a small lane (leaving the Feitian Hotel on the right). The hotel is about 300 metres down the lane on the left hand side, in a low white-tiled building; look for the restaurant which is next door. It's a friendly place, and a double here is Y160.

Where to eat

Tourists staying in the Yungang Guesthouse tend to eat in one of the two or three restaurants that are directly across the road from the hotel gates, all of which have English menus and reasonable prices. Apart from these Datong is not a great place for restaurants, although the one at the **Tianhe Guesthouse** on Xinjian Beilu is worth trying. Another good spot, particularly if you're staying near the railway station, is the small restaurant next to the 'Police Hotel'. The food here is excellent, the place is quite amazingly clean and the staff are fun.

What to buy

You might find something at the stalls near the car park at the Hanging Monastery or you could buy your own

railway cap badge from the railway museum but Datong is not the ideal place for souvenir-hunting.

Moving on

By rail Datong, for some reason is one of the most frustrating places in China to get hold of a train ticket. According to CITS the following rules apply:

1. CITS, and therefore foreign tourists, get only eight sleeper tickets in total per day out of Datong.

2. No tickets are available for sale in Datong until the day of travel itself.

3. The ticket office at the railway station will only sell Hard Seat tickets.

Either you can get CITS to buy your tickets for you (and they will probably not confirm them until the day of travel), or you can buy your own Hard Seat tickets on the morning of the day you are due to leave. Hence the advice earlier in the chapter, that Datong is best visited when you're en route to Beijing, or possibly Taiyuan, as both cities are only eight hours away, and Hard Seat tickets are easy to come by. For train times see p367-75.

By bus Another CITS story is that foreigners are not permitted to use the long distance buses and minibuses operating in and out of Datong. A cynic might suggest that this is so that CITS can corner the market for train tickets, but who knows? The only place you are likely to want to catch a bus to around here is Wutaishan, and as a precaution it might be easier to get a bus from Taiyuan instead, there being no restrictions there. I caught a minibus from Yingxian into Datong without any problems at all, so it's definitely worth a try, though perhaps you should keep a low profile when you do.

By air Again according to CITS, the airport was closed for repairs at the time of writing, although they inferred that it would be open 'soon'.

PART 7: THE NORTH-EAST

Harbin to Beijing

This route crosses the vast flat plains of Manchuria running over 1200 kilometres along the route of the old South Manchurian Railway, towards Vladivostok and the border with Russia. This is the area where the Qing dynasty, or Manchus, came from: a wasteland outside the protection of the Great Wall, as far as generations of Chinese were concerned.

The area consists of a huge central plain which, despite its fertile soils, remained largely unsettled until the early twentieth century. The reasons for this scarcity of population were simply that the area was populated by tribes who were enemies to the Han Chinese. After their accession to power in 1644 the Qing emperors deliberately preserved their homeland from settlement. This policy was reversed at the turn of the present century when fears started to grow about the encroachment of both the Russians and then more particularly the Japanese. Suddenly Manchuria was not only opened up but migration of peasant families to claim land in the great north-eastern plains was actively encouraged.

The advent of intensive agriculture made the north-east a valuable area of food production but, just as importantly, it became apparent that there were vast mineral reserves in Manchuria. Political manoeuvring started in the late nineteenth century, and within the next 50 years both Russia and Japan had occupied the north-east and fought to keep hold of it. For over ten years in the 1930's and early 1940's, Manchuria was officially called Manchukuo and was the puppet regime of the Japanese. In order to give the military occupation a veneer of respectability, the last Qing ruler, Henry Puyi, was installed as a 'puppet emperor'.

Finally, Manchuria was the scene of the great showdown between the Nationalist forces of Chiang Kaishek and the People's Liberation Army in 1948 and 1949. Since then, Manchuria has become a power house of Chinese industry – there are large oilfields north of Harbin, major steelworks in Anshan, huge port facilities at Dalian, and a multitude of other industries.

North-east China sees few tourists – in comparison to the rest of China, at least. The reason for this is simple: since Manchuria remained thinly populated until about 100 years ago, there simply isn't the wealth of historical sites that one finds elsewhere in China. It is, however, a fascinating area for those with an interest in the history of the railways. Manchuria was a prime target for 'railway colonialism', and as well as being home to one of two railway museums in China (Shenyang), the North-East contains the majority of working steam locomotives in China. Equally, if you're prepared to spend a bit of time getting outside the large cities, you can visit two of the largest nature reserves in the country.

Unfortunately accommodation in all the major cities listed in this section is very expensive. Hotels in Harbin, Changchun and Shenyang cater for business travellers rather than tourists. Accommodation is much more reasonable, however, in Shanhaiguan and Beidahe, both of which make excellent excursions from Beijing.

HARBIN TO CHANGCHUN
[242km, 4hrs]

The railway itself, now named the **Jing Ha line**, is steeped in history. Built originally as a branch line from the Chinese Eastern Railway (the Trans-Manchurian), this stretch of railway was instrumental in the Russian annexation of Port Arthur (now called Lushun). In order to present the Chinese government with a fait accompli, the Russians built the railway first, and then moved their fleet into the harbour. Only after both of these moves were complete did they start negotiations to 'lease' the port itself.

In 1905, at the end of the Russo-Japanese war, the Japanese took over the lower section of the line (south of Changchun) and renamed it the South Manchurian Railway. Conversion to standard gauge, provision of new equipment and extension of the existing lines subsequently took place. Japanese investment in the railways was, exactly as Russian investment had been, only a means to an end. The railways were the key to con-

MAP 17

HARBIN

Wanggan

Wujia

HEILONGJIANG PROVINCE

Cajiagou

Sangahe

Taolaizhou

Dajiagou

JILIN PROVINCE   Dehui

Buhai

Wopi

CHANGCHUN

Datun

Fanjiatun

Gongzhuling

Siping

Shungmaji

LIAONING PROVINCE

Changtu

Caiyuan

N

0   10km

Tieling

MAP 18

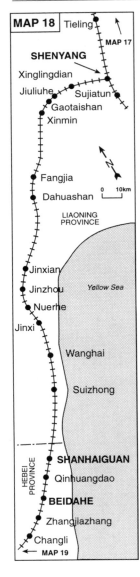

MAP 18 | Tieling
MAP 17
SHENYANG
Xinglingdian
Jiuliuhe   Sujiatun
Gaotaishan
Xinmin
Fangjia
Dahuashan   0   10km
LIAONING
PROVINCE
Jinxian
Jinzhou   Yellow Sea
Nuerhe
Jinxi
Wanghai
Suizhong
SHANHAIGUAN
HEBEI PROVINCE
Qinhuangdao
BEIDAHE
Zhangjiazhang
Changli
← MAP 19

trolling the whole of Manchuria, and provided the means to support an advance into northern and central China.

Unfortunately, although the history of this area and its railways is eventful, the scenery along this route is rather less exciting. Manchuria is really just one vast flat plain.

Km 242: Harbin For information on the provincial capital of Heilongjiang province, see p271. From here, as the line runs south-west, the kilometre markers count down towards Changchun, and are on the right of the track.

Km 163: Cajiagou Shortly before arriving at this station, the train crosses into Jilin province.

Km 115: The train crosses a large tributary of the Songhua River.

Km 0: Changchun Changchun, under the name Hsinking was the capital of the Japanese puppet state of Manchukuo. For more information see p277.

CHANGCHUN TO SHENYANG
[305 km, 5hrs]

Km 705: Changchun From Changchun the km markers start again at Km705, counting down towards Dalian on the coast (a scale on which Shenyang is at Km400).

Changchun was the point where the Russian-controlled branch of the Chinese Eastern Railway met the Japanese-administered South Manchurian Railway. Because of the difference in rail gauge, all passengers had to change trains. The *Imperial Japanese Government Railways Guide to East Asia*, published in 1913, reminded its readers to change their watches here: 'the Russian railway time being 23 minutes earlier than the Japanese'.

Km 584: Siping The line crosses into Liaoning province.

Km 403: Some three kilometres north-east of Shenyang is the spot where, on September 18th 1931, a bomb exploded in front of a Japanese train as it approached the city. It is now fairly commonly accepted that the bomb was planted by the Japanese themselves. Citing the need to guarantee greater security to their railway and possessions, they immediately began to annex Manchuria, and declared the state of Manchukuo in March 1932.

Km 400: Shenyang **Shenyang North** railway station is a huge modern place which is the main station for the city. **Shenyang**, confusingly, is the older, green domed station, four kilometres further down the line. If you are planning to stay at the Zhong Xing Hotel, get out at the latter. Check with the railway staff to see whether the train is due to stop at both stations. See p283.

❏ The intrepid Harold Rattenbury (*China-Burma Vagabond*), travelling in 1939, records his memories of a train journey in northern China thus: 'Our second class carriage was full of Japanese commercial travellers and other Japanese civilians. We noticed them comparing their samples of the goods with which their portmanteaux were stuffed. There were no Chinese at all in our carriage. They were only permitted to travel third, which was described as "coolie class"...The first class was reserved, as usual, for high Japanese officers and officials. The whole service was, of course, run by the Japanese. We'd to show our passports on the train, but there was neither difficulty nor delay. We were classed, I suppose, as belonging to the superior nations grade, along with the Japanese'.

SHENYANG TO SHANHAIGUAN [425 km, 6-9hrs]

Kilometre markers are on the left of the track and count upwards from zero as you leave Shenyang.

Km 0: Shenyang There are usually several steam locomotives at work just beyond the railway station.

Km 242: Jinzhou From here onwards the railway follows the coastline, although for many miles the sea itself is just out of sight.

Km 425: Shanhaiguan Shanhaiguan – the traditional eastern entrance to the Central Kingdom, via the First Pass Under Heaven. If you look to the right of the train on the final approach to Shanhaiguan you should be able to see the **Great Wall** as it disappears into the mountains. See p289.

SHANHAIGUAN TO BEIJING [315 km, 5hrs]

The route from Shanhaiguan to Beijing goes via Beidahe (see p295). Kilometre numbering initially continues counting down from Km425, although the train changes lines when it gets nearer to Beijing.

Trains either go via Tianjin, or head directly west towards Beijing in a straight line from Beidahe and Qinhuangdao. This more direct route is described below. There are several things to look out for, although the scenery, it has to be said, is rather dull.

Km 425: Shanhaiguan As the train leaves Shanhaiguan it crosses into Hebei province.

Km 387: Beidahe For more information about this beach resort see p295.

Km 321: Lan Xian Just past Lan Xian is the parting of the ways: trains going via Tianjin head south-west, while those bound directly for Beijing go due west. The area through which the train is passing is really the 'cradle' of China's railways. If you're on the southern line (to Tianjin) you will pass through Kaiping station. This stretch of line was the first to be laid (and remain laid) in China, and the first locomotive to run along it was CW Kinder's home-made *Chinese Rocket* (see p66).

Near Lan Xian station, the railway crosses the Lan River. Writing in 1907, PH Kent (*Railway Enterprise in China*) noted that 'the bridge over the Lan Ho...is the most notable piece of engineering to be found throughout the length of [the railways], representing the first attempt on a large scale to bridge a Chinese river'.

Km 291/153: Just to the west of Langwopu the lines divide and the kilometre markers (still on the right) are now counting down towards Beijing.

This area, which is only a few kilometres north of the city of Tangshan, was devastated by an earthquake on 28th July 1976. The epicentre was in Tangshan itself and the city was flattened. The official death toll stands at 150,000, but it was probably as high as 750,000.

Km 0: Beijing As the train approaches Beijing the km markers become almost impossible to follow. For the Beijing city guide, see p72.

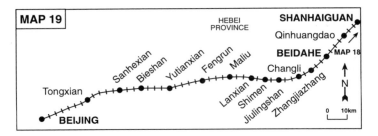

Harbin
哈尔滨

Harbin, over 1000 km east of Beijing and the closest large city to the Russian border, has a unique feel to it. Old Russian houses still grace the streets in some districts, and Western faces are common as shopping in China is popular with the Russians who live just across the border. Indeed, just when you thought you were getting to grips with a bit of Chinese vocabulary, some people may start addressing you in Russian.

Harbin is an expensive place to stay, and the city centre is ugly, but it's a pleasant place to visit, particularly in the summer, when it is relatively cool compared to central China. According to one Chinese oil worker I met, the winters are so bitter up here, and hence the area has become so unpopular to work in, that a bonus scheme operates for employees. There's certainly an affluent feel to Harbin, and the main pedestrian shopping road in the north-east of the city has a distinctly European character, with expensive boutiques alongside street market stalls. Rather like Urümqi, or Kunming, Harbin seems to be more relaxed and cosmopolitan than its central Chinese counterparts; somehow whatever Beijing may be up to, one imagines that life in Harbin continues pretty much at its own pace.

Even though it's so far east, like the rest of the country Harbin operates on Beijing Time; it gets light early in the morning while evenings are short.

HISTORY

Harbin was established at the turn of the century, as a direct result of the railways. In 1897, when there was only a small fishing village on today's site, it was chosen as a base by the Russian engineers of the new Chinese Eastern Railway, which was to connect the Trans-Siberian line with Vladivostok. Harbin became not only the depot for the railway builders, but also the junction for the branch line that was soon running south-west towards Port Arthur (which was 'leased' from the Chinese in 1898). The city sprang up at an amazing speed, although it was some considerable time before it lost its frontier feel. The Hon Maurice Baring visited Harbin in 1904, expecting to find a modern industrial metropolis but judging by the tone of his comments was not impressed: 'Harbin is now called the Chicago of the East. This is not a compliment to Chicago'. In 1905 during the Russo-Japanese war Harbin boomed as a Japanese supply base, reaching a population of over 100,000. Although there was a subsequent decline, growth started again after the First World War. The population increased eightfold from 1911-1930, partly as a result of Harbin's being opened to foreign trade in 1905. The other and equally important reason for the boom was the arrival, after 1917, of large numbers of White Russians who fled across the border after the Russian Revolution; at one stage Harbin had the largest Russian population of any city in the world outside the Soviet Union.

Russian motives for building the Trans-Siberian had been economic as well as political, and while the rail link fulfilled its promise of greater trade, it also made Harbin unique in China. The new rail route cut the journey from Europe to China to some 10 to 14 days, compared with a month by sea, and hence fashions, newspapers, and music arrived in Harbin before they made it to the rest of China. Harbin became a cross between a frontier trading town and an unusually cosmopolitan city. Peter Fleming noted his stay here in 1934 in his diary (which was subsequently published as the travelogue *A Forgotten Journey*):

'**Nov 17** In the end we had a pretty late party, dining at the American Bar and getting to bed via the Fantasia at 5am...In the American Bar was a large party of American consulars, very dashing in their pince-nez; an aloof but sufficiently British vice consul and his wife, he being an ex president of the Oxford Union to whom no doubt I was rude in my day; one coarse Japanese getting tight on beer; one intellectual Chinese in an Edwardian stiff collar, very ridiculous; many sordid white Russians; dashing and beautiful girls dancing unhappily with this and that... **Nov 18** A typical Harbin man deduced that I was a correspondent; finally insisted on giving me his name, written on a piece of paper with the word "drunk" written after it. The only Russian in Harbin with a sense of humour.'

With the proclamation of Manchukuo in 1932, Harbin was renamed Pinkiang although many people continued to use the city's old name. In 1945-6 it briefly came under Russian control again.

Harbin today is the capital of Heilongjiang province and is a large modern city with a population of somewhere around two and a half million. Despite the occasional Russian-style building, the city centre is predominantly modern and is centred round the massive main thoroughfare, Zhongshan Lu. The station is huge, and the size of the railway marshalling yards which stretch through the middle of the city should also leave you in no doubt of Harbin's industrial importance. Just up the line from Harbin is Daqing, the centre of the Chinese oil industry.

Harbin is touristically undistinguished until the winter when it hosts the largest and most famous **Ice Festival** in China. In January each year, the frozen river is turned into a carnival ground, and ice sculptures, many with lanterns built in to them, are the main attraction. The festival draws tourists from all around China and beyond; you must be prepared for the cold: temperatures can easily fall below minus 20° C in mid-winter.

WHAT TO SEE

Steam locomotive yard

This is a chance to explore and take as many photos as you like in one of the last working steam yards in the world. The staff of the yard seemed unbothered by my presence and having met me at the gates, took my money and told me I had an hour to look around, without any (apparent) supervision. If you want a guided tour of a working steam yard, however, it would be better to wait until Shenyang (see p285).

Although this is a rare opportunity, a visit can be expensive to organise. At CITS I was told it would cost Y500 for up to five people, and Y100 for every individual after that. When I said I couldn't afford Y500 just for myself, the price dropped to Y300, and then Y200. In the end, the staff at the yard didn't seem to mind how much money was involved.

Sun Island Park

The park is a nice place for a stroll, and involves a boat trip across the river, and a wander through a pleasant area of old, and imitation, Russian-style houses. It's Harbin's newest addition to the leisure scene, and apart from the usual boating lakes etc, it also has a small water slides enclosure, and various other amusements. Entry to the park is Y3, and the ferry across the river, which departs from the area of the monument on the river front, costs Y1 each way.

Market areas

The markets in Harbin are rather different from many other markets in China, and fun to wander in. Possibly it's the proximity of Russia, and the Russian-style foods and goods on sale, (dried sausage, for example), or the fact that, so far from central China, the mood is simply mellower. Two areas in particular are worth a look. The market to the north of the Heping Cun Hotel is mostly devoted to food, and is a good place to see some of the local fare on offer. By far the best is the area of Zhongyang Lu (Central St). Here the side streets are crammed with market stalls, while the shops on Zhongyang Lu itself are filled with designer names in clothes, jewellery and other goods. A small part of Harbin's cosmopolitan ambience has been preserved; the pedestrianised street has a European atmosphere, and there's even a croissant shop off to one side.

Parks

Harbin's parks are extremely well maintained. The **Children's Park** near the centre of town boasts a small railway which is run by the children themselves; it is also notable for its colourful flower beds – anywhere else in China these would be empty. In the centre of the park there are a number of concrete ping-pong tables, where the locals get serious over one of their national sports. In the north of the city, near the river, the **Zhaolin Park** is equally well-kept and attractive, and, overlooked as it is by a number of old-style buildings, it has something of the atmosphere of a leafy park in a European city. Perhaps the best area to sit and watch the world go by, in summer at least, is along the **river front**, to the south-west of the memorial. The paths along the river turn into promenades at weekends especially, and there is a relaxed atmosphere as families take a Sunday stroll together.

Provincial Museum

There are only two exhibitions, one of which consists of three dinosaur skeletons and several rooms full of stuffed animals. The rest of the museum is given over to the Heilongjiang Historical Relics Exhibition.The museum is distinctly overpriced at Y20 and not really worth a visit.

HARBIN – KEY

Where to stay

1	New World Beifang Hotel	1 新世界北方酒店
2	Holiday Inn	2 万达假日酒店
3	Zhong Da Hotel	3 中大宾馆 (音译)
4	Gloria Inn	4 凯莱酒店
5	Modern Hotel	5 现代宾馆
6	Swan Hotel	6 天鹅饭店
7	Heping Cun Hotel	7 和平屯宾馆
8	Aviation Hotel	8 民航大厦
9	Longmen Hotel	9 龙门宾馆 (音译)
10	Tianzhu Hotel	10 天竹宾馆
11	Beiyuan Hotel	11 北苑饭店

What to see

12	Steam Locomotive Yard	12 蒸汽机车场
13	Sun Island Park	13 太阳岛公园
14	Children's Park	14 儿童公园
15	Zhaolin Park	15 兆麟公园
16	Provincial Museum	16 省博物馆

Where to eat

17	Expensive Restaurants	17 高档餐厅
18	Food Stalls	18 小食摊
19	Paris Bakery and Cheap Restaurants	19 巴黎烤面包和便宜饭馆
20	Kentucky Fried Chicken	20 肯塔基烤鸡店

Other

21	Railway Station	21 火车站
22	Main Post Office	22 中心邮局
23	Bank of China	23 中国银行
24	Telecom Office	24 邮电大楼

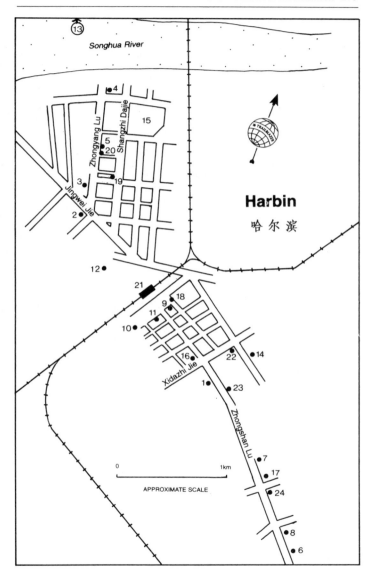

PRACTICAL INFORMATION
Orientation and services
The city is bounded to the north and west by the Songhua River, the site of the famous Ice Festival. The railway station is near the city centre, and running south-east from it is the main street, Zhongshan Lu. The hotels tend to lie either along Zhongshan Lu, or to the north-west of the station along Zhongyang Lu, also known as Central St, the main shopping area and the road running up to the river.

There's a **small post office** on the east side of the station, while the **main post office** is just a block east of the roundabout on Zhongshan Lu; and the main **telecom office** is about one and a half kilometres down Zhongshan Lu from the station. The main branch of the **Bank of China** is also on Zhongshan Lu, about three quarters of a kilometre south-east of the station.

CITS have their office in the compound of the Swan Hotel in Building B behind the hotel. The **CAAC** have an office next door to the Aviation Hotel.

Local transport
The public bus service is good, and many of the buses start from stands opposite the station. Unfortunately, the bus routes printed on the city maps seem to be inaccurate in some places, so a small amount of lateral thinking is required; check your destination with the conductor. Buses 21 and 103 head straight south-east along Zhongshan Lu, to the Swan Hotel and CITS.

Tours
CITS organise visits to the steam locomotive yard (see p273).

Where to stay
Harbin boasts a number of high quality hotels, among the best of which is the *New World Beifang Hotel* (☎ 0451-3628888), just off Zhongshan Lu, where the cheapest double rooms are US$58 and suites start at US$102.

In the same price bracket, the newly opened *Holiday Inn* (☎ 0451-4226666) had, at the time of writing, an opening promotion with standard twin rooms from Y468. A short way up Zhongyang Lu, the *Zhong Da Hotel* (☎ 0451-4638888) has doubles from Y488, but you'd probably be better off at the Holiday Inn for the same price.

Right next to the river, the *Gloria Inn* (☎ 0451-4638855) has just opened its doors, and has double rooms from Y399 (although this price may rise when it gets established). If you've got the money, this would be a good place to stay when visiting the Ice Festival. Another good option in this part of town is the *Modern Hotel* (☎ 0451-4615846). Situated about mid-way down Zhongyang Lu, the hotel first opened in 1906, and although much of the original interior has gone, it still retains some of its atmosphere. Double rooms here start at Y230.

On the other side of the railway lines, at the south side of town, the *Swan Hotel* (☎ 0451-2300201) is a smart place which unfortunately is a long way from anything else you're likely to want to see. Double rooms here start at Y450. Just up the road to the north, however, the *Heping Cun Hotel* (☎ 0451-2620101) is much better value; it's an up-market hotel where a clean triple room with a private bathroom costs Y262. In this area there is also the *Aviation Hotel* which is fine but over priced and serves best as a landmark for the CAAC office.

Near the station there are several cheaper hotels although none of these is good value by the rest of China's standards. The *Longmen Hotel* (☎ 0451-3639701), on the north corner of the square opposite the station is the best of the three, and also the most expensive, with single rooms from Y298. You may have a problem getting in here, however, as the place seems to be permanently booked solid. On the south corner of the square, the *Tianzhu Hotel* (☎ 0451-3643725) is chaotic (at reception level anyway) but has single rooms for Y160 and double rooms for Y180. The cheapest of the three, however, is the *Beiyuan Hotel* which is directly opposite the station and which has double rooms of a reasonable standard for Y130.

Where to eat
There are two or three nice but expensive restaurants in the south of the city, next to the flyover just south of the Heping Cun Hotel. Another good place to try, and with much more reasonable prices, is at the south-west corner of Zhaolin Park.

Just off Shangzhi Dajie, which runs parallel to Zhongyang Lu, is a small side road with several cheap restaurants, and in particular the *Paris Bakery* which sells great coffee and pastries. There is a *Kentucky Fried Chicken* outlet on Zhongyang Lu.

Moving on
By rail Trains out of Harbin shouldn't be a problem, although if you are having difficulty getting tickets you could try getting help from either CITS or the travel service in the Swan Hotel. For train times see p367-75.

By air Harbin has good air connections with other major cities in China, and the best place to find out prices is either at the CAAC office, or at the China Northern Airlines Office on Xinyang Lu.

Changchun
长 春

Changchun really has little to attract tourists apart from the palace of the puppet emperor, and while this is of passing interest, if you're running short of time I'd recommend that you skip this city altogether. Like Harbin, Changchun is an expensive place to stay, but if that's not a problem and you fancy a day or so where you are unlikely to bump into other tourists, you may feel it merits a visit.

HISTORY

Like Harbin, Changchun is a city of the modern era, dating from the mid-nineteenth century, when it was known as Kwancheng. With the advent of the railways, the city grew enormously not only because it was on the main line south from Harbin towards Beijing but also because, after 1905, it was the point where the wide (5') gauge Chinese Eastern Railway met the Standard Gauge (4' 8 $\frac{1}{2}$") South Manchurian Railway. Although various schemes were mooted at the time, including the addition of a third rail to allow trains of either gauge to use the track, no technical solution was found, and Changchun became a major transhipment point between north Manchuria and the southern port cities. From 1912 onwards, when Changchun was connected by rail to Jilin and the East Manchurian highlands, it also became a major link in Manchuria's lumber industry.

Because of its central position in the north-east and the fact that it was at the hub of four main railway lines, the city was selected by the Japanese to be the capital of Manchukuo in 1932, and was renamed Hsinking (New Capital). Under Japanese direction the city was greatly enlarged, and a series of enormous public buildings were erected, many of which can still be seen today. With the arrival of the Russians in 1945, the 'Puppet Emperor', Puyi was taken prisoner, and then, after the Russians withdrew, the fight between the Communists and Nationalists began, ending only with Changchun's fall to the PLA in 1948. After Liberation, Changchun continued to grow in importance as an industrial centre, and the first car factory in Mao's China was opened here in 1953. Changchun also became the centre of the Chinese film industry.

The Japanese made a start at redesigning the city with the huge buildings and wide avenues required of a capital, and the work has been continued by the Chinese. Changchun today, more even than Harbin or Shenyang, is a huge modern city. The oldest buildings you are likely to come across in Changchun date from the Japanese occupation, and there aren't many of these; the rest are all glistening high-rise structures. Somehow the planners of Changchun have managed to combine a huge scale of layout with a pleasant atmosphere, so that a walk through the city can be quite enjoyable. Changchun is the capital of Jilin province.

WHAT TO SEE

Palace of the Puppet Emperor

The palace itself is hardly what one might expect for the last of the Qing line, particularly in comparison with the Forbidden City, which is where he would have lived had the dynasty survived. The complex is really just a large house, with living quarters in the front buildings and official rooms including the reception room, mini-throne room, and tiny official dining room in the rear building. The displays bring the place to life, even

❏ Henry Puyi's life was immortalised in the film *The Last Emperor*. He ascended the imperial throne in 1908 aged two, but with the establishment of the Republic just three years later he was forced to step down. He was allowed to continue living in the Forbidden City for a while before finally taking refuge in the foreign concession area of Tianjin. Photographs of him there show him growing up as a thoroughly Westernised, and rather frail-looking young man: there are pictures of him in his golfing gear, and in top hat and tails. In 1932 he was made emperor of Manchukuo by the Japanese to give their presence in the north-east respectability. He occupied the position until 1945, when he was taken prisoner by the Russians, and disappeared from view for some time. Several years later he was given a job as a gardener in Beijing, where he died in 1967. His autobiography is appropriately entitled *From Emperor to Citizen*.

for a non-Chinese speaker, and it's possible to visualise how the place must have run as it perpetuated a myth of government in exile. To the left hand side of the main courtyard as you enter the gate there is also a small photo display of Puyi's life.

Entry is Y10 and you should note that the entrance is right next to the entrance for the provincial museum; it's easy to pay to go into the wrong one by mistake.

Jilin Provincial Museum
The museum is housed in the buildings next to the residence of the puppet emperor, and the access to it is via the right hand of the two gates as you approach from the outside. The place is well laid out, and the exhibits are clean and well cared for, which alone makes it better than many Chinese museums. There are no English titles, however, and without any sort of explanation it is really just another collection of pottery, clothing and pieces of metal work. Entry is Y15.

Steam locomotives
Changchun is just as busy for steam as either Harbin or Shenyang. It's also a good jumping off point for a trip to visit the narrow gauge steam trains which are still in use on forestry operations, although you'll need at least a couple of days to make this trip.

The **East Junction** is the place where the lines to Jilin and Harbin separate, and hence the traffic is heavy. It used to be a good place to photograph steam locomotives on the move, and although you have as good a chance here as anywhere, you should be prepared for a long wait, as steam trains moving between cities are becoming increasingly rare. The junction is about 20-30 minutes from the city centre, and CITS can explain how to get there.

In comparison with the huge price they demand in Harbin, CITS can arrange a visit to the **Steam Engine Depot** for Y80 (or more if you want an English-speaking guide). Alternatively, if you just want to have a quick look at the yards without paying to get in, walk a few hundred metres west from the railway station. The entire yard can be seen from the road although a wall prevents you getting very close.

Finally, the **miniature trains** on the logging railways attract many enthusiasts. The 762mm gauge trains are operated by the Forestry Bureau, and although there are 36 forestry railways in China, they are all either in the North-East or the South-West. Again CITS can explain how to visit the railways, and can make the arrangements for you if necessary. In outline however, you will need to take an overnight train to Dunhua, and then catch a local bus on to Dashitou Forestry Bureau. You are unlikely to be able to see the railway and get back to Dunhua in time to catch a night train back to Changchun. You will, therefore, have to stay overnight in Dunhua.

CHANGCHUN – KEY

Where to stay

1	Shangri-La Hotel	1	香格里拉饭店
2	Changchun Noble Hotel	2	长春贵宾馆 (意译)
3	Chunyi Hotel	3	春谊宾馆
4	International Building	4	国际大厦
5	Changbaishan Hotel	5	长白山宾馆
6	Tianhu Binguan	6	天湖宾馆 (拼音)
7	Good Luck Hotel	7	好运宾馆
8	Jilin University Guesthouse	8	吉林大学招待所
9	North East Normal University Guesthouse	9	东北师大招待所

What to see

10	Palace of the Puppet Emperor	10	伪皇宫
11	Jilin Provincial Museum	11	吉林省博物馆
12	Shengli Park	12	胜利公园

Where to eat

13	Chongqing Lu	13	重庆路
14	PaPa's	14	爸爸饭店
15	French Bakery	15	法国烤面包店

Other

16	Railway Station	16	火车站
17	Bank of China	17	中国银行
18	Bank of China	18	中国银行
19	Renmin Square	19	人民广场
20	Post Office	20	市邮政局
21	CITS	21	中国国际旅行社

PRACTICAL INFORMATION
Orientation and services

The railway station is at the north end of town and Renmin Lu, Changchun's main avenue, runs due south from it. Approximately halfway down Renmin Lu is Renmin Square, a large roundabout with roads heading off it in several directions. Most of the main services are on or near Renmin Lu. The **post office** is at the north end of the road, just south of the station. The **Bank of China** has its main branch about three quarters of a kilometre south of Renmin Square, and another large branch next to the Changbaishan Hotel.

CITS are in the same high rise building as this second branch of the Bank of China: they have a ticketing office (air tickets only) on the ground floor and a main office on the 7th floor (☎ 0431-609039). The staff are extremely helpful and really are worth contacting for advice, in particular the sales manager for the English department, Mrs Zhang Lei.

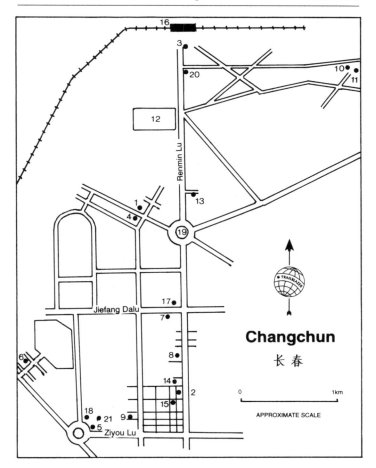

Changchun

长 春

APPROXIMATE SCALE

Local transport

The **buses** are easy to get the hang of, and Bus 6 is particularly worthy of note as it runs from the station straight south along Renmin Lu.

Taxis are cheaper in Changchun than elsewhere in China; flag fall is Y5.

Tours

If you are really keen to take a tour, CITS will certainly help you out, although there are no organised tours (there are rarely any tourists). All the places within the city are easy to get to by yourself.

Where to stay
There aren't any cheap places to stay in Changchun but there are a couple of moderately-priced places, so if there are two of you, you should be able to avoid paying too much.

The most expensive hotel in the city is the *Shangri La Hotel* (☎ 0431-8981818), on Xi'an Lu, which was still being completed at the time of writing but had single rooms from US$140. Three and a half kilometres south of the station, on Renmin Lu, the *Changchun Noble Hotel* actually puts the Shangri La in the shade, although it's a bit cheaper with rooms from US$100. If nothing else this gleaming white high-rise building is a good landmark if you're looking for either of the university guest-houses. The tower is clearly seen by day, and even easier to see at night when it is lit up by spotlights. Just opposite the station, the *Chunyi Hotel* (☎ 0431-2799966) was founded in 1909, and has a faintly period atmosphere to it. Unfortunately this extends to a slightly battered appearance, and it's doubtful whether it's worth the Y380 asking price for the cheapest rooms here.

Opposite the Shangri La Hotel, the *International Building* (☎ 0431-8981977) is better value and has rooms from Y280. Better still though further from the city centre is the *Changbaishan Hotel* (☎ 0431-5669911) which is next to the roundabout where Ziyou Lu and Yan'an Lu meet. They appear to be more used to foreigners here and charge Y300 for a standard double room. Those looking for cheaper hotels could try the *Tianhu Binguan* (☎ 0431-5607600) which is on a backstreet; it is very friendly and has doubles from Y150. The *Good Luck Hotel* (☎ 0431-5620111), just off Renmin Lu is also worth while, as they have some double rooms without bathroom for Y150.

If you can speak Chinese or produce some Chinese student ID you can try either of the foreigners' guest-houses run by the Jilin University or the North East Normal University. You can, of course, try them anyway, but their first reaction is to tell you to go away, and only production of Chinese student ID or a convincing argument is likely to make them think again. I was finally allowed to stay in the latter place, after a lot of help from a local student, and had a very clean pleasant double room for Y100.

Where to eat
There are plenty of up-market restaurants. A good place to start looking is on Tongzhi Jie, just north of Ziyou Avenue. For the best food in town you're probably best going straight to the *Shangri La Hotel*.

For the cheaper meals, try Chongqing Lu, which runs east of Renmin Lu, just to the north of Renmin Square. For a taste of home, however, there's *Pa Pa's* which is on a side street just north of the Changchun Noble Hotel. They serve Western style food here at not too outrageous prices in a very mellow atmosphere. If, however, the resident guitarist in Pa Pa's is playing, you may prefer moving on to the *French Bakery* which is on a side street just to the south of the Changchun Noble Hotel.

Just opposite the North East Normal University's Foreigners' Guesthouse, there is a small friendly Western style *bar*, although it's rather overpriced.

Moving on
By rail The ticket office in Changchun is a real struggle for sleeper tickets, although Hard Seat tickets will be relatively easy to get hold of. CITS don't deal with rail tickets but there is a travel service in the same building which will help. For train times see p367-75.

By air The airport is to the west of the city, and the CITS ticketing centre is a good place to approach for prices.

Shenyang
沈 阳

Shenyang, like Harbin and Changchun, is a large modern city, although it has managed to retain some of its old character in places. The street layout and the market area around the south railway station are fun to explore, and Shenyang also has far more on offer in the way of tourist sights than either Harbin or Changchun. Unfortunately, Shenyang is probably the most expensive of the three for accommodation.

HISTORY

Although Changchun was chosen by the Japanese as the capital of Manchukuo, Shenyang has traditionally been the political and economic centre of Manchuria. Mukden (the city's Manchu name) was the Manchu capital from 1625 to 1644 and the base from which invasions were launched on Korea and Inner Mongolia. The city still has reminders of its past, notably the tombs of the two great Manchu leaders and the palace.

Mukden's modern development began with the arrival of the railways, just after the turn of the century. In 1905, during the Russo-Japanese war a decisive battle was won here by the Japanese. After 1911 the name was changed to Shenyang, after an original 12th century name Shen. During the 1920's and 1930's Shenyang was home to one of the most powerful warlords in China, Chang Tsolin, who controlled most of Manchuria and, for a while, Beijing too. After fixing Chang Tsolin's death by arranging for his train to be blown up, the Japanese used much the same tactics to engineer the take-over of Manchuria. On 18th September 1931 a bomb exploded in front of a train as it approached Shenyang, killing (reportedly) a Japanese general. In order to restore order and protect its interests, Japan proceeded to occupy Manchuria.

Following the end of the Anti-Japanese War, Shenyang was at the heart of the fighting which took place between Mao's and Chiang Kaishek's forces. The city surrendered to the People's Liberation Army on 2 November 1948, and with it Manchuria passed into Communist hands, a crucial turning point in the war. Shenyang today is the capital of Liaoning province, and at the centre of the North-East's industrial effort.

WHAT TO SEE

Shenyang Palace Museum

The Palace Museum is Shenyang's most famous tourist attraction. It is one of only two intact imperial palaces in China, the other being the

Forbidden City in Beijing. Comparison of the two is misleading, however, for it's easy to come expecting another Forbidden City, in which case you will be extremely disappointed. This is actually a fairly small place, which has been preserved amidst the modern developments that are going up on all sides. In the process it seems to have become rather drab and battered. The palace was built between 1625 and 1636, during the reigns of Nurhachi and Huang Taiji, the founders of the Qing Dynasty.

On the eastern side of the palace is a large paved area which holds the **Dazheng Hall** and **Pavilions of the Ten Kings**. The layout reflects the Manchu style of government. In organising and unifying the Manchus, Nurhachi had split the people into 'banners' or tribes, and each of the ten pavilions was designated for the leader of one of the banners. At the end of the courtyard the Dazheng Hall (Hall of Great Government) was where the regional leaders were called to discuss matters with the emperor. The pavilions now have weapon displays which are moderately interesting.

The rest of the palace grounds is devoted mainly to living quarters which have been well preserved. It's all fairly interesting but the Y45 entry fee is way over the top.

North Tomb (Zhaoling)

The North Tomb is Shenyang's second biggest tourist attraction. The tomb was built for Emperor Huang Taiji and his wife, and construction began in 1643, taking eight years. In many ways it is similar to the Ming Tomb in Nanjing. The avenue leading to the tomb is lined with large statues of animals guarding the approach, and the tomb itself is surrounded by several layers of fortifications, including huge walls round the inner courtyard.

To get to the tomb you have to walk through the North Park (entry is Y10), and entry to the tomb itself is a further Y10.

East Tomb (Fuling)

Although the North Tomb is the more famous of the two, its eastern counterpart is the more pleasant to visit, set as it is outside the city in an area of pine and cypress trees. The East Tomb is the same in design as the North Tomb but very slightly smaller. Built for Emperor Nurhachi and his wife, the tomb took over 20 years to build (1629-51).

From the front gate a paved avenue leads between statues of lions, tigers and horses, to a 108-step staircase. At the top the Longen Gate guards the main entrance of the tomb, while inside the courtyard are a number of temples and other buildings.

Entry is Y10 but in addition you pay Y1 to walk into the car park, Y3 to look around inside the buildings and Y2 if you want to climb the tower above the gate. The tomb is eight kilometres north-east of the city centre; to get there, take bus 230 from the north station and then change to bus 218.

Shenyang Steam Locomotive Museum

The museum, which is next to the steam marshalling yards, is not actually in Shenyang itself, but in **Sujiatun**, a small satellite town, about half an hour by train from Shenyang. If you are interested at all in China's railways, this is the best place to see something of their history; the museum is better than the one in Datong, the lines next to the museum are busy with working engines, and it's all costs far less than a visit to the yards in Harbin.

There is a unique collection to be seen, ranging from a couple of American locomotives, built in 1907, to a Chinese GK 1038, built in 1960. The collection also includes trains made in Japan, the USSR, Czechoslovakia, Romania and Poland.

Entry to the museum is accompanied by a guided tour, and although you're unlikely to understand a word, the enthusiasm is obvious. It's best to come here first, as the guy who runs the museum can then take you on a guided tour of the working yard; the whole lot (museum and tour round the yard) costs Y40.

To get to Sujiatun, take a local train south, (towards Dalian) from the south railway station. The trip takes about half an hour and costs Y1.5, and two trains which you might want to consider are T470 which departs at 08.45 and T536 which departs at 11.40. From Sujiatun station you could easily walk, but it's far easier to take a moped rickshaw; about Y5 is probably the right sort of fare. For the return to Shenyang you can simply catch the first train back once you've finished. T555 is one possibility, which departs at 10.45, and the ticket back to Shenyang is, for some reason, cheaper than the outward journey – it costs Y1.

General Chang's Mansion

This large complex was the official residence of Chang Tsolin, the Old Marshal, who was one of the most powerful men in China during the period after the fall of the Qing Dynasty.

In the late 1920's Chang held almost complete power in north-east China. Despite the cruelty which certainly accompanied his 'rule', Chang Tsolin is remembered for his patriotism, for although he accepted the financial aid of the Japanese, he attempted to marginalise their power, and manoeuvred to force them out of Manchuria. Eventually the Japanese arranged for the Old Marshal to be assassinated. His place was taken by his son Chang Xueliang who supported Chiang Kaishek's Nationalist government. It was the Young Marshal who was responsible almost ten years later for arresting Chiang during the Xi'an Incident (see p318), in an attempt to force the president to join with the Communists resisting the Japanese.

For a while in the 1920's and 1930's the mansion became the political and military centre of northeast China. The place seems to hold a fascination for the Chinese (judging by the reactions of the other visitors) but it's less interesting for foreigners. There's little to be seen now apart from a few scrappy photos. Entry is Y10.

Liaoning Provincial Museum

The ground floor of this museum is entirely taken up by two huge dinosaur skeletons, and on the second floor there are a number of rooms devoted to the development of culture in Liaoning. Labels are in Chinese only. This is not the best museum you'll see in China by any means, but it's well laid out and worth a look if you have time. Entry is Y10.